Artificial Intelligence for Fault Detection and Diagnosis

Artificial Intelligence for Fault Detection and Diagnosis

Guest Editors

Ying Bi
Mengjie Zhang
Bing Xue
Bo Peng

MDPI

Basel • Beijing • Wuhan • Barcelona • Belgrade • Novi Sad • Cluj • Manchester

Guest Editors
Ying Bi
School of Electrical and Information Engineering
Zhengzhou University
Zhengzhou
China

Mengjie Zhang
School of Engineering and Computer Science (SECS)
Victoria University of Wellington (VUW)
Wellington
New Zealand

Bing Xue
School of Engineering and Computer Science (SECS)
Victoria University of Wellington (VUW)
Wellington
New Zealand

Bo Peng
College of Mechatronical and Electrical Engineering
Hebei Agriculture University
Baoding
China

Editorial Office
MDPI AG
Grosspeteranlage 5
4052 Basel, Switzerland

This is a reprint of the Special Issue, published open access by the journal *Algorithms* (ISSN 1999-4893), freely accessible at: https://www.mdpi.com/journal/algorithms/special_issues/AI_FD.

For citation purposes, cite each article independently as indicated on the article page online and as indicated below:

Lastname, A.A.; Lastname, B.B. Article Title. *Journal Name* **Year**, *Volume Number*, Page Range.

ISBN 978-3-7258-4913-0 (Hbk)
ISBN 978-3-7258-4914-7 (PDF)
https://doi.org/10.3390/books978-3-7258-4914-7

Contents

algorithms

MDPI

Review

A Survey on Fault Diagnosis of Rolling Bearings

Bo Peng [1], Ying Bi [2,3,*], Bing Xue [3], Mengjie Zhang [3] and Shuting Wan [4]

1 College of Mechanical and Electrical Engineering, Hebei Agricultural University, Baoding 071000, China
2 School of Electrical and Information Engineering, Zhengzhou University, Zhengzhou 450001, China
3 School of Engineering and Computer Science, Victoria University of Wellington, Wellington 6140, New Zealand
4 Hebei Key Laboratory of Electric Machinery Health Maintenance & Failure Prevention, North China Electric Power University, Baoding 071003, China
* Correspondence: ying.bi@ecs.vuw.ac.nz

Abstract: The failure of a rolling bearing may cause the shutdown of mechanical equipment and even induce catastrophic accidents, resulting in tremendous economic losses and a severely negative impact on society. Fault diagnosis of rolling bearings becomes an important topic with much attention from researchers and industrial pioneers. There are an increasing number of publications on this topic. However, there is a lack of a comprehensive survey of existing works from the perspectives of fault detection and fault type recognition in rolling bearings using vibration signals. Therefore, this paper reviews recent fault detection and fault type recognition methods using vibration signals. First, it provides an overview of fault diagnosis of rolling bearings and typical fault types. Then, existing fault diagnosis methods are categorized into fault detection methods and fault type recognition methods, which are separately revised and discussed. Finally, a summary of existing datasets, limitations/challenges of existing methods, and future directions are presented to provide more guidance for researchers who are interested in this field. Overall, this survey paper conducts a review and analysis of the methods used to diagnose rolling bearing faults and provide comprehensive guidance for researchers in this field.

Keywords: rolling bearing; diagnosis; fault detection; fault type recognition; signal processing; machine learning

1. Introduction

With the rapid development of technology and science, modern industry has become increasingly important in our daily life. The advancement of science and technology has led to the gradual development of large-scale and high-speed rotating machinery with integration, precision, and intelligence. Rotating machinery is an essential part of modern industry and is widely used in many fields, including energy and power, machinery manufacturing, transportation, and aerospace. Once mechanical equipment is successfully developed for production, the reliability and safety of the equipment become increasingly crucial, and the fault diagnosis and condition monitoring of the core components become an arduous task [1–3].

Roller bearings are widely used in rotating machinery and are an indispensable component that supports the rotating shaft and serves as a connector between stationary and rotating parts. Although rolling bearing damage occurs at the component level, it frequently leads to more severe equipment failures. According to statistics, rolling bearing failures account for 40–90% of all rotating machinery failures [4]. The initial failure of the rolling bearing of a wind turbine will only affect itself, and the unit will remain operational. However, as the times of abnormal operations increase, external excitations caused by broken bearings will cause the traditional system to malfunction, resulting in a fire in extreme cases. Roll bearing failure in the rolling mill will cause a reduction in the quality of rolled products, which will lead to the production line being stopped and result in significant economic losses. Due to the complex and changing conditions operating in rotating machinery, rolling bearings often fail before their designed life ends, and their actual service life is often shorter than their design life, so a routine shutdown inspection is not the best way. Therefore, an effective and intelligent fault diagnosis of rolling bearings is of considerable practical significance for ensuring the health of rotating equipment and machinery.

Fault diagnosis of rolling bearings is a multidisciplinary field that incorporates computer science, mathematics, electronics, signal processing, engineering, and other modern technologies. Rolling bearing fault diagnosis is to diagnose the bearing health status through the collected operation data. Fault diagnosis can be broadly categorized into fault detection and fault type recognition. Fault detection is to detect faults from the collected data, while fault type recognition is to recognize faults and their types from the data. During the past ten years, fault diagnosis of rolling bearings has attracted considerable attention from both academics and the industry. Figure 1 shows the number of publications on the topic of rolling bearing fault diagnosis extracted from the Scopus database. It is clear that the number of publications has gradually increased from 2011 to 2021. There are several survey papers on fault diagnosis. However, most of them focus on specifical tasks or methods, such as machine learning-based methods [5] for prognostics and health management of rolling element bearings [6], Fourier transform and enhanced fast Fourier transform algorithms [7], artificial intelligence methods [8], spectral kurtosis [9], and signal processing techniques [10]. Very few of them provide a general and comprehensive survey on rolling bearing fault diagnosis using vibration signals from the perspectives of fault detection and fault type recognition.

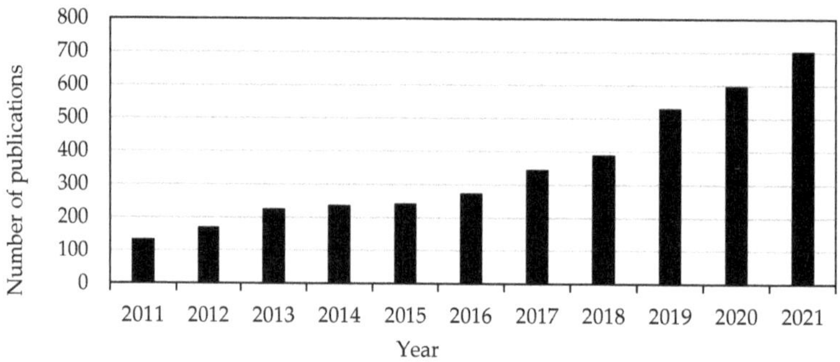

Figure 1. The number of publications on rolling bearing fault diagnosis from 2011 to 2021.

To address the above limitations, this paper reviews over 150 related publications in recent years, including over 100 publications from 2016 to 2021. These publications are well-known or representative ones in the rolling bearing fault diagnosis community. This survey discusses not only traditional methods based on signal processing and analysis but also machine learning and artificial intelligence methods, including feature extraction/reduction methods, deep learning methods, and evolutionary learning methods, to present a relatively full picture of this field. In addition, this survey summarizes commonly used datasets, existing limitations/challenges, and future research trends to provide researchers with useful guidance.

The structure of the survey is task-based, including tasks for fault detection and fault type recognition. The organization of this paper is as follows. The primary fault forms of rolling bearings and the major research topics of rolling bearing fault diagnosis are presented in Section 2. Then, Sections 3 and 4 review the typical works on rolling bearing fault detection and fault type recognition, respectively. Section 5 summarizes datasets and the limitations/challenges of existing methods and discusses future research trends in rolling bearing fault diagnosis. Finally, Section 6 draws the conclusions.

2. Background, Taxonomy, and Scope

2.1. Fault Forms/Types of Rolling Bearing

Rolling bearings have several types, but their basic structures remain the same. Typically, a rolling bearing consists of four parts: the inner ring, the outer ring, the rolling element, and the cage. There are four types of corresponding faults, i.e., the inner ring fault, the outer ring fault, the rolling element fault, and the cage fault. A rolling bearing may fail due to internal and/or external problems/factors. Nowadays, bearing failures are mainly caused by external factors, including improper assembly, oil lubrication failure, pollution corrosion, and overloading. Rolling bearing faults often have the following forms [3]:

(1) Fatigue

Rolling bearings operate with great periodic contact stress between the rolling element and the inner/outer ring surface, causing the contact surface (generally the track surface) to fatigue and crack, which gradually extends to the raceway surface. Fatigue causes the bearing surface material to fall off and form pits. In severe cases, the material on the surface may fall off in large areas. Fatigue pitting and fatigue peeling are commonly used terms for describing fatigue.

(2) Wear

The failures of the rolling bearing sealing system cause bearing wear. When the sealing system fails, foreign matter will enter the bearing, resulting in abnormal friction between the inner ring/outer ring and the rolling elements. Additionally, improper lubrication will further aggravate wear, resulting in continuous material loss, increased surface roughness, increased clearance between bearings, and decreased running accuracy.

(3) Deformation

Deformation means that the bearing surface has undergone plastic deformation, or more specifically, a permanent indentation will appear on the bearing surface if the load borne by the bearing exceeds the yield strength limit of the material. Incorrect assembly methods and foreign matter appearance are the main reasons for the bearing deformation.

(4) Corrosion

Corrosion of rolling bearings occurs when chemical reactions occur on their surface. The first one is the oxidation reaction between the water in the lubricating oil and the bearing surface. The second one is fretting friction between components that leads to the oxidation of surface materials. The last one is abnormal current/voltage that causes local overheating of the bearing, resulting in welding of the element contact surface.

(5) Fracture

Rolling bearing fractures are the damage caused by local stresses exceeding the material's tensile strength limit. Generally, the crack propagates over time and penetrates part of the bearing component, causing complete separation of the material and fracture of the bearing. In addition, violent loading and unloading can also lead to bearing fracture.

2.2. Taxonomy and Scope

The purpose of rolling bearing fault diagnosis is to determine the bearing health status by analyzing the collected operation data. Diagnostics of faults revolve primarily around fault detection and fault type identification. Figure 2 shows the general flowchart of fault detection and fault type recognition. Although fault detection and fault type recognition may have some overlap, they are two different types of tasks in fault diagnosis. Specifically, fault detection is to detect faults or non-faults from the collected data, and fault type recognition is to recognize faults and their types from the data. Therefore, to solve these two tasks, different procedures are often used. For fault detection, the collected bearing signals are utilized to determine bearing status. The process often includes removing the noise and harmonic interference from the monitoring signal using signal processing methods and then manually identifying the fault by finding its characteristic frequency. Fault type recognition refers to using the existing bearing signals to construct a diagnostic system to evaluate the unknown bearing signals. Unlike fault detection, fault type recognition methods automatically extract or construct fault features from the signals and determine the bearing health status using machine learning algorithms.

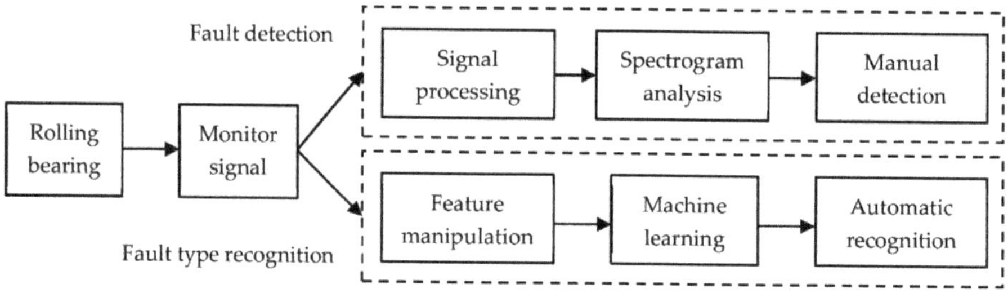

Figure 2. General flowchart of rolling bearing fault diagnosis.

The monitoring data of rolling bearings can be collected from oil [11], temperature [12], sound [13], vibration [14], and other media. Performing an oil analysis affects production continuity because it involves shutting down equipment and opening the cover to collect lubricant and other oil samples. Temperature measurement equipment is expensive and cannot provide a promising monitoring effect. Temperature analysis neither has good accuracy at the early stage of bearing fault nor distinguishes the fault types. Sound analysis has high technical demands for signal acquisition and identification because the acoustic signal attenuates and is susceptible to environmental noise interference. In contrast, vibration signal characteristics are stable and easy to collect, making vibration analysis a suitable condition monitoring technique. Vibration analysis has a firm theoretical basis. Research on the fault diagnosis method of rolling bearings based on vibration signal has long been a hot issue concern by domestic and foreign experts and scholars.

This survey paper summarizes the fault diagnosis methods of rolling bearings based on vibration signals from the perspectives of fault detection and fault type recognition. First, four types of signal processing methods commonly used for fault detection of rolling bearings, i.e., morphological transformation-based methods, filter-based methods, decomposition-based methods, and deconvolution-based methods, are discussed. Then, the classical fault type recognition methods are discussed from three aspects: feature extraction, feature reduction, and classification. In addition, the recently popular deep learning based-fault type recognition methods such as convolutional neural networks, Autoencoder, deep belief networks, and recursive neural networks, are also discussed and reviewed. The taxonomy of this survey is shown in Figure 3.

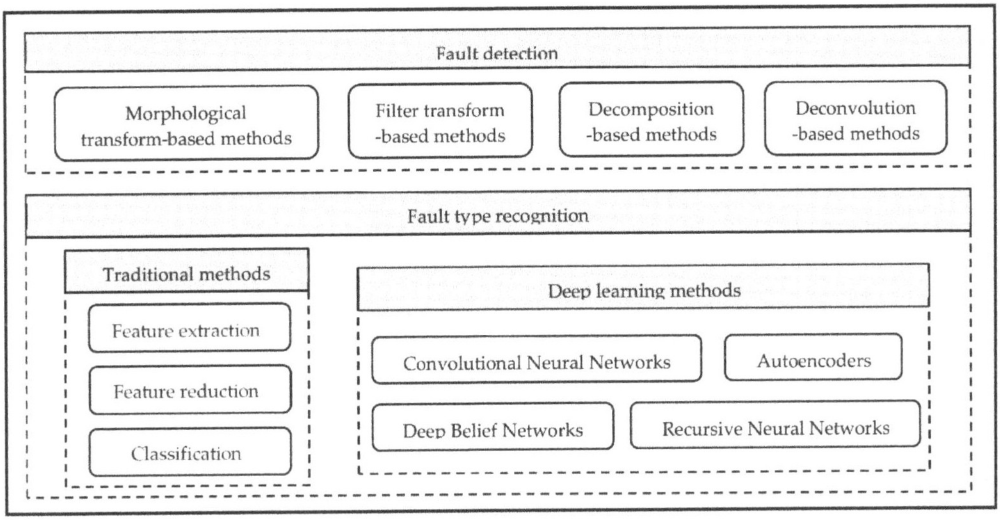

Figure 3. The taxonomy of this survey.

3. Rolling Bearing Fault Detection

The failure of rolling bearings will break the original energy balance of the system, and the most intuitive performance is abnormal vibration. The bearing fault vibration signal shows an increase or fluctuation in amplitude in the time domain and spectrum lines of fault characteristic frequency with prominent amplitude in the frequency domain. In [15], four empirical formulas were summarized for calculating the theoretical fault frequencies of the inner ring (F_{inner}), outer ring (F_{outer}), rolling element (F_{ball}), and cage (F_{cage}), as shown in Equation (1).

$$\begin{cases} F_{inner} = \frac{N_b S_{sh}}{2}(1 - \frac{d_b}{D_p}\cos\varphi) & F_{outer} = \frac{N_b S_{sh}}{2}(1 + \frac{d_b}{D_p}\cos\varphi) \\ F_{ball} = \frac{D_p S_{sh}}{2d_b}(1 - (\frac{d_b}{D_p}\cos\varphi)^2) & F_{cage} = \frac{S_{sh}}{2}(1 - \frac{d_b}{D_p}\cos\varphi) \end{cases} \quad (1)$$

where D_p is pitch diameter, d_b is rolling element diameter, N_b is rolling element number, φ is contact angle, and S_{sh} is shaft speed, which are basic parameters. It is possible to detect a bearing fault by observing the fluctuation of the time-domain waveforms or observing spectral lines associated with the fault characteristic frequency. Directly measuring rolling bearing vibrations is impossible in the real world. Generally, the sensor installed on the bearing pedestal is used to collect the signals indirectly, resulting in a significant amount of noise and harmonic interference in the collected vibration signals. The polluted bearing vibration signal is not effective for detecting bearing faults. Therefore, a series of fault detection methods based on vibration analysis was proposed to remove the noise and harmonic interference components in the signals, enhance the fault-related pulses, reduce the difficulty of fault detection, and improve the effectiveness of detection. Based on the difference in signal processing principles, the fault detection methods are mainly divided into four categories: morphological transformation-based methods, filter-based methods, decomposition-based methods, and deconvolution-based methods.

The common rolling bearing fault detection methods are summarized in Figure 4. The morphological transform-based methods can extract harmonic or impact components of signals by using morphological operators with different structures, whose appropriateness directly influences performance. The filter-based methods can adaptively identify the resonance frequency band that contains rich fault information, where the division of frequency band and the choice of subband are the key factors affecting the results. The decomposition-based methods refer to decomposing the complex signals into simple subband signals, and these methods should address modal aliasing, parameter setting, manually tuning, etc. The deconvolution-based detection methods belong to blind signal processing technology, which recovers fault characteristic signals by designing the appropriate inverse filters and setting the deconvolution period and filter length. In addition to the method based on recursive decomposition, which typically lacks the mathematical model as theoretical support, other methods have the complete mathematical theory.

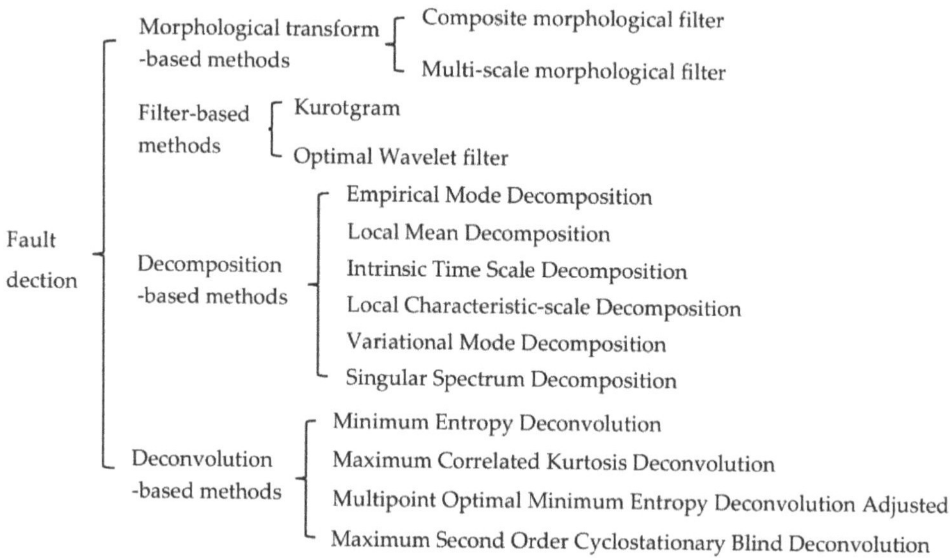

Figure 4. Summary of rolling bearing fault detection methods.

3.1. Morphological Transform-Based Fault Detection Methods

The morphological transform-based detection method is a signal processing method based on mathematical morphology theory that can capture the fault-related components in the bearing vibration signals through morphological operators, such as erosion, dilation, open, and close. Matheron introduced mathematical morphology as a denoising method for image processing [16], and then Maragos extended it to the field of signal processing [16, 17]. Given the characteristic of morphological transformation to remove signal noise, several researchers have applied it to the fault diagnosis of components of mechanical systems and conducted a great deal of research in recent years. Wang et al. [18] used a morphological close operator to process vibration signals for extracting fault impulses. Shen et al. [19] proposed morphological close–open transform and morphological open–close transform by cascading the close or open operator of the morphology. Li et al. [20] and Raj et al. [21] calculated the gradient (difference) between the dilation and erosion operator of the morphology to obtain the vibration impact component in the signal and defined this procedure as morphological gradient transformation. Following this, some improved methods based on morphological gradient transformation were developed that integrated the close and open operators [22,23] and the close–open and open–close operators [24, 25]. These morphological gradient transform methods typically change the negative impact to positive impact, resulting in the change of signal impact components. To ensure that the positive and negative impulses of the signal do not change after morphological transformation, Wang et al. [26] and Meng et al. [27] utilized the mean value operator to fuse the results of the closed and open operators. In addition, Deng et al. [28] and Yan et al. [29] further developed the morphological hat-transform technology, which can enhance the weak impact in the signal by subtracting the morphological transformation result from the original signal. Recently, Li et al. [30] proposed a morphological gradient product method by multiplying the results of two morphological transforms through a product operator. In addition to developing new morphological transformation methods, multi-scale analysis was used to improve the efficiency of the existing morphological transformation methods [31–38]. To sum up, by analyzing the available morphological transform methods and using cascade operator, gradient operator, hat-transform, product operator, and multi-scale analyses, researchers have developed a series of morphological transform-based fault detection methods with excellent performance.

3.2. Filter-Based Fault Detection Methods

The filter-based detection method is to construct a narrow-band filter to remove the noise and interference components from the bearing vibration signals and retain the fault-related pulses. The key to the filter-based method is to determine the center frequency and bandwidth of the narrow-band filter. A typical filter-based detection method is Kurotgram, proposed by Antoni et al. [39,40] in 2006, which uses the bandpass filter of a tree structure to divide the signal spectrum and then calculates the time-domain kurtosis of the filtered signal as a measure of fault information to adaptively select a narrow-band signal with the most fault information for subsequent analysis. The Kurotgram method has two shortcomings: one is that the parameters (center frequency and bandwidth) of the constructed filter are not accurate enough; the other is that the Kurtosis index is easily disturbed by noise, resulting in interference with the selection of the optimal filter. For this reason, Lei et al. [41] and Wang et al. [42] performed a wavelet packet transform on the bearing signal and used each wavelet node as a narrow-band filter to replace the tree structure filter of Kurotgram and proposed two new indicators for evaluating the fault information in the filtered signal, i.e., power spectral kurtosis and power spectral sparsity, to select the optimal filter. Similarly, Chen et al. [43] and Moshrefzadeh et al. [44] used the dual-tree complex wavelet transform and the maximum overlapping discrete wavelet packet transform to generate a series of narrow-band filters, respectively. In addition, many improvements to Kurotgram focus on proposing new evaluation indexes to replace kurtosis, such as spatial spectrum set kurtosis [43], envelope spectrum correlation kurtosis [45], l2/l1 norm [46], negative entropy [47,48], Gini index [49], and weighted cyclic harmonic noise ratio [50], to avoid the wrong selection of filters in the case of excessive non-Gaussian noise or accidental impact.

Although Kurtogram and its improved methods can remove fault-independent noise and harmonic interference from vibration signals, there is still a problem with the accuracy of filter construction, which may lead to the loss of the signal information and affect the extraction of fault-related pulses. As opposed to the traditional method of dividing the frequency band layer by layer, the optimal wavelet filter methods are proposed [51–55]. Tse et al. [51] used the Morlet wavelet as the filter, took maximizing sparsity of the filtered signal as the objective, and applied a genetic algorithm (GA) to locate the center frequency and bandwidth of the optimal Morlet wavelet for automatic filter construction. Similarly, Gu et al. [52] utilized the asymmetric real Laplace wavelet as the filter and determined its center frequency and bandwidth by simultaneously maximizing the impulse and cyclostationary characteristics of the filtered signal.

3.3. Decomposition-Based Fault Detection Methods

The decomposition-based detection method involves decomposing the raw vibration signal into several components, such as the fault-related pulse, the noise, and the harmonic interference. Analyzing only the fault-related pulses can simplify the process of detecting the fault. In 1998, Huang et al. [56,57] proposed the empirical mode decomposition (EMD) method, which provides a new idea for analyzing non-stationary signals. Gao [58] utilized EMD to decompose a bearing vibration signal into a series of eigenmode components with inherent oscillation attributes and then conducted envelope spectral analysis to realize bearing fault detection. The EMD method achieved promising performance, but it also has a number of deficiencies, such as end effect, modal aliasing, and over/under envelope, that limit its applications. Huang et al. [59] proposed ensemble empirical mode decomposition (EEMD), where Gaussian white noise is introduced in EMD to assist signal decomposition. Li et al. [60] used EEMD to analyze bearing signals and extract bearing fault features effectively. Even though EEMD can overcome the mode aliasing problem to some degree, it still suffers from problems, such as low decomposition efficiency and the inability to determine white noise amplitude adaptively. Torres et al. [61] proposed complete ensemble empirical mode decomposition with adaptive noise (CEEMDAN), where Gaussian white noise is adaptively added to each stage of the decomposition process. CEEMDAN can improve computing efficiency and reduce construction errors and was successfully applied to detect rolling bearing faults [62–64].

In 2005, Smith et al. [65] proposed the local mean decomposition (LMD), which gradually decomposes a non-stationary signal into a linear combination composed of multiple product function components through the moving average method. In essence, LMD is to separate the pure FM signal and envelope signal from the original signal and multiply the pure FM signal and envelope signal to obtain the product function component with instantaneous frequency and physical significance. LMD shows good performance for bearing fault detection, i.e., can avoid some over/under envelopes and has better signal local characteristics and fewer decomposition components than EMD [65–68]. However, the LMD method can encounter several problems in practical application, such as signal mutation, modal aliasing, and computational inefficiency [69]. In 2007, Frei et al. [70] proposed the intrinsic time scale decomposition (ITD), which can obtain the baseline signal by linear transformation and can adaptively decompose a complex vibration signal into a combination of several proper rotation components (PRCs) and a residual. ITD for bearing fault diagnosis displays significant advantages in end effect, envelope error, and calculation speed over EMD. However, the components decomposed by ITD produce burrs, resulting in distortion of the instantaneous amplitude and frequency [71,72]. Local characteristic-scale decomposition (LCD) was proposed by Cheng et al. [73,74] in 2012, which simultaneously considers the position information of non-stationary signals in the time domain and the frequency domain, avoiding the frequency confusion of EMD and the signal mutation of ITD [75]. Although LCD overcomes the shortcomings of EMD and ITD, there are still some drawbacks, such as the end effect, which often affect the processing results [76].

All the EMD, LMD, ITD, and LCD methods adopt the idea of recursive decomposition, which shares several similar defects. First, the end effect and the mode confusion; Second, the recursive procedure lacks error feedback and correction; Third, the decomposition results are easily affected by noise and abnormal components and have no physical meaning. Dragomiretskiy et al. [77] transformed signal decomposition into a constrained variational problem and proposed variational mode decomposition (VMD), in which the central frequency and bandwidth of each mode depend on the optimal solution variational model found iteratively, avoiding mode aliasing and improving the decomposition accuracy. The decomposition effect of VMD is affected by the number of decomposed modes K and the penalty factor α. The particle swarm optimization (PSO) and GA were applied to search the parameter values to enhance the performance of VMD for fault detection [78–80]. Bonizzi et al. [81] proposed the singular spectrum decomposition (SSD), which can adaptively determine the embedding dimension required for each singular value decomposition process and decompose the original signal in narrow-banded components. SSD has the advantages of small end effect, weak mode aliasing and no parameter selection. EMD does not require parameter selection either, but SSD is more effective in decomposing nonlinear and nonstationary time series. There was the development of SSD methods that could improve the decomposition accuracy and the detection ability of weak fault signals, which could be applied more effectively for the fault detection of mechanical equipment [82–84].

3.4. Deconvolution-Based Fault Detection Methods

The deconvolution-based detection method is to find an inverse filter to eliminate the transmission path influence in the signal acquisition process and extract the fault pulse from the noise-contaminated vibration signal. The research on deconvolution-based methods can be dated back to 1980. Wiggins et al. [85] proposed the minimum entropy deconvolution (MED) method to maximize the kurtosis of filtered signals and used it to analyze seismic signals. However, MED is easily affected by a random pulse with a large amplitude, making it impossible to accurately extract the periodic pulses corresponding to the fault in the signal [86]. To address this, McDonald et al. [87] developed a new index called correlation kurtosis to evaluate the periodicity and sparsity of signals and proposed maximum correlated kurtosis deconvolution (MCKD) for maximizing the correlation kurtosis value. MCKD overcomes the shortcomings of MED and can effectively extract the periodic pulse corresponding to the fault when there is a single abnormal pulse in the signal. However, the processing performance of MCKD is affected by two parameters, i.e., the inverse filter length and the fault cycle size. Whether the parameter setting is accurate directly affects the final processing result of MCKD. To address this issue, Miao et al. [88] proposed sparse maximum harmonics-noise-ratio deconvolution (SMHD), which can adaptively estimate the fault period by calculating the harmonic noise ratio of the envelope of the filtered signal. However, SMHD generally suffers diminished performance when analyzing the signals with harmonic components. MCKD and SMHD require a long calculation time due to the deconvolution operation based on iteration analysis. Therefore, McDonald et al. [89] proposed a method that does not require iterations, namely, multipoint optimal minimum entropy deconvolution adjusted (MOMEDA), which can complete the deconvolution in a short time but is adversely affected by the periodic oscillations of fault pulse. Recently, Buzzoni et al. [90] introduced the second order cyclostationary index to deconvolution methods and proposed the maximum second order cyclostationary blind deconvolution (CYCBD) method. The performance of CYCBD is better than that of MCKD and MOMEDA, but the fault cycle frequency needs to be set accurately to ensure the processing effect. In order to overcome the shortcomings of these methods, researchers have proposed some improved deconvolution methods by combining other processing methods or using optimization algorithms to determine the optimal parameters required for deconvolution, such as EMD combined with MED [91], PSO optimized MCKD [92], and CS optimized CYCBD [93].

4. Rolling Bearing Fault Type Recognition

Unlike the fault detection method, machine learning algorithms were used in the rolling bearing fault type recognition system to replace the manual observation of the fault-related spectral lines. These methods can achieve automatic recognition of different types of faults in rolling bearings.

A summary of the commonly used methods of rolling bearing fault type recognition is shown in Figure 5. These traditional methods need multiple independent steps, such as feature extraction, feature transform or feature selection, and classifier selection and optimization, which often need to be manually set to achieve effective fault recognition performance. The results of the previous step often significantly affect the results of the latter step. Rich domain knowledge is required in the process of fault recognition. The deep-learning-based fault type recognition methods can automatically learn features from the original signals and train classifiers for effective fault recognition without human intervention. However, the deep architecture used in these methods needs rich expertise to design and a large number of samples to train.

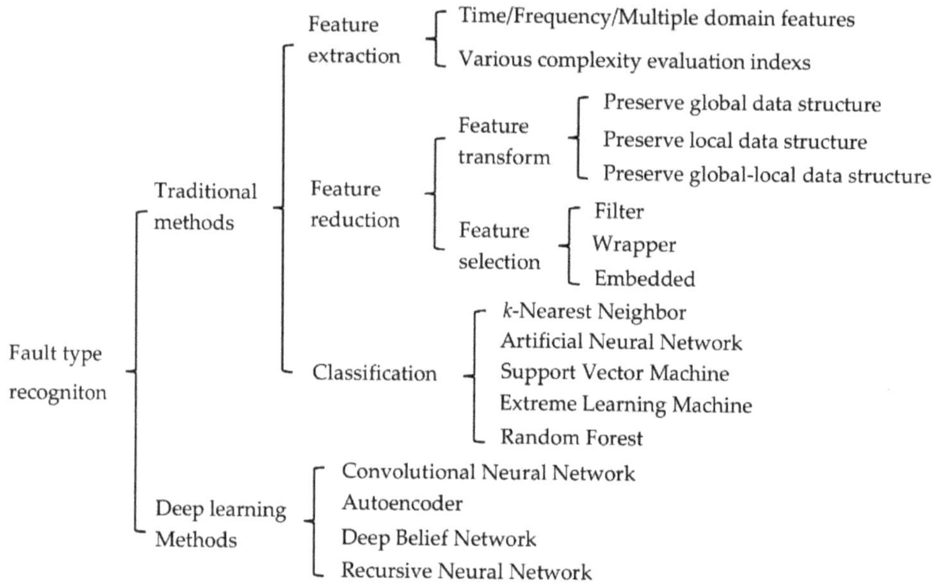

Figure 5. Summary of rolling bearing fault type recognition methods.

4.1. *Traditional Fault Type Recognition Methods*

Traditional rolling bearing fault type recognition methods usually include three steps: feature extraction, feature reduction, and classification.

(1) Feature extraction

Extracting fault-related features from vibration signals is the first step to perform rolling bearing fault type recognition. It is necessary to map the original bearing signals to statistical features to reflect the health status of bearings. Early work on feature extraction of rolling bearing vibration signals mainly focused on calculating various types of time-domain or frequency-domain statistical descriptive indexes [94,95], such as root mean square, kurtosis, skewness, average frequency, and root mean square frequency. These indexes are easy to calculate and intuitive to understand; their values vary with the running state of the rolling bearing.

Complexity can describe the dynamic characteristics of bearing signals under different running conditions. More and more attention is paid to applying various complexity evaluation indexes to fault type recognition. Yang et al. [96] used fractal dimension (FD) to evaluate bearing signals, but the calculation speed of FD is slow, which limits its use in online diagnosis. Caesarendra et al. [97] calculated the Lyapunov exponent of bearing vibration signal as a feature, but its stability is vulnerable to noise interference. The entropy of a time series is an index commonly used to quantify the degree of uncertainty or irregularity. Approximate entropy (AE), sample entropy (SE), fuzzy entropy (FE), permutation entropy (PE), and dispersion entropy (DE) were applied to fault type identification [98–102]. AE has good anti-noise performance when analyzing signals with more data points, but it may cause inaccurate estimation when analyzing signals with fewer data points [103,104]. As an improved form of AE, SE has the advantage of low dependence on the signal length and improved immunity to interference from noise. The disadvantage of SE is that its computation cost is high, and it may not be appropriate for analyzing signals containing similar information [103]. Based on SE, FE introduced a fuzzy membership function and was capable of assessing signal uncertainty more effectively [105]. PE offers simplicity, high robustness to dynamic noise, and a fast calculation speed and can effectively analyze non-stationary signals with complex components [106]. Rostaghi and Azami [107] developed

DE and proved that it was reliable in quantifying the complexity and uncertainty of time signals through the comparative test of various time series. The computational efficiency of DE is significantly better than that of SE, FE, and PE. Instantaneous energy distribution (IED) of bearing vibration signals can describe the time-varying process between fault states. Based on these characteristics, instantaneous energy distribution permutation entropy (IED-PE) [108] and instantaneous energy distribution permutation dispersion entropy (IED-DE) [109] were developed to enhance the accuracy of identifying fault types.

As performing the single-scale analysis of bearing vibration signals with complexity and uncertainty may lead to loss of information, multiscale analysis is introduced to entropy calculation to more accurately evaluate the vibration signals [110–115]. Costa et al. [110] and Aziz et al. [113] used the coarsening method to calculate the entropy of signals on multiple scales and proposed multi-scale sample entropy (MSE) and multi-scale permutation entropy (MPE), respectively. MSE and MPE investigate the irregularity of bearing vibration signals from multiple scales and have made significant progress toward fault diagnosis. In addition, when MSE and MPE are used to analyze signals with fewer data points, their calculation values will fluctuate with the increase in the scale factor, potentially leading to evaluation results instability. Azami et al. [116,117] further proposed multi-scale dispersion entropy (MDE) and refine composite multi-scale dispersion entropy (RCMDE) based on the advantages of DE and the coarse-graining method to address the shortcomings of MSE and MPE. RCMDE and MDE offer much greater computational efficiency than MSE and MPE. Multi-group experiments have shown that RCMDE is more valuable for identifying bearing fault types [117].

(2) Feature reduction

The more statistical features are used to describe signals, the more comprehensively the inherent information of signals is expressed. However, the high-dimensional feature set includes many redundant and negative-effect indexes/features. Dealing with such a large number of useless features typically increases the computational complexity and affects the recognition accuracy. In addition, using too many features to describe a large number of signals may lead to dimensional disaster. Therefore, it is necessary to reduce and compress the tremendous data resources effectively for extracting valuable information and knowledge. Feature transformation and feature selection methods can generate a low-dimensional feature set for fault type recognition.

Feature transformation methods are categorized based on how they preserve data structure. Two types of feature transformation methods exist, the global preservation-based methods, such as principal component analysis (PCA) and linear discriminant analysis (LDA), and the local preservation-based methods, such as local preserving projections (LPP) and margin Fisher analysis (MFA). In [118–121], the sample features reduced by different feature transformation methods were used to perform the identification of bearing fault types. The works in [122–124] show that the feature subset obtained by considering the local and global information in signals with different statuses is more effective for improving recognition performance. Chen et al. [123] proposed the Laplacian LDA (Lap-LDA) method based on least square LDA, which can not only obtain the global structure information of the data using LDA but also obtain the local structure information of the data using the Laplacian map. Zhang et al. [124] proposed global–local structure analysis (GLSA), combining the advantages of LPP and PCA.

Feature selection methods can be divided into three categories, i.e., filter-based methods, wrapper-based methods, and embedded-based methods. In the filter-based method, the features of the original dataset are evaluated and selected according to similarity, dependency, and correlation. This kind of method has fast calculation speed and low complexity. The commonly used methods include Fisher score (FS), Laplacian score (LS), Relief-F, and minimum redundancy maximum relevance (mRMR), which were applied to remove irrelevant features from bearing vibration [125–128]. The wrapper-based feature selection methods use a classifier to evaluate feature subsets for determining the most useful feature subset for classification. Compared with filter-based methods, wrapper-based methods require a longer computing time, but the quality of the feature subset obtained is higher. The wrapper-based feature selection methods could be more efficient through heuristic search algorithms. GA, PSO, and ant colony optimization (ACO) were used for subset search in wrapper-based feature selection methods [129–131]. In order to rapidly and accurately obtain the optimal feature subset for fault type identification, the hybrid feature selection method combining the advantages of the two methods above developed, in which the filter-based method is used as the first selection and the wrapper-based method is used as a second selection [132,133]. The embedded-based methods integrate feature selection and classifier learning, including classification and regression tree (CART) and C4.5 decision tree, which were applied to rolling bearing fault type recognition [134].

(3) Classification

After feature extraction and feature reduction, it is necessary to train a classifier to learn the mapping between the features and the class labels of existing bearing signals for conducting automatic fault type recognition. The known instances with the transformed/selected features and the corresponding class labels are fed into a classification algorithm as the training set. The class label of each instance in the test set can be predicted by the trained classifier according to their features. In the past decade, various classification methods have been applied to rolling bearing fault type recognition, such as k-nearest neighbor (KNN), artificial neural network (ANN), support vector machine (SVM), extreme learning machine (ELM), and random forest (RF).

KNN has the advantages of only one parameter and easy implementation by making classification decisions vis identifying the attributes of a limited number of neighboring training samples around the unknown/testing sample. Yan et al. [108] calculated IDE-PE of the bearing signal and used KNN to classify bearing fault types. It should be noted that the performance of KNN depends on the quality of sample features. ANN is a multilayer feedforward neural network and can perform fault type recognition by adjusting the association relationship between a large number of network nodes [135,136]. SVM has good generalization ability, but the kernel function and related parameters need to be selected. Zhu et al. [137] proposed a new rolling element bearing fault diagnosis method based on multi-scale fuzzy entropy, multiple class feature selection, and SVM. Chen et al. [138] input the symbolic entropy of the bearing signals into SVM for fault type identification and obtained good results. ELM is a feedforward neural network that uses random weights between the hidden layer and the input layer, and the output weights of its output layer are calculated through regular processes. With ELM, only the number of hidden layer neurons needs to be set. It has the advantage of rapid processing and good generalization but the disadvantage of overfitting [139]. RF can handle high-dimensional data effectively without a long running time, but the parameter selection of RF often affects the classification accuracy [140]. To avoid setting classifier parameters manually, PSO is used to adaptively determine the optimal parameters of classifiers, e.g., PSO optimized SVM, PSO optimized ELM, and PSO optimized RF, which were proposed to improve the accuracy of fault identification [141–143].

4.2. Deep Learning Based Fault Type Recognition Methods

Deep learning techniques have strong learnability. By stacking non-linear processing units layer by layer, it can automatically learn effective features from the raw data without manual feature extraction and manipulation. Deep learning methods are primarily implemented based on ANN, including convolutional neural networks (CNNs), Autoencoder (AE), deep belief networks (DBNs), and recursive neural networks (RNNs). Deep learning methods were used to address machine vision, image processing, speech recognition, text analysis, and other problems. Inspired by these successful applications, deep learning methods have been gradually introduced into the field of fault diagnosis over the past five years [144].

CNNs is the most commonly used deep learning method for fault diagnosis. The network structure is usually composed of convolution layers and pooling layers. The convolution layer convolutes with the original input data to obtain shallow features, and then the pooling layer captures the relatively important features through down sampling. The deep characteristics of the data are gradually obtained by alternately stacking the convolution layer and the pooling layer. CNNs were first used to identify the fault types of rolling bearings in 2016 [145], and then it was widely used and improved [146–148]. The input data of a CNN can be one-dimensional bearing vibration signals or two-dimensional images (i.e., spectrogram, texture, and grayscale) converted from one-dimensional vibration signals. Accordingly, 1D-CNNs and 2D-CNNs methods were developed. Wen et al. [146] transformed the one-dimensional time series signals into two-dimensional image signals through random sampling segments of the original signals and fed these images into Lenet-5, which achieved satisfactory results in three different mechanical fault diagnosis tasks. In [147], Wang et al. applied Morlet wavelet decomposition and bilinear interpolation to convert the vibration signal into grayscale images and then used rectified linear units and the appropriate dropout strategy to improve the generalization performance of CNNs for fault diagnosis. Zhang et al. [148] proposed an improved CNN model using the original vibration signals as inputs. This method uses a wide convolution kernel for extracting features and suppressing high-frequency noise and small convolutional kernels in the preceding layers for performing multilayer nonlinear mapping. The CNN-based fault recognition methods typically extract the internal features of bearing signals through multiple convolution layers and pooling layers and perform fault type recognition by using the fully connected layer, which has a layer with Softmax or Signmoid function for classification, or using other classifiers, such as KNN, to perform classification

AE is a special neural network that consists of two parts, i.e., encoding and decoding, which is to reconstruct input data for obtaining the discriminative data information. The use of improved AE methods has enhanced the processing performance of fault diagnosis. For example, the denoising AE method was proposed by adding noise to the original data, the sparsity AE method was implemented by introducing sparse constraints to the output layer, and the stacking AE method was developed by combining multiple AEs. In [149–152], AE and its improved versions were utilized for extracting discriminative features from the original vibration of signals, based on which bearing fault types may be accurately recognized. Sun et al. [149] used AE to fuse the extracted features of the bearing signals, thereby reducing the redundancy of signals. Shi et al. [150] developed the sparsity AE by adding a sparse penalty to AE for high-level feature learning and bearing fault recognition. Zhou et al. [151] proposed a novel diagnosis method based on Teager computed order spectrum and stacking AE. The results demonstrated that the proposed method could extract features adaptively from bearing vibration signals regardless of the speed or load changes. Gu et al. [152] used a denoising AE to extract features from the bearing original vibration signals and inputted the extracted features to the BP network classifier.

DBN is formed by stacking multiple restricted Boltzmann machines (RBMs), where the output layer of the former RBM is used as the input layer of the latter RBM. These RBMs are trained in a greedy hierarchical manner and can gradually learn expressive features from the data. Oh et al. [153] used the directional gradient histogram of the vibration signals as input features to the DBN model for bearing fault recognition. In [154], the time-domain and frequency-domain features extracted from the different sensor signals were fused as the machine health indicators through a multiple two-layer sparsity AE and used to train a DBN for further classification. Shao et al. [155] developed a novel rolling bearing fault recognition method called continuous DBN with locally linear embedding, which computes a new comprehensive feature index based on locally linear embedding to quantify rolling bearing performance degradation and uses a GA to optimize the DBN parameters for adapting to the signal characteristics.

Considering that the rolling bearing vibration signal is essentially a time series, RNNs with time memory functions have gradually attracted attention. RNNs can effectively analyze and process the time information of the data by establishing the connection between multiple cycle units and mapping the whole history of the input data to the target vector. To address the long-term dependency, improved methods of RNNs were developed, such as long-short-term memory (LSTM) and gated recurrent units (GRUs), which are more effective for bearing fault recognition [156–158]. Yuan et al. [156] investigated the performance of RNN, LSTM, and GRU in fault diagnosis, finding that LSTM performed the best and the ensemble of RNN, LSTM, and GRU could not enhance its performance. Zhao et al. [157] developed convolutional bi-directional LSTM combining CNN and LSTM, where CNN extracted the robust local features from original signals and LSTM encoded temporal information on the outputs of CNN. Zhao et al. [158] constructed a deep GRU for effectively learning features of bearing vibration signals and applied the artificial fish swarm algorithm to obtain the optimal parameters of the GRUs.

5. Datasets, Practices, Limitations/Challenges, and Future Research Trends

In this section, commonly used datasets are discussed to provide useful guidance and practices for researchers and practitioners. This section also summarizes the limitations and challenges of existing works and points out future research directions.

5.1. Commonly Used Datasets and Practices

In addition to the development of fault diagnosis methods, the collection and establishment of benchmark datasets are also necessary. The commonly used fault diagnosis datasets are Case Western Reserve University [159], IEEE PHM 2012 Data Challenge [160], University of Cincinnati [161], University of Ottawa [162], and Xi'an Jiao Tong University [163]. They are publicly available and state-of-the-art datasets in the rolling fault diagnosis community. These datasets contain a wide range of rolling bearing operation data, which are described in detail in the corresponding references. For the fault detection problem, a representative signal segment is subjectively intercepted from the collected rolling bearing data for analysis. The detection performance of the same method will vary with different intercepted signals. For the fault type recognition problems, these datasets cannot be directly used to test the effectiveness of the proposed methods. Data preprocessing may be needed to solve the task. For example, the original rolling bearing data of these datasets are often divided to form the training set and the test set to train and test the machine learning-based methods, respectively. In addition to these datasets, there are also some other fault diagnosis datasets that were used in the literature, but they are not publicly available. To make fair comparisons between existing methods, it is important to use the same experimental settings including data preprocessing and splitting. However, this is very hard to achieve at the current stage. On the other hand, to enrich the field of fault diagnosis, it is also necessary to develop/share good datasets of various rolling bearing fault diagnosis tasks, such as the ImageNet [164] dataset in the computer vision community.

5.2. Limitations and Challenges

Although many rolling bearing fault diagnosis methods were proposed and achieved promising results. They have limitations. Most of these methods essentially focus on how to increase the effectiveness of the diagnosis whilst paying little attention to the intelligence and adaptability of the diagnosis systems. Specifically, the limitations/challenges of existing techniques are summarized as follows. Some research directions/topics were also pointed out to address these limitations.

(1) **Limitations of fault detection methods:** Some rolling bearing fault detection methods, such as morphological transform-based methods, filter-based methods, decomposition-based methods, and deconvolution-based methods, often need rich domain/prior knowledge to design and use. For example, it should be known in advance how these methods operate, what their advantages and disadvantages are, and whether they are suitable or effective for the task at hand. However, experts with such knowledge are often costly to employ. In addition, the running condition of

rolling bearings in actual services is complex and dynamic, making it very hard to develop a method to meet the actual environment. Capturing the periodic impact component caused by the fault in the signal is a good way to achieve fault detection but very challenging. To address this limitation, it is promising to develop an intelligent method that can automatically generate a detection model to adaptively remove the background interference and effectively retain the fault-related impulses.

(2) **Limitations of traditional fault type recognition methods:** Traditional rolling bearing fault type recognition methods often include three key steps, i.e., feature extraction, feature reduction, and classification. The results of a previous step may influence the outcomes of the following step. To ensure the whole diagnostic process is feasible and effective, each step must be designed elaborately by experienced researchers, such as determining which type of features to choose/extract, which features to use, which classifier to use, and whether the classifier needs to be optimized. However, it should be noted that such a well-designed diagnostic method may only be effective for a specific fault diagnosis task. Therefore, it is promising to design methods that can automatically deal with these subtasks of fault type recognition. In addition, obtaining representative features of sample signals is the key to achieving good results. Therefore, it is a good research direction that develops a diagnostic method to automatically and simultaneously extract and construct representative features from the original bearing signals, to reduce the difficulty of distinguishing samples and improve the accuracy of fault type recognition.

(3) **Limitations of deep learning-based fault type recognition methods:** Although the deep-learning-based rolling bearing fault type recognition methods can automatically achieve feature extraction, feature reduction, and classification, most of the methods are based on neural networks, which need researchers to design their architectures and adjust the corresponding parameters. The process of model design and parameter adjustment process will consume a significant amount of time and resources. Moreover, the interpretability of the neural network-based methods is not good, i.e., cannot directly express the fault identification process. In addition, these methods usually require a large number of samples to train. However, in practical engineering applications, it is typically difficult to obtain a large number of fault samples, which will limit the use of deep learning-based diagnosis methods.

Therefore, it is necessary to develop new rolling bearing fault type recognition methods that do not need rich manual effort to design the architectures and select the parameters, can effectively deal with limited training data, and learn interpretable models for fault type recognition. These are very challenging research directions, but it is worth investigating them to make the fault type recognition methods more applicable to real-world scenarios.

In summation, the existing rolling bearing fault diagnosis methods require rich prior knowledge and expert experience and lack intelligence and flexibility; therefore, these methods have not been fully explored from a universal perspective. Therefore, it is necessary to develop a rolling bearing fault diagnosis approach that relies less on prior knowledge, domain expert experience, or human intervention and can be effectively applied to a wide range of applications.

5.3. Future Research Directions

In addition to the aforementioned research directions/topics, there are some other research topics that are becoming popular in this field. This subsection will discuss these research trends.

(1) **Transfer learning-based methods:** The effective performance of the fault type recognition methods usually needs to meet a basic assumption, namely, that the training samples and test samples are independent and identically distributed. However, the monitor information of rolling bearing is generally subject to working conditions, such as the characteristic frequency and amplitude changing with rotational speed, resulting in a large distribution difference between training data and test data, thereby

presenting a domain migration issue. Transfer learning (TL) can extract knowledge from one or more related scenes to help improve the learning performance of scenarios in the target domain [165]. TL can relax the assumption of independent and identical distributions and provide a new solution to address the above deficiencies. The TL-based rolling bearing fault type recognition methods were proposed and achieved desirable results [166–168]. The TL-based recognition model, learning the common feature space from the source domain data and the target domain data to reduce the distribution difference between different domains, cannot adaptively adjust its parameters for target domain tasks, thereby affecting its domain adaptability and recognition accuracy. Thus, the further development of TL-based fault type recognition methods is a good direction for future research to improve the classification performance, recognition accuracy, and generalization under variable operating conditions.

(2) **Few-shot learning methods:** A large amount of labelled data is also the key to ensuring the performance of existing fault type recognition methods, especially for deep learning-based methods. In real-world scenarios, it is easy to obtain enough normal samples due to the rolling bearing mostly running under normal conditions, but the fault samples are typically difficult to obtain and require extensive manual effort to label. The absence of labelled fault samples will either lead to overfitting in the training process or the class imbalance problem. Few-shot learning (FSL) is effective for distinguishing failure attribution accurately under very limited data conditions [169,170]. Data augmentation, data/model transfer, and meta-learning constitute the three main threads of FSL methods. Thus, the comprehensive exploration of FSL-based fault type recognition methods is a good direction for future research for reducing the dependence on large amounts of data, avoiding the risk of overfitting, and improving the applicability and recognition performance.

(3) **Evolutionary deep learning methods:** Evolutionary deep learning methods aim to deal with the limitations of deep learning methods, particularly neural networks, by using evolutionary computation (EC) techniques. This direction includes two main topics, i.e., using EC methods to automatically design neural networks and using EC methods to evolve deep models by themselves. On the first topic, some work was performed to evolve neural networks for fault diagnosis by finding the optimal numbers of layers, network connections, numbers of filters, etc. [171–175]. These methods can reduce the requirement of expertise from both the neural network domain and the problem domain, improve recognition performance, and decrease the number of parameters in the evolved models. On the second topic, pure EC methods, particularly genetic programming methods, are used to evolve deep models. GP is a computational intelligence algorithm to achieve automatic programming without human intervention and domain knowledge [176,177]. With a flexible program expression, GP can automatically evolve variable-length models to solve a task. GP has shown promise in the computer vision domain by evolving deep models [178–181]. The models evolved by GP typically have better interpretability than neural networks. However, there is little work on GP for fault diagnosis [182–184]. Figure 6 shows an example of using GP to solve fault type recognition, where the GP method is used to automatically generate informative and discriminative features from original vibration signals for recognizing different fault types. The left example tree of Figure 6 is the solution evolved by GP, showing high interpretability. In addition, the solutions are often creative and even not considered by human experts [183,184]. However, both topics have not been fully investigated in the fault diagnosis community. Therefore, it is promising to develop effective evolutionary deep learning approaches to fault diagnosis.

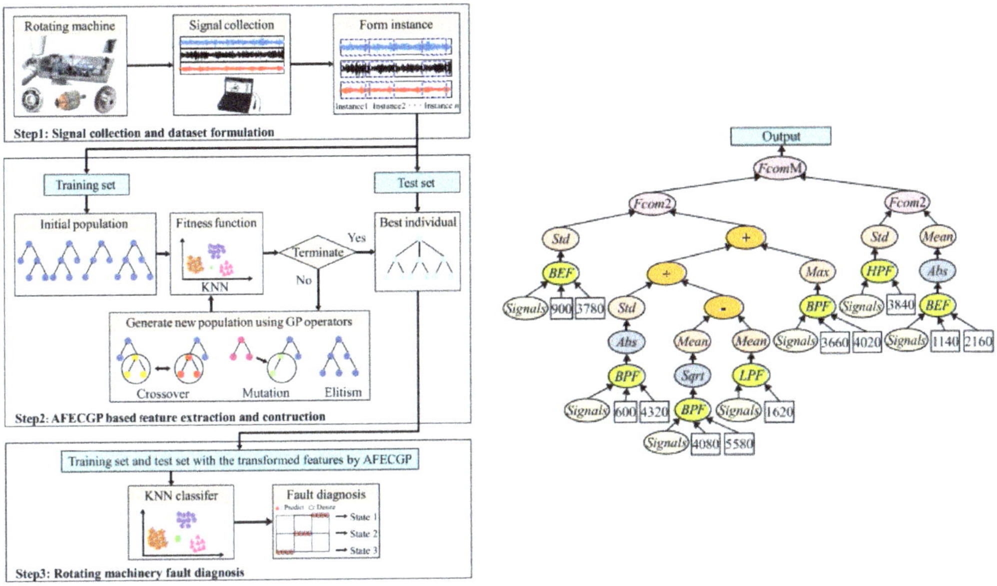

(**a**) Flowchart (**b**) Solution

Figure 6. Illustrations of the proposed GPAFEC method in [183]. (**a**) Flowchart of GPAFEC, (**b**) Solution evolved by GP.

6. Conclusions

The rolling bearing is an indispensable part of rotating machinery, and its running status typically affects the operation of the whole equipment. The research into rolling bearing fault diagnosis technology is of great significance to ensure the safe and stable operations of rotating machinery. This paper comprehensively reviewed existing fault diagnosis methods of the rolling bearing in terms of fault detection and fault type recognition. For fault detection, the methods, i.e., morphological transformation-based methods, filter-based methods, decomposition-based methods, and deconvolution-based methods, were discussed. For fault type recognition, traditional methods and deep learning-based methods were discussed. The commonly used datasets of fault diagnosis were presented for better practices. In addition, we summarized the limitations of existing methods and pointed out future research directions, which provides helpful guidance for researchers who are interested in this field. Overall, this field of fault diagnosis has potential for future study. Given the current limitations, it is still needed to develop automatic, intelligent, effective, and efficient methods for rolling bearing fault diagnosis under real-world scenarios. In addition, some topics such as transfer learning, few-shot learning, and evolutionary deep learning can also be further investigated to enrich this field.

Author Contributions: B.P.: writing—original draft preparation; Y.B.: writing—review and editing; B.X., M.Z. and S.W.: supervision and revision. All authors have read and agreed to the published version of the manuscript.

Funding: This research was funded by the Scientific Research Foundation for the Talents of Hebei Agricultural University (No: YJ2021056) and Hebei Key Laboratory of Electric Machinery Health Maintenance and Failure Prevention Fund (No.: KF2021-01).

Data Availability Statement: Not applicable.

Conflicts of Interest: The authors declare no conflict of interest.

References

1. Chen, S.; Peng, Z.; Zhou, P. Review of signal decomposition theory and its applications in machine fault diagnosis. *J. Mech. Eng.* **2020**, *56*, 91–107.
2. Yan, G.; Chen, J.; Bai, Y.; Yu, C.; Yu, C. A Survey on Fault Diagnosis Approaches for Rolling Bearings of Railway Vehicles. *Processes* **2022**, *10*, 724. [CrossRef]
3. Kuang, P.; Xu, F.; Liu, Y. *Modern Machinery Fault Diagnosis: Principles and Techniques*; China Agriculture Press: Beijing, China, 1991.
4. Wang, X. Research on Fault Diagnosis Method of Rolling Bearing Based on Vibration Signal Processing. Ph.D. Thesis, North China Electric Power University, Beijing, China, 2017.
5. Zhang, X.; Zhao, B.; Lin, Y. Machine Learning Based Bearing Fault Diagnosis Using the Case Western Reserve University Data: A Review. *IEEE Access* **2021**, *9*, 155598–155608. [CrossRef]
6. Singh, J.; Azamfar, M.; Li, F.; Lee, J. A systematic review of machine learning algorithms for prognostics and health management of rolling element bearings: Fundamentals, concepts and applications. *Meas. Sci. Technol.* **2020**, *32*, 012001. [CrossRef]
7. Lin, H.; Ye, Y. Reviews of bearing vibration measurement using fast Fourier transform and enhanced fast Fourier transform algorithms. *Adv. Mech. Eng.* **2019**, *11*, 1687814018816751. [CrossRef]
8. Liu, R.; Yang, B.; Zio, E.; Chen, X. Artificial intelligence for fault diagnosis of rotating machinery: A review. *Mech. Syst. Signal Process.* **2018**, *108*, 33–47. [CrossRef]
9. Wang, Y.; Xiang, J.; Markert, R.; Liang, M. Spectral kurtosis for fault detection, diagnosis and prognostics of rotating machines: A review with applications. *Mech. Syst. Signal Process.* **2016**, *66*, 679–698. [CrossRef]
10. Rai, A.; Upadhyay, S. A review on signal processing techniques utilized in the fault diagnosis of rolling element bearings. *Tribol. Int.* **2016**, *96*, 289–306. [CrossRef]
11. Neupane, D.; Seok, J. Bearing fault detection and diagnosis using case western reserve university dataset with deep learning approaches: A review. *IEEE Access* **2020**, *8*, 93155–93178. [CrossRef]
12. Yang, Z. Oil Liquid State Monitoring technolgoy and application in equipment maintenance management. *Mech. Manag. Dev.* **2006**, *89*, 51–52.
13. Sun, B.; Wang, Y.; Yang, L. Study of fault diagnosis of induction motor bearing based on infrared inspection. *Elect. Mach. Control* **2012**, *16*, 50–55.
14. Wang, Y. Acoustic-Based Condition Monitoring of Machinery Using Blind Signal Processing. Ph.D. Thesis, Kunming University of Science and Technology, Kunming, China, 2010.
15. Singh, S.; Vishwakarma, M. A review of vibration analysis techniques for rotating machines. *Int. J. Eng. Res. T.* **2015**, *4*, 757–761.
16. Randall, R.; Jérme, A. Rolling element bearing diagnostics—A tutorial. *Mech. Syst. Signal Process.* **2011**, *25*, 485–520. [CrossRef]
17. Ripley, B.; Matheron, G. Random sets and integral geometry. *J. R. Stat. Soc.* **1975**, *139*, 277–278. [CrossRef]
18. Maragos, P.; Schafer, R. Morphological filters. Part 1. Their set-theoretic analysis and relations to linear shift-invariant filters. *IEEE Trans. Acous. Speech Signal Process.* **1987**, *35*, 1153–1169. [CrossRef]
19. Maragos, P.; Schafer, R. Morphological filters. Part 2. Their set-theoretic analysis and relations to linear shift-invariant filters. *IEEE Trans. Acous. Speech Signal Process.* **1987**, *35*, 1170–1184. [CrossRef]
20. Wang, J.; Xu, G.; Zhang, Q.; Liang, L. Application of improved morphological filter to the extraction of impulsive attenuation signals. *Mech. Syst. Signal Process.* **2009**, *23*, 236–245. [CrossRef]
21. Shen, C.; Zhu, Z.; Kong, F.; Huang, W. An improved morphological filtering method and its application in bearing fault feature extraction. *J. Vib. Eng.* **2012**, *25*, 468–473.
22. He, W.; Jiang, Z.; Qin, Q. A joint adaptive wavelet filter and morphological signal processing method for weak mechanical impulse extraction. *J. Mech. Sci. Technol.* **2010**, *24*, 1709–1716. [CrossRef]
23. Raj, A.; Murali, N. Early classification of bearing faults using morphological operators and fuzzy inference. *IEEE Trans. Ind. Electron.* **2013**, *60*, 567–574. [CrossRef]
24. Osman, S.; Wang, W. An Hilbert-huang spectrum technique for fault detection in rolling element bearings. *IEEE Trans. Instrum. Meas.* **2016**, *65*, 2646–2656. [CrossRef]
25. Li, Y.; Liang, X.; Zuo, M. A new strategy of using a time-varying structure element for mathematical morphological filtering. *Measurement* **2017**, *106*, 53–65. [CrossRef]
26. Li, Y.; Zuo, M.; Lin, J.; Liu, J. Fault detection method for railway wheel flat using an adaptive multiscale morphological filter. *Mech. Syst. Signal Process.* **2017**, *84*, 642–658. [CrossRef]
27. Li, Y.; Liang, X.; Zuo, M. Diagonal slice spectrum assisted optimal scale morphological filter for rolling element bearing fault diagnosis. *Mech. Syst. Signal Process.* **2017**, *85*, 146–161. [CrossRef]
28. Wang, D.; Tse, P.; Tse, Y. A morphogram with the optimal selection of parameters used in morphological analysis for enhancing the ability in bearing fault diagnosis. *Meas. Sci. Technol.* **2012**, *23*, 65001–65015. [CrossRef]
29. Meng, L.; Xiang, J.; Wang, Y.; Jiang, Y.; Gao, H. A hybrid fault diagnosis method using morphological filter-translation invariant wavelet and improved ensemble empirical mode decomposition. *Mech. Syst. Signal Process.* **2015**, *50–51*, 101–115. [CrossRef]
30. Deng, F.; Tang, G.; He, Y. Fault feature extraction for rolling element bearings based on cepstrum pre-whitening and morphology self-complementary top-hat transformation. *J. Vib. Shock* **2015**, *34*, 77–81.
31. Yan, X.; Jia, M. Parameter optimized combination morphological filter-hat transform and its application in fault diagnosis of wind turbine. *J. Mech. Eng.* **2016**, *52*, 103–110. [CrossRef]

32. Li, Y.; Zuo, M.; Chen, Y.; Feng, K. An enhanced morphology gradient product filter for bearing fault detection. *Mech. Syst. Signal Process.* **2018**, *109*, 166–184. [CrossRef]
33. Deng, F.; Yang, S.; Guo, W.; Liu, Y. Fault feature extraction method for rolling bearing based on adaptive multi-scale morphological AVG-Hat filtering. *J. Vib. Eng.* **2017**, *30*, 178–187.
34. Zou, F.; Zhang, H.; Sang, S.; Li, X.; He, W.; Liu, X. Bearing fault diagnosis based on combined multi-scale weighted entropy morphological filtering and bi-LSTM. *Appl. Intell.* **2021**, *51*, 6647–6664. [CrossRef]
35. Li, Y.; Liang, X.; Lin, J.; Chen, Y.; Liu, J. Train axle bearing fault detection using a feature selection scheme based multi-scale morphological filter. *Mech. Syst. Signal Process.* **2018**, *101*, 435–448. [CrossRef]
36. Zhu, D.; Zhang, Y.; Zhu, Q. Fault feature extraction for rolling element bearings based on multi-scale morphological filter and frequency-weighted energy operator. *J. Vibroeng.* **2018**, *20*, 2892–2907. [CrossRef]
37. Wu, Z.; Yang, S.; Ren, B.; Ma, X.; Zhang, J. Rolling element bearing fault diagnosis method based on NAMEMD and multi-scale morphology. *J. Vib. Shock* **2016**, *35*, 127–133.
38. Chen, Q.; Chen, Z.; Sun, W.; Yang, G. A new structuring element for multi-scale morphology analysis and its application in rolling element bearing fault diagnosis. *J. Vib. Control* **2015**, *21*, 765–789. [CrossRef]
39. Antoni, J. The spectral kurtosis: A useful tool for characterising non-stationary signals. *Mech. Syst. Signal Process.* **2006**, *20*, 282–307. [CrossRef]
40. Antoni, J.; Randall, R. The spectral kurtosis: Application to the vibratory surveillance and diagnostics of rotating machines. *Mech. Syst. Signal Process.* **2006**, *20*, 308–331. [CrossRef]
41. Lei, Y.; Lin, J.; He, Z.; Zi, Y. Application of an improved kurtogram method for fault diagnosis of rolling element bearings. *Mech. Syst. Signal Process.* **2011**, *25*, 1738–1749. [CrossRef]
42. Wang, D.; Tse, P.; Tsui, K. An enhanced kurtogram method for fault diagnosis of rolling element bearings. *Mech. Syst. Signal Process.* **2013**, *35*, 176–199. [CrossRef]
43. Chen, B.; Zhang, Z.; Zi, Y.; He, Z.; Sun, C. Detecting of transient vibration signatures using an improved fast spatial-spectral ensemble kurtosis kurtogram and its applications to mechanical signature analysis of short duration data from rotating machinery. *Mech. Syst. Signal Process.* **2013**, *40*, 1–37. [CrossRef]
44. Moshrefzadeh, A.; Fasana, A. The autogram: An effective approach for selecting the optimal demodulation band in rolling element bearings diagnosis. *Mech. Syst. Signal Process.* **2018**, *105*, 294–318. [CrossRef]
45. Gu, X.; Yang, S.; Liu, Y.; Liao, Y. An improved kurtogram method and its application in fault diagnosis of rolling element bearings under complex interferences. *J. Vib. Shock* **2017**, *36*, 187–193.
46. Tse, P.; Wang, D. The design of a new sparsogram for fast bearing fault diagnosis: Part 1 of the two related manuscripts that have a joint title as "Two automatic vibration-based fault diagnostic methods using the novel sparsity measurement-Parts 1 and 2". *Mech. Syst. Signal Process.* **2013**, *40*, 499–519. [CrossRef]
47. Antoni, J. The infogram: Entropic evidence of the signature of repetitive transients. *Mech. Syst. Signal Process.* **2016**, *71*, 73–94 [CrossRef]
48. Wan, S.; Zhang, X.; Dou, L. Shannon entropy of binary wavelet packet subbands and its application in bearing fault extraction. *Entropy* **2018**, *20*, 260. [CrossRef]
49. Miao, Y.; Zhao, M.; Lin, J. Improvement of kurtosis-guided-grams via Gini index for bearing fault feature identification. *Meas. Sci. Technol.* **2017**, *28*, 125001. [CrossRef]
50. Mo, Z.; Wang, J.; Zhang, H.; Miao, Q. Weighted cyclic harmonic-to-noise ratio for rolling element bearing fault diagnosis. *IEEE Trans. Instrum. Meas.* **2020**, *69*, 432–442. [CrossRef]
51. Tse, P.; Wang, D. The automatic selection of an optimal wavelet filter and its enhancement by the new sparsogram for bearing fault detection. *Mech. Syst. Signal Process.* **2013**, *40*, 520–544. [CrossRef]
52. Gu, X.; Yang, S.; Liu, Y.; Ren, B.; Zhang, J. Fault Feature Extraction of Wheel-bearing Based on Multi-objective Cross Entropy Optimization. *J. Mech. Eng.* **2018**, *54*, 304–311. [CrossRef]
53. Wan, S.; Peng, B. Adaptive asymmetric real Laplace wavelet filtering and its application on rolling bearing early fault diagnosis. *Shock Vib.* **2019**, *2019*, 7475868. [CrossRef]
54. Xu, Y.; Zhang, K.; Ma, C.; Sheng, Z.; Shen, H. An adaptive spectrum segmentation method to optimize empirical wavelet transform for rolling bearings fault diagnosis. *IEEE Access* **2019**, *7*, 30437–30456. [CrossRef]
55. Guo, J.; Shi, Z.; Zhen, D.; Meng, Z.; Gu, F.; Ball, A.D. Modulation signal bispectrum with optimized wavelet packet denoising for rolling bearing fault diagnosis. *Struct. Health Monit.* **2022**, *21*, 984–1011. [CrossRef]
56. Huang, N.; Shen, Z.; Long, S.; Wu, M.; Shih, H.; Zheng, Q.; Yen, N.; Tung, C.; Liu, H. The empirical mode decomposition and the Hilbert spectrum for nonlinear and non-stationary time series analysis. *Proc. R. Soc. Lond. Ser. Math. Phys. Eng. Sci.* **1998**, *454*, 903–995. [CrossRef]
57. Huang, N.; Zheng, S.; Long, S. A new view of nonlinear water waves: The Hilbert spectrum. *Annu. Rev. Fluid Mech.* **1999**, *31*, 417–457. [CrossRef]
58. Gao, Q.; Du, X.; Fan, H.; Meng, Q. An empirical mode decomposition based method for rolling bearing fault diagnosis. *J. Vib. Eng.* **2007**, *20*, 19–22.
59. Wu, Z.; Huang, N. Ensemble empirical mode decomposition: A noise-assisted data analysis method. *Adv. Adapt. Data Anal.* **2009**, *1*, 1–41. [CrossRef]

60. Li, H.; Liu, T.; Wu, X.; Chen, Q. Application of EEMD and improved frequency band entropy in bearing fault feature extraction. *ISA Trans.* **2019**, *88*, 170–185. [CrossRef]
61. Tomes, M.; Colominas, M.; Schlotthauer, G.; Flandrin, P. A complete ensemble empirical mode decomposition with adaptive noise. In Proceedings of the IEEE International Conference on Acoustics, Speech and Signal Processing, Prague, Czech Republic, 22–27 May 2011.
62. Rabah, A.; Abdelhafid, K.; Azeddine, B.; Derouiche, Z. Rolling bearing fault diagnosis based on an improved denoising method using the complete ensemble empirical mode decomposition and the optimized thresholding operation. *IEEE Sens. J.* **2018**, *18*, 7166–7172.
63. Huang, H.; Sun, S.; Ren, X.; Liu, H. Early fault diagnosis of rolling bearing based on CEEMDAN and 1.5 dimension spectrum. *China Meas. Test* **2019**, *4*, 155–160.
64. Gao, S.; Wang, Q.; Zhang, Y. Rolling bearing fault diagnosis based on CEEMDAN and refined composite multiscale fuzzy entropy. *IEEE Trans. Instrum. Meas.* **2021**, *70*, 1–8. [CrossRef]
65. Smith, S. The local mean decomposition and its application to EEG perception data. *J. R. Soc. Interface* **2005**, *2*, 443–454. [CrossRef]
66. Cheng, J.; Yang, Y.; Yang, Y. A rotating machinery fault diagnosis method based on local mean decomposition. *Digital Signal Process.* **2012**, *22*, 356–366. [CrossRef]
67. Wang, L.; Liu, Z.; Miao, Q.; Zhang, X. Complete ensemble local mean decomposition with adaptive noise and its application to fault diagnosis for rolling bearings. *Mech. Syst. Signal Process.* **2018**, *106*, 24–39. [CrossRef]
68. Xu, Y.; Zhang, K.; Ma, C.; Li, S.; Zhang, H. Optimized LMD method and its applications in rolling bearing fault diagnosis. *Meas. Sci. Technol.* **2019**, *30*, 125017. [CrossRef]
69. Li, X.; Ma, J.; Wang, X.; Wu, J.; Li, Z. An improved local mean decomposition method based on improved composite interpolation envelope and its application in bearing fault feature extraction. *ISA Trans.* **2020**, *97*, 365–383. [CrossRef]
70. Frei, M.; Osorio, I. Intrinsic time-scale decomposition: Time-frequency-energy analysis and real-time filtering of non-stationary signals. *Proc. Math. Phys. Eng. Sci.* **2007**, *463*, 321–342. [CrossRef]
71. Yu, J.; Liu, H. Sparse coding shrinkage in intrinsic time-scale decomposition for weak fault feature extraction of bearings. *IEEE Trans. Instrum. Meas.* **2018**, *67*, 1579–1592. [CrossRef]
72. Ma, J.; Zhan, L.; Li, C.; Li, Z. An improved intrinsic time-scale decomposition method based on adaptive noise and its application in bearing fault feature extraction. *Meas. Sci. Technol.* **2020**, *32*, 025103. [CrossRef]
73. Yang, Y.; Zeng, M.; Cheng, J. A New Time-frequency analysis method-the local characteristic-scale decomposition. *J. Hunan Univ. (Nat. Sci.)* **2012**, *39*, 35–39.
74. Cheng, J.; Yang, Y.; Yang, Y. Local characteristic-scale decomposition method and its application to gear fault diagnosis. *J. Mech. Eng.* **2012**, *48*, 64–71. [CrossRef]
75. Cheng, J.; Yang, Y.; Li, X.; Pan, H.; Cheng, J. An early fault diagnosis method of gear based on improved symplectic geometry mode decomposition. *Measurement* **2019**, *151*, 107140. [CrossRef]
76. Luo, S.; Yang, W.; Luo, Y. A novel fault detection scheme using improved inherent multiscale fuzzy entropy with partly ensemble local characteristic-scale decomposition. *IEEE Access* **2020**, *8*, 6650–6661. [CrossRef]
77. Dragomiretskiy, K.; Zosso, D. Variational mode decomposition. *IEEE Trans. Signal Process.* **2014**, *62*, 531–544. [CrossRef]
78. Bian, J. Fault Diagnosis of bearing combining parameter optimized variational mode decomposition based on genetic algorithm with 1.5-dimensional spectrum. *J. Propul. Technol.* **2017**, *38*, 1618–1624.
79. Yan, X.; Jia, M. Application of CSA-VMD and optimal scale morphological slice bispectrum in enhancing outer race fault detection of rolling element bearings. *Mech. Syst. Signal Process.* **2019**, *122*, 56–86. [CrossRef]
80. Li, H.; Liu, T.; Wu, X.; Chen, Q. An optimized VMD method and its applications in bearing fault diagnosis. *Measurement* **2020**, *166*, 108185. [CrossRef]
81. Bonizzi, P.; Karel, J.; Meste, O.; Peeters, R. Singular spectrum decomposition: A new method for time series decomposition. *Adv. Adapt. Data Anal.* **2014**, *6*, 107–109. [CrossRef]
82. Xu, Y.; Zhang, Z.; Ma, C.; Zhang, J. Improved singular spectrum decomposition and its applications in rolling bearing fault diagnosis. *J. Vib. Eng.* **2019**, *32*, 168–175.
83. Wang, X.; Tang, G.; He, Y. Weak fault diagnosis for rolling bearing based on COT-SSD under variable rotating speed. *Elec. Power Autom. Equip.* **2019**, *39*, 187–193.
84. Mao, Y.; Jia, M.; Yan, X. A new bearing weak fault diagnosis method based on improved singular spectrum decomposition and frequency-weighted energy slice bispectrum. *Measurement* **2020**, *166*, 108235. [CrossRef]
85. Wiggins, R. Minimum entropy deconvolution. *Geophys. Prospect. Petrole* **1980**, *16*, 21–35. [CrossRef]
86. Endo, H.; Randall, R. Enhancement of autoregressive model based gear tooth fault detection technique by the use of minimum entropy deconvolution filter. *Mech. Syst. Signal Process.* **2007**, *21*, 906–919. [CrossRef]
87. McDonald, G.; Zhao, Q.; Zuo, M. Maximum correlated kurtosis deconvolution and application on gear tooth chip fault detection. *Mech. Syst. Signal Process.* **2012**, *33*, 237–255. [CrossRef]
88. Miao, Y.; Zhao, M.; Lin, J.; Xu, X. Sparse maximum harmonics-to-noise-ratio deconvolution for weak fault signature detection in bearings. *Meas. Sci. Technol.* **2016**, *27*, 105004. [CrossRef]
89. McDonald, G.; Zhao, Q. Multipoint optimal minimum entropy deconvolution and convolution fix: Application to vibration fault detection. *Mech. Syst. Signal Process.* **2017**, *82*, 461–477. [CrossRef]

90. Buzzonia, M.; Antoni, J.; D'Elia, G. Blind deconvolution based on cyclostationarity maximization and its application to fault identification. *J. Sound Vib.* **2018**, *432*, 569–601. [CrossRef]
91. Zhang, Z.; Entezami, M.; Stewart, E.; Roberts, C. Enhanced fault diagnosis of roller bearing elements using a combination of empirical mode decomposition and minimum entropy deconvolution. *Proc. Inst. Mech. Eng. Part C J. Mech. Eng. Sci.* **2017**, *231*, 655–671. [CrossRef]
92. Cheng, Y.; Wang, Z.; Zhang, W.; Huang, G. Particle swarm optimization algorithm to solve the deconvolution problem for rolling element bearing fault diagnosis. *ISA Trans.* **2019**, *90*, 244–267. [CrossRef]
93. Wang, X.; Yan, X.; He, Y. Weak fault detection for wind turbine bearing based on ACYCBD and IESB. *J. Mech. Sci. Technol.* **2020**, *34*, 1399–1413. [CrossRef]
94. Hu, Q.; He, Z.; Zhang, S.; Zi, Y.; Lei, Y. Intelligent diagnosis for incipient fault based on lifting wavelet package transform and support vector machines ensemble. *J. Mech. Eng.* **2006**, *42*, 20–26. [CrossRef]
95. Lei, Y.; He, Z.; Zi, Y. Fault diagnosis based on novel hybrid intelligent model. *J. Mech. Eng.* **2008**, *44*, 112–117. [CrossRef]
96. Yang, J.; Zhang, Y.; Zhu, Y. Intelligent fault diagnosis of rolling element bearing based on SVMs and fractal dimension. *Mech. Syst. Signal Process.* **2007**, *21*, 2012–2024. [CrossRef]
97. Caesarendra, W.; Kosasih, B.; Tieu, A.; Moodie, C. Application of the largest Lyapunov exponent algorithm for feature extraction in low speed slew bearing condition monitoring. *Mech. Syst. Signal Process.* **2015**, *50–51*, 116–138. [CrossRef]
98. Yan, R.; Gao, R. Approximate entropy as a diagnostic tool for machine health monitoring. *Mech. Syst. Signal Process.* **2007**, *21*, 824–839. [CrossRef]
99. Su, W.; Wang, F.; Zhu, H.; Guo, Z.; Zhang, Z.; Zhang, H. Feature extraction of rolling element bearing fault using wavelet packet sample entropy. *J. Vib. Meas. Diag.* **2011**, *31*, 33–37+134.
100. Zheng, J.; Cheng, J.; Yang, Y. A rolling bearing fault diagnosis approach based on LCD and fuzzy entropy. *Mech. Mach. Theory* **2013**, *70*, 441–453. [CrossRef]
101. Yan, R.; Liu, Y.; Gao, R. Permutation entropy: A nonlinear statistical measure for status characterization of rotary machines. *Mech. Syst. Signal Process.* **2012**, *29*, 474–484. [CrossRef]
102. Fu, W.; Tang, J.; Wang, K. Semi-supervised fault diagnosis of bearings based on the VMD dispersion entropy and improved SVDD with modified grey wolf optimizer. *J. Vib. Shock* **2019**, *38*, 190–197.
103. Pincus, S. Approximate entropy (ApEn) as a complexity measure. *Chaos* **1998**, *5*, 110–117. [CrossRef]
104. Richman, J.; Randall, M. Physiological time-series analysis using approximate entropy and sample entropy. *Am. J. Physiol. Heart C.* **2000**, *278*, 2039–2049. [CrossRef]
105. Chen, W. A Study of Feature Extraction from sEMG Singal Based on Entropy. Ph.D. Thesis, Shanghai University, Shanghai, China, 2008.
106. Bandt, C.; Pompe, B. Permutation entropy: A natural complexity measure for time series. *Phys. Rev. Lett.* **2002**, *88*, 174102. [CrossRef] [PubMed]
107. Rostaghi, M.; Azami, H. Dispersion entropy: A measure for time-series analysis. *IEEE Signal Process. Lett.* **2016**, *23*, 610–614. [CrossRef]
108. Yan, X.; Jia, M.; Zhao, Z. A novel intelligent detection method for rolling bearing based on IVMD and instantaneous energy distribution-permutation entropy. *Measurement* **2018**, *130*, 435–447. [CrossRef]
109. Tang, G.; Pang, B.; He, Y.; Tian, T. Gearbox fault diagnosis based on hierarchical instantaneous energy density dispersion entropy and dynamic time warping. *Entropy* **2019**, *21*, 593. [CrossRef]
110. Costa, M.; Goldberger, A.; Peng, C. Multiscale entropy analysis of complex physiologic time series. *Phys. Rev. Lett.* **2007**, *89*, 705–708. [CrossRef]
111. Liu, H.; Han, M. A fault diagnosis method based on local mean decomposition and multi-scale entropy for roller bearings. *Mech. Mach. Theory* **2014**, *75*, 67–78. [CrossRef]
112. Zhang, L.; Huang, W.; Xiong, G. Assessment of rolling element bearing fault severity using multi-scale entropy. *J. Vib. Shock* **2014**, *33*, 185–189.
113. Aziz, W.; Arif, M. Multiscale permutation entropy of physiological time series. In Proceedings of the INMIC 2005 9th International Multitopic Conference, Karachi, Pakistan, 1–5 December 2005.
114. Tiwari, R.; Gupta, V.; Kankar, P. Bearing fault diagnosis based on multi-scale permutation entropy and adaptive neuro fuzzy classifier. *J. Vib. Control* **2015**, *21*, 461–467. [CrossRef]
115. Zheng, J.; Cheng, J.; Yang, Y. Multi-scale Permutation entropy and its applications to rolling bearing fault diagnosis. *China Mech. Eng.* **2013**, *24*, 2641–2646.
116. Azami, H.; Kinney-Lang, E.; Ebied, A.; Fernández, A.; Escudero, J. Multiscale dispersion entropy for the regional analysis of resting-state magnetoencephalogram complexity in Alzheimer's disease. In Proceedings of the 39th Annual International Conference of the IEEE Engineering in Medicine and Biology Society, Jeju Island, South Korea, 11–15 July 2017.
117. Azami, H.; Rostaghi, M.; Abasolo, D.; Escudero, J. Refined composite multiscale dispersion entropy and its application to biomedical signals. *IEEE Trans. Biomed. Eng.* **2017**, *64*, 2872–2879.
118. Xu, Z.; Liu, K.; Zhang, H.; Wnag, D.; Zhang, M. A fault diagnosis method for rolling bearings based on empirical mode decomposition and principal component analysis. *J. Vib. Shock* **2014**, *33*, 133–139.

119. Ahmed, H.; Nandi, A. Three-stage hybrid fault diagnosis for rolling bearings with compressively-sampled data and subspace learning techniques. *IEEE Trans. Ind. Electron.* **2018**, *66*, 5516–5524. [CrossRef]
120. Ding, X.; He, Q.; Luo, N. A fusion feature and its improvement based on locality preserving projections for rolling element bearing fault classification. *J. Sound Vib.* **2015**, *335*, 367–383. [CrossRef]
121. Jiang, L.; Shi, T.; Xuan, J. Fault diagnosis of rolling bearings based on marginal fisher analysis. *J. Vib. Control* **2014**, *20*, 470–480. [CrossRef]
122. Yu, J. Local and global principal component analysis for process monitoring. *J. Process Control* **2012**, *22*, 1358–1373. [CrossRef]
123. Chen, J.; Ma, Z.; Liu, Y. Local coordinates alignment with global preservation for dimensionality reduction. *IEEE Trans. Neural Netw. Learn.* **2013**, *24*, 106–117. [CrossRef]
124. Zhang, M.; Ge, Z.; Song, Z.; Fu, R. Global-local structure analysis model and its application for fault detection and identification. *Ind. Eng. Chem. Res.* **2011**, *50*, 6837–6848. [CrossRef]
125. Gao, Y.; Yu, D.; Wang, H.; Chen, T. Fault feature extraction method of rolling bearing based on spectral graph indices. *J. Aeronaut. Power* **2018**, *33*, 2033–2040.
126. Cheng, J.; Zheng, J.; Yang, Y.; Luo, S. Fault diagnosis model for rolling bearing based on partly ensemble local characteristic-scale decomposition and Laplacian score. *J. Vib. Eng.* **2014**, *27*, 942–950.
127. Vakharia, V.; Gupta, V.; Kankar, P. Efficient fault diagnosis of ball bearing using ReliefF and Random Forest classifier. *J. Braz. Soc. Mech. Sci. Eng.* **2017**, *39*, 2969–2982. [CrossRef]
128. Li, Y.; Yang, Y.; Li, G.; Xu, M.; Huang, W. A fault diagnosis scheme for planetary gearboxes using modified multi-scale symbolic dynamic entropy and mRMR feature selection. *Mech. Syst. Signal Process.* **2017**, *91*, 295–312. [CrossRef]
129. Wang, X.; Qiu, J.; Liu, G. New feature selection method in machine fault diagnosis. *Chin. J. Mech. Eng.* **2005**, *18*, 251–254. [CrossRef]
130. Pan, X.; Huang, J.; Mao, H.; Liu, Z. Fault-characteristic extracting technology based on particle swarm optimization. *J. Vib. Shock* **2008**, *27*, 144–147.
131. Kadri, O.; Mouss, L.; Mouss, M. Fault diagnosis of rotary kiln using SVM and binary ACO. *J. Mech. Sci. Technol.* **2012**, *26*, 601–608. [CrossRef]
132. Zhang, X.; Zhang, Q.; Chen, M.; Sun, Y.; Qin, X.; Li, H. A two-stage feature selection and intelligent fault diagnosis method for rotating machinery using hybrid filter and wrapper method. *Neurocomputing* **2017**, *275*, 2426–2439. [CrossRef]
133. Xue, R.; Zhao, R. The fault feature selection algorithm of combination of ReliefF and QPSO. *J. Vib. Shock* **2020**, *39*, 176–181+213.
134. Zhu, X.; Zhang, Y.; Zhu, Y. Intelligent fault diagnosis of rolling bearing based on kernel neighborhood rough sets and statistical features. *J. Mech Sci. Technol.* **2012**, *26*, 2649–2657. [CrossRef]
135. Zhao, X.; Tang, X.; Zhao, J.; Zhang, Y. Fault diagnosis of asynchronous induction motor based on BP neural network. In Proceedings of the International Conference on Measuring Technology and Mechatronics Automation, Changsha, China, 13–14 March 2010.
136. Gunerkar, R.S.; Jalan, A.K.; Belgamwar, S.U. Fault diagnosis of rolling element bearing based on artificial neural network. *J. Mech. Sci. Technol.* **2019**, *33*, 505–511. [CrossRef]
137. Zhu, K.; Chen, L.; HU, X. Rolling element bearing fault diagnosis based on multi-scale global fuzzy entropy, multiple class feature selection and support vector machine. *Trans. Inst. Meas. Control* **2019**, *41*, 4013–4022. [CrossRef]
138. Chen, X.; He, W.; Ma, D.; Zhao, D. Symbol entropy and svm based rolling bearing fault diagnosis. *China Mech. Eng.* **2010**, *21*, 67–70.
139. Tian, Y.; Ma, J.; Lu, C.; Wang, Z. Rolling bearing fault diagnosis under variable conditions using LMD-SVD and extreme learning machine. *Mech. Mach. Theory* **2015**, *90*, 175–186. [CrossRef]
140. Han, T.; Jiang, D. Rolling bearing fault diagnostic method based on VMD-AR model and random forest classifier. *Shock Vib.* **2016**, *6*, 1–11. [CrossRef]
141. Zhang, X.; Zhang, Q.; Qin, X.; Sun, Y. Rolling bearing fault diagnosis based on ITD Lempel-Ziv complexity and PSO-SVM. *J. Vib. Shock* **2016**, *35*, 102–107+138.
142. Tang, G.; Pang, B.; Tian, T.; Zhou, C. Fault diagnosis of rolling bearings based on improved fast spectral correlation and optimized random forest. *Appl. Sci.* **2018**, *8*, 1859. [CrossRef]
143. Wu, J.; Qin, W.; Liang, H.; Jin, S.; Luo, W. Transformer fault identification method based on self-adaptive extreme learning machine. *Elec. Power Autom. Equip.* **2019**, *39*, 181–186.
144. Zhao, R.; Yan, R.; Chen, Z.; Mao, K.; Wang, P.; Gao, R. Deep learning and its applications to machine health monitoring. *Mech. Syst. Signal Process.* **2019**, *115*, 213–237. [CrossRef]
145. Singh, S.; Howard, C.; Hansen, C. Convolutional neural network based fault detection for rotating machinery. *J. Sound Vib.* **2016**, *377*, 331–345.
146. Wen, L.; Li, X.; Gao, L.; Zhang, Y. A new convolutional neural network-based data-driven fault diagnosis method. *IEEE Trans. Ind. Electron.* **2017**, *65*, 5990–5998. [CrossRef]
147. Wang, J.; Zhuang, J.; Duan, L.; Cheng, W. A multi-scale convolution neural network for featureless fault diagnosis. In Proceedings of the International Symposium on Flexible Automation, Cleveland, OH, USA, 1–3 August 2016.
148. Zhang, W.; Peng, G.; Li, C.; Chen, Y.; Zhang, Z. A new deep learning model for fault diagnosis with good anti-noise and domain adaptation ability on raw vibration signals. *Sensors* **2017**, *17*, 425. [CrossRef]

149. Sun, W.; Deng, A.; Deng, M.; Zhu, J.; Zhai, Y. Multi-view feature fusion for rolling bearing fault diagnosis using random forest and autoencoder. *J. Southeast Univ.* **2019**, *35*, 33–40.
150. Shi, P.; Guo, X.; Han, D.; Fu, R. A sparse auto-encoder method based on compressed sensing and wavelet packet energy entropy for rolling bearing intelligent fault diagnosis. *J. Mech. Sci. Technol.* **2020**, *34*, 1445–1458. [CrossRef]
151. Zhou, X.; Zhang, X.; Zhang, W.; Xia, X. Fault diagnosis of rolling bearing under fluctuating speed and variable load based on TCO spectrum and stacking auto-encoder. *Measurement* **2019**, *138*, 162–174.
152. Gu, Y.; Cao, J.; Song, X.; Yao, J. A Denoising autoencoder-based bearing fault diagnosis system for time-domain vibration signal. *Wirel. Commun. Mob. Com.* **2021**, *2021*, 9790053. [CrossRef]
153. Oh, H.; Jung, J.H.; Jeon, B.C.; Youn, B.D. Scalable and unsupervised feature engineering using vibration-imaging and deep learning for rotor system diagnosis. *IEEE Trans. Ind. Electron.* **2018**, *65*, 3539–3549. [CrossRef]
154. Chen, Z.; Li, W. Multisensor feature fusion for bearing fault diagnosis using sparse autoencoder and deep belief network. *IEEE Trans. Instrum. Meas.* **2017**, *66*, 1693–1702. [CrossRef]
155. Shao, H.; Jiang, H.; Li, X.; Liang, T. Rolling bearing fault detection using continuous deep belief network with locally linear embedding. *Comput. Ind.* **2018**, *96*, 27–39. [CrossRef]
156. Yuan, M.; Wu, Y.; Lin, L. Fault diagnosis and remaining useful life estimation of aero engine using LSTM neural network. In Proceedings of the IEEE International Conference on Aircraft Utility Systems, Austin, TX, USA, 30 October 2016.
157. Zhao, R.; Wang, J.; Yan, R.; Mao, K. Machine health monitoring with LSTM networks. In Proceedings of the International Conference on Sensing Technology, Nanjing, China, 11–13 November 2016.
158. Zhao, K.; Shao, H. Intelligent fault diagnosis of rolling bearing using adaptive deep gated recurrent unit. *Neural Process. Lett.* **2020**, *51*, 1165–1184. [CrossRef]
159. Case Western Reserve University Bearing Data Center. Available online: http://csegroups.case.edu/bearingdatacenter/home/ (accessed on 1 April 2018).
160. Nectoux, P.; Gouriveau, R.; Medjaher, K.; Ramasso, E.; Chebel-Morello, B.; Zerhouni, N.; Varnier, C. PRONOSTIA: An experimental platform for bearings accelerated degradation tests. In Proceedings of the IEEE International Conference on Prognostics and Health Management, PHM'12, Mineapollis, MN, USA, 23–27 September 2012.
161. Gousseau, W.; Antoni, J.; Girardin, F.; Griffaton, J. Analysis of the Rolling Element Bearing data set of the Center for Intelligent Maintenance Systems of the University of Cincinnati. In Proceedings of the CM2016, Paris, France, 10–12 October 2016.
162. Huang, H.; Baddour, N. Bearing vibration data collected under time-varying rotational speed conditions. *Data Brief* **2018**, *21*, 1745–1749. [CrossRef]
163. Wang, B.; Lei, Y.; Li, N.; Li, N. A hybrid prognostics approach for estimating remaining useful life of rolling element bearings. *IEEE Trans. Reliab.* **2020**, *69*, 401–412. [CrossRef]
164. Deng, J.; Dong, W.; Socher, R.; Li, L.; Li, K.; Li, F. ImageNet: A large-scale hierarchical image databas. In Proceedings of the IEEE Conference on Computer Vision and Pattern Recognition, Miami, FL, USA, 20–25 June 2009.
165. Weiss, K.; Khoshgoftaar, T.M.; Wang, D. A survey of transfer learning. *J. Big Data* **2016**, *3*, 1–40. [CrossRef]
166. Guo, L.; Lei, Y.; Xing, S.; Yan, T.; Li, N. Deep convolutional transfer learning network: A new method for intelligent fault diagnosis of machines with unlabeled data. *IEEE Trans. Ind. Electron.* **2018**, *66*, 7316–7325. [CrossRef]
167. Zhang, M.; Wang, D.; Lu, W.; Yang, J.; Li, Z.; Liang, B. A deep transfer model with wasserstein distance guided multi-adversarial networks for bearing fault diagnosis under different working conditions. *IEEE Access* **2019**, *7*, 65303–65318. [CrossRef]
168. Li, X.; Zhang, W.; Ma, H.; Luo, Z.; Li, X. Deep learning-based adversarial multi-classifier optimization for cross-domain machinery fault diagnostics. *J. Manuf. Syst.* **2020**, *55*, 334–347. [CrossRef]
169. Wang, D.; Zhang, M.; Xu, Y.; Lu, W.; Yang, J.; Zhang, T. Metric-based meta-learning model for few-shot fault diagnosis under multiple limited data conditions. *Mech. Syst. Signal Process.* **2021**, *155*, 107510. [CrossRef]
170. Wu, J.; Zhao, Z.; Sun, C.; Yan, R.; Chen, X. Few-shot transfer learning for intelligent fault diagnosis of machine. *Measurement* **2020**, *166*, 108202. [CrossRef]
171. Fuan, W.; Hongkai, J.; Haidong, S.; Wenjing, D.; Shuaipeng, W. An adaptive deep convolutional neural network for rolling bearing fault diagnosis. *Meas. Sci. Technol.* **2017**, *28*, 095005. [CrossRef]
172. Gao, S.; Xu, L.; Zhang, Y.; Pei, Z. Rolling bearing fault diagnosis based on intelligent optimized self-adaptive deep belief network. *Meas. Sci. Technol.* **2020**, *31*, 055009. [CrossRef]
173. Tong, J.; Luo, J.; Pan, H.; Zheng, J.; Zhang, Q. A Novel Cuckoo Search Optimized Deep Auto-Encoder Network-Based Fault Diagnosis Method for Rolling Bearing. *Shock Vib.* **2020**, *2020*, 8891905. [CrossRef]
174. Xiao, M.; Zhang, W.; Wen, K.; Zhu, Y.; Yiliyasi, Y. Fault Diagnosis Based on BP Neural Network Optimized by Beetle Algorithm. *Chin. J. Mech. Eng.* **2021**, *34*, 119. [CrossRef]
175. Chen, J.; Jiang, J.; Guo, X.; Tan, L. A self-Adaptive CNN with PSO for bearing fault diagnosis. *Syst. Sci. Control Eng.* **2021**, *9*, 11–22. [CrossRef]
176. Koza, J. *Genetic Programming: On The Programming of Computers by Means of Natural Selection*; MIT Press: Cambridge, MA, USA, 1992.
177. Bi, Y.; Xue, B.; Zhang, M. *Genetic Programming for Image Classification: An Automated Approach to Feature Learning*; Springer International Publishing: Berlin/Heidelberg, Germany, 2021.

178. Shao, L.; Liu, L.; Li, X. Feature learning for image classification via multiobjective genetic programming. *IEEE Trans. Neural Netw. Learn. Syst.* **2014**, *25*, 1359–1371. [CrossRef]
179. Fu, W.; Johnston, M.; Zhang, M. Genetic programming for edge detection: A Gaussian-based approach. *Soft. Comput.* **2016**, *20*, 1231–1248. [CrossRef]
180. Bi, Y.; Xue, B.; Zhang, M. Genetic programming with image-related operators and a flexible program structure for feature learning in image classification. *IEEE Trans. Evolut. Comput.* **2020**, *25*, 87–101. [CrossRef]
181. Bi, Y.; Xue, B.; Zhang, M. An effective feature learning approach using genetic programming with image descriptors for image classification. *IEEE Comput. Intell. Mag.* **2020**, *15*, 65–77. [CrossRef]
182. Guo, H.; Jack, L.; Nandi, A. Feature generation using genetic programming with application to fault classification. *IEEE Trans. Syst. Man Cyber. Part B* **2005**, *35*, 89–99. [CrossRef]
183. Peng, B.; Wan, S.; Bi, Y.; Xue, B.; Zhang, M. Automatic feature extraction and construction using genetic programming for rotating machinery fault diagnosis. *IEEE Trans. Cyber.* **2020**, *51*, 4909–4923. [CrossRef]
184. Peng, B.; Bi, Y.; Xue, B.; Zhang, M.; Wan, S. Multi-view feature construction using genetic programming for rolling bearing fault diagnosis. *IEEE Comput. Intell. Mag.* **2021**, *16*, 79–94. [CrossRef]

algorithms

MDPI

Article

Machine Learning-Based Monitoring of DC-DC Converters in Photovoltaic Applications

Marco Bindi [1,*], Fabio Corti [2], Igor Aizenberg [3], Francesco Grasso [1], Gabriele Maria Lozito [1], Antonio Luchetta [1], Maria Cristina Piccirilli [1] and Alberto Reatti [1]

[1] Department of Information Engineering, University of Florence, 50139 Firenze, Italy; francesco.grasso@unifi.it (F.G.); gabrielemaria.lozito@unifi.it (G.M.L.); antonio.luchetta@unifi.it (A.L.); mariacristina.piccirilli@unifi.it (M.C.P.); alberto.reatti@unifi.it (A.R.)
[2] Department of Industrial Engineering, University of Perugia, 06125 Perugia, Italy; fabio.corti@unipg.it
[3] Department of Computer Science, Manhattan College, Riverdale, NY 10471, USA; igor.aizenberg@manhattan.edu
* Correspondence: m.bindi@unifi.it

Abstract: In this paper, a monitoring method for DC-DC converters in photovoltaic applications is presented. The primary goal is to prevent catastrophic failures by detecting malfunctioning conditions during the operation of the electrical system. The proposed prognostic procedure is based on machine learning techniques and focuses on the variations of passive components with respect to their nominal range. A theoretical study is proposed to choose the best measurements for the prognostic analysis and adapt the monitoring method to a photovoltaic system. In order to facilitate this study, a graphical assessment of testability is presented, and the effects of the variable solar irradiance on the selected measurements are also considered from a graphical point of view. The main technique presented in this paper to identify the malfunction conditions is based on a Multilayer neural network with Multi-Valued Neurons. The performances of this classifier applied on a Zeta converter are compared to those of a Support Vector Machine algorithm. The simulations carried out in the Simulink environment show a classification rate higher than 90%, and this means that the monitoring method allows the identification of problems in the initial phases, thus guaranteeing the possibility to change the work set-up and organize maintenance operations for DC-DC converters.

Keywords: DC-DC converters; prognostic analysis; multi-valued neuron neural network; support vector machine; Zeta converter

1. Introduction

The development of smart cities leads to an increase in the complexity of electrical grids, and new challenges need to be addressed, such as the spread of electric vehicles and the management of renewable energy systems [1,2]. In this sense, new devices, control techniques and monitoring methods are needed for proper energy management [3–7]. The technical optimization of the new electrical generators allows an increase in efficiency for renewable systems, but it is not sufficient for the correct distribution of this energy, which is difficult to predict and highly variable [8,9]. For this reason, the development of new algorithms capable of predicting production from renewable sources and managing electrical loads will be a very important field of interest for many researchers [10–12]. Furthermore, the development and control of devices used as an interface between generators and the grid, or generators and other devices, play a fundamental role in the correct distribution of energy [13–17]. In this sense, the control of DC-DC converters represents a very important aspect because they can be used as an interface with renewable energy systems producing a Direct Current (DC) and are essential for all those systems powered by batteries, such as electric vehicles. In addition to controlling these devices, it is very important to monitor their state of health during the operation of the electrical system.

In traditional diagnostic systems, the main objective is to identify and localize faults, which leads to a complete loss of functionality. On the other hand, in prognostic systems, the subject of the analysis is the malfunction condition. This means that the prognostic system focuses on slight variations from the nominal point of work, identifying partial losses of functionality that precede catastrophic failures. In this way, it is possible to organize maintenance operations, increasing the reliability of the electrical system and reducing recovery times.

In this paper, the definition of a prognostic analysis for DC-DC converters is carried out and verified through a simulation procedure in a Matlab-Simulink environment. The converter taken into consideration is a Zeta converter, which allows for a high voltage gain and low ripple in the output current using four passive components [18–20]. These components are the main subjects of the prognostic analysis, and their variations with respect to the nominal values are used as indexes of the state converter of health. In fact, when a malfunction occurs on a passive component, its value changes; this introduces a variation of the working point [21,22] and could produce catastrophic consequences. To make the simulations as close as possible to the real functioning of the converter, the parasites of the real active and passive components are considered in Simulink.

The specific case of prognostics addressed in this paper involves the DC-DC converter featuring a photovoltaic (PV) input. This introduces two additional challenges to the prognostic problem. The first is the non-linear current-voltage characteristic of the source, which can result in irregular trends (if compared with ideal voltage and current sources, often used in diagnostics and prognostics problems) of the converter current and voltages. The second is the functional relationship between the characteristics and the environmental quantities of temperature and irradiance. Both difficulties might lead to erroneous classifications of the working condition of the converter. To address this problem, a specific normalization approach is used to decouple the prognostic-sensitive quantities from the environmental-dependent nature of the source.

Prognosis is performed by means of a supervised machine-learning approach. Several sensitive electrical quantities are measured on the passive elements of the operating circuit in the time domain and are processed by a Multilayer neural network with Multi-Valued Neurons (MLMVN). This classifier falls in the category of supervised learning algorithm, and it presents three layers with complex weights. Thanks to its complex nature, the MLMVN is easily adaptable to the classification of electrical quantities, which are usually expressed by phasors. Compared to real feed-forward neural networks, this classifier presents a derivative-free learning algorithm that facilitates the correction of the weights and reduces the computational cost. In several applications, MLMVN offers a better generalization capability than other machine learning techniques and its implementation in power line monitoring is presented in [23], where frequency response measurements are processed. The performance of the MLMVN in this new application is compared to that obtained by using a Support Vector Machine (SVM), which is one of the most used techniques in the field of data classification [24,25].

The paper is organized as follows: Section 2 shows the main characteristics of the renewable energy system taken into consideration, the theoretical aspects of the prognostic procedure, and the use of the MLMVN, Section 3 presents the main results of the simulation procedure, Section 4 reports the result discussion, and Section 5 shows the conclusions.

2. Materials and Methods

The analysis method proposed focuses on a photovoltaic system constituted by a 230 W solar panel and a Zeta converter connected to a DC microgrid (48 V). The DC-DC converter must guarantee the energy transfer from the source to the grid, and several techniques can be used to achieve this goal, such as the Maximum Power Point Tracking (MPPT) control [26,27]. The MPPT algorithm's purpose is to control the converter duty-cycle (D) to ensure an optimal operating point is achieved on the PV source. If no condition is required on the output current and voltage, classic MPPT aims at setting the source voltage as close as possible to the maximum power voltage. Since this voltage changes according to the environmental conditions, either a tracking algorithm (e.g., the Perturb & Observe) or a model-based algorithm (also based on machine-learning methods) should be used. In this paper, the MPPT algorithm is not simulated because it does not represent a fundamental aspect of the prognostic analysis. The main idea the monitoring procedure is based on is to fix the duty-cycle for the short time interval necessary to extract the voltage and current measurements. This avoids putting the converter out of service and allows the definition of its state of health without interrupting the energy transfer. Therefore, during the prognostic analysis, the duty-cycle of the converter is not varied to reach the maximum power point, thus limiting the variability of the measurements and facilitating the localization of malfunctions. Once the prognosis is finished, the MPPT algorithm can vary the duty-cycle again. Since the measurement procedure requires only a few periods at the converter switching frequency, the prognostic analysis does not significantly affect the energy production.

2.1. Photovoltaic Source

The energy source considered in this paper is a 230 W solar panel with 60 multicrystalline cells TW230P60-FA by Tianwei New Energy [28]. The main electrical characteristics of the panel are extracted from its datasheet and reported in Table 1, where V_{MPP} and I_{MPP} are the maximum power point voltage and current, respectively, V_{OC} is the open-circuit voltage, and I_{SC} is the short-circuit current.

Table 1. Characteristics of the photovoltaic panel at the Standard Test Condition.

V_{MPP}	I_{MPP}	V_{OC}	I_{SC}	α_T	*N Cell*
29.4 V	7.82 A	37.3 V	8.22 A	0.06%/°C	60

Based on these characteristics, it is possible to implement an equivalent circuit model in a Simulink environment for the panel and extract the voltage–current curves as the solar irradiance and the working temperature change. Figure 1a,b shows these curves obtained for different values of irradiance and temperature.

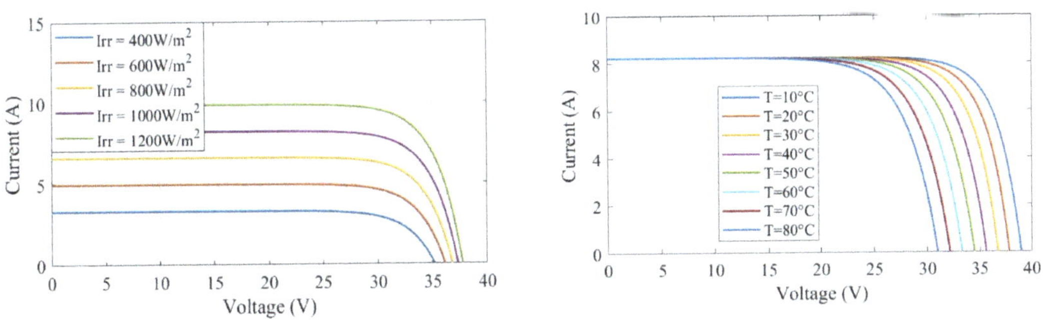

(**a**) (**b**)

Figure 1. Voltage–Current curves of the photovoltaic panel; (**a**) curves obtained with fixed temperature (25 °C) as the irradiance varies, (**b**) curves obtained with fixed irradiance (1000 W/m^2) as the temperature varies.

Obviously, the input current and voltage depend on the environmental conditions, and this is reflected in the internal electrical quantities of the DC-DC converter. Since the measurements extracted from the DC-DC converter for evaluating its state of health are sensitive to the changes in the input current and voltage, those measurements are sensitive to the environmental conditions of the PV device as well. This can create confusion during the classification of malfunctions because the monitoring system must be able to discriminate the variations introduced by the aging of the components from those caused by changes in solar irradiance and working temperature.

To avoid this problem, a simple solution could be to add the values of the irradiance and temperature to the set of measurements processed by the classifier. However, these quantities are not easily measurable from a practical point of view, and this solution makes the training stage more complex by requiring a very large dataset. In this paper, a graphical method is proposed for choosing the time-domain measurements less sensitive to variations in solar irradiance and temperature.

2.2. Zeta Converter

The DC-DC converter considered in this paper is a Zeta converter, which is a fourth-order non-inverted step-up/step-down circuit that guarantees high voltage gain and low ripples in the output voltage and current [18,29]. A Simulink model is used to verify the operation of the converter connected to the photovoltaic source and that of the monitoring method.

Figure 2 shows the whole system reproduced in Simulink and used during the simulation procedure: a Pulse Width Modulation (PWM) technique is implemented to drive the converter switches S_1 and S_2 (N-channel Power MOSFET) with opposite phases.

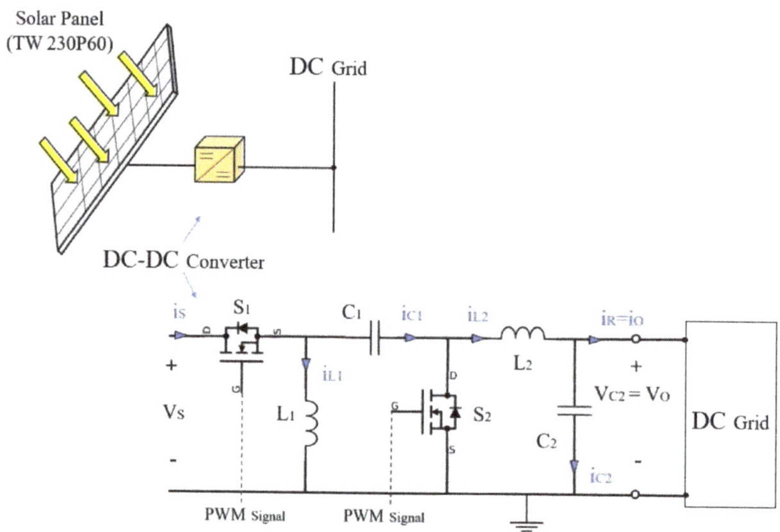

Figure 2. General diagram of the photovoltaic system and Zeta converter circuit.

When the switch S_1 is in conduction mode, the inductor L_1 absorbs energy from the DC source, and, at the same time, L_2 absorbs energy from the source and capacitor C_1. This means that the input current $i_S(t)$ is equal to the sum $i_{L1}(t) + i_{L2}(t)$, and these two currents increase linearly, as shown in Figure 3a,b, which are extracted from the Simulink model considering a solar irradiance of 1000 W/m^2 and an operating temperature of 25 °C. In the opposite condition (S_1 Off and S_2 On), the input current is zero, and the current $i_{L1}(t)$ flows through S_2 to charge capacitor C_1. Simultaneously, $i_{L2}(t)$ crosses the circuit (C_2-R) and returns through the closed switch S_2.

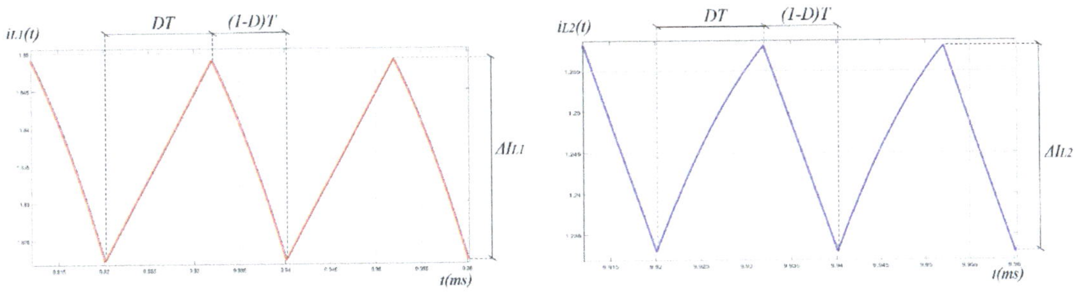

(**a**) (**b**)

Figure 3. Converter currents in time domain: (**a**) current I_{L1}; (**b**) current in the inductor I_{L2}.

The currents $i_{L1}(t)$, $i_{L2}(t)$, and $i_{S2}(t)$ present three different ripples, $\Delta i_{L1}(t)$, $\Delta i_{L2}(t)$, and $\Delta i_{S2}(t)$, respectively. The latter is the most important to define the conduction mode of the circuit: if current $i_{S2}(t)$ becomes zero during the Switch-Off period, the converter works in the Discontinuous Conduction Mode (DCM). Otherwise, the Continuous Conduction Mode (CCM) requires a non-zero current in S_2 when the switching from off to on mode occurs. By operating in CCM, it is possible to reduce the electrical stress on the converter components and obtain a lower ripple on the output quantities. For this reason, only the CCM is considered in this work, and the dimensioning of the analog components has been performed to ensure this condition.

As shown in [18], the voltage gain G of the Zeta converter can be calculated through Formula (1), where V_S is the input voltage imposed by the photovoltaic source and V_O is the output voltage of the converter. Consequently, Formula (2) is used to describe the relationship between the mean value of the input current I_S and the output current I_O.

$$G = \frac{V_O}{V_S} = \frac{D}{1-D} \tag{1}$$

$$I_O = \frac{1-D}{D} I_S \tag{2}$$

As for the dimensioning of the passive components, one of the main aspects is to ensure a sufficient margin between CCM and DCM. In addition, ripples of voltages and currents are also considered, as shown in [18]. The variation ratios of the currents i_{L1} and i_{L2} are expressed by the terms η and ζ, respectively, and are calculated as follows,

$$\eta = \frac{\Delta_{i_{L1}}/2}{I_{L1}} = \frac{1-D}{2\,G}\,\frac{R}{f\,L_1} \tag{3}$$

$$\zeta = \frac{\Delta_{i_{L2}}/2}{I_{L2}} = \frac{D}{2\,G}\,\frac{R}{f\,L_2} \tag{4}$$

where capital letters are used to indicate the average values of the quantities, and R represents the load resistance. Similarly, the variation ratios of the voltages are calculated as,

$$\rho = \frac{\Delta_{v_C}/2}{V_{C1}} = \frac{D}{2}\,\frac{1}{f\,C_1\,R} \tag{5}$$

$$\varepsilon = \frac{\Delta_{v_0}/2}{V_o} = \frac{D}{8\,G}\,\frac{1}{f^2\,C_2\,L_2} \tag{6}$$

where ρ is the variation ratio of the voltage across C_1, and ε is that of the output voltage.

Table 2 summarizes the nominal values of the converter components that ensure CCM operation and limit the output ripple to 5%.

Table 2. Converter components.

L_1 [mH]	L_2 [mH]	C_1 [μF]	C_2 [μF]
5	5	2.4	2.4

2.3. *Fault Classes*

To propose a prognostic approach for photovoltaic systems focused on parametric faults, the corresponding classes must be defined starting from tolerance ranges around the component nominal values. In fact, parametric faults are deviations of components from the nominal values that produce a partial loss of functionality. These variations could introduce undetectable consequences from a general point of view in the functioning of the system but by choosing appropriate measurements, the variations can be identified and localized in a specific component or in a group of components.

The nominal intervals of the four passive components are defined, starting from the nominal values shown in Table 2 and applying a 15% tolerance. These variations are considered acceptable as they guarantee an output ripple lower than 10% and maintain CCM operation. The parametric failure conditions correspond to a maximum decrease of 70% for each passive component. Table 3 summarizes the operating ranges of each component.

Table 3. Operating ranges.

	L_1 (mH)	L_2 (mH)	C_1 (μF)	C_2 (μF)
Nominal Range	(4.25–5.75)	(4.25–5.75)	(2.04–2.76)	(2.04–2.76)
Malfunction Condition	(1.5–4.25)	(1.5–4.25)	(0.72–2.04)	(0.72–2.04)

It is necessary to highlight that the single failure hypothesis is assumed because it is the most likely, and no-fault propagation is expected. This means that only one passive component at a time can be considered defective, and five classes of failure are used. The nominal working condition of the converter is called "class 0", and it presents all components in their nominal ranges. The other classes are summarized in Table 4.

Table 4. Fault Classes.

Fault Class	Description
0	Each component is in the nominal range
1	Malfunction on L_1
2	Malfunction on L_2
3	Malfunction on C_1
4	Malfunction on C_2

Therefore, the main objective of the classifier is to identify these working conditions starting from specific measurements extracted from the DC-DC converter. To make the monitoring system suitable from a practical point of view, it is important to offer a low intrusive level using as few measures as possible. For this reason, in the next paragraphs of this paper, a selection method of the measurements is proposed based on the testability level of the circuit and on the influence of the environmental conditions.

All the time-domain measures considered in this work have two information contents: the first is linked to the average value of the quantities and the second to their ripples. Therefore, the dataset matrix used to train the neural classifier must contain two columns for each measurement and one column for the corresponding class. The general form of the dataset is (7),

$$\begin{bmatrix} Q^1_{1,m} & Q^1_{1,r} & \dots & 0 \\ Q^2_{1,m} & Q^2_{1,r} & \dots & 0 \\ \vdots & \vdots & \dots & \vdots \\ Q^{N_S}_{1,m} & Q^{N_S}_{1,r} & \dots & 4 \end{bmatrix} \tag{7}$$

where, for example, $Q^1_{1,m}$ is the first measure of the mean value of the quantities Q_1 (voltage or current) and $Q^1_{1,r}$ is its ripple. A significant number of samples are used for each fault class, and the total number of rows belonging to the dataset is N_S. It should be noted that keeping the duty cycle fixed; it is possible to reduce the size of the dataset matrix and the variability of the measurements. In fact, the values of the measured quantities in the nominal conditions are known, and the recognition of malfunctions is facilitated. If the duty-cycle is continuously changed, it would be necessary to add a column containing the different values of D and replicate the structure shown in (7) for each value of D.

2.4. Testability Analysis

Testability analysis represents a fundamental step in each diagnostic and prognostic system. Thanks to this study, the identifiable components are defined, thus facilitating the selection of test points and the definition of the achievable objectives.

Since the Simulation After Test (SAT) techniques are usually used to detect parametric faults in analog circuits, the main step is the definition of the failure equations. These equations present the component values as unknowns and are obtained by comparing the circuit responses at specific points with their nominal forms. The solvability level of the failure equations corresponds to the testability of the circuit, and its maximum value is the total number of passive components. If the testability is less than the maximum value, one or more ambiguity groups can be defined: they are sets of components that cannot be uniquely determined starting from the selected measurements.

Several methods have been developed in recent years in order to facilitate the calculation of testability in different types of electrical circuits [30]. The study of linear time-invariant circuits is widespread in the literature, and the calculation methods in the frequency domain can be easily adapted to different topologies [31]. Regarding the non-linear time-variant circuits, the testability evaluation presents many complexities due to the different topologies that the circuit assumes during operation. In the case of DC-DC converters, two different topologies are used in Continuous Conduction Mode (CCM), one for each switching period, while in Discontinuous Conduction Mode (DCM), the topologies become three due to the cancellation of the inductor current.

In such cases, a time-domain method can be used [32]. The first step is to choose a specific switching period in steady-state conditions and to sample the inputs, which are the circuit power supply quantities. In this way, vector $\boldsymbol{u}_0$ is obtained. The second step is the definition of the output vector, as shown in (8), where $\boldsymbol{p}$ is the vector of the unknown parameters and $\boldsymbol{y}_T$ is a vector of measurements obtainable from the circuit.

$$\boldsymbol{y}_T(\boldsymbol{p}, \boldsymbol{u}_0) = \left[y(t_1, \boldsymbol{p}, \boldsymbol{u}_0)^{tr}, y(t_2, \boldsymbol{p}, \boldsymbol{u}_0)^{tr}, \ldots, y(t_n, \boldsymbol{p}, \boldsymbol{u}_0)^{tr} \right]^{tr} \quad (8)$$

Then, the failure equations can be obtained by (9),

$$\boldsymbol{y}_T(\boldsymbol{p}, \boldsymbol{u}_0) = \boldsymbol{y}_T{}^* \quad (9)$$

where $\boldsymbol{y}_T{}^*$ is the vector of measurements extracted from the circuit. Finally, testability is calculated as the rank of the Jacobian matrix obtained stating from these equations.

The equivalence between the time-domain procedure proposed here and the testability analysis performed in the Laplace domain is presented in [33]. In this paper, the testability assessment of the Zeta converter is carried out through SapWinPE (SapWin for Power Electronics), which is a program for simulating analog switching circuits. A specific algorithm called TAPSLIN (Testability Analysis for Periodically switched Linear Networks) is implemented on SapWinPE to perform the testability analysis in symbolic form [32].

2.5. Multilayer Neural Network with Multi-Valued Neurons (MLMVN) and Its Adaptation to a Zeta Convertor

2.5.1. Main Characteristics

The main tool proposed in this paper for identifying the state of health of DC-DC converters is a neural network-based classifier. It is a feed-forward Multilayer neural network with Multi-Valued Neurons that uses a derivative-free learning algorithm during the backpropagation procedure. Each neuron is a Multi-Valued Neuron (MVN) with multiple complex-valued inputs ($X_1, \ldots, X_n$) and complex-valued weights ($W_1, \ldots, W_n$). This neural network might be used either in a continuous or in a discrete version.

A three-layer neural network with discrete output neurons is used in this paper: each neuron belonging to the last layer employs a discrete activation function dividing the complex plane into k equal sectors and adjusting the output to the lower border of the sector that contains the weighted sum of the inputs z ($z = X_1 W_1 + X_2 W_2 + \ldots + X_s W_n$). The discrete activation function is represented by Formula (10), as it is described in [34].

$$P(z) = Y = \varepsilon_k^j = e^{i2\pi j/k} \quad if \ 2\pi j/k \leq \arg(z) < 2\pi(j+1)/k \tag{10}$$

where j is an index of a sector where the weighted sum is located, k is the total number of the sectors, and arg(z) represents the argument of the weighted sum.

Since this neural network is feed-forward, the backpropagation of the output errors is the main procedure for the correction of the complex weights during the training phase. These errors are calculated starting from a dataset containing corrected classification examples and applying the correction rules in a supervised procedure. As it is shown in (3), the last column of the dataset matrix contains the desired outputs, which are the fault classes corresponding to the time-domain measurements. The dataset rows are processed in succession during the training phase, and the error value for each neuron in the output layer is calculated by the difference between the number (a root of unity) determining the lower border of the desired sector and the actual output. Therefore, the error for each sample belonging to the dataset corresponds to the difference between two complex numbers located on the unit circle.

Applying the standard correction rules presented in detail in [34], it is possible to modify the complex weights without introducing derivative terms, thus facilitating the backpropagation procedure compared to other feed-forward neural networks and reducing the computational cost. Formula (11) shows how to calculate the adjustment of a neural network weight,

$$\Delta W_i^{k,m} = \frac{\alpha_{k,m}}{(n_{m-1}+1)\left|z_{k,m}^s\right|} \delta_{k,m}^s \overline{Y}_{i,m-1}^s \tag{11}$$

where $\Delta W_i^{k,m}$ is the adjustment for the i-th weight of the k-th neuron belonging to the layer m, $\alpha_{k,m}$ is the corresponding learning rate (complex-valued in general, but set equal to 1 in all actual applications), n_{m-1} is the number of the neuron inputs equal to the number of the outputs of the previous layer, $\left|z_{k,m}^s\right|$ is the magnitude of the weighted sum, $\delta_{k,m}^s$ is the neuron error obtained through the backpropagation method, and $\overline{Y}_{i,m-1}^s$ is the conjugate-transposed of the input.

This learning rule allows the correction of the weights for each sample of the dataset s ($s = 1, \ldots, N_S$). While the error should be backpropagated starting from the output neurons up to the input ones, after all the neurons errors were found, the weights should be adjusted starting from the first hidden layer to the last one. Figure 4 shows the initial error definition for a neuron in the output layer.

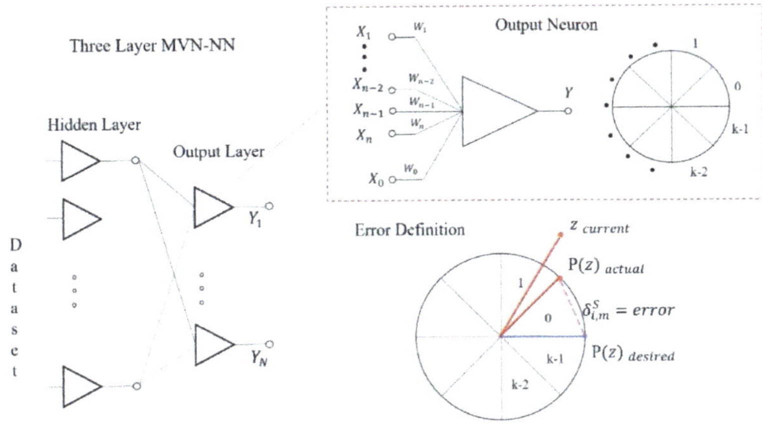

Figure 4. General configuration of the MLMVN and error definition in the output layer.

Once the errors have been calculated for the output layer neurons, the errors should be backpropagated by applying Formula (12).

$$\delta^S_{k,m-1} = \frac{1}{(n_{m-2}+1)} \sum_{i=1}^{n_m} \delta^S_{i,m} \left(W_k^{i,m}\right)^{-1} \tag{12}$$

In order to simplify the training procedure reducing the computational cost, a batch algorithm based on the Linear Least Square (LLS) method can be introduced, as shown in [35]. In this case, the errors calculated for each sample belonging to the dataset are saved in a specific matrix without correcting the complex weights. When all samples have been processed, this matrix presents N_S rows, as shown in (13). Since the number of samples is greater than the number of weights, an oversized system of equations is obtained, and different techniques can be applied, such as Q-R decomposition and Singular Value Decomposition (SVD), reducing the number of iterations required for the calculation of the corrections.

$$\begin{bmatrix} \delta^1_{1,m} & \delta^1_{2,m} & \cdots & \delta^1_{n,m} \\ \delta^2_{1,m} & \delta^2_{2,m} & \cdots & \delta^2_{n,m} \\ \vdots & \vdots & \cdots & \vdots \\ \delta^{N_S}_{1,m} & \delta^{N_S}_{1,m} & \cdots & \delta^{N_S}_{n,m} \end{bmatrix} \tag{13}$$

To improve the performance of the classifier, the soft margin technique described in [36] is used. In this case, the purpose of the correction is not only to position the outputs within the desired sectors but, for each of them, to minimize the distance of all output neuron-weighted sums from the bisector of the desired sector as much as possible. In this way, better classification results are obtained avoiding the ambiguity caused by outputs close to the boundary of two different sectors.

2.5.2. Neural Classifier for Zeta Converter

In order to adapt the MLMVN to the objective of the paper, a number of binary neurons equal to that of the passive components are used in the output layer. The binary neurons divide the complex plane into two different sectors: the first corresponds to the upper half plane $[0\ \pi)$ and is identified by the value 0; the second sector corresponds to the phase interval $[\pi\ 2\pi)$ and is encoded by the number 1. As it is shown in Figure 5, the first (labeled by 0) sector is used to indicate the nominal behavior of the corresponding component, while the second sector (labeled by 1) is used to describe its malfunction condition.

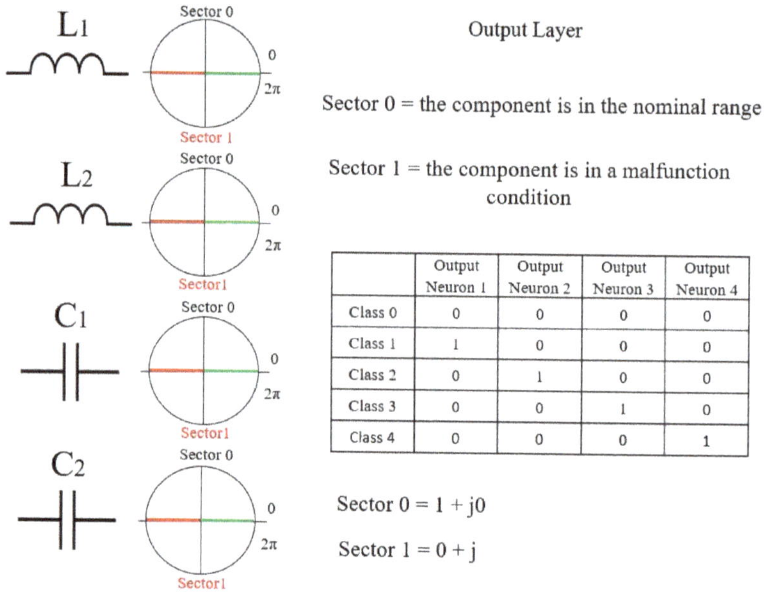

Figure 5. Set-up of the output layer and coding of the classes.

When, for example, only the first output neuron is "high", the first fault class is identified, which means that a problem is detected on L_1. This rule is used for classes 1 to 4, while class 0 corresponds to a "low" value on each output neuron. It is necessary to highlight that the "winner take all" technique is used to avoid the presence of two outputs on the "high" value at the same time. This means that only the minor error output is considered equal to 1. Formula (14) describes the dataset matrix introducing the coding of the fault classes.

$$\begin{bmatrix} Q_{1,m}^{1} & Q_{1,r}^{1} & \cdots & 0\ 0\ 0\ 0 \\ Q_{1,m}^{2} & Q_{1,r}^{2} & \cdots & 0\ 0\ 0\ 0 \\ \vdots & \vdots & \cdots & \vdots \\ Q_{1,m}^{N_S} & Q_{1,r}^{N_S} & \cdots & 0\ 0\ 0\ 1 \end{bmatrix} \tag{14}$$

As for the measurements belonging to the dataset, they are used to create complex inputs as follows: each value corresponds to the phase of a complex number with a magnitude equal to 1. These numbers are the inputs of the MLMVN.

3. Results

This paragraph presents the simulation results obtained by applying the prognostic approach to the photovoltaic system described above. The main steps of the simulation procedure can be summarized as follows:

- first selection of measurements;
- testability analysis;
- neural network training.

3.1. First Selection of the Measurements

The first step of the prognostic procedure is the selection of the most significant measurements to obtain a correct evaluation of the converter status. Since the DC source corresponds to a photovoltaic panel, the input voltage and current are highly variable and depend on the incident solar irradiance and the temperature of the panel. This means that variations in measured quantities can be introduced due to changes in environmental conditions. If these measurements are used as inputs to the monitoring system, classification errors may occur. To avoid this issue, measurements on the component's quantities are first normalized against input quantities (which are in general known due to their use in almost any MPPT algorithm). Among the normalized quantities, the ones with lower sensitivity towards irradiance and temperature are chosen as inputs for the prognostic classification.

Therefore, the best choice of measurements includes all voltages and currents with low sensitivity compared to the input ones.

As said before, the dataset used to train the neural network-based classifier contains measurements of ripples and mean values. Initially, all currents and voltages on the passive components are taken into consideration, and their variations with respect to the irradiance and temperature are graphically evaluated through the Simulink model. The operating points considered for this simulation are extracted from [37] and represent common situations with a realistic relationship between irradiance and working temperature. Table 5 summarizes these working points.

Table 5. Operating conditions.

Operating Point	Irradiance (W/m^2)	Temperature (°C)
A	400	15
B	800	45
C	1200	65

Starting from a common situation characterized by an irradiance of 1000 W/m^2 and a working temperature of 55 °C, and considering the fixed grid voltage of 48 V, the maximum power point is obtained with a duty cycle of 0.6. This working condition is chosen as the starting point to evaluate the effects of changes in environmental conditions. Therefore, the duty-cycle is set at 0.6, and the changes in voltages and currents across the passive components are analyzed by moving to the three operating conditions presented in Table 5. Since the environmental situation changes but the duty-cycle is kept constant, the three working points shown in Figure 6 are obtained. These three points indicate three different pairs of input voltage and current. As previously said, to correctly choose the quantities to be measured during the monitoring procedure, the sensitivity of all voltages and currents with respect to these changes is studied.

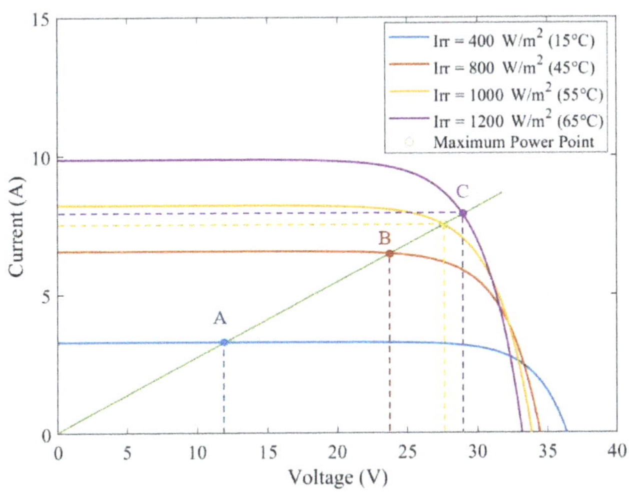

Figure 6. Variations of the working point and variations of the input current and voltage.

It should be noted that the duty-cycle value used in this paper is not mandatory and that several methods can be used to choose it. In this case, the starting point is a condition of maximum power transfer, and this value of D is maintained. Once this parameter has been chosen, it is necessary to keep it constant during the generation of all the samples belonging to the dataset matrix.

In this paper, the sensitivity analysis is performed graphically by using the Simulink model described above.

Analyzing the simulation results, it can be observed that the voltage ripples on the passive components and the average values of the currents exhibit a low level of sensitivity with respect to the irradiance and temperature variations. For this reason, the average values of the inductor currents and the ripples of the capacitor voltages are selected as possible measurements. Figure 7a–d presents the approximately constant behavior of these quantities with respect to the changes in input current and voltage.

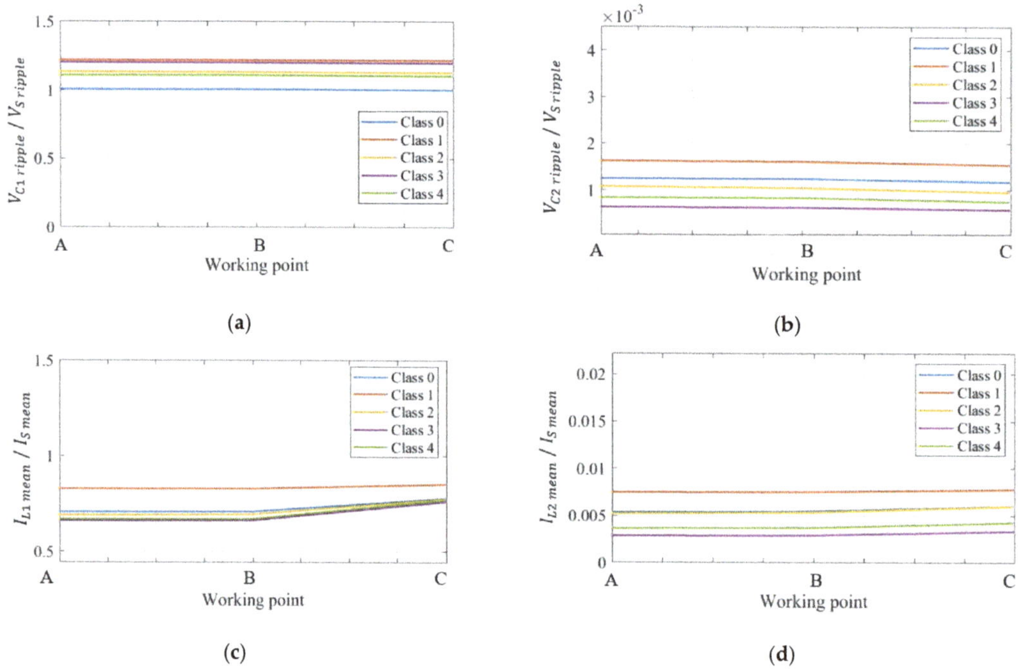

Figure 7. Sensitivity of the measurements with respect to the variation of environmental conditions; (**a**) ripple of the voltage on the first capacitor $V_{C1ripple}$; (**b**) ripple of the voltage on the second capacitor $V_{C2ripple}$; (**c**) mean value of the current through the first inductor I_{L1mean}; (**d**) mean value of the current through the second inductor I_{L2mean}.

3.2. *Testability Assessment of the Zeta Converter*

The testability analysis of the Zeta converter is performed following the theoretical approach described above and using the software TAPSLIN. Figure 8 shows the symbolic circuit developed on SapWin and the consequent analysis in the Laplace domain. The test points used in this case are those corresponding to the previously selected measurements. Therefore, the voltages across the capacitors and currents flow through the inductors are considered for the testability evaluation.

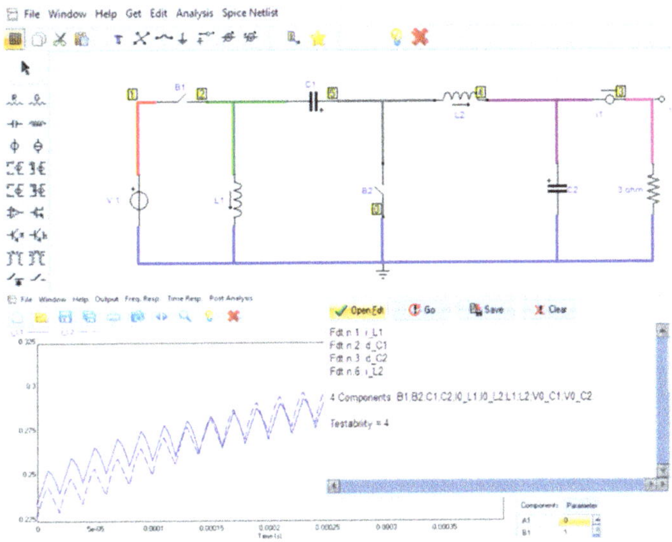

Figure 8. Testability analysis of the Zeta converter through SapWin and TAPSLIN.

The results obtained show the absence of ambiguity groups and guarantee the possibility of detecting malfunctions in each passive component. Therefore, the dataset used to train the classifier contains the measurements of two voltage ripples and two current average values (15).

$$\begin{bmatrix} V^1_{C1\,r} & V^1_{C2\,r} & I^1_{L1\,m} & I^1_{L2\,m} & 0\;0\;0\;0 \\ & & \vdots & & \\ V^{N_S}_{C1} & V^{N_S}_{C2\,r} & I^{N_S}_{L1\,m} & I^{N_S}_{L2\,m} & 0\;0\;0\;1 \end{bmatrix} \quad (15)$$

3.3. Neural Network Training and Validation

The training of the MLMVN is performed through a Matlab application developed by the authors. This algorithm processes the dataset matrix (11), modifying the complex weights through a Q-R decomposition. The simulation procedure used to create the dataset can be summarized as follows:

- the first step is the creation of 400 random values in the nominal range and 100 random values in the malfunction condition for each passive component;
- using these values, 100 samples for each fault class can be obtained in the hypothesis of a single failure;
- the values of the components are used in Simulink to simulate different working conditions and extract the corresponding measurements (voltage ripple on capacitors and mean current values on inductors);
- repeating these steps for three irradiance values (400, 800, and 1200 W/m^2), a dataset matrix containing 1500 samples is obtained.

The three environmental conditions used to create the dataset matrix allow the covering of an extremely wide range of possible scenarios. In this way, it is possible to train MLMVN in a very short time and to exploit its generalization capability to correctly classify many operating conditions not present during the learning phase. Once the dataset has been created, the cross-validation method is used to perform the training of the MLMVN. This means that two phases are performed: the first, called the learning phase, uses 80% of the samples belonging to the dataset for the correction of the weights, while in the second step, called the test phase, the performance of the classifier is verified using the remaining 20% of the samples. The same data split is maintained for complete training, and then it is changed five times to use all samples both in the learning and test phases. Whenever the data for training and testing are changed, the weights are initialized to random values.

Figure 9a shows the global classification results obtained during the training procedure, while in Figure 9b, the performance of the classifier for each fault class is presented in a histogram chart. In both cases, the index used to evaluate the accuracy of the MLMVN is the Classification Rate (CR), defined as the ratio between the number of correctly classified data and the total number of processed data.

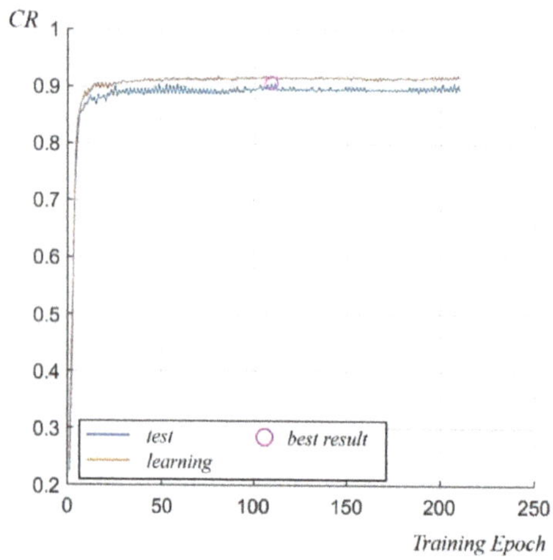

(a)

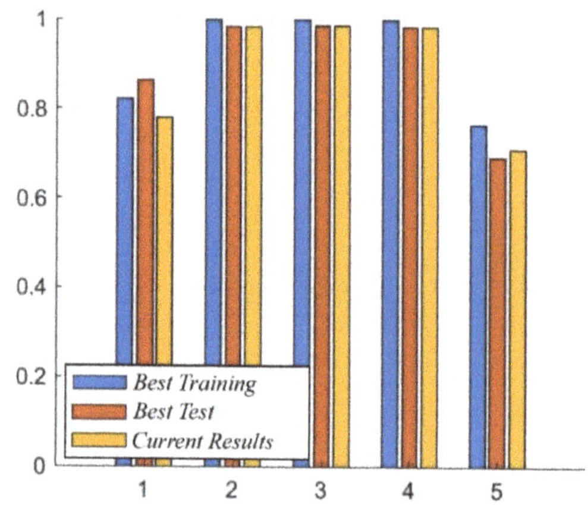

(b)

Figure 9. Classification Results; (**a**) performance of the classifier during the training phase: the red line represents the CR of the learning phase, and the blue line is the CR obtained in the test phase; (**b**) classification results for each fault class shown in the Matlab application at the end of each training epoch.

In order to compare the performance of the MLMVN with that of the other machine learning techniques, a quadratic SVM algorithm is considered. During the training phase, the SVM presents a classification rate of 88.7%. This result has been obtained by processing the same dataset used for the MLMVN-based classifier and using a cross-validation method. Since the one-against-one method is used during the training phase of the SVM algorithm, 10 binary classifiers are defined, each of which presents 13 support vectors.

As shown in Figure 10a,b, further validations of the results can be achieved using these two classifiers for processing new measurements extracted directly from the Simulink model. Two validations are proposed in this paper: the first is obtained by processing new measurements under the same conditions of the training phase (Figure 10a), while the second uses different values of irradiance and temperature (Figure 10b). In particular, the results shown in Figure 10b have been obtained by randomly setting the four fault conditions in some of the environmental situations shown in Table 6. These operational situations represent some typical values of environmental conditions systems in Italy.

Table 6. Real working conditions used for validation.

Irradiance 1 W/m^2	Temperature 1 °C	Irradiance 2 W/m^2	Temperature 2 °C	Irradiance 3 W/m^2	Temperature 3 °C
500	25	705	40	390	19

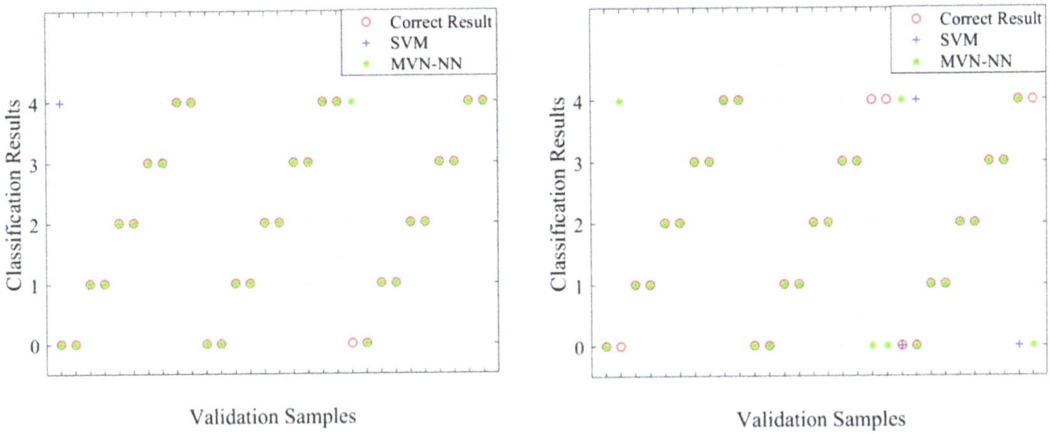

(a) (b)

Figure 10. Comparison between MLMVN and SVM; (**a**) performance obtained by processing measurements under the same conditions of the training phase; (**b**) performance obtained by processing measurements with different irradiance and temperature values.

Finally, Table 7 summarizes the results obtained during the simulation procedure.

Table 7. Simulation Results.

Classifier	Hyperparameters	Learning Phase	Test Phase	Validation 1	Validation 2
MLMVN	75 Neurons	92%	91.66%	96.66%	86.66%
SVM	13 Support Vectors	88.7%	-	93.33%	83.33%

4. Discussion

The results reported in the previous paragraph show excellent performances of the MLMVN-based classifier both in training and in validation.

During the training procedure, the neural classifier with 75 neurons in the hidden layer allows a classification rate of 92% in the learning phase and 91.66% in the test phase. Comparable results can be obtained by increasing the number of neurons in the hidden layer, but this produces a greater difference between the two phases. Therefore, the generalization capability of the neural network decreases by using more than 75 neurons, which means that the CR, obtained by processing new measurements during validation, decreases. Figure 11 summarizes the heuristic procedure used to select the best number of neurons.

As regards the validations, it can be stated that the MLMVN confirms a classification rate higher than 90% using the same conditions as the training, while in the second validation, there is a reduction of up to 86.66%. These results show the possibility of obtaining good performances even without introducing numerous environmental conditions into the dataset used during the training phase.

However, one consideration is needed: observing the results obtained for each class of failure, it can be stated that the main problem is to correctly classify the presence of malfunctions on C_2. This aspect is not particularly important when the environmental conditions are similar to those used in training but becomes relevant otherwise. In fact, two false negatives are presented in Figure 10b, and this could be a problem for practical applications. Therefore, even if the classification rate does not decrease significantly, it is advisable to use a dataset with various environmental conditions during the training phase.

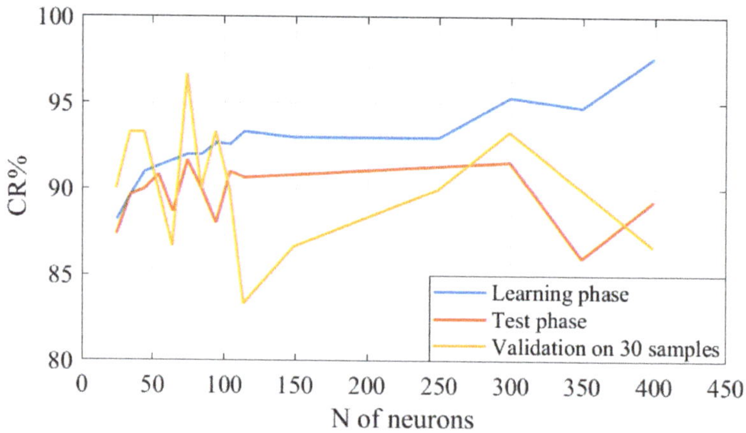

Figure 11. Classification rate with respect to the number of neurons in the hidden layer.

5. Conclusions

In this paper, a prognostic procedure to monitor the operating conditions of a power converter in photovoltaic applications was proposed. The approach is based on a machine-learning classifier that receives, as inputs, a subset of time-domain measurements of the DC-DC converter and produces, as output, a class that identifies one of four possible faulty components.

To achieve proper fault classification in the presence of an environmental-dependent source, such as a PV device, a normalization procedure was implemented. Among the normalized quantities, a selection of those relevant for testability but insensitive to the irradiance and temperature of the PV source was used. The full system was implemented in Matlab Simulink to generate the datasets used for the classifier training and validation, considering operating conditions compatible with the common operation of a power-producing PV device.

The results from the MLMVN are compared against a standard SVM classifier. The proposed classifier outperforms the SVM both in the training accuracy and in the validation set generalization capabilities.

The simple computational nature of the classifier makes it a prime candidate to be implemented in the embedded environment as well since, differently from deep-learning classification strategies, it shows a very small memory footprint.

Author Contributions: Problem identification, I.A.; investigation and conceptualization, F.C. and A.R.; testability analysis and symbolic analysis, M.C.P. and F.G.; neural network application, I.A. and A.L.; procedure development, M.B., G.M.L. and F.C.; simulations, M.B., G.M.L. and F.C. All authors have read and agreed to the published version of the manuscript.

Funding: This research received no external funding.

Institutional Review Board Statement: Not applicable.

Informed Consent Statement: Not applicable.

Conflicts of Interest: The authors declare no conflict of interest.

References

1. Rahbar, K.; Xu, J.; Zhang, R. Real-Time Energy Storage Management for Renewable Integration in Microgrid: An Off-Line Optimization Approach. *IEEE Trans. Smart Grid* **2015**, *6*, 124–134. [CrossRef]
2. Wang, W.; Liu, L.; Liu, J.; Chen, Z. Energy management and optimization of vehicle-to-grid systems for wind power integration. *CSEE J. Power Energy Syst.* **2021**, *7*, 172–180. [CrossRef]

3. Olivares, D.E.; Mehrizi-Sani, A.; Etemadi, A.H.; Canizares, C.A.; Iravani, R.; Kazerani, M.; Hajimiragha, A.H.; Gomis-Bellmunt, O.; Saeedifard, M.; Palma-Behnke, R.; et al. Trends in Microgrid Control. *IEEE Trans. Smart Grid* **2014**, *5*, 1905–1919. [CrossRef]
4. Ahmed, W.; Ansari, H.; Khan, B.; Ullah, Z.; Ali, S.M.; Mehmood, C.A.A.; Qureshi, M.B.; Hussain, I.; Jawad, M.; Khan, M.U.S.; et al. Machine Learning Based Energy Management Model for Smart Grid and Renewable Energy Districts. *IEEE Access* **2020**, *8*, 185059–185078. [CrossRef]
5. Cardelli, E. A general hysteresis operator for the modeling of vector fields. *IEEE Trans. Magn.* **2011**, *47*, 2056–2067. [CrossRef]
6. Quondam, A.S.; Ghanim, A.M.; Faba, A.; Laudani, A. Numerical simulations of vector hysteresis processes via the Preisach model and the Energy Based Model: An application to Fe-Si laminated alloys. *J. Magn. Magn. Mater.* **2021**, *539*, 168372. [CrossRef]
7. Li, X.; Chen, C.; Xu, Q.; Wen, C. Resilience for Communication Faults in Reactive Power Sharing of Microgrids. *IEEE Trans. Smart Grid* **2021**, *12*, 2788–2799. [CrossRef]
8. Mahmoud, K.; Lehtonen, M. Comprehensive Analytical Expressions for Assessing and Maximizing Technical Benefits of Photovoltaics to Distribution Systems. *IEEE Trans. Smart Grid* **2021**, *12*, 4938–4949. [CrossRef]
9. Kong, W.; Dong, Z.Y.; Jia, Y.; Hill, D.J.; Xu, Y.; Zhang, Y. Short-Term Residential Load Forecasting Based on LSTM Recurrent Neural Network. *IEEE Trans. Smart Grid* **2019**, *10*, 841–851. [CrossRef]
10. Zheng, R.; Gu, J.; Jin, Z.; Peng, H. Probabilistic Load Forecasting with High Penetration of Renewable Energy Based on Variable Selection and Residual Modeling. In Proceedings of the 2019 IEEE Power & Energy Society General Meeting (PESGM), Atlanta, GA, USA, 4–8 August 2019; pp. 1–5. [CrossRef]
11. Grasso, F.; Talluri, G.; Giorgi, A.; Luchetta, A.; Paolucci, L. Peer-to-Peer Energy Exchanges Model to optimize the Integration of Renewable Energy Sources: The E-Cube Project. *Energ. Elettr. Suppl.* **2020**, *96*, 1–8. [CrossRef]
12. Lee, W.; Jung, J.; Lee, M. Development of 24-hour optimal scheduling algorithm for energy storage system using load forecasting and renewable energy forecasting. In Proceedings of the 2017 IEEE Power & Energy Society General Meeting, Chicago, IL, USA, 16–20 July 2017; pp. 1–5. [CrossRef]
13. Dedeoglu, S.; Konstantopoulos, G.C. Three-Phase Grid-Connected Inverters Equipped with Nonlinear Current-Limiting Control. In Proceedings of the 2018 UKACC 12th International Conference on Control (CONTROL), Sheffield, UK, 5–7 September 2018; pp. 38–43. [CrossRef]
14. Bindi, M.; Garcia, C.I.; Corti, F.; Piccirilli, M.C.; Luchetta, A.; Grasso, F.; Manetti, S. Comparison Between PI and Neural Network Controller for Dual Active Bridge Converter. In Proceedings of the 2021 IEEE 15th International Conference on Compatibility, Power Electronics and Power Engineering (CPE-POWERENG), Florence, Italy, 14–16 July 2021; pp. 1–6. [CrossRef]
15. Quondam, A.S.; Faba, A.; Rimal, H.P.; Cardelli, E. On the Analysis of the Dynamic Energy Losses in NGO Electrical Steels under Non-Sinusoidal Polarization Waveforms. *IEEE Trans. Magn.* **2020**, *56*, 8960638. [CrossRef]
16. Guarino, A.; Vanel, L.; Scorretti, R.; Ciliberto, S. The cooperative effect of load and disorder in thermally activated rupture of a two-dimensional random fuse network. *J. Stat. Mech. Theory Exp.* **2006**, *2006*, P06020. [CrossRef]
17. Divyasharon, R.; Narmatha Banu, R.; Devaraj, D. Artificial Neural Network based MPPT with CUK Converter Topology for PV Systems Under Varying Climatic Conditions. In Proceedings of the 2019 IEEE International Conference on Intelligent Techniques in Control, Optimization and Signal Processing (INCOS), Tamilnadu, India, 11–13 April 2019; pp. 1–6. [CrossRef]
18. Luo, F.L. Luo-converters, voltage lift technique. In Proceedings of the PESC 98 Record, 29th Annual IEEE Power Electronics Specialists Conference (Cat. No.98CH36196), Fukuoka, Japan, 22 May 1998; Volume 2, pp. 1783–1789. [CrossRef]
19. Woranetsuttikul, K.; Pinsuntia, K.; Jumpasri, N.; Nilsakorn, T.; Khan-ngern, W. Comparison on performance between synchronous single-ended primary-inductor converter (SEPIC) and synchronous ZETA converter. In Proceedings of the 2014 International Electrical Engineering Congress (iEECON), Chonburi, Thailand, 19–21 March 2014; pp. 1–4. [CrossRef]
20. Luo, F.L. Double output Luo-converters-voltage lift technique. In Proceedings of the 1998 International Conference on Power Electronic Drives and Energy Systems for Industrial Growth, Perth, WA, Australia, 1–3 December 1998; Volume 1, pp. 342–347. [CrossRef]
21. Tadeusiewicz, M.; Hałgas, S. A Method for Local Parametric Fault Diagnosis of a Broad Class of Analog Integrated Circuits. *IEEE Trans. Instrum. Meas.* **2018**, *67*, 328–337. [CrossRef]
22. Aizenberg, I.; Belardi, R.; Bindi, M.; Grasso, F.; Manetti, S.; Luchetta, A.; Piccirilli, M.C. A Neural Network Classifier with Multi-Valued Neurons for Analog Circuit Fault Diagnosis. *Electronics* **2021**, *10*, 349. [CrossRef]
23. Bindi, M.; Aizenberg, I.; Belardi, R.; Grasso, F.; Luchetta, A.; Manetti, S.; Piccirilli, M.C. Neural Network-Based Fault Diagnosis of Joints in High Voltage Electrical Lines. *Adv. Sci. Technol. Eng. Syst. J.* **2020**, *5*, 488–498. [CrossRef]
24. Li, H.; Yin, B.; Li, N.; Guo, J. Research of fault diagnosis method of analog circuit based on improved support vector machines. In Proceedings of the 2010 The 2nd International Conference on Industrial Mechatronics and Automation, Wuhan, China, 30–31 May 2010; pp. 494–497. [CrossRef]
25. Ni, Y.; Li, J. Faults diagnosis for power transformer based on support vector machine. In Proceedings of the 2010 3rd International Conference on Biomedical Engineering and Informatics, Yantai, China, 16–18 October 2010; pp. 2641–2644. [CrossRef]
26. González-Castaño, C.; Lorente-Leyva, L.L.; Muñoz, J.; Restrepo, C.; Peluffo-Ordóñez, D.H. An MPPT Strategy Based on a Surface-Based Polynomial Fitting for Solar Photovoltaic Systems Using Real-Time Hardware. *Electronics* **2021**, *10*, 206. [CrossRef]
27. Laudani, A.; Fulginei, F.R.; Salvini, A.; Lozito, G.M.; Mancilla-David, F. Implementation of a neural MPPT algorithm on a low-cost 8-bit microcontroller. In Proceedings of the 2014 International Symposium on Power Electronics, Electrical Drives, Automation and Motion, Ischia, Italy, 18–20 June 2014; pp. 977–981. [CrossRef]

28. Available online: https://it.enfsolar.com/tianwei-new-energy (accessed on 11 February 2022).
29. Khatab, A.M.; Marei, M.I.; Elhelw, H.M. An Electric Vehicle Battery Charger Based on Zeta Converter Fed from a PV Array. In Proceedings of the 2018 IEEE International Conference on Environment and Electrical Engineering and 2018 IEEE Industrial and Commercial Power Systems Europe (EEEIC/I&CPS Europe), Palermo, Italy, 12–15 June 2018; pp. 1–5. [CrossRef]
30. Fontana, G.; Luchetta, A.; Manetti, S.; Piccirilli, M.C. A Fast Algorithm for Testability Analysis of Large Linear Time-Invariant Networks. *IEEE Trans. Circuits Syst. I Regul. Pap.* **2017**, *64*, 1564–1575. [CrossRef]
31. Fontana, G.; Luchetta, A.; Manetti, S.; Piccirilli, M.C. A Testability Measure for DC-Excited Periodically Switched Networks with Applications to DC-DC Converters. *IEEE Trans. Instrum. Meas.* **2016**, *65*, 2321–2341. [CrossRef]
32. Aizenberg, I.; Bindi, M.; Grasso, F.; Luchetta, A.; Manetti, S.; Piccirilli, M.C. Testability Analysis in Neural Network Based Fault Diagnosis of DC-DC Converter. In Proceedings of the 2019 IEEE 5th International forum on Research and Technology for Society and Industry (RTSI), Florence, Italy, 9–12 September 2019; pp. 265–268. [CrossRef]
33. Luchetta, A.; Manetti, S.; Piccirilli, M.C.; Reatti, A.; Corti, F.; Catelani, M.; Ciani, L.; Kazimierczuk, M.K. MLMVNNN for Parameter Fault Detection in PWM DC–DC Converters and Its Applications for Buck and Boost DC–DC Converters. *IEEE Trans. Instrum. Meas.* **2019**, *68*, 439–449. [CrossRef]
34. Aizenberg, I. *Complex-Valued Neural Networks with Multi-Valued Neurons*; Springer: New York, NY, USA, 2011.
35. Aizenberg, I.; Luchetta, A.; Manetti, S. A modified learning algorithm for the multilayer neural network with multi-valued neurons based on the complex QR decomposition. *Soft Comput.* **2012**, *16*, 563–575. [CrossRef]
36. Aizenberg, I. MLMVN With Soft Margins Learning. *IEEE Trans. Neural Netw. Learn. Syst.* **2014**, *25*, 1632–1644. [CrossRef]
37. Laudani, A.; Lozito, G.M.; Riganti Fulginei, F. Irradiance Sensing through PV Devices: A Sensitivity Analysis. *Sensors* **2021**, *21*, 4264. [CrossRef] [PubMed]

algorithms

MDPI

Article

A Data-Driven Fault Tree for a Time Causality Analysis in an Aging System

Kerelous Waghen and Mohamed-Salah Ouali *

Mathematics and Industrial Engineering Department, Polytechnique Montreal, 2500 Chemin de Polytechnique, Montreal, QC H3T 1J4, Canada; kerelous.waghen@polymtl.ca
* Correspondence: msouali@polymtl.ca

Abstract: This paper develops a data-driven fault tree methodology that addresses the problem of the fault prognosis of an aging system based on an interpretable time causality analysis model. The model merges the concepts of knowledge discovery in the dataset and fault tree to interpret the effect of aging on the fault causality structure over time. At periodic intervals, the model captures the cause–effect relations in the form of interpretable logic trees, then represents them in one fault tree model that reflects the changes in the fault causality structure over time due to the system aging. The proposed model provides a prognosis of the probability for fault occurrence using a set of extracted causality rules that combine the discovered root causes over time in a bottom-up manner. The well-known NASA turbofan engine dataset is used as an illustrative example of the proposed methodology.

Keywords: knowledge discovery in dataset; fault tree; causality analysis; aging system

1. Introduction

The aging of a system is characterized by the progressive deterioration of its initial performance over time, including—among other factors—the occurrence of faults that adversely affect the system's reliability [1]. Causality analysis methods aim to diagnose the fault event through identifying, isolating and quantifying the effect of the root causes on the system performance so that the appropriate maintenance actions can be performed to restore the system to good condition [2]. The future fault behaviour and its drawback on the system's performance are essential in order to optimize the maintenance decision-making [3]. Gao et al. [4] proposed a comprehensive survey of real-time fault diagnosis methods that are mainly categorized into model-, signal-, and knowledge-based techniques. The fault prognosis task provides a model that depicts the progression of a specific failure mode from its inception until the time of failure [5]. The time causality analysis builds a prognostic model that captures the fault causality behaviour over time [6].

A prognostic model may use a mathematical expression that quantifies the fault causality evolution or a graphical representation that depicts the changes in the causality structure over time [7]. Both the event-based and the data-driven methods are commonly deployed to provide relevant fault prognostic models. The event-based method requires the involvement of experts from different fields with detailed prior knowledge about the fault time causality. However, this knowledge could be biased and reflects only the expert opinions about the fault development [8]. On the other hand, the data-driven method can directly extract the fault evolution knowledge from the data, which is unbiased knowledge and reflects the fault causality. However, it lacks the interpretability and the expert knowledge representation to identify fault hierarchical causality over time [9].

Waghen and Ouali [10] have developed a data-driven fault tree method for causality analysis which addresses the lack of interpretability of the data-driven model and overcomes the model-based limitation regarding the expert prior knowledge. The method visualizes the fault causality architecture of a simple system using one-level fault tree that consists of three layers. The condition layer identifies the fault root causes and their coverage ranges within the dataset. The pattern layer arranges the root causes in the form of interpretable conjunctions. The solution layer combines some selected patterns that depict the fault event. Although the proposed tree is interpretable for the expert, the model hides the fault hierarchical cause-and-effect relations in a complex system. Moreover, it reflects the fault causality in a static way without considering the influence of a system's aging on the change in the fault causality structure over time.

From a practical point of view, human experts look for models that are able to explain and represent the fault causality structure in addition to having prediction capability. Ensuring that the fault and its impact and consequences are well represented to human experts guarantees optimal preventive maintenance actions. Another challenge in a complex system with regard to data-driven fault prognosis models is graphically modeling the deterioration and performance degradation. Consequently, the fault causality structure can be changed over a system's life. Therefore, these complex systems need models that are able to capture these changes in an interpretable manner. This is a crucial feature that helps anticipate the impacts of a fault and provides more precise knowledge about the processes that will be affected in the future by a currently occurring fault.

In this paper, an interpretable time causality analysis (ITCA) methodology is developed to address the problem of fault prognosis in an aging system using a data-driven fault tree model. We aim to build a time-dependent multilevel causality model based on the selection of feasible solutions that characterize the fault occurrence at a certain period from a set of representative time series historical datasets to address the causality analysis over time in a meaningful way. The ITCA model is a combination of different common one-level fault trees that depict the changes of the fault causality structure at periodic intervals. At each defined period, the ITCA methodology identifies, isolates, and represents the possible causes of the fault event in the form of the interpretable one-level fault tree. These constructed trees over defined periods are merged into a common one-level fault tree that graphically summarizes the changes in the fault causality structure over time. This procedure is iteratively repeated for each unexplained cause from the previous level until the final multilevel ITCA model is constructed. The proposed construction procedure ensures that redundant knowledge is eliminated within the ITCA model, while maximizing its interpretability over the time. Finally, a set of causality rules are deduced from the ITCA fault tree that characterize the dynamic change effect of the causality structure in the causes of a fault occurrence.

The rest of the paper is organized into four sections. Section 2 reviews the available methods for achieving the fault prognosis based on time causality analysis and discusses the main challenges. Section 3 develops the ITCA methodology. It explains the data preparation, the construction of the fault tree models over time, and the deduction of the time causality rules for fault prognosis. Section 4 illustrates the ITCA methodology using the NASA turbofan engine degradation dataset. The performance of the ITCA model to predict the fault is demonstrated by the fault trend over time. Section 5 concludes the paper and discusses the contribution of the ITCA methodology in achieving the fault prognosis task.

2. Time Causality Analysis Methods

Time causality analysis is a causal interference over time where the temporary dependency between events over the stochastic process is captured and represented using analytical methods. The time causality analysis can achieve the fault prognosis task by providing the expert with the essential knowledge regarding the fault evolution and the change in its causality structure over time [11]. Schwabacher distinguishes the model-based and data-driven methods to address the fault prognosis issue. In what follows, a brief literature review of each prognostic method is discussed, and their strengths and limitations are highlighted to clarify the research gap [7].

The model-based method for time causality analysis relies heavily on human expertise to describe the system's behaviour over time in degraded conditions [12]. Lu, Jiang [13] address the drawback of the system downtime due to fault evolution in complex industrial process by expert knowledge enrichment. First, the time-delayed mutual information (TDMI) is employed to model the fault causality in the form of a time-delayed signed digraph (TD-SDG) mode. Then, a general fault prognosis strategy is used to optimize the system's downtime based on TD-SDG and the principal component analysis (PCA) technique. Darwish, Almouahed [14] propose an enriched fault tree for Active Assisted Living Systems (AALS). The fault tree basic events are ranked according to the degree of their importance based on the expert prior knowledge and the imprecise failure probabilities of those basic events. Ragab, El Koujok [15] combine the domain knowledge with the extracted knowledge from the database to build an enriched fault tree. First, the expert constructs the fault tree skeleton, which represents the main causality structure for the fault event. Then, some extracted patterns from the database that may depict unknown combinations of root causes are deployed to enrich the initial fault tree. Yunkai, Bin [16] integrate the bond graph modelling technique with the Bayesian network to predict the faults in a high-speed train traction system. The bond graph represents the system structure that is mainly constructed based on expert prior knowledge, while the Bayesian network enriches the expert prior knowledge represented by the bond graph through discovering the hidden causal relations.

Indeed, the model-based time causality approach can provide interpretable and relatively accurate models that can be built from the first principle of the system's faults. It is mainly applicable on simple systems with well-known causes where human knowledge about the faults, their occurrence and development is clear. Its limited implementation in complex systems has been overcome by enriching those models based on data-driven techniques, in which the unseen events are discovered and added to the model's prior knowledge. However, forming the model skeleton prior to knowledge by the expert in complex systems to identify the principal causality structure of the faulty situation and combining and positioning the extracted hidden fault knowledge from the data in the constructed model is a challenging task.

Unlike the model-based methods, the data-driven time causality method explores the data using machine learning (ML) techniques and does not impose a model to predict the behaviour of a complex system [17]. The ML data-driven methods build unbaised models and are able to deal with noisy and correlated variables [18]. Zhang, Wang [19] proposed a methodology to predict the remaining useful time (RUL) using the Wavelet Packet Decomposition of the vibration signal and Fast Fourier Transform. The pre-processed signals are treated as input features to learn the Artificial Neural Network (ANN) that predicts the RUL. Wu, Ding [20] implemented the long short-term memory (LSTM) neural network rather than relying on feature engineering and an ANN for fault prognosis in aircraft turbofan engines. The main advantage of LSTM over an ANN is its ability to learn long-term dependencies between input features and over the equipment lifetime to give accurate RUL prediction. Razavi, Najafabadi [21] developed an adaptive neuro-fuzzy inference system (ANFIS) algorithm that combines the ANN and a fuzzy rule-based model to predict the RUL of aircraft engines. The ANFIS algorithm has been applied to maintenance scheduling problems.

Although the data-driven models offer an accurate prediction of the RUL, they suffer from a lack of interpretability [22]. This is because they are too shallow to understand the fault causality structure and its changes over time. Therefore, an expert may not be able to deeply understand the cause–effect relations within a complex system. With regard to this challenge, several methods have been proposed to simplify and unlock the model interpretability. Li, Wang [23] employed the Deep Belief Network (DBN) to model the geometric error structure of the backlash error. The DBN was built using restricted Boltzmann machines and energy-based models to predict the fault geometric. Su, Jing [24] have proposed a dynamic extraction knowledge method that illustrates the relationship between the environmental stresses and the system failure modes using a fuzzy causality diagram and a Bayesian rough set of multiple decision classes to weigh the extracted knowledge. Kimotho, Sondermann-Woelke [25] addressed the challenge of maintenance action recommendation for industrial systems based on remote monitoring and diagnosis. They proposed an interpretable event-based decision tree that graphically identifies some problems associated with particular events and conducts evidence-based decisions. Medjaher, Moya [26] used Dynamic Bayesian Networks (DBNs) to quantify the failure prognostic in complex systems. The fault time series data are divided into several periods and a Bayesian network is constructed for each period. The obtained networks are connected through the chronology of periods to depict the changes in the fault causality structure over time and quantify the fault behaviour.

On the other hand, the achieved data-driven methods attempt to unlock the time-dependent relations between the system variables in an interpretable manner in addition to capturing the change in the fault causality through the periods. However, building an interpretable data-driven model that can directly grasp the influence of the system aging on the fault causality structure and summarize the fault behaviour in one model, is a challenge that still needs to be overcome. The main motivation of this study is to build an interpretable time causality analysis model that characterizes, first, the hierarchical causality structure between the fault event, intermediate causes, and root-causes; and second, the influence of the system aging on that structure over time. Thus, the proposed ITCA methodology will achieve the fault prognosis task in an efficient way through anticipating the fault event based on the causal relations discovered over time. It will be developed in the following section.

3. The ITCA Methodology

Figure 1 depicts the four-phase ITCA methodology. The main input dataset is an unlabelled timestamp of observations that can represent sequential data. We assume that the system undergoes a certain degradation trend, depicted by the sequential data, from a normal state to a failure state, represented by green and red colors, respectively. Phase 1 prepares several labelled subsets from the input data. Each subset is formed by a sub-sequence of degraded observations, beginning from normal observations (green colors) to failure ones (red colors), gradually. Phase 2 iteratively builds the appropriate logic tree corresponding to each subset of data, and then aggregates them into one common fault tree. Phase 3 constructs the ITCA model by going deeply through each variable in the above common fault tree and seeks its root-causes. Phase 4 deduces the time causality rules that determine the effects that the system aging has on the evolution of the fault occurrence over time. In what follows, each phase of the proposed methodology is explained in detail.

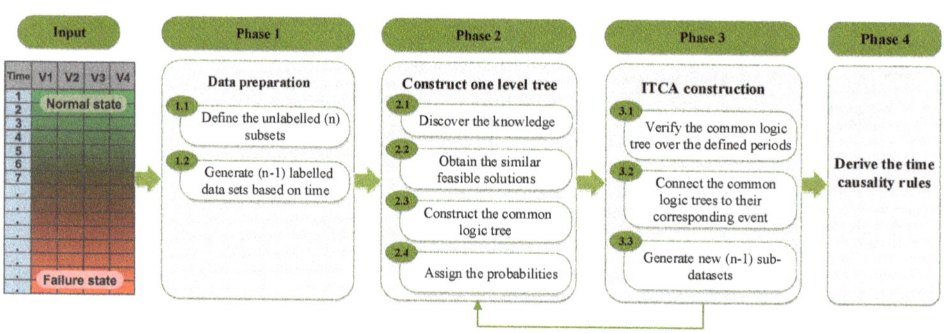

Figure 1. The four-phase ITCA methodology.

3.1. Phase 1: Data Preparation

Phase 1 splits the main input data into several subsets according to the expert's prior knowledge about the process degradation trend. Each subset contains the sequential observations that represent the system state at a certain period and the observations that characterise the failure state or the worst deterioration condition of the system. The expert should identify the observations that represent the failure before splitting the rest of the data into equal or non-equal sizes of subsets, according to his judgment about the amount of system degradation. Equal and non-equal sizes of subsets are suitable for linear and nonlinear degradation processes, respectively. Hence, the original main data are divided into n subsets, where the last one contains the failure observations and the others contain degraded observations. Those n subsets will be concatenated to form $(n-1)$ datasets. Each dataset will contain two classes of observations corresponding to failure and degraded data.

Figure 2 depicts the data preparation procedures, in which X_1 and X_2 are two variables. Beginning from the main timestamped dataset, the observations in the last period Δ_n belong to the failure state. Then, $(n-1)$ subsets are extracted. Each subset SS_i contains the observations of the period Δ_i, $I = 1, \ldots, J$, where (j) is the index of the last observation for a given period. At the end, $(n-1)$-labelled datasets are concatenated. Each dataset D_i contains the observations of the period Δ_i, labelled as class i and the observations of the last period Δ_n, labelled as class n.

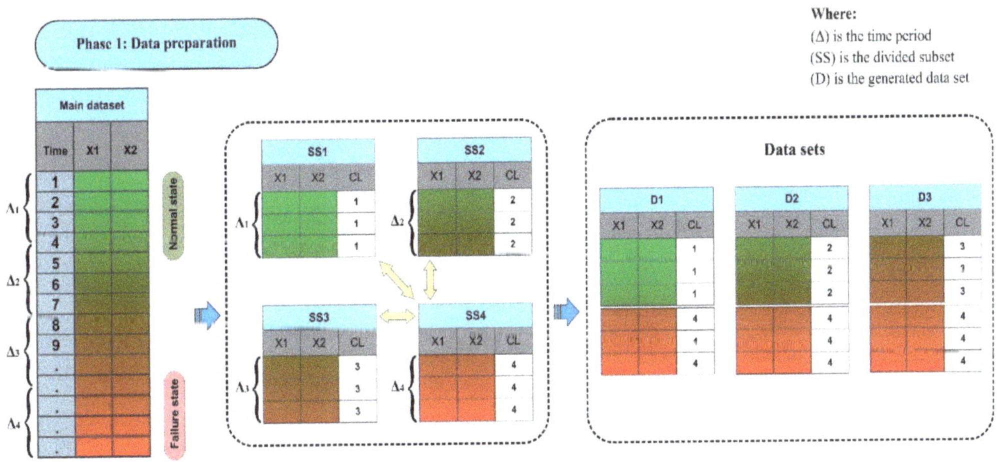

Figure 2. Data preparation phase.

3.2. Phase 2: Build a One Level Fault Tree

Phase 2 iteratively extracts all of the logic trees that differentiate the fault event (class n) from each class i, $i = 1, \ldots, (n-1)$ of the degraded observations individually. Each logic tree highlights the relevant variables that discriminate the observations of the failure state from the degraded ones, from one period to another. Then, the obtained logic trees are merged into one common fault tree, which identifies and isolates the variables that discriminate the failure state from the degraded ones over time. To do so, Waghen and Ouali [10] developed a four-stage methodology, named Interpretable Logic Tree Analysis (ILTA), to build a one-level fault tree from a two-class dataset (i.e., normal and failure classes). The methodology discovers the knowledge from the dataset (Stage 1); forms feasible solutions (Stage 2); constructs the fault tree (Stage 3); and finally quantifies the fault tree using Bayes' theorem (Stage 4). Although such a methodology can be applied separately with each dataset D_i, $i = 1, \ldots, (n-1)$, the merged fault tree may be difficult to interpret due to the dependence of the datasets over time. To overcome this limitation, Stage 2 of the ILTA methodology needs to be improved. Nevertheless, for the convenience of the reader, we briefly recall the four stages of the ILTA methodology and highlight the improvements to Stage 2 in the following.

- Stage 1: Discover knowledge. Discovering knowledge from a two-class dataset can be achieved through different pattern generation and extraction techniques, such as the logic analysis of data (LAD) [27] and prediction rule ensembles (PRE) [28]. The pattern is a conjunction of certain conditions that discriminate one class of observations from another class. Each condition includes a variable, an inequality sign, and a cut point value. Furthermore, the percentage of observations covered by a given pattern may characterize the knowledge expanse caught by that pattern. However, when the observations of the same class are covered by more than one pattern, an overlap between those patterns may occur, with a certain percentage leading to redundant knowledge.
- Stage 2: Obtain similar feasible solutions. A solution is defined as a combination of certain patterns that cover the observations of the same class. Each solution can be characterized by its coverage (Cov) and overlap (OL) percentages. The feasible solution is a solution that respects certain criteria. In the ILTA methodology, only the feasible solution that maximizes the class Cov and minimizes the class OL is selected, which leads to maximizing the interpretability and minimizing the redundancy of the discovered knowledge. However, in the ITCA methodology, we need to search for all of the feasible solutions that respect not only the Cov and OL threshold percentages, but also with minimal number of patterns to capture the common knowledge at the same level over time. In other words, the minimal number of patterns having the maximum Cov and the minimum OL allows us to characterize the fault using global knowledge at the first levels of the tree. When this causality is represented in the tree and the related knowledge is removed from the dataset, the subsequent feasible solutions will reveal other knowledge that depicts sub-causalities not yet discovered and represented in the tree. As Stage 2 aims to select similar feasible solutions that characterize knowledge discovery over time, we seek the most frequent patterns over the predefined periods of time. In addition, the frequent pattern involves the same variable and inequality sign in the shared conditions, independent of the cut-point values. Therefore, the initial version of the burn-and-build algorithm proposed in [10] is improved to form a set of feasible solutions instead of only one for each period, using another decision criterion called the solution tolerance selection (STS) threshold. Hence, a time-based searching algorithm is developed in the ITCA methodology to obtain all the similar feasible solutions over time. It is depicted in the following Algorithm 1.

Figure 3 illustrates the proposed time-based searching algorithm using the above three concatenated datasets D_1, D_2 and D_3 of the toy example (Figure 1). Applying Step 1 to Step 4, the algorithm finds a set of five feasible solutions that respect the STS threshold of 90%. To clearly understand this, we assume that each solution consists of only one pattern. From D_1, $S_1 : P_1 : (X_1 \leq 30)$ and $S_2 : P_2 : (X_2 > 10)$ are obtained with 98% and 100% of Cov, respectively. From D_2, there is only one formed solution $S_3 : P_3 : (X_1 \leq 20)$ with a Cov of 90%. From D_3, the obtained solutions $S_4 : P_4 : (X_1 \leq 10)$ and $S_5 : P_5 : (X_2 > 20)$ have 95% and 100% Cov, respectively. Note that the patterns P_1, P_3 and P_4 share the same condition on X_1 except the cut points. Consequently, at Step 5, the algorithm selects S_1, S_3 and S_4 as the only three similar solutions that characterize the evolution of the same condition through the three periods Δ_1, Δ_2, and Δ_3, respectively. However, the algorithm does not select S_2 and S_5 because there is a loss of information during the period Δ_2, even though they are similar, by sharing the same condition of X_2 during Δ_1 and Δ_3. Hence, the algorithm evaluates all of the similar feasible solutions and selects the ones that dominate the maximum number of periods.

Algorithm 1. Time-based searching algorithm: ***Search for similar feasible solutions over time.***

Input.

(i) (n-1)-labelled datasets corresponding to the defined time periods (Δ);

(ii) Set of generated patterns: $P_{gen} = \{P_1, P_2, \ldots, P_l\}$*; where (l) is the number of the discovered patterns;*

(iii) Overlap (OL) threshold;

(iv) Solution tolerance selection (STS) threshold.

***For** each (n-1)-labelled dataset that represents a defined time period (Δ):*

***Step 1.** Select a start pattern* (P_i) *and calculate its coverage.*

1.1. *Remove the overlapped patterns with* P_i *based on the preset overlap threshold:*
    i. *At number of combination (n) = 2;*
    ii. *Select the combination with* P_i *that has the maximum coverage.*

1.2. *Repeat (the sub-steps 1.1-i and ii) until the number of combinations (n) = number of the discovered patterns;*

1.3. *Compare the selected combinations at each n and select the combination that maximizes the coverage with a minimal number of patterns.*

***Step 2.** Select another pattern* (P_i) *as a start point and repeat 1.1, 1.2 and 1.3.*

***Step 3.** Repeat 2 until considering each pattern as a start point.*

***Step 4.** Compare the selected combinations over the start patterns* P_i *and select the combination that includes the minimal number of patterns and its coverage value within the STS threshold.*

End

***Step 5.** Compare the selected combinations that represent (n-1)-labelled datasets and select the combinations that maximize the similarity over the defined periods (Δ), where each period (Δ) is represented by only one combination.*

Output.

Set of similar feasible solutions: $Sol = \{S_1, S_2, \ldots, S_k\}$*; where (k) is the number of similar feasible solutions.*

Figure 4 depicts the curve of the cut-point values that reflect the evolution of similar feasible solutions obtained over the three periods Δ_1, Δ_2, and Δ_3. Note that these periods are consecutive, and the cut-point curve may have a positive, negative, or constant trend over time depending on how the cut-point values change over time.

- Stage 3: Construct a common logic tree over time. The similar feasible solutions obtained are visualized in a one-level fault tree through the condition, pattern, and solution layers. At the condition layer, all the involved conditions are connected to their respective patterns using the AND gate. At the pattern layer, all the patterns of the similar feasible solutions are connected to that solution using the OR gate. Similarly, at the solution layer, all the selected similar feasible solutions are connected to the fault event using the OR gate.
- Stage 4: Assign the probabilities. The common logic tree is quantified using the probabilities of the solutions, patterns and conditions involved in similar feasible solutions obtained from the concatenated dataset individually. Let N_k and N_T be the number of observations covered by the condition C_k and the total number of observations in one concatenated dataset, respectively. Equations (1) to (4) calculate the probabilities of the fault class $\mathcal{P}(CL)$ and the involved solutions $\mathcal{P}(S_q)$ $q = 1, 2, \ldots Q$, patterns $\mathcal{P}(P_j)$ $j = 1..J$, and conditions $\mathcal{P}(C_k)$ $k = 1..K$ as follows:

$$\mathcal{P}(C_k) = \frac{N_k}{N_T} \tag{1}$$

$$\mathcal{P}(P_j) = \prod_{k=1}^{n_j-1} \mathcal{P}(C_k \mid C_{k+1}) \cdot P(C_{k+1}) \tag{2}$$

$$\mathcal{P}(S_q) = \mathcal{P}\left[\bigcup_{j=1}^{J} P_j\right] \tag{3}$$

$$\mathcal{P}(CL) = \mathcal{P}\left[\bigcup_{q=1}^{Q} S_q\right] \tag{4}$$

Figure 3. Example of selecting similar feasible solutions over the periods Δ_1, Δ_2, and Δ_3.

For a simple cause–effect relation between the fault event and its root causes, the common one-level logic tree can depict the fault causality structure at each period, as well as over time through the trend of cut-point curves of similar feasible solutions employed in the tree. For a complex causality structure, the one-level logic tree is not sufficient to completely represent a fault occurrence because the variables involved at the condition layer may represent the intermediate causes, and not necessarily the root causes of the fault event. Therefore, each one of those variables needs a second level of decomposition or more to explore the solution that will explain its causality structure at each period. Accordingly, Phase 3 constructs many levels of the tree to address the complex causality structure over time.

Periods	Δ1	Δ2	Δ3
Sol.	S1: X1 ≤ 30	S3: X1 ≤ 20	S4: X1 ≤ 10

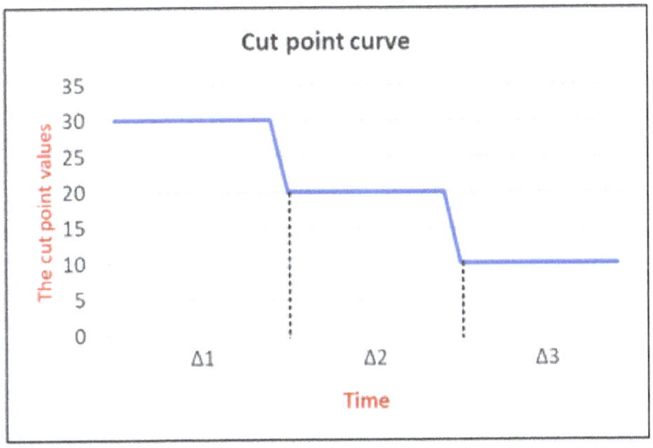

Figure 4. Curve of the cut-point values of similar feasible solutions obtained over time.

3.3. Phase 3: The ITCA Model Construction

Phase 3 builds, in a sequential up-bottom structure, several connected common logic trees to depict unexplained causes through multilevel structure. Each level includes three stages: verify the common logic trees' construction, connect those trees to their corresponding causes, and generate new labelled sub-datasets that exclude the variables associated with causes already explained from the concatenated datasets. In Phase 3, each cause (i.e., condition) of the obtained common logic trees in Phase 2 is considered as a new event that needs to be explained in a lower level using a new common logic tree. This procedure is iteratively repeated to construct a multilevel tree that represent the fault causality structure over time. In such hierarchical structures, the common feasible solutions at the first level characterize the fault event using general fault indicators, while the common feasible solutions at the lower levels will use specific fault indicators to explain the last causes of the tree.

- Stage 1: Verify the common logic trees' construction over the defined periods. This stage verifies the knowledge representability of the constructed logic tree for each defined period of time and decides whether the further decomposition of its involved condition is required or not. At each decomposition level, verification of the tree knowledge is characterized by the coverage of the common feasible solution, which assists in avoiding decomposing the weak information branches. Therefore, the model construction is verified to sustain the tree at a non-redundant knowledge level based on the pre-set coverage threshold. Meanwhile, the construction phase can be interpreted if there is no common tree that is able to provide sufficient knowledge representability, or if there are no more variables in the dataset for any further root cause explorations.
- Stage 2: Connect the common logic trees to their corresponding causes. The applied relaxation in selecting a common feasible solution over the defined periods is very useful in constructing a common logic tree that easily demonstrates the change in the causality at a given level of decomposition in the ITCA model. However, it could happen if the time-based searching algorithm fails to form only one common logic tree that dominates all the defined periods at a certain decomposition level. This case could happen if there is a lack of extracted knowledge or a tight range in the solution tolerance selection (STS). To solve this situation, different common logic trees may be found by the algorithm, but each period is dominated by only one common feasible solution. Therefore, if such a situation rises, a time–OR gate is proposed to connect the different common logic trees to represent the change in the event causality

knowledge over all the defined periods at a given decomposition level. The time–OR gate acts as a time switch that shifts between the common logic trees according to their corresponding periods. Hence, an expert could observe the fault behaviour over time based on the proposed common similar solution trees at a certain decomposition level of the ITCA model.

Figure 5 presents an example of the time–OR gate functionality in a one-level ITCA model. Two common feasible solutions, S_1 and S_2, are found by the time-based searching algorithm. S_1 characterizes the fault event at only Δ_1 and Δ_2 using the OR gate (G2) between the patterns P_1 and P_2. While S_2 represents the fault even only at only Δ_3 with one pattern, P_3. This allows P_3 to be connected directly to S_2 without any need for an OR gate. The time–OR gate (G1) enables ITCA to fully demonstrate the fault event causality over the three defined periods (Δ_1, Δ_2 and Δ_3). It switches between S_1 and S_2 according to the selected corresponding period that is dominated by the solution. For instance, at the periods Δ_1 and Δ_2, the time–OR gate (G1) enables only S_1 to depict the fault event causality. On the other hand, during the period Δ_3, the fault causality is explained only by S_2.

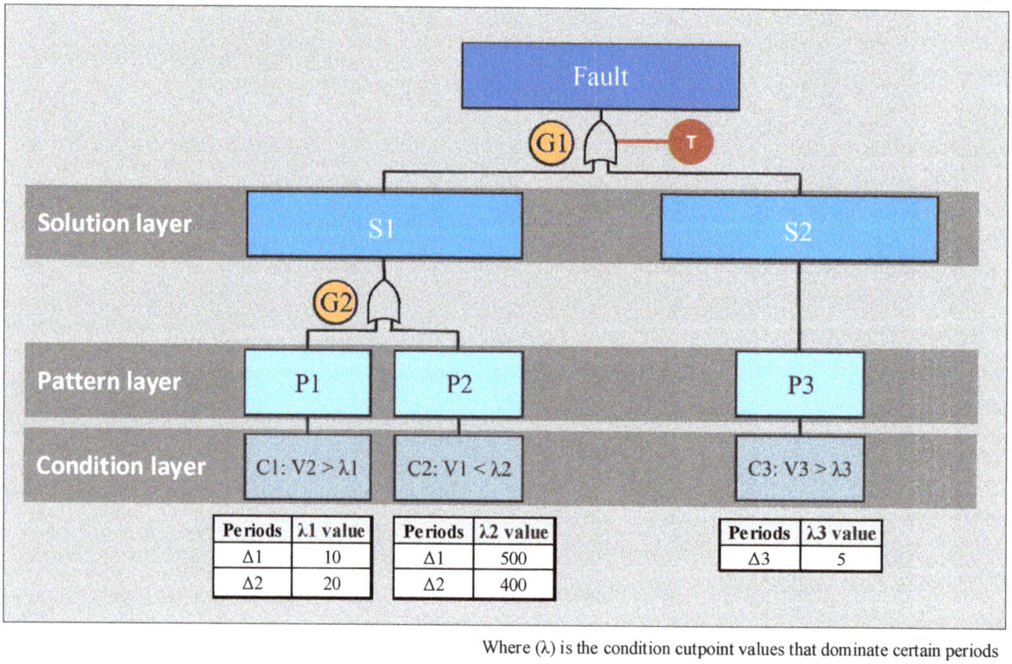

Figure 5. Time–OR gate functionality in the ITCA model.

- Stage 3: Generate new (m − 1) sub-datasets. In a case in which the added common logic trees are verified at a certain decomposition level of the ITCA model, each one of the involved conditions in the tree is used to generate new labelled sub-datasets based on the condition variable cut-point values. Figure 6 takes the example of Figure 3. It presents the generation of the three two-class sub-datasets $D_1^{(2)}$, $D_2^{(2)}$ and $D_3^{(2)}$ at the second decomposition level using the variable X_1 cut-point values 10, 20 and 30, respectively. Note that the generated new sub-datasets contain (m − 1) columns each time that a variable is removed from the data.

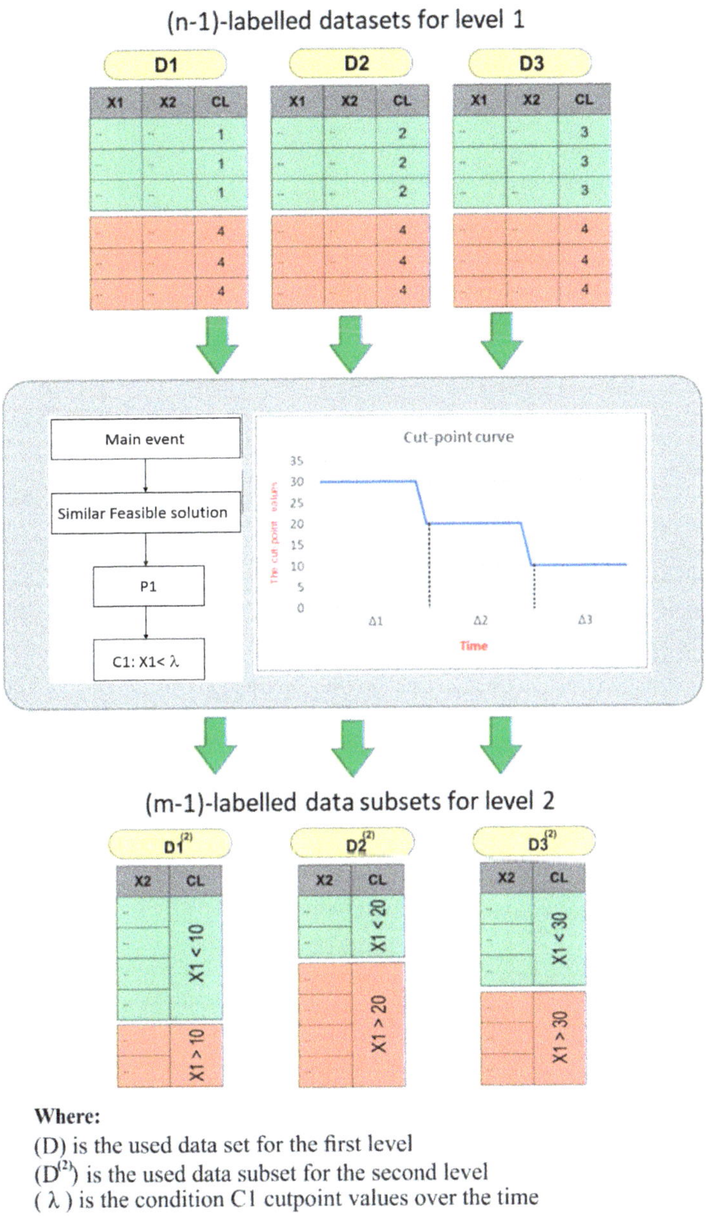

Figure 6. Generating new labelled data subsets in the ITCA methodology.

3.4. Phase 4: Derive the Time Causality Rules

Based on the calculation of the probabilities of root causes, causes and fault events in the final ITCA model, Phase 4 derives the time causality rules that represent the change in occurrence probabilities from one period to another. Each time causality rule summarizes a specific structure of the cause–effect relations over the time between the root causes, causes and fault events within the ITCA model in the form of an algebraic formula based on the above Equations 1 to 4 (Stage 4, Phase 2). The obtained time causality rules allow the fault event occurrence to be controlled based only on its root causes. Moreover, these rules enable managing the fault occurrence over the defined time horizon, which makes them more suitable and appropriate for the task of making a prognosis.

4. Case Study

Most aging systems that include bearings, seals, glands, shafts, and couplings are more likely to suffer from several degradation processes due to harsh operating constraints such as high temperatures, vibration, and dynamic load, and likely the deficiency of the maintenance plan as well. In this section, the ITCA methodology is deployed on simulated data that reproduce the degradation of a turbofan engine proposed by NASA. It is known as the PHM08 challenge dataset. The dataset is generated by the Commercial Modular Aero-Propulsion System Simulation (C-MAPSS) simulator based on MATLAD® and Simulink® [29]. The simulator uses the combination of three specific operation variables to generate different degradation profiles. The high-pressure compressor (HPC) degradation fault mode is selected as an illustrative example.

Based on the C-MAPSS user guide, as shown in Figure 7A, the engine consists of several interconnected subsystems (inlet, bypass nozzle, fan, low-pressure compressor (LPC), high-pressure compressor (HPC), combustor, high-pressure turbine (HPT), low-pressure turbine (LPT), and core nozzle). The fuel valve controls the fuel flow into the combustor that turns the HPT. The HPT rotates the HPC, LPT, LPC and the inlet fan. The turbofan engine has two state variables: the fan speed and the core speed [30]. Based on the thermodynamic cycle, the air is compressed and combusted by the engine to produce propelling. Figure 7B describes the ambient airflow to the engine. First, the air enters the engine through the inlet and the fan. Then, it is divided by the splitter into two portions. One portion passes through the compressor and then the burner to mix with fuel and produces combustion. The hot exhaust passes through the core and fan turbines to the nozzle, while the other portion is bypassed to the back of the engine. The airflow is controlled by the bypass ratio, which is the ratio of the bypassed mass airflow to the mass airflow that goes through an engine core [31]. The HPC's main functionality drives the airflow to higher pressure and temperature states to prepare it for combustion by using its spinning blades. Therefore, the change in the bypass ratio is the main control element for controlling the HPC outlet air pressure and its temperature for the burning phase.

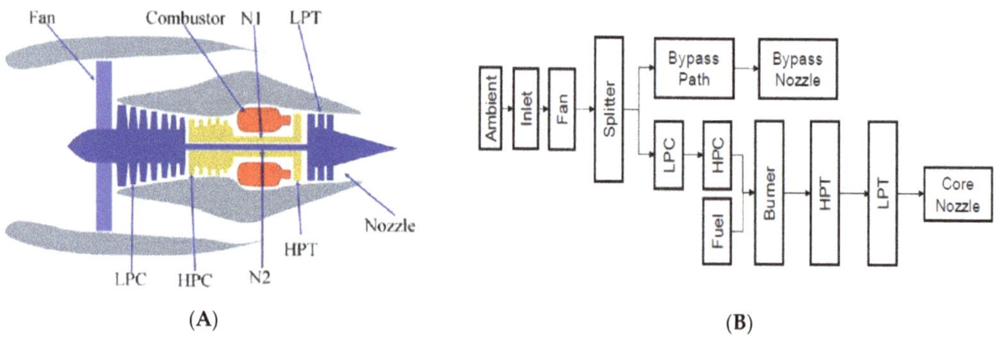

Figure 7. The simulated turbofan engine based on C-MAPSS [32] (images courtesy of NASA). (**A**) Simplified diagram of the turbofan engine; (**B**) Turbofan engine modules layout and connections.

The challenge addressed by the ITCA methodology is to model the HPC fault causality structure in a dynamic manner so that the model can demonstrate the effect of the root cause changes over time on the main HPC degradation curve.

4.1. Dataset Description

The dataset consists of 21 measurement variables that describe the HPC fault mode (Table 1) and 465 timestamp observations. The generated data are divided into training and testing sets with 258 (60%) and 207 observations (40%), respectively. The constant (—), increasing (↑) or decreasing (↓) trend that depicts each variable over time is mentioned in Table 1.

Table 1. Variable descriptions of the HPC fault mode.

Variable	Description (Unit)	Trend (—, ↑, ↓)	Variable	Description (Unit)	Trend (—, ↑, ↓)
T2	Total temperature at fan inlet (R)	—	phi	Ratio of fuel flow to Ps30 (pps/psi)	↓
T24	Total temperature at LPC outlet (R)	↑	NRf	Corrected fan speed (rpm)	↑
T30	Total temperature at HPC outlet (R)	↑	NRc	Corrected core speed (rpm)	↓
T50	Total temperature at LPT outlet (R)	↑	BPR	Bypass ratio (rpm)	↑
P2	Pressure at fan inlet (psia)	—	farB	Burner fuel–air ratio (without unit)	—
P15	Total pressure in bypass duct (psia)	—	htBleed	Bleed enthalpy (without unit)	↑
P30	Total pressure at HPC outlet (psia)	↓	Nf_dmd	Demanded fan speed (rpm)	—
Nf	Physical fan speed (rpm)	↑	W31	HPT coolant bleed (lbm/s)	↓
Nc	Physical core speed (rpm)	↓	W32	LPT coolant bleed (lbm/s)	↓
epr	Engine pressure ratio	—	Ps30	Static pressure at HPC outlet (psia)	↓
PCNfR_dmd	Demanded corrected fan speed (rpm)	—			

Note that the majority of the variables have an increasing or decreasing trend over the time, except T2, P2, P15, epr, farB, Nf_dmd and PCNfR_dmd, which are constant no matter the fault mode.

4.2. The HPC Fault Prognosis Using the ITCA Model

In what follows, the main results of the proposed four-phase ITCA methodology applied on the NASA turbofan engine dataset are presented and discussed to perform the HPC fault prognosis task. As per the first phase, the training dataset is ordered according to the timestamp variable and divided into six equal, unlabelled subsets, where each subset SS_i $i = 1..6$ depicts the period of time Δ_i $i = 1..6$. The subsets are ordered in a timely manner, where SS_1 represents the best normal state of the turbofan while SS_6 depicts its worst or failure state. Consequently, five labelled datasets are concatenated from those 6 subsets as follows D_i: SS_i versus SS_6 $i = 1..5$. Each dataset has 86 labelled observations. Note that the dataset is divided by fixed width for simplicity. However, the expert can assign different width thresholds to produce non-equal data subsets. Meanwhile, the number of subsets is important to capture the evolution of the faults over time. This is a trade-off between time step resolution and ITCA construction time. Phase 2 and Phase 3 are iteratively repeated to construct the ITCA model. The coverage tolerance selection STS threshold used by the time-based searching algorithm (Stage 2 of Phase 2) is set to 10%. In addition, the coverage threshold is set to 90% to control redundant knowledge in the common trees at Stage 1 of Phase 3, when a new level is considered in the ITCA model.

Figure 8 depicts the final ITCA model of the HPC fault mode. It includes six levels of decomposition to reproduce the causality structure between the HPC fault and its root-causes over six periods of time. Note that each level of the ITCA model consists of three layers that represent the solutions, patterns, and conditions related to the fault event or to one of its causes. The first level includes only one common feasible solution S_1 over the five defined time periods (Δ_1 to Δ_5). S_1 has only one pattern, P_1, which includes only one condition: $C_1 : P30 > \lambda_1$. The plot A1 of Figure 8 characterizes the degradation of the variable P30 over time. Note that the cut-point curve (blue line) bounds the trend of the variable P30 in time. Additionally, the plot A2 of Figure 8 shows the common feasible solution coverage and the overlap percentages over the five time periods. Regarding Level 2 of the ITCA model, the same interpretation above can be performed for the variable T50. It is clear that the ITCA model captures the trend of the involved variables based on the cut-point curves.

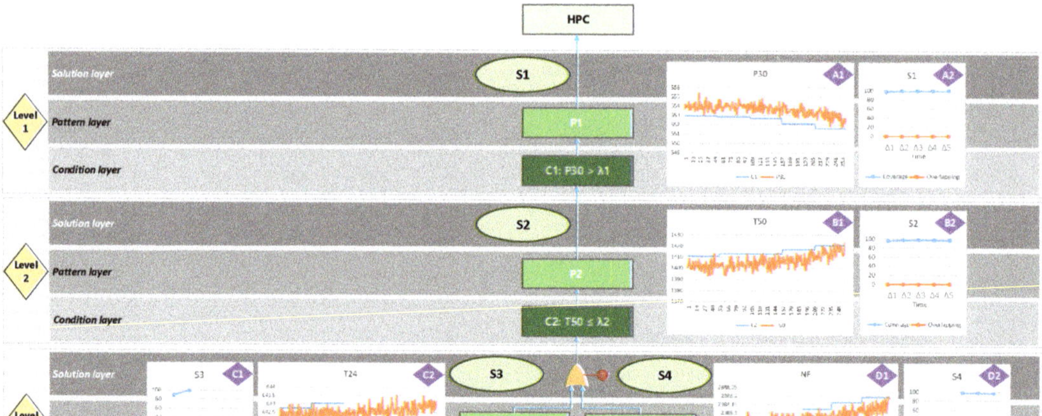

Figure 8. Obtained ITCA model of the HPC degradation mode.

At Level 3, two common feasible solutions, S_3 and S_4, are found by the time-based searching algorithm. These solutions respect the construction setting; S_3 explains the cause ($C_2 : T50 \leq \lambda_2$) at the time periods Δ_1 and Δ_2, while S_4 dominates the three other periods Δ_3 to Δ_5. S_3 and S_4 each have only one pattern and condition. The plots C2 and D1 of Figure 8 depict the bordering of the cut-point curves that represent the degradation trends of the variables T24 and NF, respectively. Meanwhile, the C1 and D2 plots show the solution coverage and overlap percentages over the corresponding time periods. S_3 and S_4 describe the full-time causality of the cause event ($C_2 : T50 \leq \lambda_2$) through the time–OR gate by toggling between the two feasible solutions. Hence, S_3 explains the event causality at only Δ_1 and Δ_2, while S_4 illustrates the causality of the same event at Δ_3, Δ_4 , and Δ_5.

At Level 4, two other feasible solutions, S_5 and S_6, are found that explain the events $C_3 : T24 \leq \lambda_3$) and $C_4 : NF > \lambda_4$, respectively. At Level 5, only one common feasible solution S_7 is found that explains both events' ($C_5 : Ps30 \leq \lambda_5$ and $C_6 : Phi \leq \lambda_6$) causality over the five periods of time. This solution includes one pattern P_7 with only one condition $C_7 : NRF \leq \lambda_7$. The same reasoning can be made with the only common feasible solution S_8, which explains the condition C_7 at the last level of the ITCA model using only one pattern P_8 that consists of one root cause: $C_8 : BPR \leq \lambda_8$. The cut-point curve of Figure 8. H1 bounds the trend of C_8.

From the obtained logic tree of Figure 8, the ITCA model confirms the discussion above about the main root cause of the HPC fault mode. Effectively, the first level of the ITCA model identifies the variable P30 (total pressure at HPC outlet) as the only fault indicator of the HPC degradation over time. Therefore, P30 can be employed to predict the remaining useful time of the turbofan engine according to the HPC fault mode. At the second level, the variable T50 (total temperature at an LPT outlet) is discovered to explain the effect of the temperature of combustion on the total pressure at the HPC outlet. T50 refines the knowledge discovered about P30. The same reasoning continues until reaching the final Level, 6, where the ITCA model discovers the variable BPR (bypass ratio), which is identified by the expert as the main control element that affects the occurrence of the HPC fault mode over time. Therefore, the ITCA model provides the expert with more refined knowledge, outlining the effects of the root causes on the fault trend over time, which help him to achieve the prognosis task in an efficient way.

The probabilities associated with the ITCA model are calculated using Equations (1) to (4) of Stage 4, Phase 2. They quantify the occurrence of similar feasible solutions, patterns, and associated conditions, period after period, at each level of the ITAC model. Figure 9 plots the probabilities of the eight discovered conditions over five periods of time. Note that the occurrence of each feasible solution is equal to the probability of its associated conditions due to the structure of the obtained logic tree. For example, plot A in Figure 9 represents the probability curve of $S_1 : P_1 : C_1$ over the periods Δ_1 to Δ_5. The maximum probability value is equal to 0.16 at each period, since the original data are divided into six equal-size data subsets. Therefore, each subset represents 0.16 from the original data size. Note that each common feasible solution tries to maximize its class coverage, so that the associated condition probability value may not exceed that coverage value over the five periods.

Based on the ITCA model and the calculation of probabilities, only one time causality rule can be derived over five investigated periods, as follows:

$$\mathcal{P}(HPC(\Delta_i)) = \mathcal{P}(C_8(\Delta_i)) \; i = 1 \ldots 5 \tag{5}$$

The time causality rule expresses the contribution of the root-cause on the occurrence of the HPC fault, period after period, according to the C_8 cut-point curve. Each cut-point value provides the essential knowledge to sustain the turbofan for more or less time in each defined period interval through the maintenance action. For instance, the turbofan can spend more time in Δ_1 by making the C_8 variable (BPR) value under the corresponding cut-point value for a set of time.

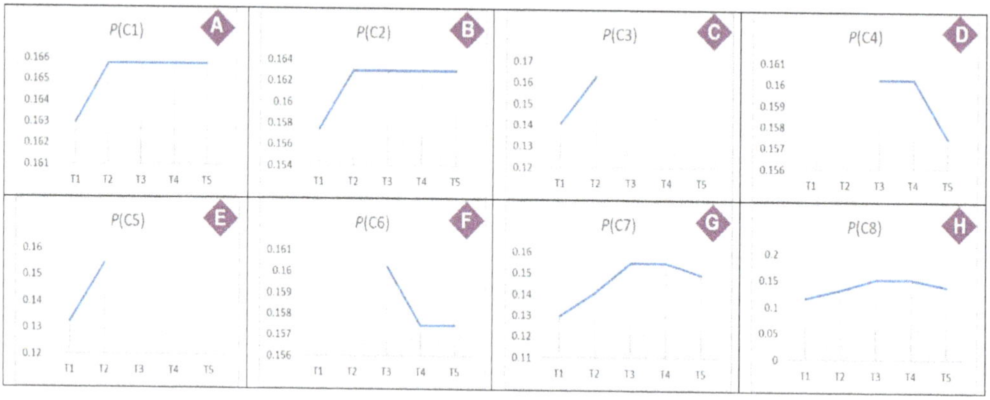

Figure 9. Probability calculations of the HPC fault mode.

4.3. Validation of the ITCA Model

The accuracy of the obtained ITCA model is quantified using the testing dataset. Five concatenated datasets are formed to represent the five periods of time in the same manner as the data preparation of the training datasets. The mean and the standard error for each period are calculated using the time causality rule and 1000 random data samples; each has a size of 135 observations that provides a 95% confidence level, as shown in Figure 10. Based on the error in each period, an average error distribution is generated over the five periods.

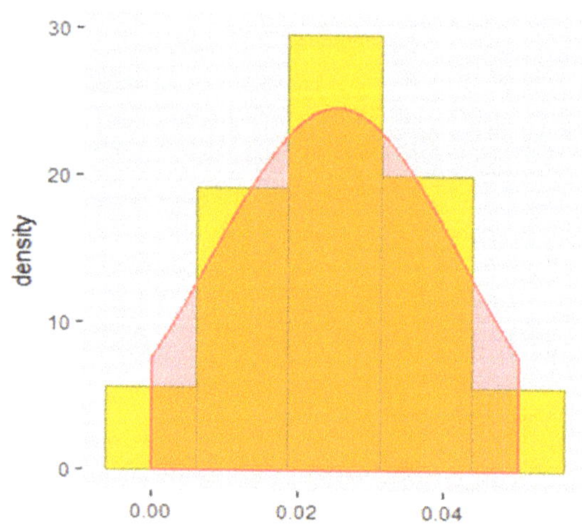

$$M_{error} = 2.51\ 10^{-2} \cdot \text{and} \cdot S_{error} = 1.29\ 10^{-2}$$

Figure 10. Accuracy of the ITCA model.

From another point of view, the variables T2, P2, P15, epr, farB, Nf_dmd and PCNfR_dmd are not considered in the ITCA model of Figure 8 because they have a constant trend over time (see Table 1). However, the variables NC, NRc, htBleed, W31 and W32 have a changeable trend, but are not included in the ITCA model. To investigate this situation, the correlation matrix between those omitted variables and those already considered in the ITCA model are measured, as depicted in Table 2. In each column, the bold value shows the maximum correlation value. The variables NRc, htBleed, and both W31 and W32 are correlated to the variables phi, Nrf and Ps30, respectively, with a correlation value that is higher than 0.6. Except for the variable NC, which measures the physical core speed, and is correlated to P30 with the highest absolute value of 0.17. Accordingly, it seems to be relevant for the HPC degradation. This could be overlooked by the ITCA model.

Table 2. Correlation matrix. The bold cell shows the maximum correlation value.

	NC	NRc	htBleed	W31	W32
T24	−0.159	−0.502	0.595	−0.629	−0.614
T30	−0.211	−0.459	0.534	−0.543	−0.582
T50	−0.153	−0.548	0.644	−0.727	−0.699
P15	−0.001	−0.014	0.065	−0.059	−0.107
P30	**0.175**	0.588	−0.651	0.718	0.739
Nf	−0.167	−0.594	0.707	−0.750	−0.743
Ps30	−0.171	−0.594	0.689	**−0.761**	**−0.742**
phi	0.158	**0.616**	−0.688	0.722	0.721
NRf	−0.169	−0.582	**0.708**	−0.746	−0.715
BPR	−0.184	−0.575	0.605	−0.663	−0.714

5. Conclusions

This paper has proposed an interpretable time causality analysis (ITCA) methodology for aging systems. The ITCA model represents the fault hierarchy causality by using the logic of the graphical fault tree and the knowledge discovery in the dataset. The obtained tree models the effect of the system's aging on the changes in the fault causality structure over time to better achieve fault prognosis. The illustrated case study demonstrates its usefulness and ability to discover only the relevant root cause that impacts the fault behaviour. Based on the model's interpretability, the expert is able to use the time causality structure of the turbofan HPC degradant performance to support his decision. Thus, the ITCA model provides the expert with the deep causality knowledge that explains the fault evolution over time. Unlocking the data-driven model's complexity by providing an interpretable graphical model, in addition to summarizing the evolution of the fault over time in one interpretable model are the two major contributions of the ITCA model over the current time causality data-driven models for fault prognosis. The ITCA model takes a further step towards reinforcing the link between experts and data-driven models. Such a model will help experts elucidate and implement the maintenance decision-making process.

Our next research work will be to assist the expert by better optimizing the system performance through a set of control actions to maximize the RUL. We hope to allow our future ITCA model to demonstrate the system's reaction regarding a set of proposed control actions based on its causality rules and link the impact of a given proposed action to the RUL. The expert still needs to observe this system's reaction, represented by the new fault causality structure that reflects the system's response to the causality rule control actions that are taken, and note how this improves the RUL. Therefore, the future ITCA model must include different scenarios for fault causality structures that reflect the impact of the different combinations of control actions based on the derived causality rules.

Author Contributions: K.W.: Methodology, Data curation, Formal Analysis, Validation, Investigation, Software, Writing—Original draft preparation. M.-S.O.: Conceptualization, Formal Analysis, Writing—Reviewing and Editing, Supervision, Resources, Funding. All authors have read and agreed to the published version of the manuscript.

Funding: The Natural Sciences and Engineering Research Council of Canada [grant number 231695] supported this work.

Institutional Review Board Statement: Not applicable.

Informed Consent Statement: Not applicable.

Data Availability Statement: NASA turbofan engine degradation dataset available at https://data.nasa.gov/Aerospace/Turbofan-engine-degradation-simulation-data-set/vrks-gjie (accessed on 15 July 2019).

Conflicts of Interest: The authors declare that they have no known competing financial interests or personal relationships that could have appeared to influence the work reported in this paper.

References

1. Vogl, G.W.; Weiss, B.A.; Helu, M. A review of diagnostic and prognostic capabilities and best practices for manufacturing. *J. Intell.Manuf.* **2019**, *30*, 79–95. [CrossRef] [PubMed]
2. Ming, L.; Yan, H.-C.; Hu, B.; Zhou, J.-H.; Pang, C.K. A data-driven two-stage maintenance framework for degradation prediction in semiconductor manufacturing industries. *Comput. Ind. Eng.* **2015**, *85*, 414–422.
3. de Jonge, B. Discretizing continuous-time continuous-state deterioration processes, with an application to condition-based maintenance optimization. *Reliab. Eng. Syst. Saf.* **2019**, *188*, 1–5. [CrossRef]
4. Gao, Z.; Cecati, C.; Ding, S.X. A survey of fault diagnosis and fault-tolerant techniques—Part I: Fault diagnosis with model-based and signal-based approaches. *IEEE Trans. Ind. Electron.* **2015**, *62*, 3757–3767. [CrossRef]
5. Wang, K.S. Key techniques in intelligent predictive maintenance (IPdM)—A framework of intelligent faults diagnosis and prognosis system (IFDaPS). In Proceedings of the 4th International Workshop of Advanced Manufacturing and Automation (IWAMA 2014), Shanghai, China, 27–28 October 2014.
6. Bousdekis, A.; Magoutas, B.; Apostolou, D.; Mentzas, G. Review, analysis and synthesis of prognostic-based decision support methods for condition based maintenance. *J. Intell. Manuf.* **2018**, *29*, 1303–1316. [CrossRef]
7. Schwabacher, M.A. A survey of data-driven prognostics. In Proceedings of the Infotech@ Aerospace 2005, Arlington, VA, USA, 26–29 September 2005; p. 7002.
8. Aggab, T.; Kratz, F.; Avila, M.; Vrignat, P. Model-based prognosis applied to a coupled four tank MIMO system. *IFAC PapersOnline* **2018**, *51*, 655–661. [CrossRef]
9. Schwabacher, M.; Goebel, K. A survey of artificial intelligence for prognostics. In Proceedings of the Artificial Intelligence for Prognostics—Papers from the AAAI Fall Symposium, Arlington, VA, USA, 9–11 November 2007.
10. Waghen, K.; Ouali, M.-S. Interpretable logic tree analysis: A data-driven fault tree methodology for causality analysis. *Expert Syst. Appl.* **2019**, *136*, 376–391. [CrossRef]
11. Chen, H.-S.; Yan, Z.; Zhang, X.; Liu, Y.; Yao, Y. Root Cause Diagnosis of Process Faults Using Conditional Granger Causality Analysis and Maximum Spanning Tree. *IFAC PapersOnLine* **2018**, *51*, 381–386. [CrossRef]
12. Vania, A.; Pennacchi, P.; Chatterton, S. Fault diagnosis and prognosis in rotating machines carried out by means of model-based methods: A case study. In Proceedings of the ASME 2013 International Design Engineering Technical Conferences and Computers and Information in Engineering Conference, IDETC/CIE 2013, Portland, OR, USA, 4–7 August 2013.
13. Lu, N.; Jiang, B.; Wang, L.; Lü, J.; Chen, X. A Fault Prognosis Strategy Based on Time-Delayed Digraph Model and Principal Component Analysis. *Math. Probl. Eng.* **2012**, *2012*, 937196. [CrossRef]
14. Darwish, M.; Almouahed, S.; de Lamotte, F. The integration of expert-defined importance factors to enrich Bayesian Fault Tree Analysis. *Reliab. Eng. Syst. Saf.* **2017**, *162*, 81–90. [CrossRef]
15. Ragab, A.; El Koujok, M.; Ghezzaz, H.; Amazouz, M.; Ouali, M.-S.; Yacout, S. Deep understanding in industrial processes by complementing human expertise with interpretable patterns of machine learning. *Expert Syst. Appl.* **2019**, *122*, 388–405. [CrossRef]
16. Yunkai, W.; Jiang, B.; Lu, N.; Zhou, Y. Bayesian Network Based Fault Prognosis via Bond Graph Modeling of High-Speed Railway Traction Device. *Math. Probl. Eng.* **2015**, *2015*, 321872.
17. Jin, S.; Zhang, Z.; Chakrabarty, K.; Gu, X. Failure prediction based on anomaly detection for complex core routers. In Proceedings of the 37th IEEE/ACM International Conference on Computer-Aided Design, ICCAD 2018, San Diego, CA, USA, 5–8 November 2018.
18. Niu, G. *Data-Driven Technology for Engineering Systems Health Management: Design Approach, Feature Construction, Fault Diagnosis, Prognosis, Fusion and Decisions*; Springer: Singapore, 2016; pp. 1–357.
19. Zhang, Z.; Wang, Y.; Wang, K. Fault diagnosis and prognosis using wavelet packet decomposition, Fourier transform and artificial neural network. *J. Intell. Manuf.* **2013**, *24*, 1213–1227. [CrossRef]
20. Wu, Q.; Ding, K.; Huang, B. Approach for fault prognosis using recurrent neural network. *J. Intell. Manuf.* **2020**, *31*, 1621–1633. [CrossRef]
21. Razavi, S.A.; Najafabadi, T.A.; Mahmoodian, A. Remaining Useful Life Estimation Using ANFIS Algorithm: A Data-Driven Approcah for Prognostics. In Proceedings of the 2018 Prognostics and System Health Management Conference, PHM-Chongqing 2018, Chongqing, China, 26–28 October 2018.
22. Doukovska, L.; Vassileva, S. Knowledge-based Mill Fan System Technical Condition Prognosis. *WSEAS Trans. Syst.* **2013**, *12*, 398–408.
23. Li, Z.; Wang, Y.; Wang, K. A data-driven method based on deep belief networks for backlash error prediction in machining centers. *J. Intell. Manuf.* **2020**, *31*, 1693–1705. [CrossRef]

24. Su, Y.; Jing, B.; Huang, Y.-F.; Tang, W.; Wei, F.; Qiang, X.-Q. Correlation analysis method between environment and failure based on fuzzy causality diagram and rough set of multiple decision classes. *Instrum. Tech. Sens.* **2015**, 100–103.
25. Kimotho, J.K.; Sondermann-Woelke, C.; Meyer, T.; Sextro, W. Application of Event Based Decision Tree and Ensemble of Data Driven Methods for Maintenance Action Recommendation. *Int. J. Progn. Health Manag.* **2013**, *4* (Suppl. S2), 1–6. [CrossRef]
26. Medjaher, K.; Moya, J.Y.; Zerhouni, N. Failure prognostic by using Dynamic Bayesian Networks. *IFAC Proc. Vol.* **2009**, *42*, 257–262. [CrossRef]
27. Hammer, P.L.; Bonates, T.O. Logical analysis of data—An overview: From combinatorial optimization to medical applications. *Ann. Oper. Res.* **2006**, *148*, 203–225. [CrossRef]
28. Fokkema, M. PRE: An R package for fitting prediction rule ensembles. *arXiv* **2017**, arXiv:1707.07149. [CrossRef]
29. May, R.; Csank, J.; Litt, J.; Guo, T.-H. Commercial Modular Aero-Propulsion System Simulation 40k (C-MAPSS40k) User's Guide. NASA TM-216831. 2010. Available online: https://www.researchgate.net/publication/273755967_Commercial_Modular_Aero-Propulsion_System_Simulation_40k_C-MAPSS40k_User\T1\textquoterights_Guide (accessed on 30 September 2021).
30. Frederick, D.K.; de Castro, J.A.; Litt, J.S. User's Guide for the Commercial Modular Aero-Propulsion System Simulation (C-MAPSS): Version 2. 2012. Available online: https://ntrs.nasa.gov/citations/20120003211 (accessed on 30 September 2021).
31. National Aeronautics and Space Administration NASA. Turbofan Engine. 2015. Available online: https://www.grc.nasa.gov/www/k-12/airplane/Animation/turbtyp/etfh.html (accessed on 30 September 2021).
32. Frederick, D.K.; de Castro, J.A.; Litt, J.S. User's Guide for the Commercial Modular Aero-Propulsion System Simulation (C-MAPSS). 2007. Available online: https://ntrs.nasa.gov/citations/20070034949 (accessed on 30 September 2021).

algorithms

MDPI

Article

Lessons for Data-Driven Modelling from Harmonics in the Norwegian Grid

Volker Hoffmann [1], Bendik Nybakk Torsæter [2], Gjert Hovland Rosenlund [2] and Christian Andre Andresen [2,*]

[1] Department of Sustainable Communication Technologies, SINTEF Digital, Forskningsveien 1, 0373 Oslo, Norway; volker.hoffmann@sintef.no
[2] Department of Energy System, SINTEF Energi AS, Sem Sælands vei 11, 7034 Trondheim, Norway; bendik.torsater@sintef.no (B.N.T.); gjert.h.rosenlund@gmail.com (G.H.R.)
* Correspondence: christian.andresen@sintef.no; Tel.: +47-957-79-331

Abstract: With the advancing integration of fluctuating renewables, a more dynamic demand-side, and a grid running closer to its operational limits, future power system operators require new tools to anticipate unwanted events. Advances in machine learning and availability of data suggest great potential in using data-driven approaches, but these will only ever be as good as the data they are based on. To lay the ground-work for future data-driven modelling, we establish a baseline state by analysing the statistical distribution of voltage measurements from three sites in the Norwegian power grid (22, 66, and 300 kV). Measurements span four years, are line and phase voltages, are cycle-by-cycle, and include all (even and odd) harmonics up to the 96th order. They are based on four years of historical data from three ELSPEC Power Quality Analyzers (corresponding to one trillion samples), which we have extracted, processed, and analyzed. We find that: (i) the distribution of harmonics depends on phase and voltage level; (ii) there is little power beyond the 13th harmonic; (iii) there is temporal clumping of extreme values; and (iv) there is seasonality on different time-scales. For machine learning based modelling these findings suggest that: (i) models should be trained in two steps (first with data from all sites, then adapted to site-level); (ii) including harmonics beyond the 13th is unlikely to increase model performance, and that modelling should include features that (iii) encode the state of the grid, as well as (iv) seasonality.

Keywords: machine learning; power systems; harmonic distortion; power quality

1. Introduction

1.1. Motivation and Background

The introduction of ever-increasing amounts of intermittent renewable generation, coupled with the increasing electrification of European societies, leads to an increased strain on the power grid and its operation [1–3]. In order to maintain high security of supply, it is paramount to evolve the tools used for power systems operations [4]. One such tool would be the ability to predict undesired events with sufficient prediction horizon to facilitate mitigating actions [5–7].

The development of such tools is encouraged by recent advancements in data-driven techniques, machine learning (ML), available data volumes, and computational resources [8–10]. These algorithms can derive insights from data without being explicitly told what to look for in the vast data steams [11,12], which is particularly beneficial in the domain of power system fault prediction. An explicit detailed modeling of the power system is cumbersome and would not encapsulate conditions the modeler does not know about, that could lead to faults, such as icing on transmission lines, faults in critical components or reoccurring abnormalities.

Data driven methods are only as good as the data they rely on, and only have the capability to predict situations that the model have been trained on [13–15]. In a best case scenario, the models are trained on a complete and large dataset, and it can rely on the automatic tuning of model parameters [16,17]. This is, however, often not the case in real word applications. In the case of fault prediction in the power system, the number of faults occurring are very small compared to normal operating conditions [18].

To achieve high performance with data driven methods, the analyst must therefore pre-process the data—essentially guiding the algorithms in selecting their focus. This type of pre-processing includes dimensionality reduction, feature selection, feature engineering, and rescaling of features and prediction targets [19,20]. While there are aspects of an art (or, more precisely, intuition based on experience and domain knowledge) to these activities, they depend on an understanding of the behaviour of the underlying power system.

This paper seeks to establish (aspects of) the statistical foundation of the behaviour of the power system at the levels of transmission and distribution, cf. Figure 1. By establishing the statistical and temporal behaviour of cycle-by-cycle voltage harmonics from three sites in the Norwegian grid, we derive implications for the data-driven modelling of power grid events. Although the data are sourced from the Norwegian grid, we expect results to apply to other national grids.

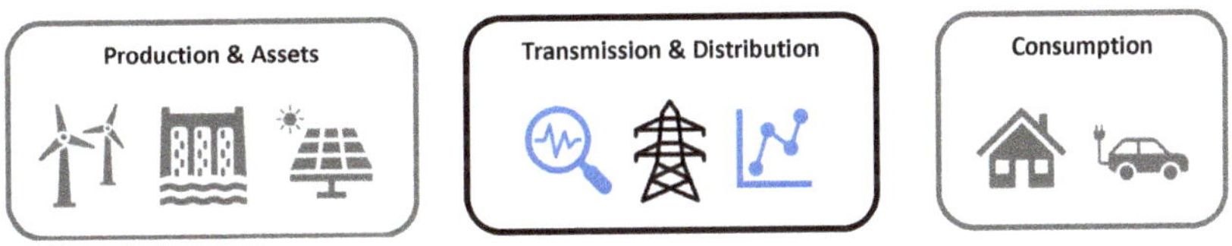

Figure 1. Illustration of the scope of the paper. The figure shows the entire value chain of electricity (from left to right—generation, distribution, and consumption). Machine learning techniques are relevant in all links of the chain (see also our literature overview). Our focus (highlighted in blue and black) is on the background state of the grid at transmission and distribution voltage levels.

1.2. *Relevant Literature*

1.2.1. Data-Driven Methods in Power Grids

Applications of data-driven methods in power grids are motivated by the need to predict and mitigate intermittency in a grid that leans heavily on renewables [21,22]. Works tend to focus on: (i) equipment degradation; (ii) forecasting (and control) of demand and production; or (iii) grid-scale power quality (PQ) and continuity of supply. For equipment degradation, focus is either on individual assets (usually with the aim of predictive maintenance) or their interaction with the grid at large. The most relevant assets are wind turbines, hydroelectric power plants, photovoltaic power plants, and distribution transformers.

Focusing on key assets (and their subcomponents), refs. [23,24] used event and state logs from wind-turbine control systems to train supervised learning algorithms (neural networks, boosted trees, and support vector machines). They report successful prediction of fault states with lead times in the order of five minutes to an hour. In a similar vein, refs. [25,26] monitoring data from sub-components (e.g., compressors, generators, turbines) are used to detect and predict anomalous behaviour in hydro power stations. They demonstrate implementations of self-organizing maps and neural networks within the control loops, but unfortunately do not report on model performance. For photovoltaic systems, forecasting of faults appears to be less advanced and the literature focuses on fault detection and characterization. For example, ref. [27] integrates system data (currents, voltages, temperature) and uses neural networks to detect and classify abnormal operating conditions. Based on multispectral drone imagery, ref. [28] deploys convolutional neural networks (CNNs) to detect various types of panel damage. Overall, there is significant potential in machine learning approaches to predicting the condition of photovoltaic system due to the large amount of non-correlated data sources (weather, system data, and imagery), see also [29,30]. Finally, multiple works attempt to predict failure of distribution transformers by combining event logs and data from outgassing of insulating oil. While [31] deploys a fairly complicated scheme involving agents, neural networks, and evolutionary methods, ref. [32] uses gradient boosted trees and claims a superior performance compared to their reviewed literature. The state-of-the-art in the use of machine learning to predict transformer failures is reviewed in [33].

On the production side, data-driven forecasting methods for wind and photovoltaic systems are mainly concerned with: (i) using (and improving upon) numerical weather prediction models; and (ii) relating the weather conditions to actual power output. For example, ref. [34] uses neural networks to accelerate wind-field computation for a complicated topography while [35] uses model ensembles (k-nearest neighbours, support vector regression, and decision trees) to relate local wind-speed measurements to turbine power output. For solar forecasting, ref. [36] compare 68 machine learning-based forecasting models and find that (a) tree-based methods perform best but (b) that there is significant variation between the performance of different models in space and time. See also [37,38] for reviews. Hydro power forecasting, on the other hand, is more often cast as a scheduling problem. For example, ref. [39] feeds climate data, expected demand curves, and market conditions into a reinforcement learning system for optimal (most profitable) long-term scheduling. See also [40] for a recent review. Research on demand forecasting, on the other hand, is frequently coupled to control schemes for residential and commercial smart buildings [41,42] or vehicle-to-grid technologies [43,44]. In addition, there is a sprawling literature on customer segmentation [45,46], building performance assessments [47], and residential level demand forecasting [48,49].

With a focus on components and their impact on the remainder of the grid, ref. [50] uses the recurrent incidence of minor events to predict major outages, ref. [51] couple event logs from distribution transformers to meteorological data, and ref. [52] connects meteorological data to component states to predict the impact of extreme weather. Focusing on power quality alone, refs. [53,54] detect and identify PQ anomalies using either neural networks and decision trees, extensive feature engineering, or semi-supervised learning approaches, respectively. Finally, ref. [55] include anomaly prediction and—by using random forests—obtains inherently explainable models. Similarly, our own recent works have also focused on predicting PQ disturbances using a variety of data sources, methods, and features [56–61]. Unfortunately, most works (including our own) omit describing the underlying data, and instead jump straight to feature engineering and machine learning.

1.2.2. Harmonic Distortions

In this work, we will focus on voltage harmonics in the distribution and transmission grid. These have previously been analyzed in [62–64]. The first two characterize harmonics (and THD) time-series by control limit violations and build statistics thereof. Limits are either derived from probability of occurrence or national standards. The latter focuses on how voltage flicker is coupled to harmonic distortions near four industrial sites. The statistical analyses of [62,63] revolve around control limits and their violations with little focus on the statistical distributions of the underlying measurements. The analysis in [64] summarizes the statistical distribution into the 95 percentile of observed values. All analyses are based on data aggregated to the order of minutes.

1.2.3. The Literature Gap

Based on our review, most works appear to focus on data-driven modelling of asset state and performance as well as scheduling, forecasting, and the control of production and consumption. There are few works focusing on the conditions of the grid itself. Those that do tend not to discuss the underlying state. We therefore attempt to answer two open questions. First, what the underlying statistical distribution of harmonics measurements are, especially at aggregation intervals below 60 s? Second, how should the underlying state of the power grid influence the design of data-driven fault prediction methodologies?

1.3. Contributions and Organization

In Section 2, the underlying data and data sources are described, as well as a brief introduction to the power system being analyzed and the methodology utilized in the later results section. Section 3 offers insights into the key statistical properties that are found in the data. Finally, the discussion and conclusions are presented in Sections 4 and 5.

2. Methodology

We focus on the voltage harmonics component of power quality data. We consider the statistical properties of (time-series of) harmonic power up to a particular order, total harmonic distortion (THD), as well as the contribution of each order to THD. We further analyze how the largest (>99 percentile) values for THD are distributed in time. We compute THD from harmonics measurements and consider up to six voltage channels.

Figure 2 shows the flow of harmonics measurements from source to analysis. Roughly following the figure from left to right, we will discuss data sources and the data flow, as well as the various data processing steps. We also address the three largest challenges encountered when working with the data.

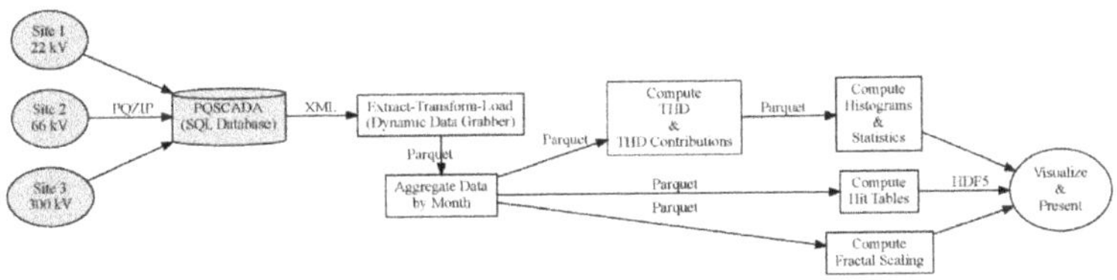

Figure 2. Dataflow (left to right) from source to analysis. Boxes indicate processing steps and text on arrows indicates the file format used. Grey shading indicates proprietary technology. Unshaded steps are our own scripts (based on the Python). The ETL (Extract-Transform-Load) steps interact with ELSPEC's proprietary PQSCADA system (using our own *Dynamic Data Grabber* package) to extract voltage and harmonics data as dataframes into Parquet files. Dataframes are aggregated by month and then consumed by various analysis scripts. These output data in HDF5 format for use by plotting scripts.

2.1. Data Origin

SINTEF has conditional access to power quality data for the majority of the Norwegian power system through agreements with distribution system operators (DSOs) and the Norwegian transmission system operator (TSO) Statnett. The data cover the period from January 2009 to early March 2020. The nominal line voltages at the locations where the measuring instruments are installed varies from 10 to 420 kV. A total of roughly 270 years of PQ data have been collected from 49 measurement nodes, giving on average 5–6 years of historical data from each node. However, the number of years of available data varied significantly from node to node.

In this work, we focus on three sites as full coverage of the available data would either: (i) require a different analytical approach; or (ii) clutter the presentation needlessly. The three sites were chosen to have different voltage levels, are placed in different locations in the Norwegian power grid and have long and robust time series. In conjunction, these sites constitute the basis for the below analysis and discussion.

All sites are located in the Norwegian grid so they are exposed to the Norwegian power mix, barring bottlenecks between price zones. The power mix is dominated by power from hydroelectric plants (85%), followed by biomass (12%) and wind (4%) [65], (data from 2018).

2.2. Data Flow, Extraction, and Processing

Raw data are recorded by ELSPEC Power Quality Analyzers (PQAs), https://www.elspec-ltd.com/metering-protection/ (accessed on 26 April 2022) compressed, and then forwarded to a PQSCADA, https://www.elspec-ltd.com/power-quality-software-pqscada-software/ (accessed on 26 April 2022) database for permanent storage. The Elspec PQAs sample voltage, current, power waveforms at up to 50 kHz, but employ lossy compression (at the edge) to reduce the data volume and velocity. Due to their proprietary nature, the details of the compression are not well documented. The PQSCADA database can be queried for a wide range of performance parameters, including—but not limited to—aggregated voltage and harmonics data. We extract data from this database through a small stack of Python [66] scripts that abstract away various data engineering complications. These depend heavily on Numpy [67] and Pandas [68].

We extract data from sites at three different grid voltage levels. For each level, there are two data packages. The first covers four years, six voltage (three phase-to-ground, three phase-to-phase) channels, and eight harmonics. The second covers a month, three voltage channels (phase-to-ground), and 96 harmonics. Data are aggregated by calculating mean values in intervals of 1/50 Hz. Each site in the first (second) package contains 3.6×10^{11} (3.9×10^{10}) samples. See also Table 1.

Table 1. We extract two data packages. The first covers four years, six voltage channels, eight harmonics. The second covers a month, three voltage channels, 96 harmonics. They contain 3.6×10^{11} and 3.9×10^{10} samples, respectively.

Site	Voltage	Period	$V_{\mathbf{Phases}}^{\mathbf{Harmonics}}$	Aggregation
1	22 kV	2015 to 2018	$V_{1,2,3,12,23,31}^{0\cdots 8}$	1/50 Hz, Mean
2	66 kV	2015 to 2018	$V_{1,2,3,12,23,31}^{0\cdots 8}$	1/50 Hz, Mean
3	300 kV	2015 to 2018	$V_{1,2,3,12,23,31}^{0\cdots 8}$	1/50 Hz, Mean
1	22 kV	January 2017	$V_{1,2,3}^{0\cdots 96}$	1/50 Hz, Mean
2	66 kV	January 2017	$V_{1,2,3}^{0\cdots 96}$	1/50 Hz, Mean
3	300 kV	January 2017	$V_{1,2,3}^{0\cdots 96}$	1/50 Hz, Mean

Uncompressed sizes for the data packages are ∼2.8 TB and 240 GB, respectively. To deal with this amount of data efficiently, we use column storage with lossless compression (Parquet (https://parquet.apache.org (accessed on 26 April 2022))) and slice data into subsets for processing.

2.3. Data Processing: THD and Harmonic Contributions

For each harmonic component, querying the database of ELSPEC data returns the harmonic voltage as a fraction of the fundamental voltage component. We use this value (i) directly, (ii) to calculate THD, and (iii) to calculate the contribution of the harmonic to THD. This is done as follows.

For the i-th phase, the voltage in the j-th harmonic is $v_{i,j} = c_{i,j} v_{i,0}$, where $c_{i,0}$ is the value returned by the device. $v_{i,0}$ is the value of the fundamental voltage of the i-th phase. The THD for the i-th phase is:

$$\mathrm{THD}_i = \frac{\sqrt{\sum_{j=1}^{j,\max} v_{i,j}^2}}{\sqrt{v_{1,0}^2}} = \sqrt{\sum_{j=1}^{j,\max} c_{i,j}^2}, \tag{1}$$

and the contribution of the j-th harmonic to the overall THD is $c_{i,j}^2/\mathrm{THD}_i^2$. Depending on the site and temporal coverage, data is available for either 8 or 96 harmonics ($j, \max = \{8, 96\}$ as well as phase-to-ground ($i = \{1,2,3\}$) or phase-to-phase voltages ($i = \{12, 23, 31\}$).

2.4. Data Processing: Cumulative Distribution Functions, Histograms, and Percentiles

Statistical analysis of data in this work is fairly standard although some adaptions are made to deal with the large volumes. We explore and present the statistical distributions of measurements using their (normalized) cumulative distribution distribution functions (CDFs). For some variable x (for example, THD measurements), the normalized CDF is $C(x) = \int_0^x \rho(x')\,\mathrm{d}x' / \int_0^\infty \rho(x')\,\mathrm{d}x'$, where $\rho(x)$ is the probability density function of x. For a finite number of samples, C and ρ can be approximated by computing the (cumulative) histogram of x. In other words, given N samples, $\mathcal{C}(x_t) = N(x < x_t)/N$ is the fraction of samples with values of x below some threshold x_t.

Owing to the large amounts of data, we calculate histograms individually for each voltage channel and harmonic order in time-slices of one month. The histograms over the entire time-period are then the sums of the monthly histograms. The cumulative histograms are then computed as their cumulative sum.

All percentiles in our analysis are approximate. The standard (exact) way of calculating percentiles requires loading (and sorting) all samples in memory, which proved difficult. Instead, we estimate percentiles from the cumulative distribution functions. Numerically, for the desired percentile $\mathcal{P}$, this amounts to finding the value of x_t at $\mathcal{P} = \mathcal{C}$. This means that the numerical accuracy of our percentile calculations is limited by the binning used during histogram calculation. We use 256 logarithmically spaced bins in the range 0.01 to 10, corresponding to an upper bound on the numerical accuracy of $\approx 10^{-2}$.

2.5. Data Processing: Time-Distribution of THD Excursions

While our dataset has no information about whether events (e.g., voltage drops, rapid voltage changes, interruptions, or earth faults) occur, we can nevertheless try to understand how the largest excursions (outliers) of harmonic power behaves. In other words, we wish to determine how the largest values of harmonic power are distributed in time. Do they occur regularly? Do they cluster together? Does their distribution depend on the time-scale?

We characterize the time-distribution of excursions by determining the fractal dimension $\mathcal{D}$ of a downsampled and binarized THD signal. For each minute, we determine whether any of the samples therein have a value exceeding the 99 percentile of the (four-year) THD distribution. If it does, the minute is tagged as containing an outlier (and vice versa). We then calculate $\mathcal{D}$ by box-counting (and slope-fitting) the binarized time-series [69]. This method essentially asks how many boxes $N(s)$ of a given size s (the time-scale) are required to completely cover the binary signal. The fractal dimension is the slope $\mathcal{D}$ of the power-law $N \propto s^{-\mathcal{D}}$. We compute $\mathcal{D}$ from least-squares regression of $\log_{10}(N(\log_{10} s))$. For a given time-scale s, $\mathcal{D} = 1$ indicates that excursions are uniformly distributed. Conversely, $\mathcal{D} < 1$ indicates temporal clustering of excursions. We consider a range $s_{min} \leq s \leq s_{max}$ with $s_{min} = 300$ s (five times the time-resolution of our binary signal) and $s_{max} = 292$ days (a fifth of the four year measurement period).

2.6. Challenges

During data extraction and initial data exploration, we have encountered three challenges that constrain our analysis.

1. *Compression Thresholds*—The ELSPEC PQA instruments have a compression algorithm that introduces a lower cut-off level for the harmonic components in their compression algorithm. Contributions to the overall signal below this cut-off value for each harmonic component will not be recorded in the stored data from the instrument. This threshold may vary between measuring devices, depending on the harmonic noise and the needs of the measurements at the given site. The threshold is usually set to be in a range from 0.1 to 0.2% of the base harmonic component. Values below this level will be stored as 0 values, and is referred to as such in the discussion below.
2. *Computational Tractability*—We had initially set out to load 96 harmonics and six voltages for all three nodes over the four year time period. However, the database proved uncooperative and required frequent restarts during the extraction. We therefore limited the analysis of 96 harmonics to a month.
3. *THD Calculation*—The ELSPEC instruments also record THD directly, although neither the aggregation interval nor function is clearly documented. We observe a median difference of 21% (ranging from 0 to 56% at the 1 and 99 percentile, respectively) between the THD calculated by our own procedure and the THD directly reported

by the ELSPEC instrument. We base the analysis in this paper on the above THD calculation for transparency reasons.

3. Results

3.1. Presence of Harmonics

Figure 3 shows the fraction of cycles (per month) with power > 0 for three sites in the Norwegian power grid between 2015 to 2018. By grouping data by harmonic channel, phase, month, and site, we find the following.

1. Across all voltage levels, non-negligible amounts of non-zero measurements occur only on the third, fifth, and seventh harmonics;
2. At the 22 kV level and across all phases, 95% of measurements of the seventh harmonic are non-zero. For the fifth harmonic, there are non-zero measurements in 70% of cases. The third harmonic differs across phases. On V_2, non-zero measurements are more common (40%) than on V_1 and V_3 (10% each). Non-zero observations on the third and fifth harmonic are clustered in time rather than being spread out evenly. The clusters are not evenly distributed and do not appear to correlate with seasons;
3. At the 66 kV level, we find the same patterns as at the 22 kV level, with most non-zero measurements found in the seventh, fifth, and third harmonics. Across all phases, we find non-zero values for the seventh and fifth harmonics in 75 and 55% of cases, respectively. For the third harmonic, non-zero values are unbalanced across phases. On V_1, V_2, and V_3, we count 55, 65, and 35% of non-zero values, respectively. Observing no differences in the temporal distribution of counts, V_3 appears to have a generally lower level of non-zero counts;
4. At the 300 kV level, there is a marked difference between the periods of March 2017 to July 2018 and the remainder of the observation period. Inside this period, 45% of measurements across phases (and for the third, fifth, and seventh harmonic channel) are non-zero. Outside this period (and overall), only 3 (19)% of measurements are non-zero (again, for the third, fifth, and seventh harmonic channel). The temporal patterns (in the period of March 2017 to July 2018) are identical across phases, except for the third harmonic channel on V_2, where 87% of all samples are non-zero (compared to 45 and 55% for the third and fifth harmonic, respectively).

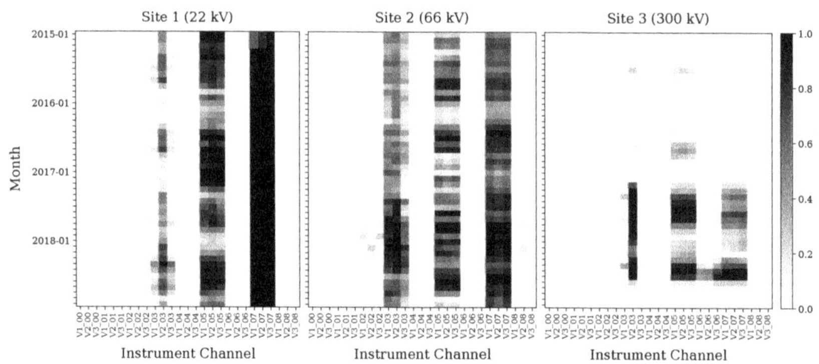

Figure 3. Fraction of non-zero observations for the first eight harmonics in each voltage channel (denoted as *Instrument Channel*), grouped by harmonic. Data for all three sites are shown, see panel titles. A period of four years is covered for each site. The fraction (see colormap on the right) is calculated over $\sim 1.3 \times 10^8$ samples in each month. It is clear that there are some channels (harmonics for each phase) that are clearly more present than others, and that the pattern is to a large degree transferable from phase to phase and from site to site. It is also clear that there is considerably less harmonic content in the higher voltage levels. This is confirmed in Figures 5 and 6.

The harmonic levels in Figures 4 and 5 show that there is some variation in harmonic levels on each site. The figures show variation detailed by harmonic number, voltage level and hour-of-day (Figure 4) and the cumulative distribution function (CDF) for each voltage level (Figure 5). As mentioned above, the non-zero values on Site 1 (22 kV) are present on the 3rd, 5th and 7th harmonics. The presence of these odd harmonics is usual in the modern power system, due to a high number of non-linear loads [70]. Both single- and three-phase converters are contributing to this type of harmonic noise, for equipment such as computers and power-intensive industry, respectively. For Site 1, the 7th harmonic is higher than 1% for the whole analysed period. The 5th harmonic also has a considerable presence throughout the period. This could suggest that the harmonic noise is caused by power-intensive industry with 6-pulse three-phase rectifiers [71]. Based on the results in Figure 4, it is clear that there is a daily variation in the harmonic levels that backs this claim.

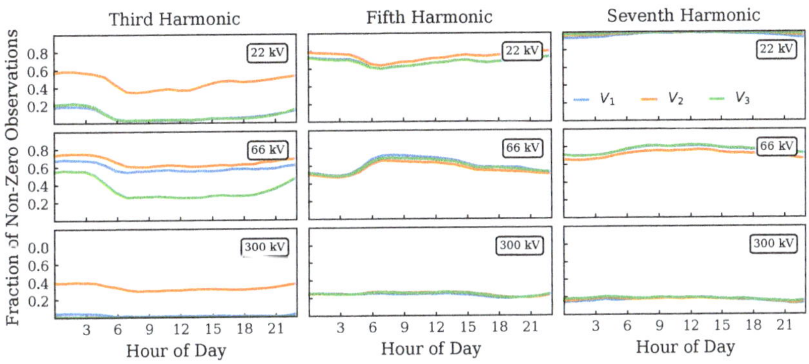

Figure 4. Variation in the occurrence of non-zero values for each node averaged on a daily basis. The 3rd, 5th and 7th harmonics have been selected.

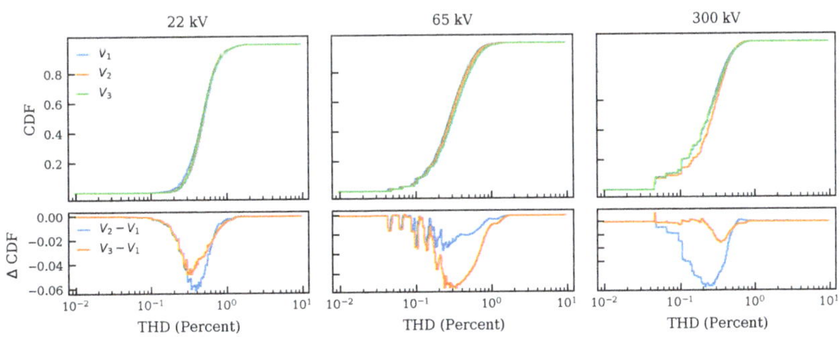

Figure 5. Cumulative distribution function (CDF) of total harmonic distortion (THD) for three sites (columns). We use 256 bins of uniform logarithmic spacing from 10^{-2} to 10. Distributions are calculated over the time range from 2015 to 2018 for a total of $\sim 5.9 \times 10^9$ samples. *Top*: CDFs for each phase (see legend). *Bottom*: Difference between the CDFs for V_2 and V_1 as well as V_3 and V_1, respectively (see legend). Statistically, the three phases always remain within six percent of each other. See Table 2 for summary statistics.

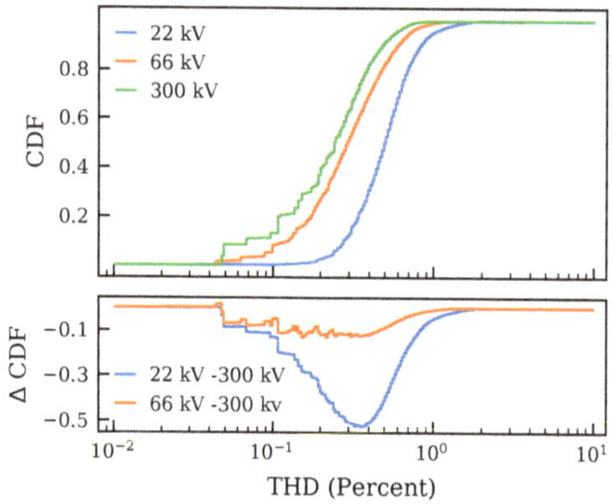

Figure 6. Cumulative distribution function (CDF) of total harmonic distortion (THD) for three sites (see legend) for the phase-to-ground voltage V_1 plotted together for comparison. Binning and data basis is the same as for Figure 5. (**Top**): CDFs for each site (see legend). (**Bottom**): Difference between the CDFs for 22 and 300 kV as well as the 66 and 300 kV sites, respectively (see legend). See Table 2 for summary statistics. For higher voltage levels, the distribution shifts to smaller THD values—there is less noise in the system.

Table 2. Summary statistics for the distribution of total harmonic distortion (THD) per site and phase.

Site	Phase	1 Percentile	Median	99 Percentile
22 kV	V_1	0.15	0.49	1.48
	V_2	0.19	0.51	1.48
	V_3	0.19	0.51	1.48
66 kV	V_1	0.04	0.29	1.01
	V_2	0.05	0.31	1.13
	V_3	0.05	0.32	1.26
300 kV	V_1	0.05	0.24	0.73
	V_2	0.05	0.28	0.73
	V_3	0.05	0.25	0.77

On Site 2 (66 kV), there is a similar harmonic pattern as on Site 1, with the most dominant harmonics being the 3rd, 5th and 7th. However, on this site, the 3rd is more dominant. This is a normal observation on this power level. In addition to these odd harmonics, there is a presence of even harmonics on the 2nd, 4th and 8th harmonics. The presence of even harmonics is more important to monitor, as they can cause early degradation and malfunction in the power system [72]. In the analysed period, however, the harmonic level never exceeds 8%, which is the acceptable 10-min average according to the Norwegian regulators requirements [73].

On Site 3 (300 kV), there is a similar harmonic pattern as on Sites 1 and 2, except that the harmonic levels are lower than on the other sites throughout the period. There are also some considerable even harmonic levels present on the 6th harmonic. It is also interesting to observe that the harmonic levels are considerably higher during the period from March 2017 to July 2018. The reason for this is not clear to the authors, but it could be caused by a change of topology due to maintenance or construction of a new line in the area during this period. It is also likely that the other seasonal variations that are present during the period from 2015–2018 are caused by changes in topology, including the changes in power generation in the area. The power generation in the areas around the analysed sites is dominated by hydro-power (and to some extent wind-power) plants, and changes in grid-connected generating units can affect the short-circuit impedance of the grid and the associated propagation of harmonic distortion [74]. For grid-connection points with a voltage level from 35 kV to 245 kV, the 10 min average of the 6th harmonic should be below 0.5% [73].

3.2. Total Harmonic Distortion, Phases & Voltage Levels

Figures 5 and 6 show the normalized cumulative distribution functions (CDF) of total harmonic distortion (THD), i.e., the fraction of samples $N(\geq \text{THD})/N$ found at or above a given THD level. Table 2 shows their respective summary statistics. We observe the following:

1. Overall, most (99%) of the THD values are small and $\lesssim$ 1% of their respective fundamental phase voltage. Distributions are narrow with most values concentrated in the range 0.1 to 1%. Difference between different phases at the same voltage level are always smaller than differences between voltage levels;
2. Across phases and voltage levels, the difference between phases is always $\leq$ 6%. Note that this only means that the phases are STATISTICALLY within 6% of one another. At any given point in time, their difference may be larger than that;
3. Difference between phases cover a wider range of THD for higher voltage levels. The largest integral difference (The area between CDF_i and CDF_j, i.e., $\int \sqrt{(\text{CDF}_i - \text{CDF}_j)^2}\, \text{dTHD}$.) between two phases is 0.024, 0.49, and 0.056) for 22, 66, and 300 kV, respectively. For 22 kV, the median values of V_1, V_2, and V_3 remain within 4% of one another. This difference grows to 10% and 15% at 66 and 300 kV, respectively;
4. At higher voltage levels, the distributions of THD consistently shift towards smaller values. For 22 kV (66, 300), 99% of THD measurements (on V_1) are $\leq$1.48 ($\leq$1.01, $\leq$0.73). Median THD values shift similarly so that the median THD (on V_1) at 300 kV (66 kV) is half (a fifth) of that measured at 22 kV. The 22 kV site is consistently about half a decade above the 300 kV site, and the 66 kV site is located between these a little towards the 300 kV site.

Regulatory requirements for THD levels are stricter for higher voltage levels, and more effort is made to keep these disturbances low at transmission level due to the potential impact on all downstream distribution feeders. The THD values are usually higher at lower voltage levels due to the proximity to the non-linear harmonic generating loads and generators. The propagation of harmonics from the polluter to higher voltage levels will usually be damped either by damping in grid components (lines, transformers etc.). However, in some cases, active or passive filters may be necessary to make sure that the harmonics do not propagate and cause damage to grid customers elsewhere in the grid. It is, however, important to understand the frequency-dependent impedance of the grid to understand the harmonic propagation and accurately calculate the resonance frequency [72]. As an example, a temporary change of topology in an area of the power system could cause harmonic levels to increase with several orders of magnitude, which as a consequence could cause instability in the power system. In general, the higher the frequency, the higher the resistance is. Consequently, damping of harmonics is stronger at higher frequencies.

Researchers or technicians that seek to utilize the development of THD level or the level of specific harmonics for predictive modelling need to take this variation in harmonic levels into account while designing and training models. This variation in harmonic levels may be an underlying reason why general-purpose models trained on data from many sites in different geographic locations may have an inferior performance compared to models trained on specific sites, even though the data volumes are considerably smaller [75].

3.3. Harmonic Contributions to Total Harmonic Distortion

In the previous subsection, a high-level picture of harmonic noise in the power system was established through an analysis of the THD level on the three investigated sites. In this subsection, the contribution from each of the individual harmonics on the THD is investigated. This will allow us to answer: (i) how many harmonics contribute (meaningfully) to the THD on different voltage levels; (ii) to what extent they are contributing; and (iii) whether there are differences in the most relevant harmonics across voltage levels. As indicated in Section 2, we consider only the month of January 2017 due to the large volume of data. Although only harmonics up to the 7th order is shown in the figures, harmonics up to the 96th order has been extracted and used for analysis. Figure 7 illustrates the average contribution of each individual harmonic to the THD over a time period of one month. The following can be concluded.

1. Across all phases and voltage levels, $\gtrsim$98% of the contribution towards the THD are concentrated in at most the 13th harmonic. The next largest contributions (1.9 percent) is the 29th harmonic on V_3 in the 66 kV site. Beyond this, all other contributions are $\lesssim$1%;
2. The highest individual harmonic with a total contribution of $\gtrsim$2 % are 11th (22 kV), 13th (66 kV), and 13th (300 kV). At 22 and 300 kV, these harmonics also have a significant (>10%) contribution on at least one phase. However, at 66 kV, the largest harmonic with a significant contribution is the 7th;
3. At 22 kV, the 7th, 11th, and 5th harmonic contribute the most to THD. In order (and averaged over phases), they contribute ~52, 37, and 11%. Across phases, the contributions to THD are balanced and remain within a few % of one another;
4. At 66 kV, the 3rd, 7th, and 5th harmonics contribute the most to the THD. When averaged over all phases, they contribute ~51, 40, and 7%, respectively. There is an imbalance in the contribution of V_3 which contributes 40% more than V_1 and V_2 to the THD on the 7th harmonic. For the 3rd harmonic, the reverse holds;
5. At 300 kV, there are large differences (20 to 40%) between the contribution of each phase to the THD across different harmonics. For example, on V_1, the 5th harmonic dominates THD with a contribution 60%. On V_3, however, the 13th harmonic dominates with a 60% contribution. On V_3, the 3rd harmonic drives THD (with a contribution of ~50%). The authors are not able to attribute this imbalance to any specific phenomena, and this may be the subject of future investigations.

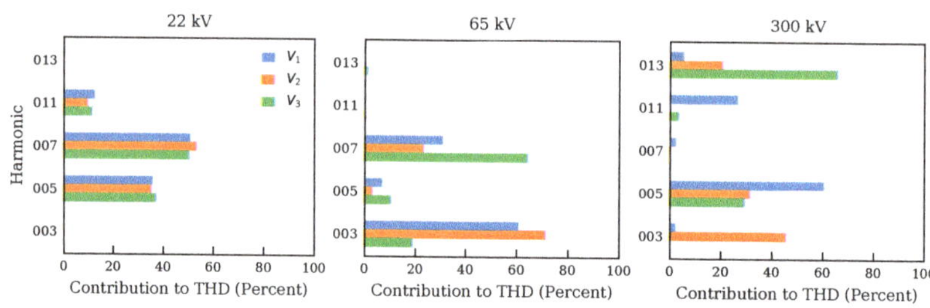

Figure 7. Total average contribution to THD over the period of one month per phase (columns) and site (rows). For each cycle, we calculate THD as well as each harmonics' contribution to THD. We then average over all samples of January 2017.

3.4. Harmonic Distortions over Time

After considering the THD and the contributions of individual harmonics, we now extend the analysis to include variations in time. Figure 8 shows the monthly statistics (median, 1 to 99, 10 to 90, and 25 to 75 percentile ranges) for the THD as well as third, fifth, and seventh harmonic for a single phase on all three sites. We find the following.

1. For Sites 1 and 2, non-zero THD values are present during the entire measurement period from 2015 to 2018. For site 3, only 16 out 24 months in 2015 and 2016 and 18 out of 24 months between 2017 and 2018 record THD values above the compression threshold;

2. For all sites, THD appears to follow a seasonal pattern. For Site 1 and Site 2, median THD is about 50% higher in summer and autumn than during the winter and spring. For Site 3, the difference is more pronounced due to many periods without observed THD. For 2015 and 2016, non-zero THD values are recorded only in the summer months;
3. The spread (difference between the 1 and 99 percentile) of observed THD values (binned monthly) decreases with voltage level. Aggregating across months, the maximum spreads are 1.71, 1.45, and 1.00% for Sites 1, 2, and 3, respectively. In the same order, the average spreads are 0.73, 0.67, and 0.27%. Independent of voltage level, larger spreads always occur in the summer and autumns months;
4. For Site 1 (and phase 1), the contribution of the third, fifth, and seventh harmonics to THD over a period of 48 months is in-line with the results for a single month (cf. Figure 7). Over time, the majority of THD is accounted for by the 5th and 7th harmonics. For most months, both harmonics track similar medians (and spreads), except in the spring and autumn of 2017. Over these periods, the 5th harmonic follows a seasonal pattern (lower during winter/spring, larger during summer/autumn) while the 7th harmonic keeps an almost constant median. Their combined contribution leads to the deviation from seasonality earlier observed in THD;
5. For Sites 2 and 3, the contribution of individual harmonics to THD is more complicated. For Site 2, considering only January 2017 suggests that the 3rd and 7th harmonic should contribute most to THD. However, over time, we observe a different pattern. Here, the 7th harmonic appears to set a baseline of distortion (with slight seasonality), the 5th harmonic modulates additional (stronger) seasonality in the median as well as additional noise (larger spread), and the 3rd harmonic adds even more noise (larger spread). This shows that the analysis of a single month is insufficient and unlikely to be representative of THD and harmonic contributions over longer time frames.

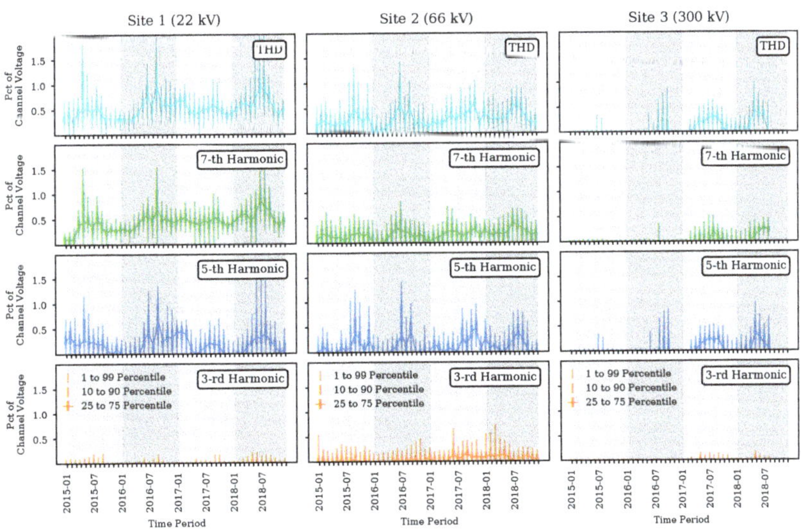

Figure 8. Statistical descriptors of the THD and selected harmonics (rows) aggregated per month for the three sites (columns). For each month, we indicate the median as well as 1, 10, 25, 75, 90, and 99 percentile (see legend). Grey shaded bands indicate the passage of one year.

3.5. Temporal Distribution of THD Excursions

Previous work [60] suggests that events in the power grid are not uniformly distributed in time, but rather occur in clusters. While not having access to event data, we can analyze the temporal distribution of THD excursions (values > 99 percentile) for the three sites on a signal downsampled a time-resolution of one minute. For each site, there are a total $\sim 2 \times 10^6$ samples (minutes). For the 22, 66, and 300 kV sites, we find 34362, 39015, and 22063 min with excursions, respectively.

Figure 9 show a temporal scatterplot of THD excursions as well as the fractal dimension $\mathcal{D}$ as a function of time-scale s, on the left and right panel respectively. We find that—irrespective of voltage level—the fractal dimension $\mathcal{D}$ depends on the time-scale. In particular:

1. At timescales 300 s $< s \leq 10^5$ s (a few days), we find $\mathcal{D} \sim 0.34 < 1$ (with slight variations across voltage levels, but a goodness of fit $R \sim 0.99$ for each level). This suggest multi-scale substructure of THD excursions in time. Visually, this is manifested as clumping of THD excursions (see Figure 9, lower panel). Clusters also vary in size (duration) and can be decomposed into further (sub-)clusters;
2. At time-scale $s \geq 10^5$ s, we find $\mathcal{D} \sim 1$ ($R \sim 0.99$). This suggests no (or at least very little) temporal substructure in the distribution of THD excursions. Visually speaking, there are long sequences of THD excursions with similar timing (Figure 9, upper panel). There are only occasional large gaps in time.

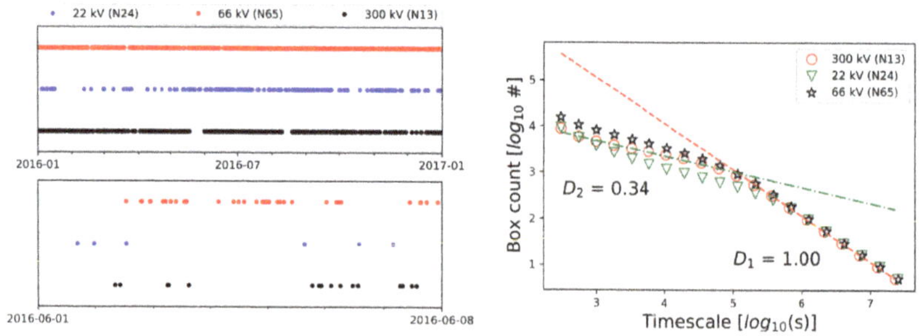

Figure 9. Left panel: Illustration of the temporal distribution of 99 percentile harmonic occurrence for all three sites spanning one year (top-left-panel) and one week (lower-left-panel). Lower time resolution in the figure is one minute. Right panel: Result from the application of the box-counting algorithm for determining the fractal nature of the distribution of the events in time.

The fractal dimension is essentially a measure of signal roughness. At timescales $\gtrsim 10^5$ s, our binary signal of THD excursions is fairly smooth (visually, excursion appear equally spaced in time). Statistical measures will weakly depend on the timescale over which they are calculated. For example, the mean return interval computed over a period of a weeks, a months, or years will be similar. At timescales $\lesssim 10^5$ s, excursions clump together (the signal is rough) so that statistical measures will strongly depend on the timescale over which they are calculated. The mean return intervals computed over a few minutes or over a few hours will be different.

Published works using fractal analysis apply a variety of measures and is therefore difficult to compare to. For example, refs. [76,77] compute the fractal dimensions of one-dimensional time-series (of power and current, respectively) to detect the presence of (artificially induced) events and loads. Closest to our work is [78], which computes the Hurst exponent $\mathcal{H}$ of a (presumably binarized) power fault time-series to determine the timescales over which faults in transmission (and distribution systems) are correlated.

While $\mathcal{D}$ measures local roughness, $\mathcal{H}$ measures long-term correlations. (Values $\mathcal{H} > 0.5$ indicate long-term dependencies, while $\mathcal{H} < 0.5$ indicates rapid mean reversion.) For self-similar (self-affine) processes, $\mathcal{D} = n + 1 - \mathcal{H}$ ($n = 0$ for a binarized time-series), so that locally defined roughness can be related to long-term correlations [79]. For $\mathcal{D} = 0.34$ and $\mathcal{D} = 1$, we find $\mathcal{H} = 0.66$ and $\mathcal{H} = 0$, respectively. In our case, this means that long-term correlations are limited to timescales $\lesssim 10^5$ s. In other words, the autocorrelation drops off at lags $\gtrsim 10^5$ s and phenomena longer than a few days ago do not influence

THD excursions. By directly computing $\mathcal{H}$, ref. [78] find $\mathcal{H} \sim 0.74$ (0.78) for transmission (distribution) system faults over a time period of a few hundred days, indicating that the power system faults have much longer correlation timescales than THD excursions. (We have not tested for self-similarity so that any comparison that involves computing $\mathcal{H}$ from $\mathcal{D}$ (instead of directly from the signal) should be taken with a grain of salt.)

4. Discussion

In this section, we summarise the discussion of the implications from the findings observed in the results section above and try to indicate the consequences for the application of data-driven predictive modelling.

4.1. Regulation on Harmonic Distortion

In Section 3.2, we found that THD and harmonic power remains well below the Norwegian regulatory requirements of $\leq$8% of the RMS voltage on the phase [73]. However, there is considerable variation across nodes, timescales, and seasons. Methodologies utilizing harmonics observations must therefore account for these. Variations can be accounted for implicitly (left to be dealt with by the model) or explicitly (by encoding into auxiliary features). Implicit processing requires sufficiently complex models (e.g., deep neural networks) while explicit encoding requires engineering of suitable features (e.g., information on time and season, node location, as well as other pertinent node metadata).

4.2. Trends in THD and Harmonic Contributions

In Section 3.2, we found that higher voltage levels have lower THD than lower voltage levels (Figure 6), but that there is large variation across phases (Figure 5). Additionally, in Section 3.3, we noted that harmonic channels contribute differently to THD depending on the node (voltage level) and phase. This strongly suggests that there are site specific variations that predictive models can exploit. Explicitly exploiting these variations will require models to be exposed to harmonic information for each phase. As we find very little THD contribution beyond the 13th harmonic (independent of phase and voltage level), models are unlikely to benefit from the inclusion of data for higher orders. This is in line with previous work [80,81].

4.3. Towards Event Prediction

Training and verification of data-driven methods requires a large amount of data to be efficient. In general, more input data will provide a larger learning basis and better results. However, any and all additional data should contain new (uncorrelated) information (rather than redundant information or, even worse, noise). Which data (features) to include is often motivated by domain-expertise, and feature engineering techniques (where features are combined or augmented) can be very effective. In [82], for example, we have demonstrated a procedure to assess the value of adding additional data (or features).

We have found that THD and individual harmonics (across voltage levels, phases, and seasons) vary considerably. It is therefore unlikely that a generalized model trained on data from all sites and phases will perform particularly well for a single site and phase. The potential application of transfer learning techniques can remedy such issues [83]. Transfer learning applies a two-step training procedure. First, a model is trained on data from all sites and phases. Second, the model is refined by exposing it to data from a single target site (and phase). Such an approach is not undertaken in this paper and is left for further works.

4.4. Statistical Robustness and Time-Correlations

In Section 3.5, we have shown that statistical measures (such as the mean return interval of THD excursions) computed over timescales of a more than a few days tend to be robust. Conversely, measures computed over shorter timescales depend on the timescale over which they are computed. Additionally, THD excursions also become uncorrelated if they are more than a few days apart. Taken together, this suggests that predictive models

(a) do not need to take into account data more than a few days in the past, and (b) should include features that explicitly model temporal features such as time since last event.

4.5. Actionable Event Predictions

For predictions to be actionable for power system operators, they must be reliable (few or no false alarms), accurate (predict actual events), and timely (sufficient forecast horizon to take action). Actions would aim to mitigate or even avoid the incipient events.

Assuming the first two are met, forecasts on time horizons of a few minutes could trigger a control room response such as reconfiguring the grid or reducing the load on critical components. Over longer time horizons (hours), it may be possible to do field actions such as removing vegetation or wildlife. In some cases, an early warning could also enable early mobilization of personnel to shorten incident response times.

If systems become sufficiently robust and accurate, actions could be initiated without a human in the loop. In this case (and assuming sufficient control capabilities), very short time horizons (milliseconds) may be possible.

5. Conclusions & Future Work

We have presented a statistical analysis of time-series of harmonic components for three sites in the Norwegian power system. Variations between voltage levels, over different time periods (hourly, monthly, and seasonally), and between individual harmonics were quantified. The findings can be condensed into four major points:

1. The distribution of harmonics differs with phases and voltage level (site);
2. There is little power (below the ELSPEC instrument cut-off) beyond the 13th harmonic;
3. There is temporal clumping of events;
4. There is seasonality on different time-scales.

Each of these has an implication for the development of data-driven (machine learning) models of power system behaviour. In particular:

1. Variations in harmonic power with phase and voltage level suggests that two-step training procedures akin to transfer learning may be useful. In such a scheme, one would (i) train a baseline model on data from all nodes and all harmonics, and then (ii) fine-tune the model to with data from specific sites. This will result in a model specific to each site;
2. The lack of power beyond the 13th harmonic suggests that including higher-order harmonics will not increase the predictive power of models;
3. Clumping suggests that models should include features such as the time-since-last-event to distinguish between grid states (frequent alarms vs. nominal operations);
4. Seasonality suggests that models should include features such as the hour of the day or the month of the year.

Strictly speaking, these conclusions are only valid for the set of three sites we have analyzed. However, Norwegian grid operators have deployed PQA instruments at 49 sites (with more being rolled out). Most of these have at least a few years worth of measurements (and some more than a decade). Future work should therefore focus on adapting and scaling the analysis to (a) include more sites, (b) account for grid topology (and switching), as well as (c) explicitly account for local production and consumption profiles. Additionally, the statistical properties of voltages, currents, and power should be included to generalize the work even further. An early draft of this work included a preliminary statistical analysis of cycle-by-cycle RMS voltage, but we were forced to drop it due to resource constraints.

A separate thread of work should focus on applying these lessons to the development of predictive models. The development of predictive (machine learning) models comes with its own set of challenges and choices—the inclusion of which we deemed to have gone beyond the scope of this contribution.

Author Contributions: Conceptualization, V.H., B.N.T. and G.H.R.; Data curation, V.H.; Formal analysis, B.N.T. and C.A.A.; Funding acquisition, C.A.A.; Investigation, V.H., B.N.T. and G.H.R.; Methodology, V.H., B.N.T., G.H.R. and C.A.A.; Project administration, C.A.A.; Software, V.H.; Validation, V.H.; Visualization, V.H. and C.A.A.; Writing—original draft, V.H., B.N.T., G.H.R. and C.A.A.; Writing—review & editing, V.H., B.N.T., G.H.R. and C.A.A. All authors have read and agreed to the published version of the manuscript.

Funding: This work was funded by the Research Council of Norway via the EnergyX grant number 268193 and the project partners Statnett, Tensio TN, Lyse Elnett, Nettalliansen, Hydro Energi, Haugaland Kraft Nett and the Norwegian University of Science and Technology (NTNU).

Data Availability Statement: Due to the sensitive nature of the data used in this article the underlying data are not made public as required by Norwegian Law. The methodology should however be readily transferable to data obtained from similar instruments measuring power quality in other grids.

Conflicts of Interest: The authors declare no conflict of interest.

Abbreviations

The following abbreviations are used in this manuscript:

PQSCADA	Name of the Power Quality Management Software
TSO	Transmission System Operator
DSO	Distribution System Operator
PQA	Power Quality Analyzer
THD	Total Harmonic Distortion
CDF	Cummulative Distribution Function
ML	Machine Learning
PQ	Power Quality

References

1. Kumar, G.V.B.; Sarojini, R.K.; Palanisamy, K.; Padmanaban, S.; Holm-Nielsen, J.B. Large Scale Renewable Energy Integration: Issues and Solutions. *Energies* **2019**, *12*, 1996. [CrossRef]
2. Muljadi, E.; McKenna, H. Power quality issues in a hybrid power system. *IEEE Trans. Ind. Appl.* **2002**, *38*, 803–809. [CrossRef]
3. Rönnberg, S.; Bollen, M. Power quality issues in the electric power system of the future. *Electr. J.* **2016**, *29*, 49–61. [CrossRef]
4. Balasubramaniam, P.M.; Prabha, S.U. Power Quality Issues, Solutions and Standards: A Technology Review. *J. Appl. Sci. Eng.* **2015**, *18*, 371–380. [CrossRef]
5. Sallam, A.A.; Malik, O.P. *Electric Distribution Systems*; Wiley-Blackwell: Hoboken, NJ, USA, 2018; pp. 1–604.
6. Bashir, A.K.; Khan, S.; Prabadevi, B.; Deepa, N.; Alnumay, W.S.; Gadekallu, T.R.; Maddikunta, P.K.R. Comparative analysis of machine learning algorithms for prediction of smart grid stability. *Int. Trans. Electr. Energy Syst.* **2021**, *31*, e12706. [CrossRef]
7. Azad, S.; Sabrina, F.; Wasimi, S. Transformation of smart grid using machine learning. In Proceedings of the 29th Australasian Universities Power Engineering Conference (AUPEC), Nadi, Fiji, 26–29 November 2019; pp. 1–6.
8. Rangel-Martinez, D.; Nigam, K.; Ricardez-Sandoval, L.A. Machine learning on sustainable energy: A review and outlook on renewable energy systems, catalysis, smart grid and energy storage. *Chem. Eng. Res. Des.* **2021**, *174*, 414–441. [CrossRef]
9. Hossain, E.; Khan, I.; Un-Noor, F.; Sikander, S.S.; Sunny, M.S.H. Application of Big Data and Machine Learning in Smart Grid, and Associated Security Concerns: A Review. *IEEE Access* **2019**, *7*, 13960–13988. [CrossRef]
10. Ibrahim, M.S.; Dong, W.; Yang, Q. Machine learning driven smart electric power systems: Current trends and new perspectives. *Appl. Energy* **2020**, *272*, 115237. [CrossRef]
11. LeCun, Y.; Bengio, Y.; Hinton, G. Deep learning. *Nature* **2015**, *521*, 436–444. [CrossRef]
12. Shrestha, A.; Mahmood, A. Review of deep learning algorithms and architectures. *IEEE Access* **2019**, *7*, 53040–53065. [CrossRef]
13. Hastie, T.; Tibshirani, R.; Friedman, J.H.; Friedman, J.H. *The Elements of Statistical Learning: Data Mining, Inference, and Prediction*; Springer: Berlin/Heidelberg, Germany, 2009; Volume 2.
14. James, G.; Witten, D.; Hastie, T.; Tibshirani, R. *An Introduction to Statistical Learning*; Springer: Berlin/Heidelberg, Germany, 2013; Volume 112.
15. Raschka, S. Model evaluation, model selection, and algorithm selection in machine learning. *arXiv* **2018**, arXiv:1811.12808.
16. Yu, T.; Zhu, H. Hyper-parameter optimization: A review of algorithms and applications. *arXiv* **2020**, arXiv:2003.05689.
17. Probst, P.; Wright, M.N.; Boulesteix, A.L. Hyperparameters and tuning strategies for random forest. *Wiley Interdiscip. Rev. Data Min. Knowl. Discov.* **2019**, *9*, e1301. [CrossRef]
18. CEER. *6th CEER Benchmarking Report on the Quality of Electricity and Gas Supply*; CEER: Brussels, Belgium, 2016.
19. García, S.; Ramírez-Gallego, S.; Luengo, J.; Benítez, J.M.; Herrera, F. Big data preprocessing: Methods and prospects. *Big Data Anal.* **2016**, *1*, 1–22. [CrossRef]

20. Heaton, J. An empirical analysis of feature engineering for predictive modeling. In Proceedings of the SoutheastCon, Norfolk, VA, USA, 30 March–3 April 2016; pp. 1–6.
21. Al-Sheikh, H.; Moubayed, N. Fault detection and diagnosis of renewable energy systems: An overview. In Proceedings of the 2012 International Conference on Renewable Energies for Developing Countries (REDEC), Beirut, Lebanon, 28–29 November 2012; pp. 1–7. [CrossRef]
22. Pérez-Ortiz, M.; Jiménez-Fernández, S.; Gutiérrez, P.A.; Alexandre, E.; Hervás-Martínez, C.; Salcedo-Sanz, S. A Review of Classification Problems and Algorithms in Renewable Energy Applications. *Energies* **2016**, *9*, 607. [CrossRef]
23. Kusiak, A.; Li, W. The prediction and diagnosis of wind turbine faults. *Renew. Energy* **2011**, *36*, 16–23. [CrossRef]
24. Kusiak, A.; Verma, A. Analyzing bearing faults in wind turbines: A data-mining approach. *Renew. Energy* **2012**, *48*, 110–116. [CrossRef]
25. Betti, A.; Crisostomi, E.; Paolinelli, G.; Piazzi, A.; Ruffini, F.; Tucci, M. Condition monitoring and predictive maintenance methodologies for hydropower plants equipment. *Renew. Energy* **2021**, *171*, 246–253. [CrossRef]
26. Fu, C.; Ye, L.; Liu, Y.; Yu, R.; Iung, B.; Cheng, Y.; Zeng, Y. Predictive maintenance in intelligent-control-maintenance-management system for hydroelectric generating unit. *IEEE Trans. Energy Convers.* **2004**, *19*, 179–186. [CrossRef]
27. Garoudja, E.; Chouder, A.; Kara, K.; Silvestre, S. An enhanced machine learning based approach for failures detection and diagnosis of PV systems. *Energy Convers. Manag.* **2017**, *151*, 496–513. [CrossRef]
28. Li, X.; Li, W.; Yang, Q.; Yan, W.; Zomaya, A.Y. An unmanned inspection system for multiple defects detection in photovoltaic plants. *IEEE J. Photovolt.* **2019**, *10*, 568–576. [CrossRef]
29. Berghout, T.; Benbouzid, M.; Ma, X.; Djurović, S.; Mouss, L.H. Machine Learning for Photovoltaic Systems Condition Monitoring: A Review. In Proccedings of the IECON 2021—47th Annual Conference of the IEEE Industrial Electronics Society, Toronto, ON, Canada, 13–16 October 2021; pp. 1–5. [CrossRef]
30. Bosman, L.B.; Leon-Salas, W.D.; Hutzel, W.; Soto, E.A. PV System Predictive Maintenance: Challenges, Current Approaches, and Opportunities. *Energies* **2020**, *13*, 1398. [CrossRef]
31. Sica, F.C.; Guimarães, F.G.; de Oliveira Duarte, R.; Reis, A.J. A cognitive system for fault prognosis in power transformers. *Electr. Power Syst. Res.* **2015**, *127*, 109–117. [CrossRef]
32. Kabir, F.; Foggo, B.; Yu, N. Data Driven Predictive Maintenance of Distribution Transformers. In Proccedings of the 2018 China International Conference on Electricity Distribution (CICED), Tianjin, China, 17–19 September 2018; pp. 312–316. [CrossRef]
33. Mirowski, P.; LeCun, Y. Statistical Machine Learning and Dissolved Gas Analysis: A Review. *IEEE Trans. Power Deliv.* **2012**, *27*, 1791–1799. [CrossRef]
34. Donadio, L.; Fang, J.; Porté-Agel, F. Numerical Weather Prediction and Artificial Neural Network Coupling for Wind Energy Forecast. *Energies* **2021**, *14*, 338. [CrossRef]
35. Heinermann, J.; Kramer, O. Machine learning ensembles for wind power prediction. *Renew. Energy* **2016**, *89*, 671–679. [CrossRef]
36. Yagli, G.M.; Yang, D.; Srinivasan, D. Automatic hourly solar forecasting using machine learning models. *Renew. Sustain. Energy Rev.* **2019**, *105*, 487–498. [CrossRef]
37. Voyant, C.; Notton, G.; Kalogirou, S.; Nivet, M.L.; Paoli, C.; Motte, F.; Fouilloy, A. Machine learning methods for solar radiation forecasting: A review. *Renew. Energy* **2017**, *105*, 569–582. [CrossRef]
38. Foley, A.M.; Leahy, P.G.; Marvuglia, A.; McKeogh, E.J. Current methods and advances in forecasting of wind power generation. *Renew. Energy* **2012**, *37*, 1–8. [CrossRef]
39. Riemer-Sørensen, S.; Rosenlund, G.H. Deep Reinforcement Learning for Long Term Hydropower Production Scheduling. In Proceedings of the 2020 International Conference on Smart Energy Systems and Technologies (SEST), Istanbul, Turkey, 7–9 September 2020; pp. 1–6. [CrossRef]
40. Bordin, C.; Skjelbred, H.I.; Kong, J.; Yang, Z. Machine Learning for Hydropower Scheduling: State of the Art and Future Research Directions. *Procedia Comput. Sci.* **2020**, *176*, 1659–1668. [CrossRef]
41. Fotopoulou, M.C.; Drosatos, P.; Petridis, S.; Rakopoulos, D.; Stergiopoulos, F.; Nikolopoulos, N. Model Predictive Control for the Energy Management in a District of Buildings Equipped with Building Integrated Photovoltaic Systems and Batteries. *Energies* **2021**, *14*, 3369. [CrossRef]
42. Wu, X.; Hu, X.; Moura, S.; Yin, X.; Pickert, V. Stochastic control of smart home energy management with plug-in electric vehicle battery energy storage and photovoltaic array. *J. Power Sources* **2016**, *333*, 203–212. [CrossRef]
43. Mouli, G.R.C.; Kefayati, M.; Baldick, R.; Bauer, P. Integrated PV charging of EV fleet based on energy prices, V2G, and offer of reserves. *IEEE Trans. Smart Grid* **2017**, *10*, 1313–1325. [CrossRef]
44. Wang, X.; Nie, Y.; Cheng, K.W.E. Distribution system planning considering stochastic EV penetration and V2G behavior. *IEEE Trans. Intell. Transp. Syst.* **2019**, *21*, 149–158. [CrossRef]
45. McLoughlin, F.; Duffy, A.; Conlon, M. A clustering approach to domestic electricity load profile characterisation using smart metering data. *Appl. Energy* **2015**, *141*, 190–199. [CrossRef]
46. Haben, S.; Singleton, C.; Grindrod, P. Analysis and clustering of residential customers energy behavioral demand using smart meter data. *IEEE Trans. Smart Grid* **2015**, *7*, 136–144. [CrossRef]
47. Seyedzadeh, S.; Rahimian, F.P.; Glesk, I.; Roper, M. Machine learning for estimation of building energy consumption and performance: A review. *Vis. Eng.* **2018**, *6*, 1–20. [CrossRef]

48. Chou, J.S.; Tran, D.S. Forecasting energy consumption time series using machine learning techniques based on usage patterns of residential householders. *Energy* **2018**, *165*, 709–726. [CrossRef]
49. Gonzalez-Briones, A.; Hernandez, G.; Corchado, J.M.; Omatu, S.; Mohamad, M.S. Machine learning models for electricity consumption forecasting: A review. In Proceedings of the 2019 2nd International Conference on Computer Applications & Information Security (ICCAIS), Riyadh, Saudi Arabia, 1–3 May 2019; pp. 1–6.
50. Manivinnan, K.; Benner, C.L.; Don Russell, B.; Wischkaemper, J.A. Automatic identification, clustering and reporting of recurrent faults in electric distribution feeders. In Proceedings of the 19th International Conference on Intelligent System Application to Power Systems, San Antonio, TX, USA, 17–20 September 2017. [CrossRef]
51. Viegas, J.L.; Vieira, S.M.; Melicio, R.; Matos, H.A.; Sousa, J.M. Prediction of events in the smart grid: Interruptions in distribution transformers. In Proceedings of the 2016 IEEE International Power Electronics and Motion Control Conference, Varna, Bulgaria, 25–28 September 2016. [CrossRef]
52. Eskandarpour, R.; Khodaei, A. Machine Learning Based Power Grid Outage Prediction in Response to Extreme Events. *IEEE Trans. Power Syst.* **2017**, *32*. [CrossRef]
53. Kumar, R.; Singh, B.; Shahani, D.T.; Chandra, A.; Al-Haddad, K. Recognition of Power-Quality Disturbances Using S-Transform-Based ANN Classifier and Rule-Based Decision Tree. *IEEE Trans. Ind. Appl.* **2015**, *51*. [CrossRef]
54. Zyabkina, O.; Domagk, M.; Meyer, J.; Schegner, P. A feature-based method for automatic anomaly identification in power quality measurements. In Proceedings of the 2018 International Conference on Probabilistic Methods Applied to Power Systems, Boise, ID, USA, 24–28 June 2018. [CrossRef]
55. Vantuch, T.; Misak, S.; Jezowicz, T.; Burianek, T.; Snasel, V. The Power Quality Forecasting Model for Off-Grid System Supported by Multiobjective Optimization. *IEEE Trans. Ind. Electron.* **2017**, *64*. [CrossRef]
56. Hoffmann, V.; Michałowska, K.; Andresen, C.; Torsæter, B.N. Incipient Fault Prediction in Power Quality Monitoring. In Proceedings of the 25th International Conference on Electricity Distribution (CIRED), Madrid, Spain, 3–6 June 2019.
57. Andresen, C.A.; Torsæter, B.N.; Haugdal, H.; Uhlen, K. Fault Detection and Prediction in Smart Grids. In Proceedings of the 9th International Workshop on Applied Measurements for Power Systems, Bologna, Italy, 26–28 September 2018. [CrossRef]
58. Hoiem, K.W.; Santi, V.; Torsater, B.N.; Langseth, H.; Andresen, C.A.; Rosenlund, G.H. Comparative Study of Event Prediction in Power Grids using Supervised Machine Learning Methods. In Proceedings of the 2020 International Conference on Smart Energy Systems and Technologies (SEST), Istanbul, Turkey, 7–9 September 2020. [CrossRef]
59. Rosenlund, G.H.; Hoiem, K.W.; Torsater, B.N.; Andresen, C.A. Clustering and Dimensionality-reduction Techniques Applied on Power Quality Measurement Data. In Proceedings of the 2020 International Conference on Smart Energy Systems and Technologies (SEST), Istanbul, Turkey, 7–9 September 2020. [CrossRef]
60. Tyvold, T.S.; Nybakk Torsater, B.; Andresen, C.A.; Hoffmann, V. Impact of the Temporal Distribution of Faults on Prediction of Voltage Anomalies in the Power Grid. In Proceedings of the 2020 International Conference on Smart Energy Systems and Technologies (SEST), Istanbul, Turkey, 7–9 September 2020. [CrossRef]
61. Michalowska, K.; Hoffmann, V.; Andresen, C. Impact of seasonal weather on forecasting of power quality disturbances in distribution grids. In Proceedings of the 2020 International Conference on Smart Energy Systems and Technologies (SEST), Istanbul, Turkey, 7–9 September 2020. [CrossRef]
62. Li, Y.; Wang, T.; Zhou, S.; Liu, Y. Power quality data analysis based on a state-wide monitoring system in China. In Proceedings of the International Conference on Power System Technology, Guangzhou, China, 6–9 November 2018; pp. 3734–3739.
63. Santoso, S.; Sabin, D.D.; McGranaghan, M.F. Evaluation of harmonic trends using statistical process control methods. In Proceedings of the Transmission and Distribution Conference and Exposition, Chicago, IL, USA, 21–24 April 2008; p. 1169.
64. Guan, J.L.; Yang, M.T.; Gu, J.C.; Chang, H.H. Effect of harmonic power fluctuation on voltage flicker. In Proceedings of the 11th WSEAS International Conference on Systems. 2007. pp. 429–435. Available online: https://zenodo.org/record/1333048#.YpQj-1RBxPY (accessed on 26 April 2022).
65. IRENA. *Energy Profile*; IRENA: Oslo, Norway, 2018.
66. Van Rossum, G.; Drake, F.L. *Python 3 Reference Manual*; CreateSpace: Scotts Valley, CA, USA, 2009.
67. Harris, C.R.; Millman, K.J.; van der Walt, S.J.; Gommers, R.; Virtanen, P.; Cournapeau, D.; Wieser, E.; Taylor, J.; Berg, S.; Smith, N.J.; et al. Array programming with NumPy. *Nature* **2020**, *585*, 357–362. [CrossRef] [PubMed]
68. McKinney, W. Data Structures for Statistical Computing in Python. In Proceedings of the 9th Python in Science Conference, Austin, TX, USA, 28 June–3 July 2010; pp. 56–61. Available online: https://conference.scipy.org/proceedings/scipy2010/pdfs/mckinney.pdf (accessed on 26 April 2022).
69. Dubuc, B.; Quiniou, J.F.; Roques-Carmes, C.; Tricot, C.; Zucker, S.W. Evaluating the fractal dimension of profiles. *Phys. Rev. A* **1989**, *39*, 1500. [CrossRef] [PubMed]
70. Das, J. Power System Harmonics. In *Power System Harmonics and Passive Filter Designs*; John Wiley and Sons, Ltd.: Hoboken, NJ, USA, 2015; Chapter 1, pp. 1–29. [CrossRef]
71. Zare, F.; Soltani, H.; Kumar, D.; Davari, P.; Delpino, H.A.M.; Blaabjerg, F. Harmonic Emissions of Three-Phase Diode Rectifiers in Distribution Networks. *IEEE Access* **2017**, *5*, 2819–2833. [CrossRef]
72. Kanao, N.; Hayashi, Y.; Matsuki, J. Analysis of Even Harmonics Generation in an Isolated Electric Power System. *Electr. Eng. Jpn.* **2009**, *167*, 56–63. [CrossRef]

73. Norges vassdrags og energidirektorat (NVE). Forskrift om Leveringskvalitet i Kraftsystemet (FOL), 2021. Data Retrieved from Lovdata on 2021-12-21. Available online: https://lovdata.no/dokument/SF/forskrift/2004-11-30-1557#KAPITTEL_4 (accessed on 26 April 2022).
74. Das, S.; Santoso, S.; Maitra, A. Effects of distributed generators on impedance-based fault location algorithms. In Proceedings of the IEEE Power and Energy Society General Meeting, National Harbor, MD, USA, 27–31 July 2014; Volume 2014.
75. Xiao, F.; Ai, Q. Data-Driven Multi-Hidden Markov Model-Based Power Quality Disturbance Prediction That Incorporates Weather Conditions. *IEEE Trans. Power Syst.* **2019**, *34*, 402–412. [CrossRef]
76. Nandi, A.; Debnath, S. Recognition of harmonic sources in distribution network using fractal analysis. In Proceedings of the 1st International Conference on Control, Measurement and Instrumentation, Kolkata, India, 8–10 January 2016. [CrossRef]
77. Zhou, J.; LI, X.; Ren, Z. Power-Load Fault Diagnosis via Fractal Similarity Analysis. In Proceedings of the 12th IEEE PES Asia-Pacific Power and Energy Engineering Conference (APPEEC), Nanjing, China, 20–23 September 2020. [CrossRef]
78. Zhou, T.; Lu, J.; Li, B.; Tan, Y. Fractal analysis of power grid faults and cross correlation for the faults and meteorological factors. *IEEE Access* **2020**, *8*. [CrossRef]
79. Gneiting, T.; Schlather, M. Stochastic Models That Separate Fractal Dimension and the Hurst Effect. *SIAM Rev.* **2004**, *46*, 269–282. [CrossRef]
80. Santi, V.M. *Predicting Faults in Power Grids Using Machine Learning Methods*; Technical Report; Norwegian University of Science and Technology (NTNU): Oslo, Norway, 2019.
81. Meen, H.K.; Jahr, C. *Power Wave Analysis and Prediction of Faults in the Norwegian Power Grid*; Technical Report; Norwegian University of Science and Technology (NTNU): Oslo, Norway, 2020.
82. Hoffmann, V.; Klemets, J.R.A.; Torsæter, B.N.; Rosenlund, G.H.; Andresen, C.A. The value of multiple data sources in machine learning models for power system event prediction. In Proceedings of the 2021 International Conference on Smart Energy Systems and Technologies (SEST), Vaasa, Finland, 8 September 2021; pp. 1–6.
83. Weiss, K.; Khoshgoftaar, T.M.; Wang, D. A survey of transfer learning. *J. Big Data* **2016**, *3*, 1–40. [CrossRef]

algorithms

MDPI

Article

A Cost-Efficient MCSA-Based Fault Diagnostic Framework for SCIM at Low-Load Conditions

Chibuzo Nwabufo Okwuosa, Ugochukwu Ejike Akpudo and Jang-Wook Hur *

Department of Mechanical Engineering (Department of Aeronautics, Mechanical and Electronic Convergence Engineering), Kumoh National Institute of Technology, 61 Daehak-ro, Gumi-si 39177, Gyeonsang-buk-do, Korea; okwuosachibuzo333@gmail.com (C.N.O.); akpudougo@gmail.com (U.E.A.)

* Correspondence: hhjw88@kumoh.ac.kr

Abstract: In industry, electric motors such as the squirrel cage induction motor (SCIM) generate motive power and are particularly popular due to their low acquisition cost, strength, and robustness. Along with these benefits, they have minimal maintenance costs and can run for extended periods before requiring repair and/or maintenance. Early fault detection in SCIMs, especially at low-load conditions, further helps minimize maintenance costs and mitigate abrupt equipment failure when loading is increased. Recent research on these devices is focused on fault/failure diagnostics with the aim of reducing downtime, minimizing costs, and increasing utility and productivity. Data-driven predictive maintenance offers a reliable avenue for intelligent monitoring whereby signals generated by the equipment are harnessed for fault detection and isolation (FDI). Particularly, motor current signature analysis (MCSA) provides a reliable avenue for extracting and/or exploiting discriminant information from signals for FDI and/or fault diagnosis. This study presents a fault diagnostic framework that exploits underlying spectral characteristics following MCSA and intelligent classification for fault diagnosis based on extracted spectral features. Results show that the extracted features reflect induction motor fault conditions with significant diagnostic performance (minimal false alarm rate) from intelligent models, out of which the random forest (RF) classifier was the most accurate, with an accuracy of 79.25%. Further assessment of the models showed that RF had the highest computational cost of 3.66 s, while NBC had the lowest at 0.003 s. Other significant empirical assessments were conducted, and the results support the validity of the proposed FDI technique.

Keywords: machine learning; peak detection; fault diagnosis; frequency domain; low-load condition

1. Introduction

SCIMs are used to power most industrial appliances because of their robust nature and ability to generate sufficient torque to effectively drive much larger machinery at an affordable cost through the process of electromagnetic induction. Injection sea water pumps, air conditioner compressor drives, gas circulators in power generating firms, and oil exporting pumps in the oil and gas drilling industries are only a few of the well-known applications of SCIMs [1]. SCIMs are often prone to failures and breakdowns as a result of faults and prolonged operation, and, if left unmonitored, often suffer major damage or breakdowns. According to a review done by Bhowmik et al. [2], severe operating environments, insufficient insulation, purposely overloading the power supply, and factory defects are the most typical causes of breakdowns and failure. The production down-times caused by these flaws have frequently resulted in revenue loss, among other pitfalls. Therefore, early fault detection is important/crucial to avoid these occurrences [1]. The consequences of these failures have increased the need for SCIM failure diagnosis as a crucial module for overall equipment prognostics and health management (PHM).

State-of-the-art research studies on SCIM FDI and prognostics feature data-driven PHM technologies, with research ongoing; these studies show that data-driven AI-based

PHM technologies rely heavily on the quantity and quality of data to train AI-based predictive modeling [1,3]. However, the accuracy of these models is also dependent on how suitable the method befits the nature of the available data, which has led to various studies exploring numerous data-driven PHM methodologies. Researchers have used advances in artificial intelligence (AI), machine learning (ML), and deep learning to construct models that exploit current signals, vibration signals, and thermal signals generated by equipment via sensors, examining these signals separately or combining them for FDI [1,4,5]. Fourier analysis has proven to be effective among the different ways of analysis owing to its convenience and nature of application, especially when it comes to current signature analysis and/or vibration signature analysis (VSA) [5]. Fourier transforms (FTs) are essentially concerned with the decomposition of signals from their time domain to their frequency domain for analysis in both healthy and faulty motors, providing a superior platform for signal interpretation and feature extraction for FDI [3,6]. Even though it can decompose signals to their frequency domains, a FT still has limitations, such as its lack of transient information and its nature of providing only the average time of the spectrum content, thereby lacking in providing details on variations in frequency with regard to time of the signals [7]. Fast Fourier transforms with high computation speed and short-time Fourier transforms that decompose data into the time–frequency domain are frequently used to solve these challenges [7,8]. Further, according to [9], Fourier analysis is one of the highly efficient analytical tools that is compatible with MCSA for a variety of fault detection for SCIMs.

Although variable frequency drives (VFDs) have recently become more popular in industries than direct online starters due to their ability to provide flexible production control and soft motor start-up, variable frequencies, complex control systems, and harmonics generated at the drive output are still some of the major concerns they are associated with [10]. Harmonics generated by VFDs pose a significant problem for motor bearings and stator windings since they raise their level of stress. Moreover, they have an impact on signal quality in terms of noise ratio, particularly when using stator current signals for FDI [5,10].

2. Motivation and Literature Review

As dependency on SCIMs by industries is on the increase due to their robust nature, failures of these machines cannot be accommodated; therefore, the need to find solutions to these failures or to predict possible failure time cannot be overemphasized. Globally, close to 90% of industrial equipment relies on SCIMs as their prime mover [11]. According to Choudhary et al. [1], faults in SCIMs are categorized based on the location of occurrence, i.e., internal or external, and these faults are then grouped based on the nature and/or origin of the fault, i.e., mechanical or electrical faults; the severity of each fault type depends on its location. For instance, an external electrical fault is less threatening than an internal electrical issue, but if left unmonitored, it can escalate to an internal electrical fault, which can lead to a total breakdown.

Bearing and stator faults account for more than 70% of general failures in SCIMs [12]. According to an investigative report, bearing failure, unsurprisingly, has the highest percentage of occurrence in an SCIM (40–45% contribution) [1], which can be traced to the nature of SCIMs, whose bearings are susceptible to damage when overloaded, misaligned, and/or unbalanced. Moreover, the bearings are subjected to continuous loading at all times when the SCIM is in operation. Stator failures are common as well, owing to large current flows in their winding coils and insulation weakness caused by mechanical and electrical stress and/or deterioration of insulation. The most common defect in a stator is an interturn fault, which happens when two turns in a phase become linked as a result of failed insulation and, if left unchecked, can lead to phase damage or more serious stator failures, resulting in substantial maintenance costs [13]. Although not as common as stator and bearing problems, rotor faults are one of the most commonly occurring faults, accounting for over 8% of all SCIM faults [1], and can lead to poor performance and/or breakdown of the motor if left unmonitored.

For adequate FDI, signals generated from these machines are employed for condition-based monitoring, which has proven to be useful in past and present research studies [5,14,15]. Based on the nature of SCIMs, which generate vibration and thermal responses while in operation, vibration signals have been one of the most-used measurements thus far due to their efficiency in both time and frequency domains [16]. On the flip side, due to the simplicity, low cost, and non-intrusive nature of obtaining current signals, MCSA has become very popular in recent times. This can be linked to the unique current signatures from the IM's supply [5,15]. Due to the effectiveness/efficiency of this approach, MCSA has been effectively employed in both stator and rotor monitoring [1,11]. Furthermore, MCSA has also proven to be effective and compatible with Fourier analysis for discriminant feature extraction for critical FDI [6,8,12,14,17].

In the literature, various studies have been presented for fault diagnosis frameworks and classifications that exploit MCSA and spectral features extracted based on Fourier series transformations of signals from their time to frequency domains. For instance, in [15], the authors used both MCSA and FFT under different conditions. Two faults were considered in the study to evaluate their proposed algorithm using stationary and non-stationary signals. Studies presented in [5,14] employed MCSA for SCIM fault detection in broken rotor bars. In their methodologies, spectral features obtained from applying FFT analysis to MCSA were applied to independent component analysis (ICA) for improved performance; the extracted features were labeled FFT-ICA and were proven to contain a wealth of information for FDI with good outcomes when used for online fault detection. In [18], the authors capitalized on the effectiveness of current FDI monitoring. Their proposed methodology used an FFT algorithm to interpret current signals for reliable anomaly detection in the IM. The authors also used advanced signal processing techniques in their proposed method for critical FDI at the bearing and rotor bar of SCIMs to improve the interpretation of current signals. Duc Nguyen et al. [6], trained features extracted from the FFT spectrum of raw current signals using a machine learning algorithm. According to their research, their methodology presents a low-cost, accurate, and robust FDI instrument for SCIMs that uses only current signals and is also applicable to real-world data. In [17], the authors used a novel methodology that combined two techniques, wavelet and power-spectral-density (PSD), to analyze the FFT spectrum of MCSA. The technique's effectiveness was been demonstrated in diagnosing short turns and broken rotor bars in non-constant-load-torque SCIM applications, just as it does in constant-load-torque motor applications. In [8], Yoo proposed a fault detection algorithm for SCIMs using FFT and PCA. He employed FFT to analyze induction motor current in the frequency domain for fault-characteristic spectral components and used PCA for easy extraction of features from the available components.

In reality, SCIMs and induction motors are often operated under varying loads. It is not recommended to meet/exceed the motor's maximum loading specification; however, production demands may sometimes require increased loading. These situations often induce stress and/or faults in motors, which may gradually evolve into failures [19]. On the flip side, SCIMs also experience faults that are humanly undetectable under low-load conditions [20]. At low-load conditions, SCIMs often do not generate noise and/or observable fault symptoms, which makes operation riskier since abrupt failures may occur, leading to interrupted production and/or accidents. This rationale makes it necessary to develop intelligent monitoring for early fault detection in SCIMs at low-load conditions. Bessam et al. [20] exploited the Hilbert transform (HT) and a neural network for broken rotor bar intelligent diagnosis in induction machines at low load. Beyond the efficiencies and limitations of their stand-alone HT-based diagnostic technique, other signal processing techniques could be integrated for comprehensive fault diagnostic efficiencies. For instance, Das et al. used an extended Park's vector approach in conjunction with FFT, DWT, and PSD to process and extract features from current signals for distinguishing induction motor inter-turn stator winding faults from unstable supply voltage conditions [21]. The coefficient of the major peak observed in FFT was used in their methodology to indicate fault severity and load level in the IM. Hussain et al. [22] proposed a method for implementing and analyzing current signatures from a three-phase SCIM using a combination of three signal processing techniques: FFT, short-time Fourier transform, and continuous wavelet transform. Their method demonstrated that MCSA can detect changes in frequency components by obtaining the FFT-based spectrum that contains the initial information about the fault. In [23], the authors demonstrated the non-intrusive nature and simplicity of MCSA. They presented a methodology for detecting faults in an SCIM's stator winding using external flux sensors on a three-phase SCIM. The sensors were placed on the outside of the motor's body in the X, Y, and Z directions so as not to interfere with the motor's operation. FFT analysis of the stator currents revealed a short circuit fault in the SCIM stator winding.

For all these successful case studies, one major take-home is the high efficiency of FTs for MCSA and its robustness for isolating fault frequencies on frequency bands in varying magnitudes. This provides a reliable avenue for harnessing the information provided by frequency-magnitude coordinates as representative features for discriminate modeling for FDI. Peak detection offers a cost-effective diagnostic feature-extraction alternative to spectral frequency-domain extraction and was employed in our study. Its diagnostic efficiency has been recorded in [19,24]. According to Jena and Panigrahi [19], peak detection was one of the techniques employed for fault localization in an automatic gear and bearing using vibration and acoustic signals. In their study, peak detection was one of their proposed filtering techniques, which aimed to unify the approach for both acoustic and vibration signals for enabling fault detection. Further, in [24], using peak detection as one of their techniques, the authors proposed a methodology for distinguishing bearing fault signals from masking signals emitted by drive-train elements. Peaks in the frequency spectrum were used as a discriminating technique for fault classification and separation in their proposed model. In our quest to develop an FT-MCSA-based diagnostic framework for SCIMs, this study makes the following contributions:

- A proposal for a three-phase MCSA-based peak detection approach for diagnostic feature extraction. The proposed feature extraction method extracts the coordinates of the highest peaks from the FFT, PSD, and autocorrelation function (ACF) spectra as features.
- An extensive comparison of ML-based diagnostic models to provide a generalization paradigm for SCIM diagnosis.
- A computational cost assessment of ML-based diagnostic models is presented, and empirical assessments is conducted for improved diagnostic assessment of the models.

The rest of the paper is structured thus: Section 3 presents the theoretical background of the key modules of our proposed study, while Section 4 presents an overview of the proposed MCSA-based diagnostic method. Section 5 presents the experimental study on a physical case study, while Sections 6 and 7 conclude the study.

3. Theoretical Background

In this section, the theoretical background of MCSA induction motor condition monitoring, frequency domain feature extraction, and ML-based diagnostic models for fault detection and isolation are discussed.

3.1. *Review of Current Signature Analysis Methods*

MCSA has recently become one of the most popular methods for fault detection in induction motors, owing to its rich spectrum contents and non-intrusive nature of accessing machines. MCSA exploits the current in the supply phases of the SCIM, which often contains little transient and spectral characteristics. The generated current signatures leave little room for proper interpretation of the underlying harmonics generated by the SCIM during operation, which has been a significant challenge for MCSA. Spectral decomposition of these signals, on the other hand, provides a more reliable avenue for understanding system dynamics due to its robustness for representing signatures in representative spectra bands [25]. The signatures typically present a rationale for distinguishing between healthy and faulty states of the machine being monitored because variations in loading of an SCIM are often reflected in the spectral bands. When faults occur in components, they cause a magnetic field anomaly in the regular mutual and self-inductance of the motor, resulting in sidebands across the line frequency [26].

Since motor faults change the harmonic content of the supply current, several methods have been used to aid in the pre-processing stage for feature extraction from measured current signals for adequate comparison between current signatures to detect motor fault signatures. These methods are fundamentally Fourier-based, and they include: fast Fourier transform (FFT), discrete Fourier transform (FDT), mel frequency cepstral coefficient (MFCC), short-time Fourier transform (STFT), wavelet transform, empirical mode decomposition, variable mode decomposition, etc. These popular methods are quite unique in their efficiencies and have been reported in several studies [7,27–30]. Traditional DFT and FFT discretize signals by representing the signal as different sinusoidal wave components, providing a strong foundation for most other advanced discretization methods. On the bright side, PSD offers an even more-reliable alternative to FFT due to its comparatively higher sensitivity to spectral changes in a signal. PSD computes the energy densities of the constituent frequencies, thereby exaggerating relevance for high-energy signal components while suppressing the effects of lower-energy constituents [27]; however, its limitations for transient signal representation remains a major challenge [7]. These inherent challenges motivated the development of STFT, which provides time-frequency resolution of a signal by taking the Fourier transform of the signal within a time window function; however, the optimal choice of window function remains its major challenge [7].

In contrast to Fourier-based transforms, wavelet transform represents signals as wavelet-series: a representation of a square integral function by a wavelet-created orthogonal series [28,30]. Due to its unique nature, the wavelet transform has been one of the most widely used signal representation method transforms for decades and is broadly used for discretization (discrete wavelet transform) and for transient-spectral representations (continuous wavelet transform); however, the choice of mother wavelet remains an exhaustive challenge for its optimal use and remains an open area of continued research [28]. Interestingly, numerous improvements have been made on existing methods as well as novel ideas offered over the years, including variational mode decomposition (VMD)—a relatively new signal processing technique that can be used to easily decompose signals into their various band-limited intrinsic mode functions. Technically, VMD is an improved version of the wavelet transform and Hilbert Huang transforms that is noise sensitive and devoid of the modal merging effect [29,31]. Though these methods are unique in their efficiencies (and deficiencies) for diverse purposes, their use for diagnosis is often motivated by the discriminative representations they provide from input signals, which form a feature set for diagnosis.

3.2. *Review of ML-Based Classification Algorithms*

As previously stated, recent AI advancements have aided in the improvement of ML and deep learning models for effective FDI, which typically involves relying on intelligent models for improved FDI at a minimal false alarm rate even amid uncertainties. Even though the efficiencies of these methodologies have been reported in numerous studies, there are still underlying challenges associated with their use, such as computational cost and their tendency to deviate from core engineering concepts, which makes them sometimes irrelevant for cost-conscious industrial applications, as presented in this study [32]. Traditional ML algorithms, on the other hand, offer a more cost-effective and dependable platform for adequate FDI because their efficiency is rarely affected by data availability [32,33]. The effectiveness of FDI algorithms is highly dependent on the nature of the discriminative content of the input signal of the device under monitoring; thus, significant discriminative feature extraction from raw signals is critical [30]. As a result, this study was motivated to investigate various ML algorithms and their efficacy on current-based fault detection after peak-detection-based feature extraction. As a result, in this study, a handful of popular ML-based classifiers are presented and discussed to present their theoretical background for FDI.

DT is one of the most common, cost-efficient, and reliable known ML algorithms that has been effectively employed for both regression and classification problems. DT is an algorithm that uses a tree-like structure of decision-making rules to classify input data into subsets and to make predictions based on this classification [34,35]. Its two main advantages are its ease of use and its ability to present solutions with various outputs [35]. However, this model is prone to over-fitting and under-fitting, which can be overcome with pruning. Again, even with proper pruning, a perfect solution to the problem is not guaranteed [30]. Random forest (RF), on the other hand, mitigates the major challenges of DT by establishing a great number of decision trees at the same instance [30]. RF passes the presented sample through its various structures with different classifiers, computing and storing the output of each tree, which it further compares with single outputs of the popular trees to derive the final classifiers. By simply changing its key parameters, this model eliminates the major problem of DT [30]. One of the well-known disadvantages of RF is its complexity, which can result in high computational cost [36]. Booster algorithms such as Adaboost classifier (ABC), gradient boosting classifier (GBC), and XG boost (XGB) have been used to improve the efficiency and predictive accuracy of weak classifiers such as DT, regressors, and so on. These boosters are ensemble learning algorithms that combine weak learners to produce strong learners by minimizing their training errors [36]. However, these boosters have their challenges, which provides justification for further development of other algorithms to address such issues. For example, as more trees are added to their structure, these models are prone to over-fitting. However, in comparison, each booster presents a distinctive advantage over the other. GBC outperforms ABC in terms of accuracy due to its immense flexibility, which allows the algorithm as many differentiable and convex loss functions as possible [36]. On the other hand, XGB's scalability presents a structure that achieves algorithmic optimization, distinguishing it from the other boosters [37].

Interestingly, some ML algorithms make their predictions based on the assumption of a set of particular mathematical sequences or theories. For instance, k-nearest neighbor (KNN) is predicated on the assumption that any group of data with similar features will have similar feature values [38]. As a result, KNN performs better in cases where the datasets are evenly distributed; however, in cases where the datasets differ slightly, the accuracy of KNN may be affected [30]. On the plus side, normalization is critical in ensuring even representation of all feature values when feeding datasets to KNN for improved performance. Naive Bayes classifier (NBC) is a popular type of theorem-based learner; it is based on Bayes' theorem, which defines the relationship between two conditional probabilities of a specific event based on available prior information about the event under consideration [39]. NBC is a better classifier than other models whose principles are also based on Bayes' theorem because it presents a simpler model with a simpler computational procedure [30].

Overall, the accuracy of ML algorithms has improved over the years, as many algorithms employ techniques that would readily predict complex datasets to give an outstanding result—SVM is a unique ML algorithm that employs a hyper-plane to create its decision boundary using support vectors. It provides space for the user to define gamma parameters for decision boundaries, and its performance is based on: the distance of the sample on either side can change influence; its regularization parameter determines the distance between the decision boundary and separation; its various kernels (for nonlinear boundaries), radial-based function (RBF), and so on [40]. SVMs are known to be computationally efficient; however, as the parameter values increase, the computational speed significantly drops [30], which is a major drawback for its use on large datasets. Amongst ML-based learners, multi-layer perception (MLP) has a relatively high predictive accuracy compared to other methods. MLP is a feed-forward neural network (FFNN) with three structures by default: input, hidden, and output layers [41]. It is very efficient for both supervised and unsupervised situations due to its architecture, learning sequence, and flexibility, making it ideal for classification [30,41]. MLP's difficulty in implementation and interpretation are some of its significant drawbacks [41].

4. Proposed System Model

The proposed MCSA-based diagnostic framework for three-phase induction motors fundamentally features a Fourier-based peak detection module for discriminative feature extraction, interpreted by ML-based classifiers for diagnosis. Figure 1 shows the proposed diagnostic framework.

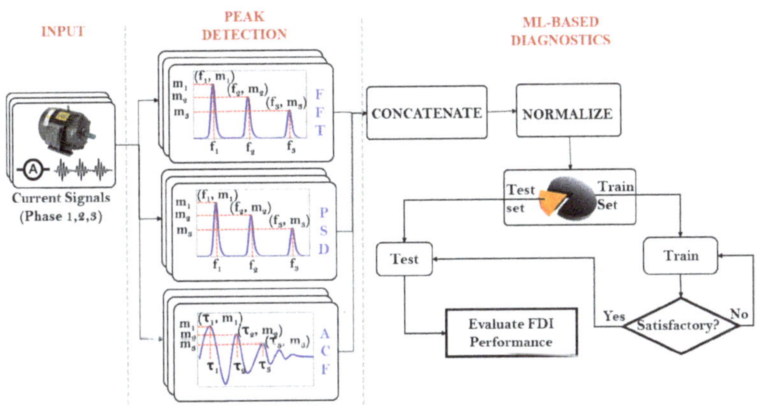

Figure 1. Proposed diagnostic model.

As shown, the model receives current signals from the three phases of the induction motor, which are simultaneously processed via FFT, PSD, and ACF for peak-based feature extraction. The Fourier transform (and its variants) is named after Joseph Fourier (21 March 1768–16 May 1830), and it serves as the foundation for most frequency-domain signal processing techniques. As previously stated, FFT and PSD provide a spectral representation of the constituent periodic components in the current signatures and can be exploited for accurate condition monitoring. In addition, ACF provides the degree of similarity between a discrete signal and its delayed copy as a function of the delay τ between them.

Feature extraction from FFT, PSD, and ACF exploits peak coordinates (f_i, m_i) from FTT and PSD spectra and (τ_i, m_i) from ACF such that for the first l tallest peaks in each of the three functions, their coordinates are concatenated to form the feature set. These labeled features are then received as input by the ML-based classifiers for discriminative modeling, validation, testing, and performance evaluation using standard classification performance evaluation metrics. The subsections below summarize the core modules of the proposed diagnostic framework.

4.1. Fourier-Based Peak Detection for Feature Extraction

Digital signal processing (DSP) has been a reliable condition monitoring paradigm in a variety of applications for decades. Particularly for induction motors, current signatures are often stationary with different periodic components that are affected by changing operating conditions. Most signals are composed of complex synthesis of sine and cosine functions under relaxable assumptions, which provides a reliable avenue for FFT to flourish.

Different parameters can be extracted from the spectra to make the necessary discriminative inferences for diagnosis. Often, there is a change in magnitude of the spectral components as the operating conditions of the induction motor change, and this presents an opportunity to exploit spectral peaks and their coordinate frequency values as representative features. Given a time-recorded signal (one-dimensional digitized current signal) $f(x) = \{x_1, x_2, \ldots, x_m\}$, the Fourier transform of $f(x)$ is traditionally denoted $F(k)$ and is computed using Equation (1):

$$F(k) = \int_{-\infty}^{\infty} f(x)e^{-j(\frac{2\pi mk}{N})}dx, 0 \leq m \leq N \tag{1}$$

where $f(x)$ is the input signal, k is the length of the transform, and $F(k)$ is the corresponding frequency-domain output of the signal.

PSD exaggerates the impact of high-energy components while reducing it for lower-energy components by computing the energy densities of the constituent frequencies. Mathematically, PSD generates a spectrum by squaring the magnitude of the FFT outputs from Equation (1), and is obtained using Equation (2):

$$PS(k) = |F(k)|^2 \tag{2}$$

where $PS(K)$ is the PSD-domain output from the FFT of the signal.

High autocorrelation (a maximum of 1) implies high similarity between the signal and its delayed component, while the reverse is the case if autocorrelation is close to zero. ACF can be computed via a convolution theorem using Equation (3):

$$y(\tau) = \sum_{i=0}^{i=N-1} f(x_i)f(x_i - \tau) = iFFT(F(k)F(k)^*) \tag{3}$$

where * means complex conjugation and $iFFT$ is the inverse FFT.

Feature extraction from FFT, PSD, and ACF exploits peak coordinates such that for the first l tallest peaks in each of these three functions, their coordinates are concatenated to form the feature set:

$$A = \{[k_1, F(k)_1, k_1, PS(k)_1, \tau_1, y(\tau_1)], [k_2, F(k)_2, k_2, PS(k)_2, \tau_2, y(\tau_2)],, \ldots, [k_n, F(k)_n, k_n, PS(k)_n, \tau_n, y(\tau_n)]\}.$$

4.2. Discriminative Performance Evaluation Metrics

Because every ML model is unique to its architecture, it becomes necessary to exhaustively explore each model's prowess for diagnostics while also considering other factors such as model complexity, computational costs, parametirization, etc. This presents the need to employ standardized diagnostic/discriminative performance evaluation metrics. These metrics include accuracy, sensitivity, precision, F1-score, and false alarm rate (FAR) [40]. These criteria are defined, respectively, as (4)–(8).

$$\text{Accuracy} = \frac{TP}{TP + FP + TN + FN} \tag{4}$$

$$\text{Sensitivity} = \frac{TP}{TP + FN} \tag{5}$$

$$\text{Precision} = \frac{TP}{TP + FP} \tag{6}$$

$$\text{F1-Score} = \frac{2 * \text{Sensitivity} * \text{Precision}}{\text{Precision} + \text{sensitivity}} \tag{7}$$

$$\text{FAR} = \frac{FP}{FP + TN} \tag{8}$$

where TP, FP, TN, and FN, respectively, are the number of correctly classified classes, number of incorrectly classified classes, number of incorrectly labeled samples belonging to a class that were correctly classified, and the number of incorrectly labeled samples belonging to a class that were incorrectly classified.

Although these metrics provide a global perspective for evaluating model classification performance, it may become necessary to evaluate each model's class-specific performance to ensure a more comprehensive performance assessment. For instance, a classifier may return an overall classification accuracy of 90% over a five-class problem set. This high accuracy may emanate from the model's strengths for correctly classifying three out of the five classes, whereas it may flaw on the remaining two classes. On the contrary, another model may return the same level of accuracy but its class-specific classification performance may be fairly uniform for each class; hence it would be more reliable than the previous model. This is usually the case, and presents the need for the confusion matrix, which provides an avenue for evaluating each model's class-specific diagnostic performance.

5. Experimental Study

This study proposes an MCSA-based diagnostic framework, which was employed on a physical testbed at the Defense Reliability Laboratory, Kumoh National Institute of Technology, Korea. The testbed consists of different four-pole, 0.25 hp, three-phase squirrel cage (delta connection) induction motors operating at different operating conditions, as summarized in Table 1.

Table 1. The different fault conditions of induction motors used in the experiment.

Label	Failure Mode	Description
ARM-1	Rotor misalignment	A condition where the center lines of coupled shafts do not coincide.
BRB-2	Broken rotor bar	A stress-induced condition whereby the rotor break and/or cracks
ISC-3	Inter-turn short circuit winding	A condition whereby two coils in a phase connect with each other
NOM-4	Normal operating condition	No fault condition

Three-phase induction motors are often exposed to different failure modes that emanate from sources ranging from environmental, thermal, electrical, and other factors. However, some failure modes are more critical than others, and they are prioritized in this study. Misalignment in a motor drive system is severe and the most frequently occurring condition in motor driven systems and may present itself in the form of angular, parallel/offset and/or a combination of parallel and angular misalignment [42]. In reality, it may be highly impossible to experience a single type of misalignment in absolute absence of the other. Often, even an acceptably aligned rotor has some level of a combination of angular and parallel misalignment (though insignificant). On the other hand, another frequently occurring (and critical) failure in induction motors is a broken rotor bar, which often occurs due to mechanical stresses emanating from variable operating conditions [43]. In addition, inter-turn short circuit winding is yet another critical and highly severe failure mode that often results in complete motor breakdown if undetected. This failure occurs as a result of aging and thermal stress to the insulator separating some turns in a particular phase of the motor [1,13,44]. Consequently, our study prioritizes these three critical failure modes, which were replicated on the testbed shown in Figure 2.

Figure 2. A pictorial view of the experimental setup.

The induction motors were loaded via a DC loading mechanism—a DC power supply was connected to the driven motor to induce a magnetic field between its rotor and stator, which causes resistance in the driver, resulting in a low-load condition. The motors were operated at a constant speed of approximately 1780 RPM (30 Hz), while data were collected via the driver's terminals using a NI 9246 module connected to a cDAQ-9178 connected to a desktop computer, as shown in Figure 2 above. The digital current signals were collected via a LabVIEW interface and stored in .csv format at a sampling rate of 50 Hz; the spectral resolution of the signals was 0.0003 Hz. Figure 3 shows the manually induced fault conditions to replicate rotor misalignment (ARM-1), a broken rotor bar (BRB-2), and inter-turn short circuit winding (ISC-3) failure modes for the experiment.

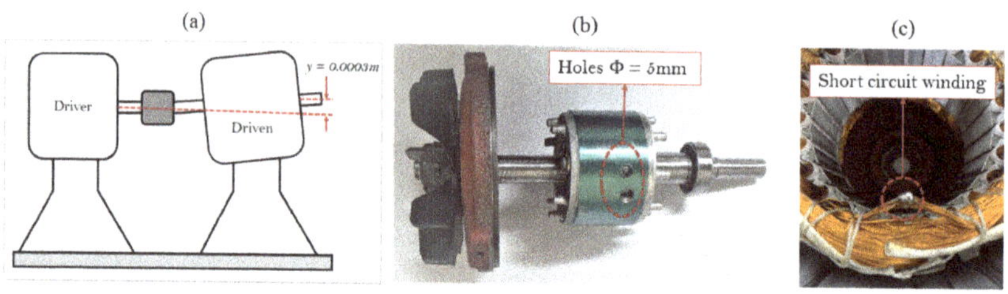

Figure 3. Fault conditions to replicate for the failure modes: (**a**) rotor misalignment, (**b**) broken rotor bar, and (**c**) inter-turn short circuit winding.

ARM-1 was achieved by first aligning the motors (driver and driven) using a precision laser alignment kit, and then to misaligned them by 0.3 mm for both parallel and angular misalignment. BRB-2 was imitated by drilling two holes of diameter 5 mm to a depth of 5 mm. ISC-3 was imitated by bridging seven (7) coils in the same phase. For control, a motor with no fault/failure mode (NOM-4) was also employed.

5.1. Signal Processing for Feature Extraction

Current data were collected from the three-phases of the motors at the different operating conditions and cleaned. Figure 4 shows a visualization of the current signals collected from the induction motors at the different operating conditions, with red, blue, and green representing phases 1, 2, and 3, respectively.

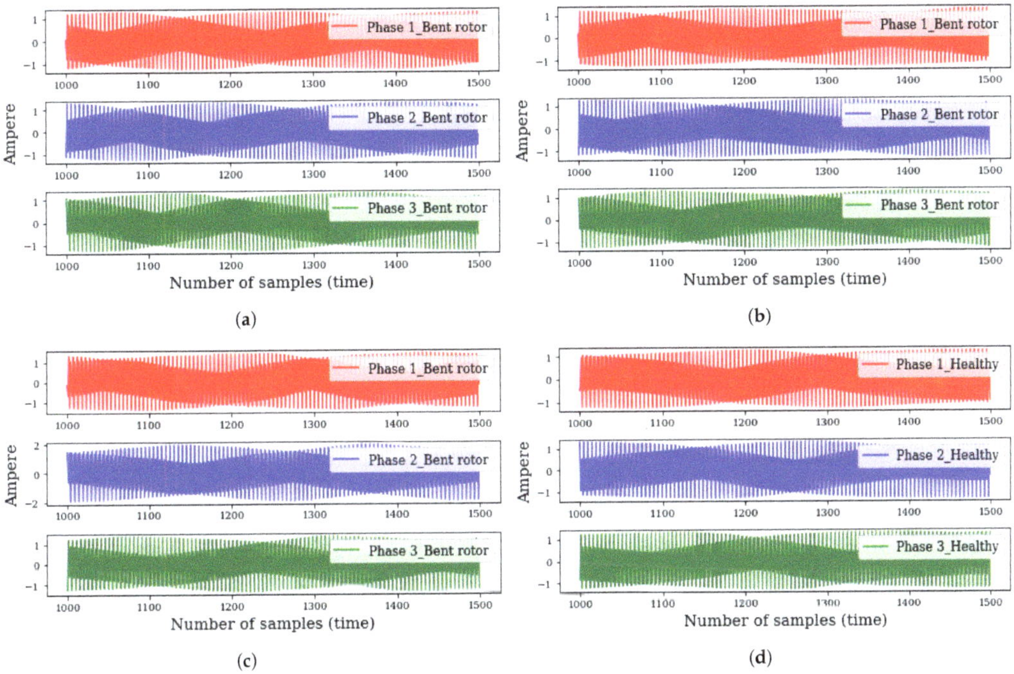

Figure 4. Current signals collected from the induction motors: (**a**) ARM-1, (**b**) BRB-2, (**c**) ISC-3, and (**d**) NOM-4.

As shown, the signals reveal some similarity in waveforms across the different operating conditions apart from the phase 2 signal (in blue) of Figure 4c, whose maximum amplitude is about 2 amperes while the rest have a magnitude of 1 ampere. Next, the signals were processed for feature extraction using the method proposed in Section 4. Figure 5 shows the respective FFT, PSD, and ACF visualizations of the signals under the different operating conditions.

As shown in Figure 5a,b, the FFT and PSD for each of the different operating conditions uniquely reflect different spectral bands of different magnitudes and frequency ranges, whereby PSD is more sensitive for the 1SC-3 condition for phase 2 signals. In addition, the ACF results in Figure 5c reveals differing ACF amplitudes over the time delay for each of the phases. These were concatenated to form the feature set for discriminative modeling for diagnosis. To develop the feature set, the proposed peak detection algorithm extracted the ten (10) tallest peaks from the FFT, PSD, and ACF spectra, respectively, from each of the current signals collected from the different operating conditions.

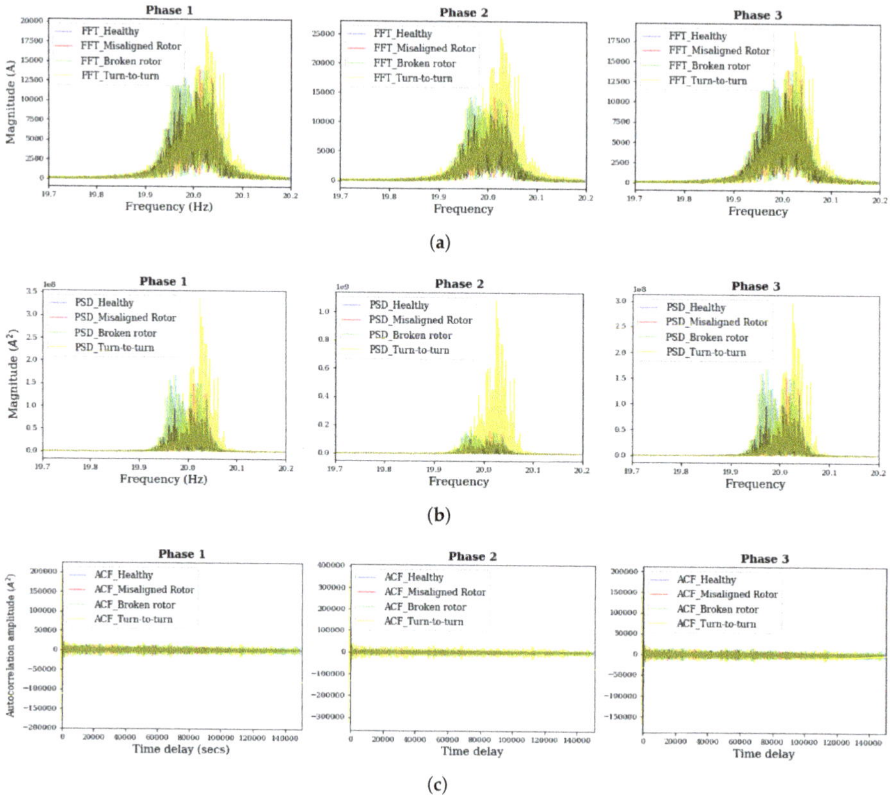

Figure 5. Phase current signal spectra for different fault conditions: (**a**) FFT (**b**) PSD, and (**c**) ACF.

5.2. Feature Evaluation

Ideally, the efficiency of traditional ML-based classifiers for diagnosis relies on the discriminative power of the input features. Interestingly, Spearman's correlation provides a reliable avenue for evaluating the discrimnance amongst the features extracted from each of the operating conditions. This tool measures the linear dependence between two continuous variables and returns a value in the range of −1 (negative correlation) and +1 (positive correlation). Apart from serving as an easy-to-use feature selection tool, it fundamentally provides a hint of the level of dsiscriminance between/amongst features, whereby a high positive and/or negative correlation implies poor discriminance in the features and vice versa. Sometimes, it is also desirable to visually assess the features for discrimnance. This is often supported by dimensionality reduction tools such as principal component analysis (PCA), locally linear embedding (LLE), independent component analysis (ICA), etc. These algorithms fundamentally reduce the dimensions of a feature set and have been employed for numerous purposes, including feature selection, feature reduction, health index construction, etc., and are unique in their individual architectures. For ease-of-use and familiarity in the domain, LLE was employed for reducing the features to a three-dimensional vector for visualizing their discriminative potentials. Accordingly, Figure 6 shows the feature assessment results.

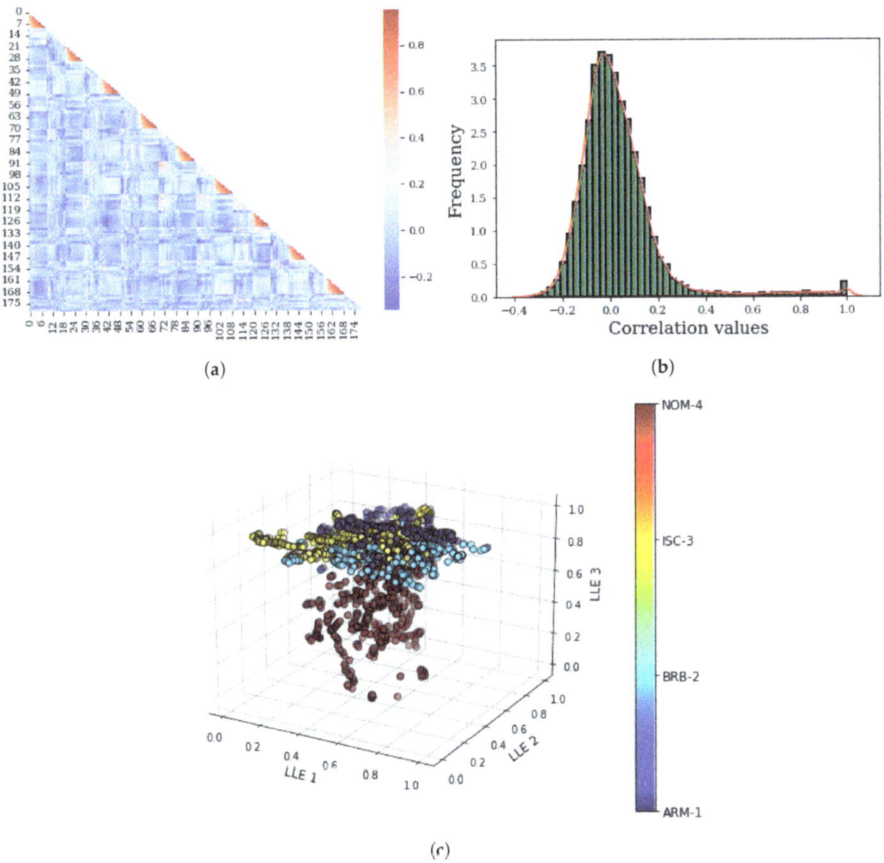

Figure 6. Feature evaluation results: (**a**) correlation heatmap between features, (**b**) probability density plot of the features, and (**c**) LLE-assisted discriminative property assessment.

Figure 6a shows the Spearman's correlation heatmap of the peak features extracted from motor current signals. Overall, the feature set, which formed a 180-dimensional feature matrix, is mostly uncorrelated, with correlation values normally distributed with a mean of zero, as shown in Figure 6b. This hints that the features are not correlated and are, hence, very useful for discriminative modeling. Further assessment of the features using the LLE-based feature visualization tool shows in Figure 6c that the dissimilarity between respective feature clusters per operating condition. They are reasonably isolated in space, as shown in the dark blue, light blue, yellow, and red circles corresponding to the ARM-1, BRB-2, ISC-3, and NOM-4 conditions, respectively.

5.3. ML-Based Diagnosis

Empirically, the feature extraction and evaluation processes described in the previous subsections provide the platform upon which traditional ML-based classifiers are deployed for fault classification. Practically, each ML-based classifier is unique in its architecture and learning principle, and this often poses a concern when choosing the most appropriate model for practical use. In addition, their respective cons and computational costs also pose valid concerns during decision making. Consequently, we explore (as much as possible) many popular traditional ML-based classifiers in our study. The classifiers summarized in

Table 2 were employed for training (using the training feature set) and testing (using the test feature set).

Table 2. Classifiers and their respective architecture.

Algorithm	Parameter	Value
Logistic regression (LR)	regularization	L1
Adaboost classifier (ABC)	*n* estimators, learning rate	50, 0.1
Naive Bayes classifier (NBC)	Gaussian	–
k-nearest neighbor (KNN)	k	5
Gaussian process classifier (GPC)	kernel	RBF
Random forest (RF)	*n* estimators	120
Gradient boosting classifier (GBC)	*n* estimators	1000
Decision tree (DT)	pruning	12
Multi-layer perceptron (MLP) classifier	*n* layers, learning rate	3, 0.001
Linear SVM	kernel	linear
Gaussian SVM	C, gamma	10, 1
Quadratic discriminant analysis (QDA)	regularization	0.001

For optimal efficiency, each algorithm has its own set of parameters and architecture, as shown in Table 2. Exhaustive parameter tuning optimized parameters for each algorithm, which are recorded in Table 2. Figure 7 illustrates the accuracy, precision, recall, and F1-scores resulting from ten-fold cross-validation of the algorithms on the test data.

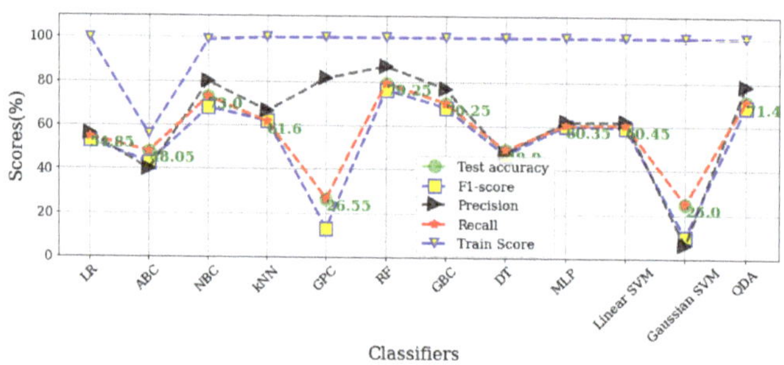

Figure 7. Global performance evaluation of the classifiers on the test data.

In general terms, accuracy measures a model's ability to predict classes correctly and is represented in Figure 7 in green circles. F-1 (represented by yellow squares with blue dotted lines) is calculated by taking the average of precision and recall, which determines the proportion of true predictions the model makes among all actual predictions. Precision determines the percentage of classes that are true and is represented by black triangles, while recall determines the percentage of predicted cases that are actually true and is represented by red stars. As observed, RF is the highest performing classifier, with a test accuracy of 79.25%. This is followed by NBC, QDA, and GBC, whose test accuracies are 73%, 71.4%, and 70.25%, respectively. On the downside, GPC and Gaussian SVM were the worst performing, with test accuracies of 26.55% and 25%, respectively, while the rest of the classifiers ranged between 40% and 62%.

It can be observed that the training scores of all the classifiers (except ABC) on the training data are almost 100%; however, their test performances are not as optimal as anticipated. This hints at the superiority of some classifiers over others. Interestingly, RF remains one of the most reliable ML-based classifiers and has been shown to be the most accurate in the proposed case study. From a different perspective, assessing the computational cost of the classifiers provides a further avenue for assessing their suitability for practical use, especially in cost-sensitive situations where computational power is a concern. Table 3 summarizes the computational costs (in seconds) of the classifiers for training and testing.

Table 3. Computational costs of training and testing process.

Classifier	LR	ABC	NBC	kNN	GPC	RF	GBC	DT	MLP	SVM-Lin	SVM-RBF	QDA
Cost (mSecs)	60	810	3	1	5030	3660	31210	72	0.71	51	370	17

Table 3 reveals that the most accurate classifier, RF, takes approximately 3660 milliseconds (3.66 s), whereas the second most accurate took much less than 1 s for the same process, yet returned a reliable test accuracy. However, its efficiency is limited to the underlying assumption that the input data distribution is Gaussian—which is not often the case for real-life applications. On the high side, GBC revealed itself as a greedy algorithm, as shown by its high computational cost of 31,210 milliseconds (31.2 s); yet it ranks third in the test comparative assessment. This is followed by GPC (whose cost is 5030 milliseconds), which is costlier than RF but still the second least accurate on the test data. Based on the comparison, a choice of classifier can be made according to the metric being assessed. Typically, computational speed is highly considered in most real-world scenarios, but not at the expense of predictive efficiency. Considering such circumstances, NBC may be preferred, since it offers both low computational cost and significantly high test accuracy. However, RF is an appropriate choice when there is abundant computing power available or when accuracy is critical.

Digging deeper into the algorithms, we assessed the class-specific predictive performance of the classifiers using the traditional confusion matrix, which reveals the probability of correct predictions of a classifier for each of the classes of interest, i.e., operating conditions. Figure 8 illustrates the confusion matrix resulting from ten-fold cross-validation of the algorithms based on the test data.

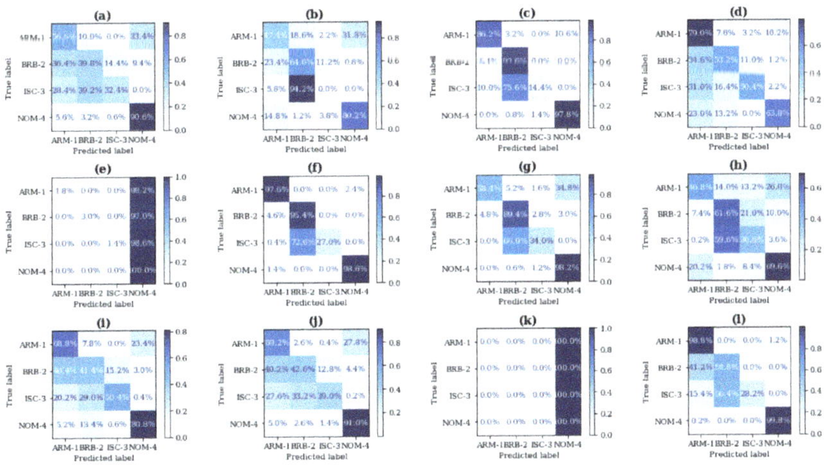

Figure 8. Confusion matrix on test data: (**a**) LR, (**b**) ABC, (**c**) NBC, (**d**) kNN, (**e**) GPC, (**f**) RF, (**g**) GBC, (**h**) DT, (**i**) MLP, (**j**) Linear SVM, (**k**) Gaussian SVM, and (**l**) QDA.

Close examination of Figure 8 reveals that GPC and Gaussian SVM returned the highest false positives (FP) per class (except NOM-4), as shown in Figure 8e,k. However, class-specific efficacy in prediction for RF (see Figure 8f) is observed in its high true positive values (across the diagonal). Unfortunately, the false-alarm rate for ISC-3 is observed in the 72.6% false negative to BRB-2. This implies that the model mostly recognizes data belonging to ISC-3 as belonging to BRB-2, and this reveals itself as a major limitation of our study.

6. Discussion, Open Issues, and Future Work

Despite the robustness and low cost of maintenance for extended use of SCIMs [1], the increasing industrial reliance on these power machines, with the critical need to assess for efficiency, reliability, and safety, as emphasized by this study's goals, cannot be overstated. This study focuses on presenting an ML model that can provide a high level of fault classification performance for various types of faults that are common in SCIMs; nevertheless, we consider the following to be some of the study's inadequacies: Although the findings revealed the cost efficiency and accuracy of the proposed peak-based feature extraction and ML-based diagnosis, the need for improved diagnostic performance is still critical considering that against the limitations of traditional ML-based algorithms (accompanied with hand-crafted feature extraction processes), the superior feature extraction and classification efficiencies of deep learning models have been shown in multiple studies. These deep learning models—convolutional neural networks, recurrent neural networks, etc.—are popular for automated feature learning; however, their mystical defiance from the statistical principles from which they were fundamentally designed has been a major issue for their adoption. In addition, other issues such as trustworthiness, computational cost, increased complexity, over-fitting/under-fitting, high stochasticity in learning, extensive parameterization/optimization, etc., contribute significantly to hesitation towards generalization. On the other hand, although the traditional, hand-crafted feature extraction process for ML-based diagnosis offers comparatively poorer diagnostic efficiencies in relation to deep learning models, it does offer a transparent architecture for ensuring explainability, empirical investigations, and trustworthiness.

Under realistic situations, the occurrence of the SCIM failure modes presented in this study are not mutually exclusive and may occur in little or intense degrees. This presents the issue of accurately identifying the fault type (or combination of fault types) in place. For example, turn-to-turn short circuit may be minimal (just two turns), intense (several turns in the same phase), or may become very intense when it grows to a phase-to-phase short circuit. Although this presents a broad opportunity for more extensive research, it becomes an endless uphill task to replicate all the possible failure modes, their individual degrees of severity, the possible failure combinations, and their respective degrees of combined severity. Nonetheless, our study offers a reliable feature extraction approach that is expected to direct continued research in the domain. On a different note, the frequency-domain approach for SCIM fault diagnosis has some limitations, which are mostly inherited from spectral leakage and lack of transient information. The models often perform poorly in finite-time window situations, require high-frequency resolution for adequate performance, and exhibit unstable variations in side-band frequencies in varying load situations. In addition, they are often flawed at detecting certain faults at no load conditions, especially the broken rotor bar [21,45]. On the other hand, deep learning and time-frequency domain signal processing techniques offer better discrimninative feature extraction efficiencies; however, they are often associated with high computational costs. Because current signals are often stationary and do not often exhibit any transient changes, we believe the proposed frequency-domain approach is more beneficial, considering that the efficiencies of its counterparts—time-domain, time-frequency-domain approaches, and deep learning methods—are insignificant, computationally expensive, and highly unexplainable, respectively.

At minimal load conditions (as presented in our study), the peak detection technique proposed herein offers reliable discrimininative efficiencies. Nonetheless, the high false negatives by the best-performing classifiers for ISC-3 poses a strong concern and is currently a major motivation for our continued research. Notwithstanding, our comparative study herein (for the ML classifiers) provides a valid yardstick for assessing the efficiencies of our future work. From a broader perspective, beyond the efficiencies of standalone sensing/monitoring methods, combination of multiple sensing techniques has been reported in several studies [45]. Such combinations may exploit vibration, temperature, acoustic emissions, and so on in a unified framework for comprehensive monitoring and/or diagnostic MCSA [29,30]. Although these sensor fusion techniques offer valid rationale, achieving a standardized approach for their use remains open for continued investigations. However, as part of our continued studies, we intend to explore deeper and more comprehensive approaches.

7. Conclusions

Squirrel cage induction motors are among the most popular industrial electrical motors due to their high motive power generation, durability, and low maintenance costs. The need for condition monitoring presents the opportunity for CS-based fault diagnosis; however, selecting the appropriate signals processing technique(s) for ML-based diagnostics remains open for continued research.

This paper presented a peak detection approach for discriminative feature extraction, which concatenates FFT, PSD, and ACF peak coordinates from the current signals sourced from a three-phase SCIM. These features are received by various ML-based classifiers, whose classification results are also presented in the study. An extensive comparison of ML-based diagnostic models provides a generalization paradigm for SCIM diagnosis. Results show that RF is the most accurate, with an accuracy of 79.25%, followed by NBC and QDA, with accuracies of 73% and 71.4%, respectively. Furthermore, computational cost assessment of the ML-based diagnostic models is conducted for improved diagnostic assessment of the models. Results show that RF's computational cost of 3.66 s is in an acceptable range, while NBC has the lowest at 0.003 seconds.

The confusion matrix of the best-performing models revealed that the turn-to-turn fault was imprecisely predicted, providing an avenue for future research. Amongst the paper's limitations, it is believed that the developed easy, nonintrusive, low-cost FDI framework offers a reliable direction for motivating future work.

Author Contributions: Conceptualization, C.N.O. and U.E.A.; methodology, C.N.O. and U.E.A.; software, U.E.A.; formal analysis, U.E.A.; investigation, C.N.O. and U.E.A.; resources, C.N.O., U.E.A., and J.-W.H.; data curation, C.N.O. and U.E.A.; writing—original draft, C.N.O. and U.E.A.; writing—review and editing, C.N.O. and U.E.A.; visualization, U.E.A.; supervision, J.-W.H.; project administration, J.-W.H.; funding acquisition, J.-W.H. All authors have read and agreed to the published version of the manuscript.

Funding: This research was supported by the Ministry of Science and ICT (MSIT), Korea, under the Grand Information Technology Research Center support program (IITP-2020-2020-0-01612) supervised by the Institute for Information & Communications Technology Planning & Evaluation (IITP).

Institutional Review Board Statement: Not applicable.

Informed Consent Statement: Not applicable.

Data Availability Statement: The data presented in this study are available on request from the corresponding author. The data are not publicly available due to laboratory regulations.

Conflicts of Interest: The authors declare no conflict of interest.

References

1. Choudhary, A.; Goyal, D.; Shimi, S.L. Condition Monitoring And Fault Diagnosis Of Induction Motors: A Review. *Arch. Comput. Methods Eng.* **2019**, *26*, 1221–1238. [CrossRef]
2. Bhowmik, P.I.; Pradhan, S.; Prakah, M. Fault Diagnostic And Monitoring Methods of Induction Motor: A Review. *IJACEEE* **2013**, *1*, 8681–8689.
3. Amanuel, T.; Ghirmay, A.; Ghebremeskel, H.; Ghebrehiwet, R.; Bahlibi, W. Comparative Analysis of Signal Processing Techniques for Fault Detection in Three Phase Induction Motor. *J. Electron. Inform.* **2021**, *1*, 61–76. [CrossRef]
4. Ali, M.Z.; Shabbir, M.N.S.K.; Zaman, S.M.K.; Liang, X. Machine Learning Based Fault Diagnosis for Single-and Multi-Faults for Induction Motors Fed by Variable Frequency Drives. In Proceedings of the 2019 IEEE Industry Applications Society Annual Meeting, Baltimore, MD, USA, 29 September–3 October 2019; pp. 1–14. [CrossRef]

5. Yang, T.; Pen, H.; Wang, Z.; Chang, C.S. Feature knowledge based fault detection of induction motors through the analysis of stator current data. *IEEE Trans. Instrum. Meas.* **2016**, *65*, 549–558. [CrossRef]
6. Nguyen, V.D.; Zwanenburg, E.; Limmer, S.; Luijben, T.; Back, T.; Olhofer, M. A Combination of Fourier Transform and Machine Learning for Fault Detection and Diagnosis of Induction motors. In Proceedings of the 8th International Conference on Dependable Systems and Their Applications (DSA), Yinchuan, China, 5–6 August 2021; pp. 344–351. [CrossRef]
7. Boudinar, A.H.; Aimer, A.F.; Khodja, M.E.A.; Benouzza, N. Induction Motor's Bearing Fault Diagnosis Using an Improved Short Time Fourier Transform. In *Lecture Notes in Electrical Engineering*; Springer: Cham, Switzerland, 2019; pp. 411–426. [CrossRef]
8. Yoo, Y.J. Fault Detection of Induction Motor Using Fast Fourier Transform with Feature Selection via Principal Component Analysis. *Int. J. Precis. Eng. Manuf.* **2019**, *20*, 1543–1552. [CrossRef]
9. Pusca, R.; Sbaa, S.; Bessous, N.; Romary, R.; Bousseksou, R. Mechanical Failure Detection in Induction Motors Using Stator Current and Stray Flux Analysis Techniques. *Eng. Proc.* **2022**, *14*, 19. [CrossRef]
10. Zaman, S.M.K.; Liang, X.; Li, W. Fault Diagnosis for Variable Frequency Drive-Fed Induction Motors Using Wavelet Packet Decomposition and Greedy-Gradient Max-Cut Learning. *IEEE Access* **2021**, *9*, 65490–65502. [CrossRef]
11. Gundewar, S.K.; Kane, P.V. Condition Monitoring and Fault Diagnosis of Induction Motor. *J. Vib. Eng. Technol.* **2021**, *9*, 643–674. [CrossRef]
12. Nakamura, H.; Asano, K.; Usuda, S.; Mizuno, Y. A Diagnosis Method of Bearing and Stator Fault in Motor Using Rotating Sound Based on Deep Learning. *Energies* **2021**, *14*, 1319. [CrossRef]
13. Sadeghi, R.; Samet, H.; Ghanbari, T. Detection of Stator Short-Circuit Faults in Induction Motors Using the Concept of Instantaneous Frequency. *IEEE Trans. Ind. Inform.* **2019**, *15*, 99. [CrossRef]
14. Garcia-Bracamonte, J.E.; Ramirez-Cortes, J.M.; de Jesus Rangel-Magdaleno, J.; Gomez-Gil, P.; Peregrina-Barreto, H.; Alarcon-Aquino, V. An Approach on MCSA-Based Fault Detection Using Independent Component Analysis and Neural Networks. *IEEE Trans. Instrum. Meas.* **2019**, *65*, 1353–1361. [CrossRef]
15. Gaeid, K.S.; Ping, H.W.; Khalid, M.; Salih, A.L. Fault Diagnosis of Induction Motor Using MCSA and FFT. *Sci. Acad. Publ.* **2011**, *1*, 85–92. [CrossRef]
16. Kafeel, A.; Aziz, S.; Awais, M.; Khan, M.A.; Afaq, K.; Idris, S.A.; Alshazly, H.; Mostafa, S.M. An Expert System for Rotating Machine Fault Detection Using Vibration Signal Analysis. *Sensors* **2021**, *21*, 7587. [CrossRef] [PubMed]
17. CusidÓCusido, J.; Romeral, L.; Ortega, J.A. GarcÍaGarcia Espinosa, A. Fault Detection in Induction Machines Using Power Spectral Density in Wavelet Decomposition. *IEEE Trans. Ind. Electron.* **2008**, *55*, 633–643. [CrossRef]
18. Benbouzid, M.E.H.; Vieira, M.; Theys, C. Induction motors' faults detection and localization using stator current advanced signal processing techniques. *IEEE Trans. Power Electron.* **1999**, *14*, 14–22. [CrossRef]
19. Jena, D.P.; Panigrahi, S.N. Automatic gear and bearing fault localization using vibration and acoustic signals. *Appl. Acoust.* **2015**, *98*, 20–33. [CrossRef]
20. Bessam, B.; Menacer, A.; Boumehraz, M.; Cherif, H. Detection of broken rotor bar faults in induction motor at low load using neural network. *Isa Trans.* **2016**, *64*, 241–246. [CrossRef]
21. Das, S.; Purkait, P.; Chakravorti, S. Separating induction Motor Current Signature for stator winding faults from that due to supply voltage unbalances. In Proceedings of the 2012 1st International Conference on Power and Energy in NERIST (ICPEN), Nirjuli, India, 28–29 December 2012; pp. 1–6. [CrossRef]
22. Hussain, M.; Soother, D.K.; Kalwar, I.H.; Memon, T.D. Stator winding fault detection and classification in three—phase induction motor. *Intell. Autom. Soft Comput.* **2021**, *29*, 869–883. [CrossRef]
23. Prahesti, F.E.; Asfani, D.A.; Yulistya Negara, I.M.; Dewantara, B.Y. Three-Phase Induction Motor Short Circuit Stator Detection Using an External Flux Sensor. In Proceedings of the 2020 International Seminar on Intelligent Technology and Its Applications (ISITIA), Surabaya, Indonesia, 22–23 July 2020; pp. 375–380. [CrossRef]
24. Peeters, C.; Guillaume, P.; Helsen, J. Vibration-based bearing fault detection for operations and maintenance cost reduction in wind energy. *Renew. Energy* **2018**, *98*, 74–87. [CrossRef]
25. Deeb, M.; Kotelenets, N.F.; Assaf, T.; Sultan, H.M.; Akayasheedept, A.S.A. Three Phase Induction Motor Short Circuits Fault Diagnosis using MCSA and NSC. In Proceedings of the 2021 3rd International Youth Conference on Radio Electronics, Electrical and Power Engineering (REEPE), Moscow, Russia, 11–13 March 2021; pp. 1–6. [CrossRef]
26. Messaoudi, M.; Flah, A.; Alotaibi, A.A.; Althobaiti, A.; Sbita, L.; Ziad El-Bayeh, C. Diagnosis and Fault Detection of Rotor Bars in Squirrel Cage Induction Motors Using Combined Park's Vector and Extended Park's Vector Approaches. *Electronics* **2022**, *11*, 380. [CrossRef]
27. Yu, H.; Wang, B.; Li, Y.; Gao, Z. Spectral decomposition-based explicit integration method for fully non-stationary seismic responses of large-scale structures. *Mech. Syst. Signal Process.* **2022**, 168, 108735. [CrossRef]
28. Rhif, M.; Ben Abbes, A.; Farah, I.R.; Martínez, B.; Sang, Y. Wavelet Transform Application for/in Non-Stationary Time-Series Analysis: A Review. *Appl. Sci.* **2019**, *9*, 1345. [CrossRef]
29. Chaitanya, B.K.; Yadav, A.; Pazoki, M.; Abdelaziz, A.Y. Chapter 8—A comprehensive review of islanding detection methods. In *Uncertainties in Modern Power Systems*; Academic Press: Cambridge, MA, USA, 2021; pp. 1664–1674. [CrossRef]
30. Lee, G.-H.; Akpudo, U.E.; Hur, J.-W. FMECA and MFCC-Based Early Wear Detection in Gear Pumps in Cost-Aware Monitoring Systems. *Electronics* **2021**, *10*, 2939. [CrossRef]

31. Chen, X.; Yang, Y.; Cui, Z.; Shen, J. Wavelet Denoising for the Vibration Signals of Wind Turbines Based on Variational Mode Decomposition and Multiscale Permutation Entropy. *IEEE Access* **2020**, *8*, 40347–40356. [CrossRef]
32. Akpudo, U.E.; Hur, J.W. Towards bearing failure prognostics: A practical comparison between data-driven methods for industrial applications. *J. Mech. Sci. Technol.* **2020**, *34*, 4161–4172. [CrossRef]
33. Han, T.; Jiang, D.; Zhao, Q.; Wang, L.; Yin, K. Comparison of random forest, artificial neural networks and support vector machine for intelligent diagnosis of rotating machinery. *Trans. Inst. Meas. Control.* **2017**, *40*, 2681–2693. [CrossRef]
34. Asman, S.H.; Ab Aziz, N.F.; Ungku Amirulddin, U.A.; Ab Kadir, M.Z.A. Decision Tree Method for Fault Causes Classification Based on RMS-DWT Analysis in 275 kV Transmission Lines Network. *Appl. Sci.* **2021**, *11*, 4031. [CrossRef]
35. Nabipour, M.; Nayyeri, P.; Jabani, S.S.; Mosavi, A. Predicting Stock Market Trends Using Machine Learning and Deep Learning Algorithms Via Continuous and Binary Data; A Comparative Analysis. *IEEE Access* **2020**, *8*, 150199–150212. [CrossRef]
36. Stavropoulos, G.; van Vorstenbosch, R.; van Schooten, F.; Smolinska, A. Random Forest and Ensemble Methods. *Compr. Chemom. Chem. Biochem. Data Anal.* **2020**, *2*, 661–672. [CrossRef]
37. Chen, T.; Guestrin, C. XGBoost: A Scalable Tree Boosting System. In Proceedings of the KDD'16: 22nd ACM SIGKDD International Conference on Knowledge Discovery and Data Minings, San Francisco, CA, USA, 13–17 August 2016; pp. 785–794. [CrossRef]
38. Yang, J.; Sun, Z.; Chen, Y. Fault Detection Using the Clustering-kNN Rule for Gas Sensor Arrays. *Sensors* **2016**, *16*, 2069. [CrossRef]
39. Pietrzak, P.; Wolkiewicz, M. On-line Detection and Classification of PMSM Stator Winding Faults Based on Stator Current Symmetrical Components Analysis and the KNN Algorithm. *Electronics* **2021**, *10*, 1786. [CrossRef]
40. Akpudo, U.E.; Hur, J.W. A Multi-Domain Diagnostics Approach for Solenoid Pumps Based on Discriminative Features. *IEEE Access* **2020**, *8*, 175020–175034. [CrossRef]
41. Carreras, J.; Kikuti, Y.Y.; Miyaoka, M.; Hiraiwa, S.; Tomita, S.; Ikoma, H.; Kondo, Y.; Ito, A.; Nakamura, N.; Hamoudi, R. A Combination of Multilayer Perceptron, Radial Basis Function Artificial Neural Networks and Machine Learning Image Segmentation for the Dimension Reduction and the Prognosis Assessment of Diffuse Large B-Cell Lymphoma. *AI* **2021**, *2*, 106–134. [CrossRef]
42. Piotrowski, J. *Shaft Alignment Handbook*, 3rd ed.; CRC Press: Boca Raton, FL, USA, 2006. [CrossRef]
43. Garcia-Calva, T.A.; Morinigo-Sotelo, D.; Fernandez-Cavero, V.; Garcia-Perez, A.; Romero-Troncoso, R.d.J. Early Detection of Broken Rotor Bars in Inverter-Fed Induction Motors Using Speed Analysis of Startup Transients. *Energies* **2021**, 14, 1469. [CrossRef]
44. Swana, E.F.; Doorsamy, W. Investigation of Combined Electrical Modalities for Fault Diagnosis on a Wound-Rotor Induction Generator. *IEEE Access* **2019**, *7*, 32333–32342. [CrossRef]
45. Bouraiou, A. A comparative investigation between the mcsa method and the hilbert transform for broken rotor bar fault diagnostics, in a closed-loop three-phase induction motor. *UPB Sci. Bull. Ser. C Electr. Eng.* **2020**, *81*, 209–296.

algorithms

MDPI

Article

Tailored Quantum Alternating Operator Ansätzes for Circuit Fault Diagnostics

Hannes Leipold [1,2,3,4,*], Federico M. Spedalieri [1,5] and Eleanor Rieffel [3]

1 Information Sciences Institute, University of Southern California, Marina del Rey, CA 90292, USA
2 Department of Computer Science, University of Southern California, Los Angeles, CA 90089, USA
3 Quantum Artificial Intelligence Laboratory (QuAIL), NASA Ames Research Center, Moffett Field, CA 94035, USA
4 USRA Research Institute for Advanced Computer Science (RIACS), Mountain View, CA 94043, USA
5 Department of Electrical and Computer Engineering, University of Southern California, Los Angeles, CA 90089, USA
* Correspondence: leipold@usc.edu

Abstract: The quantum alternating operator ansatz (QAOA) and constrained quantum annealing (CQA) restrict the evolution of a quantum system to remain in a constrained space, often with a dimension much smaller than the whole Hilbert space. A natural question when using quantum annealing or a QAOA protocol to solve an optimization problem is to select an initial state for the wavefunction and what operators to use to evolve it into a solution state. In this work, we construct several ansatzes tailored to solve the combinational circuit fault diagnostic (CCFD) problem in different subspaces related to the structure of the problem, including superpolynomially smaller subspaces than the whole Hilbert space. We introduce a family of dense and highly connected circuits that include small instances but can be scaled to larger sizes as a useful collection of circuits for comparing different quantum algorithms. We compare the different ansätzes on instances randomly generated from this family under different parameter selection methods. The results support that ansätzes more closely tailored to exploiting the structure of the underlying optimization problems can have better performance than more generic ansätzes.

Keywords: quantum algorithms; quantum computation; combinatorial optimization; circuit fault diagnostics

1. Introduction

We introduce and characterize several different quantum alternating operator ansatz (QAOA) [1] approaches to solving the combinational circuit fault diagnostic (CCFD) problem, a combinatorial optimization problem of importance for diagnosing faults in circuits. In particular, we identify different constrained spaces of interest and explore various constructions of mixing and cost operators that allow us to evolve within each constrained subspace, allowing the protocol to focus on bringing the support of the system's wavefunction to an optimal or approximately optimal state within this subspace that can be significantly smaller than the space of the physical qubits needed to run the system. There are many such relevant subspaces, and through a different selection of mixing and phase separation operators, even the same subspaces can be explored in very different ways.

After describing QAOAs for optimization problems, we delineate the stuck-at-fault model of CCFD problems considered in this paper and how they can be cast as optimization problems. We then develop several different ansätzes for solving this optimization problem, beginning with the least constrained (measured as the resulting size of the constrained space maintained) and ending with the most constrained. The most constrained ansatz has a superpolynomially smaller constrained space. For circuits with a logarithmic or lower minimum fault explanation, it can be modified to have a constrained space that grows subexponentially in the number of wires while the most generic approach grows exponentially.

The methods used for constructing ansätzes in this domain can be useful for constructing more tailored approaches for other domains, which is an interesting avenue for future quantum algorithms. The results from running each ansatz under several parameter selections indicate that ansätzes more closely tailored to a problem can have better performance than more generic ansätzes. The relative success of the simple parameter selection methods used in this manuscript are of interest to researchers focusing on QAOAs for other domains.

For many classes of combinatorial optimization problems that are NP-hard, the features of specific instances can make them, in practice, more or less accessible to different algorithms. The features of typical CCFD instances, such as a planar-like topology that is often amendable to embedding on local two-dimensional lattice quantum architectures, make them a strong candidate for quantum algorithms utilized on NISQ devices. Given the real-life applications of CCFD problems, they have become problems of interest for leveraging the potential quantum advantage for industrial purposes [2]. Our results in this manuscript support that tailored ansätzes should be explored on NISQ quantum computers to solve CCFD problems. The family of scalable, dense, and highly connected circuits we introduce is a useful testbed for such devices.

Even between different QAOA algorithms, the features of particular instances can affect which approaches are more or less promising. For example, we consider an ansatz that is similar to a recently studied CQA approach [3] that shows promise in the regime where an instance has higher degeneracy in the solution space and higher minimum fault explanations, while another approach maintains a subexponential constrained space when there is an upper bound on the minimum fault explanation. This suggests that the scaling of the minimum fault explanation for the instances of interest is important for determining the best ansatz to utilize.

However, there are still more considerations for implementing these approaches on quantum systems, including the preparation of the initial state and considering the best implementation of the required unitaries through a specific gate set. Certainly, more than the size of the constraint is important for determining the best ansatz for a problem, and it remains an open challenge to identify what specific features of the mixing operators and phase-separating operators would lead to the best performance.

In Section 2, we introduce a QAOA for combinatorial optimization problems and develop the principles around constrained quantum evolution within this context. In Section 3, we describe the single-pair input/output circuit fault diagnostic problem over the stuck-at fault (SAF) model, where circuit wires are either healthy or permanently stuck at one or zero. In Section 4, we delineate different QAOA protocols, with different resulting constrained spaces. In Section 5, we introduce a family of circuit instances to explore the suitability of our QAOA approaches for solving this problem for small sizes. In Section 6, we benchmark the approaches on the distribution of small-sized circuit instances introduced in Section 5. Our results support that tailored ansätzes can be beneficial for obtaining better performance in optimization problems such as CCFD problems, where there is structure in the underlying problem that can be exploited.

2. Constrained Evolution in Quantum Alternating Operator Ansätzes

For combinatorial optimization problems, there have been recent advances in the research of applying quantum algorithms to solve such problems that are centered around the quantum approximate optimization algorithm (QAOA1) [4], which is a very general protocol to approximately (or exactly) solve combinatorial optimization problems, such as the Max Cut problem [4–7]. However, further generalizations of this concept, such as the RQAOA [8] and quantum alternating operator ansatz (QAOA) [1,5,9], have been developed in the hope to better tailor protocols to particular problems and thereby exploit their specific structures. For the purpose of this paper, we focus on using QAOA protocols to find optimal solutions to a combinatorial optimization problem. For example, the authors of [5] demonstrated a near-optimal quantum unstructured search algorithm based on using coherent phase-separation operators in the QAOA setting. Under reasonable complexity-theoretic assumptions, the QAOA cannot be efficiently simulated by any classical computer [10]. For a small number of qubits, this has been realized on an NISQ [11] device [12].

Given a general binary optimization problem with N bits, the quantum computer works with N qubits over a space $\mathbb{C}^{2^N}$. The wavefunction of the system $|\psi\rangle$ is a normalized, complex-valued vector in this space, and potential actions on this state (i.e., algorithmic steps) are represented by unitary operators.

The QAOA works by starting the quantum system in a prepared state and then applying a series of angle-parameterized unitaries to evolve the system into a state that is then measured over a predetermined basis. The result can then be interpreted as a bit-string solution to the optimization problem. The QAOA divides the task of evolving the system into P rounds, each involving the application of two sets of operators. The first is a set of mixing operators, which are discussed in greater detail later. The second is a diagonal unitary operator associated with a classical cost function that acts to essentially evaluate the quality of different configurations.

Given a classical cost function $C(x)$, in both the QAOA and QAOA1, Hamiltonian form phase separation operators are used such that $U_c(\alpha) = \sum_{x\in\{0,1\}^N} e^{i\alpha\, C(x)}|\,x\,\rangle\langle\,x\,|$, where $|\,x\,\rangle$ are the orthonormal computational basis states in $\mathbb{C}^{2^N}$. Any such state $|\,x\,\rangle$ (a ket-state) can be written as an outerproduct state of individual qubit states $|\,x\,\rangle = |\,x_1,\ldots,x_N\,\rangle = |\,x_1\,\rangle\ldots|\,x_N\,\rangle$ with $x \in \{0,1\}^N$, $|\,x_i\,\rangle \in \mathbb{C}^2$ and $x_i \in \{0,1\}$. As such, the classical cost function is interpreted as a classical Hamiltonian $H_c = \sum_{x\in\{0,1\}^n} C(x)|\,x\,\rangle\langle\,x\,|$ (a real-valued diagonal matrix in $\mathbb{C}^{2^N}$). The complex exponentiation of a Hermitian operator is a unitary operator, and so $U_c(\alpha)$ is a diagonal unitary operator.

For example, a marked state cost function associated with a single solution state $x^* = (1,\ldots,1)$ could be $C(x) = -\prod_{i=1}^{n} x_i$. Then, $U_c(\alpha) = \mathbb{1} - (1-e^{-i\alpha})|\,x^*\,\rangle\langle\,x^*\,|$. The wave function associated with the quantum system $|\,\psi\,\rangle = \sum_{x\in\{0,1\}^n} a_x|\,x\,\rangle$ will therefore evolve to $|\,\psi\,\rangle = a_{x^*}e^{-i\alpha}|\,x^*\,\rangle + \sum_{x\in\{0,1\}^n/\{x^*\}} a_x|\,x\,\rangle$, and so the behavior of $U_c(\alpha)$ is to add the same phases to computational basis states that have the same energy evaluations according to the cost function $C(x)$.

QAOA1 is a type of QAOA approach with a specific mixing operator and a fixed starting state. Both of these conditions are replaced with a more general condition in the QAOA. In QAOA1, we begin in the uniform superposition state $|+\rangle^{\otimes n} = \frac{1}{\sqrt{2^n}}\sum_{x\in\{0,1\}^n}|\,x\,\rangle$ so that every computational basis state $|\,x\,\rangle$ has the same amplitude. The mixing operators are single local Pauli X operators:

$$U_d(\beta) = \prod_{j=1}^{n} e^{-i\beta\sigma_j^x}.$$

The action of σ_j^x on qubit j is to flip the bit, mapping $|\,1\,\rangle$ to $|\,0\,\rangle$ and vice versa. Any QAOA approach that utilizes U_d as mentioned above is considered a QAOA1 approach for the purpose of our descriptions. As such, QAOA1 proposes a very specific type of ansatz, in which the mixing operator takes this form for any problem. The QAOA will generalize this to allow for more structured ansatzes.

Then, for a single round t_i of a QAOA (including QAOA1), we pick two degrees α_i and β_i and evolve the wave function as $|\,\psi(t_i)\,\rangle = U_d(\beta_i)U_c(\alpha_i)|\,\psi(t_{i-1})\,\rangle$. U_c changes the phase of states based on their evaluation from the classical cost function in the computational basis, while U_d acts as a mixer, leading to interference between the states in the superposition and potentially leading to concentration on low-lying energy states based on the cost function $C(x)$ after several rounds. Indeed, as the number of rounds P goes to infinity, one can select α_i and β_i such that $|\,\psi(t_P)\,\rangle$ is guaranteed to minimize the cost function $C(x)$ [4].

For a given finite value P, there are $2P$ angles to select for running the algorithm which can therefore be cast as an optimization task where one wishes to find the angles that lead to a minimization of the cost function $C(x)$. QAOA1, as well as the QAOA, is a type of variational quantum algorithm (VQA) [13] for which finding the optimum parameters is typically an NP-hard problem [14]. The landscape of the final cost given by the quantum algorithm is known to suffer from a barren plateau [13,15–17], and optimization with random starts can lead to convergence to the local minima [6,13]. Nonetheless, the optimum or near-optimum solutions can follow similar patterns across instances [6,18]. For a more detailed discussion, we refer the reader to [13]. The techniques utilized in this paper will be discussed Section 6. Once the algorithm has run for P rounds, the wave function of the system is measured in the computational basis $\{|\,x\,\rangle \,|\, x \in \{0,1\}^n\}$ such that the wave function collapses to a single state in that basis according to the Born rule, where $\Pr(x) = |\langle\, x \,|\, \psi(t_P)\rangle|^2$.

For many classes of problems, including certain class of linear and quadratic constraint problems, it is possible to find alternative mixing operators that allow us to limit the evolution of the wave function to a feasible subspace of a collection of those constraints [1,19–22]. The general problem is NP-hard, but there is a simple polynomial algorithm for bounded operators [22]. In QAOA1, the mixing operator utilized can be associated with there being no constraint placed on the evolution, since every state is reachable under its action (although it is clearly not the only such mixing operator). The two essential requirements for the mixing operators are that they must take actions moving states in the constrained space to potentially any other state in that constrained space, but they cannot move such states outside of the constrained space.

As such, the QAOA describes a more general approach than QAOA1, in which the mixing operator and phase-separating operators can be much more general. In particular, they are usually tailored to the specific type of symmetries of the underlying problem (such as the ansatz to the algorithm). Notice that the QAOA shares the same acronym as QAOA1 in the literature. For example, ref. [1] lists a compendium of mixing and phase-separating operators that can be utilized for different combinatorial optimization problems. Specific types of mixers have been studied more extensively. For example, XY mixers are associated with a very simple kind of equality constraint that makes them useful for many types of combinatorial optimization problems [23] as well as quantum chemistry [24].

3. Circuit Fault Diagnostics

Diagnosing errors and faults for gate-based digital circuits is an area of intense research, as large-scale integrated circuits and specialized circuit designs have become abundant in many scientific and engineering disciplines. Increasingly sophisticated automation techniques used to check and correct errors in the circuit design and fabrication are increasingly relied upon in practice. Because of the underlying combinatorial nature of this problem as well as the local design of many modern circuits, this is a class of problems that is well suited to typical NISQ [2,11] architectures.

We employ a simple stuck-at-fault model for analyzing circuits with a given string of inputs and empirically found string of outputs [25]. Let n be the number of wires in the circuit and n_o be the number of output wires. Each wire in the circuit is either healthy or stuck at either zero (SA0) or one (SA1). Under the assumption that faults are equally likely to occur on every wire, the task of circuit fault diagnostics (CFD) is an optimization problem for finding the minimum number of faults needed to explain the input-output pair [2].

For the purpose of our discussion in this paper, we consider gates that are one-input/one-output, two-input/one-output, or one-input/two-output. One-input/one-output gates are an identity gate ID or an inverter gate INV. Two-input/one-output gates are OR, AND, XOR, NOR, NAND, or XNR. One-input/two-output gates are a fan-out gate FAN, a fan-out gate with an inverter on the first output F10, a fan-out gate with an inverter on the second output F01, or a fan-out gate with an inverter on both F11.

A configuration for the problem is a $2n$-bit string, where over bits $1, \ldots, n$ are the wire bits and over bits $n+1, \ldots, 2n$ are the fault bits. A valid configuration $(w_1, \ldots, w_n, f_1, \ldots, f_n)$ has an erroneous value of a wire w_i if the corresponding f_i is nonzero.

The inputs to a circuit are considered to also be potentially faulty such that the input wires themselves could be SA0 or SA1, but the output wires have to correspond to the empirical value they have (otherwise, this diagnosis would be invalid), but that value may come from error propagation in the circuit or from the output value itself being SA0 or SA1.

For whatever faults are present in the circuit, the output values can always be made to match the empirical value by taking the nonconforming output values and flipping their values (as well as their associated fault bit). As such, the size of the valid configuration space is 2^{n-n_o} [3], since we have precisely $n - n_o$ wire locations where the fault flag can be 0 or 1. (The fault flag on the n_o output wires is then forced to be such that the configuration is indeed valid.) Figure 1 shows all possible valid fault explanations for a small circuit. Note that there are 3 non-output wires and 2^3 valid fault configurations.

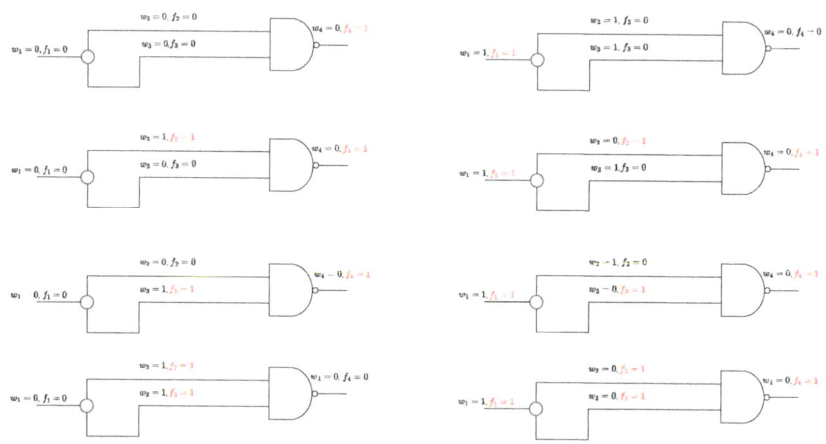

Figure 1. All possible valid fault configurations for a small circuit with one FAN gate and one NAND gate that has a faulty output. The diagrams on the top left and right show minimum fault explanations for this instance.

3.1. *Valid and Invalid Configurations Around Gates*

Enforcing the logic of the circuit on our configurations is essentially enforcing the logic of each individual gate on the part of the configuration that corresponds to that gate's inputs and outputs.

Valid configurations around gates follow the same logical delineation as valid configurations for the entire circuit. For any circuit or subcircuit, including a single gate, we can list the potential valid configurations by considering the different input/output pairs. If a configuration is valid for a particular input/output pair, it cannot be valid for any other, and so the valid configurations always make disjointed sets. For that circuit or subcircuit, as discussed before, the inputs can potentially be faulty, but the outputs must match their empirical values. However, the size of the different valid configuration sets is always the same.

As such, the valid configurations around a gate are split by what the inputs before considering the fault status are (If they differ from this value, there must be an associated fault on this input.) and what the output after considering the fault status is (i.e., the same situation as for the circuit at large). Table 1 gives a full description of all the valid subconfiguration spaces for an NAND gate, where the first element in each entry is the trivial valid configuration that exists for every subcircuit (or the whole circuit) by applying the faults on the outputs only (i.e., all wires are healthy, except the outputs that disagree with the logical value they should have).

If a configuration is valid and maintains a state status as described by an entry in Table 1, then swapping this subconfiguration with a state status in the same entry will also be valid, since we did not change the values that came from previous gates or were set as global inputs to the circuit, nor did we change the value of the output (which is then used as an input to a gate or is a global output for the circuit).

For a circuit with a collection of gates G, we consider the input and output wires (I_g and O_g) for that gate. The collection of valid configuration sets around this gate

$$V_g = \{V_g^{(S_{I_g};S_{O_g})} | S_{I_g} \in \{0,1\}^{|I_g|}, S_{O_g} \in \{0,1\}^{|O_g|}\},$$

is indexed by what the potential values the wire inputs S_{I_g} are set to without faults and what the potential wire outputs S_{O_g} are set to. For example, S_{I_g} for an NAND gate in the fault model is a collection of the possible inputs $\{(0,0),(0,1),(1,0),(1,1)\}$, and S_{O_g} is a collection of the possible outputs $\{(0),(1)\}$.

Table 1. Each kind of input/output pair for a faulty NAND is described. Each entry has different valid configurations, and configurations in the same entry form a subspace such that the action of the driver terms we construct connects the configurations of this subspace.

Entry	IO Pair	Valid Configurations
1	(0,0;0)	(0,0,0;0,0,1), (1,1,0;1,1,0), (1,0,0;1,0,1), (0,1,0;0,1,1)
2	(1,0;0)	(1,0,0;0,0,1), (1,1,0;0,1,0), (0,0,0;1,0,1), (0,1,0;1,1,1)
3	(0,1;0)	(0,1,0;0,0,1), (1,1,0;1,0,0), (0,0,0;0,1,1), (1,0,0;1,1,1)
4	(1,1;0)	(1,1,0;0,0,0), (0,0,0;1,1,1), (1,0,0;0,1,1), (0,1,0;1,0,1)
5	(0,0;1)	(0,0,1;0,0,0), (1,1,1;1,1,1), (1,0,1;1,0,0), (0,1,1;0,1,0)
6	(1,0;1)	(1,0,1;0,0,0), (1,1,1;0,1,1), (0,0,1;1,0,0), (0,1,1;1,1,0)
7	(0,1;1)	(0,1,1;0,0,0), (1,1,1;1,0,1), (0,0,1;0,1,0), (1,0,1;1,1,0)
8	(1,1;1)	(1,1,1;0,0,1), (0,0,1;1,1,0), (1,0,1;0,1,0), (0,1,1;1,0,0)

4. QAOA Approaches to CFD

In this section, we give details on the construction for several QAOA approaches to solving the CFD problem, with each constraining the evolution of the wave function to a specific subspace and using mixing terms which connect all feasible states within this space to one another in different ways. We map each bit in the $2n$-bit string to a qubit such that the wave function of our system $|\psi\rangle$ is a normalized vector in $\mathbb{C}^{2^{2n}}$. At the end of the QAOA algorithm, we measure $|\psi\rangle$ in the computational basis to extract a solution to our problem.

4.1. Approach 1: Transverse Field with a QUBO

This approach is closely related to a Hamiltonian description of this problem, which is similar to, for example, the approach described in [2] for using a transverse field and an Ising Hamiltonian with explicit fault mappings to represent this problem. As such, our approach is in the spirit of QAOA1 for Ising spin problems.

The mixing operators are the Pauli X operators:

$$U_d(\beta_t) = \prod_{i=1}^{n-n_o} e^{-i\beta_t \sigma_i^x}.$$

Since the output values of the circuit have to match the given empirical values, they are not allowed to change during the problem. As such, these qubits can be integrated out of the problem. The phase-separating operators are associated with an Ising Hamiltonian:

$$U_c(\alpha_t) = e^{i\alpha_t H_f},$$

where the Hamiltonian counts the number of faults and enforces the logic of the gates:

$$H_f = \left(\sum_{i=n-n_o+1}^{2n-n_o} (\mathbb{1} - \sigma_i^z)/2 \right) + \kappa \left(\sum_{g \in \mathcal{G}} H_g \right),$$

where $H_g = \sum_{V_g^r \in V_g} \left(\mathbb{1} - \sum_{v \in V_g^r} | v \rangle\langle v | \right)$ associates a cost to the state being in an invalid set for that particular gate. If a configuration x fails to be a valid configuration in the fault around a gate g, then H_g will associate a cost to the state x.

To ensure consistency with the model, we can set $\kappa = n_o + 1$, the number of outputs, so that it is never advantageous to break a gate over placing the faults at the very end of the circuit. The number of output bits is an upper bound on the number of faults of the minimal fault diagnosis. For individual instances, we can set κ to any value greater than the number of faulty output bits, which is less than or equal to n_o.

As in QAOA1, our initial state is the uniform superposition over $2n - n_o$ qubits: $| \psi \rangle = | + \rangle^{\otimes 2n-n_o} = \frac{1}{\sqrt{2^{n-n_o}}} \sum_{x \in \{0,1\}^{2n-n_o}} | x \rangle$.

4.2. Approach 2: Transverse and XY Mixer with a QUBO

Any solution to the single input/output CFD problem has at most n_o faults. To exploit this bound, we can employ the XY mixer such that over the fault bits $(f_1, \ldots, f_n)$, we impose the constraint $\sum_{i=1}^{n} f_i \leq n_o$. This can be achieved in different ways, for example, by introducing n_o ancilla qubits and employing the standard ring XY mixer over the n fault bits and n_o ancilla bits.

Note that the XY mixer operating on a computational basis state of N qubits keeps the number of ones fixed, so if the initial wave function only has support for the computational basis states with k ones ($| \psi \rangle = \sum_{x \in \{0,1\}^N \text{ s.t. } |x|=k} a_x | x \rangle$), then the wave function after applying any collection of XY mixers will still have support only for computational basis states with k ones.

To achieve states with a number of ones between 0 and k, we can add k ancillas and then apply the XY mixer on $N + k$ qubits such that when those mixers are applied to a wave function $\left| \psi^{N+k} \right\rangle = \sum_{x \in \{0,1\}^N \text{ s.t. } |x| \leq k} \sum_{y \in \{0,1\}^k \text{ s.t. } |y|=k-|x|} a_{x+y} | x \rangle | y \rangle$, the constraint on the number of ones in the wave function is maintained. Then, at the time of measurement, we simply discard the ancilla qubits and consider the resulting state over N qubits.

Since the outputs, as in the previous approach, can be integrated out, and so the wire bits correspond to the qubits between 1 and $n - n_o$, the fault bits correspond to qubits between $n - n_o$ and $2n - n_o$, and the ancillas correspond to qubits between $2n - n_o + 1$ and $2n$. Utilizing the XY mixer over qubits between $2n - n_o + 1$ and $2n$ and the transverse field applied on the wire bits leads to

$$H_d = \left(\sum_{i=1}^{n-n_o} \sigma_i^x \right) + \left(\sigma_n^x \sigma_{n-n_o+1}^x + \sigma_n^y \sigma_{n-n_o+1}^y \right) + \sum_{i=n-n_o+1}^{2n-1} \left(\sigma_i^x \sigma_{i+1}^x + \sigma_i^y \sigma_{i+1}^y \right),$$

which can be split into two noncommuting Hamiltonians:

$$H_1 = \left(\sum_{i=1}^{n-n_o} \sigma_i^x\right) + \left(\sigma_n^x \sigma_{n-n_o+1}^x + \sigma_n^y \sigma_{n-n_o+1}^y\right) + \sum_{i=1}^{\lfloor (n+n_o)/2 \rfloor} \left(\sigma_{n+2i}^x \sigma_{n+2i+1}^x + \sigma_{n+2i}^y \sigma_{n+2i+1}^y\right),$$

and

$$H_2 = \sum_{i=1}^{\lfloor (n+n_o)/2 \rfloor} \left(\sigma_{n+2i-1}^x \sigma_{n+2i}^x + \sigma_{n+2i-1}^y \sigma_{n+2i}^y\right).$$

When $n + n_o$ is odd, H_1 also has a noncommuting term associated with qubits $n - n_o + 1, n - n_o + 2$, and $2n$. As for the XY mixing operators [23], we can apply commuting mixing operators associated with H_1 and then H_2 as follows:

$$U_d(\beta_t) = \left(\prod_{i=1}^{n-n_o} e^{-i\beta_t \sigma_i^x}\right)\left(\prod_{i=1}^{\lfloor (n+n_o)/2 \rfloor} e^{-i\beta_t \left(\sigma_{n+2i}^x \sigma_{n+2i+1}^x + \sigma_{n+2i}^y \sigma_{n+2i+1}^y\right)}\right)$$
$$\left(e^{-i\beta_t \left(\sigma_n^x \sigma_{n-n_o+1}^x + \sigma_n^y \sigma_{n-n_o+1}^y\right)}\right)\left(\prod_{i=1}^{\lfloor (n+n_o)/2 \rfloor} e^{-i\beta_t \left(\sigma_{n+2i-1}^x \sigma_{n+2i}^x + \sigma_{n+2i-1}^y \sigma_{n+2i}^y\right)}\right).$$

The phase-separating operators are then the same as in the previous section. The initial state is an outer product (concatenation) of the uniform superposition over the wire bits and a state with a uniform superposition over $n + n_o$ states with precisely n_o bits set to one, where $|\psi\rangle = |\psi_1\rangle|\psi_2\rangle$ with $|\psi_1\rangle = \frac{1}{\sqrt{2^{n-n_o}}}\sum_{x\in\{0,1\}^{n-n_o}}|x\rangle$ and $|\psi_2\rangle = \binom{n+n_o}{n_o}^{-1/2}\sum_{x\in\{0,1\}^n \text{ s.t. } |x|_1=n_o}|x\rangle$. We discuss the preparation of the well-known entangled state $|\psi_2\rangle$, studied in several contexts with relation to the XY mixer, in Section 4.6.

4.3. Approach 3: Graph Diffusors with a Linear Field on the Fault Bits

In this approach, we tailor the mixing operators to maintain the valid fault configuration space. Around each gate, a mixing operator is associated with swapping valid fault configurations around that gate, utilizing the descriptions given in Section 3.1 such that, given a valid configuration, the mixing operators populate states that are also valid configurations.

Given a set of logical gates $G = \{g_1, \ldots, g_m\}$ in the fault model over $w_1, \ldots, w_n$ wires and $f_1, \ldots, f_n$ fault bits, define $V_g^{(S_I;S_O)}$ as detailed in Section 3.1. We wish to construct the collection of unitaries $\mathcal{U} = \{U_{g_1}^{(1)}, \ldots, U_{g_1}^{(r)}, \ldots, U_{g_m}^{(r)}\}$ associated with the mixing operator of each gate and the respective tuple of input/output pairs for each gate. (Note that the index (r) runs over a set of input/output pairs to the gate, so it is typically an n-tuple and not a single integer.) For example, as in the circuit considered in Section 3 and illustrated in Figure 1, if g_2 is an NAND gate, then $\{U_{g_2}^{(1)}, \ldots, U_{g_2}^{(8)}\}$ are associated with the eight input/output pairs for an NAND gate. We define the uniform superposition over the collections $V_{g_i}^{(j)}$ as $\left|V_{g_i}^{(j)}\right\rangle = \frac{1}{\sqrt{|V_{g_i}^{(j)}|}}\sum_{v\in V_{g_i}^{(j)}}|v\rangle$. (See Table 1 for such a description for an NAND gate) Then, we define each mixing operator associated with a specific input/output pair for a specific gate:

$$U_{g_i}^{(j)}(\beta_t) = \mathbb{1} - \left(1 - e^{-i\beta_t}\right)\left|V_{g_i}^{(j)}\right\rangle\left\langle V_{g_i}^{(j)}\right|$$
$$= \mathbb{1} - \left(1 - e^{-i\beta_t}\right)/|V_{g_i}^{(j)}| \sum_{v,u\in V_{g_i}^{(j)}} |v\rangle\langle u|.$$

Then, we define the mixing operator associated with each gate:

$$U_{g_i}(\beta_t) = \prod_{j=(1)}^{(r)} U_{g_i}^{(j)}(\beta_t).$$

Here, $U_{g_i}(\beta_t)$ are unitary because $U_{g_i}^{(j)}(\beta_t)$ are mutually commutative over the input/output pair index j. $U_{g_i}^{(j)}$, which has an eigenvalue e^{ia} for an eigenvector $\left| V_{g_i}^{(j)} \right\rangle$ and an eigenvalue of one for any vector in the range of the projector $\mathbb{1} - \left| V_{g_i}^{(j)} \right\rangle\left\langle V_{g_i}^{(j)} \right|$. Then, we define

$$U_d(\beta_t) = \prod_{i=1}^{m} U_{g_i}(\beta_t),$$

as the mixing operator for this ansatz, where we apply each gate one after another. However, for circuits with a highly regular structure (such as those introduced in Section 3), we can group many commutating unitaries together and apply all $U_i(\beta_t)$ with in two steps.

The cost function (also one-local) simply counts the number of faults of the configurations:

$$U_c(\alpha_t) = \prod_{i=n}^{2n} \left(e^{i\alpha_t(\mathbb{1}-\sigma_i^z)/2} \right).$$

The feasibility space and how it is connected through the action of U_d is more complicated for this approach than previous approaches such that it cannot be as easily described by a uniform superposition over the states. We begin with a known feasible configuration and apply $U_d(\beta_t)$ to explore the feasible configuration from there. A simple starting state used for this purpose is the state with only faults placed on the faulty output states.

We also consider a modified protocol which includes a second cost function that has this state as its minimum, in clear inspiration from a similar CQA [3] approach. A sufficient (and one-local) cost function puts a penalty on every bit that does not conform with the initial state chosen. As such, the cost associated with any state in the space is given by its Hamming distance from the initial state. Let $x^0 = \{x_1^0, \ldots, x_{2n}^0\}$ be the computational basis string associated with the initial state $|\psi\rangle = |x^0\rangle$. Then, the initial state cost function operator can be implemented as

$$U_s(\gamma_t) = \prod_{i=1}^{2n} e^{i\gamma_t(\mathbb{1}-(1-2x_i^0)\sigma_i^z)/2}.$$

For this modified protocol, we have three sets of operators: the initial state cost function operator, the mixing operators, and the phase-separating operator. As such, we generalize the QAOA protocol to have three angles to select for every round such that the state evolves under $(\alpha_1, \beta_1, \gamma_1, \alpha_2, \beta_2, \gamma_2, \ldots, \alpha_p, \beta_p, \gamma_p)$. For step t_i, $|\psi(t_i)\rangle = U_s(\gamma_i)U_d(\beta_i)U_c(\alpha_i)|\psi(t_{i-1})\rangle$. In Section 6, we consider the performance of both approaches for small circuit instances and different parameter selection methods. Since U_s and U_c are both one-local operators, it is also straightforward to apply them together in a device.

4.4. *Approach 4: Transverse Field on Faults with an Oracle Circuit Simulator*

Rather than representing the wire and fault bits explicitly, in our next approach, we focus on the space of valid fault configurations (of dimensions 2^{n-n_o}). Notice that for any invalid fault configuration, it can be made a valid configuration by simply flipping the fault bit for the output bits which are incorrect.

Consider a fault configuration $f = (f_1, \ldots, f_{n-n_o})$ over non-output wires. The energy of the state is dependent on the number of nonzero fault bits $P(f) = \sum_{i=1}^{n-n_o} f_i$ as well as the number of *implied* faults needed on the outputs to make this a valid configuration $Q(f) = \sum_{i=n-n_o}^{n}(w_i - S(f,i))^2$, where $S(f,i)$ is the value placed on the output wire w_i when simulating the circuit with the given inputs and the fault configuration f over the non-output wires.

Then, $R(f) = P(f) + Q(f)$ counts the total number of faults implied by the fault configuration f in this constrained space. By constructing an oracle that simulates the circuit and then uses this information to find the proper fault count, we have a phase separation operator with the same cost function as in Section 4.3:

$$U_c(\alpha_t) = \sum_{x\in\{0,1\}^{n-n_o}} e^{i\alpha_t R(x)} |\, x\,\rangle\langle\, x\,|.$$

As in QAOA1, our starting state will be $|\,\psi\,\rangle = |\,+\,\rangle^{\otimes n-n_o} = \frac{1}{\sqrt{2^{n-n_o}}}\sum_{f\in\{0,1\}^{n-n_o}}|\,f\,\rangle$. and we use the one-local Pauli X mixing operators:

$$U_d(\beta_t) = \prod_{i=1}^{n} e^{-i\beta_t(\sigma_i^x)}.$$

To see how $U_c(t)$ can be implemented in practice, we consider a protocol where ancilla qubits are used for the computation of the faults needed on the outputs. Let $|\,\psi(r_{i-1})\,\rangle \in \mathbb{C}^{2^{n-n_o}}$ be the wave function at the beginning of round r_i, with the initial wave function defined as shown above. We show how $|\,\psi(r_i)\,\rangle$ is then generated over the current round. For $r_i \in [r_1, r_t]$, we have

$$\begin{aligned}
|\,\nu(r_i)\,\rangle &= U_{circ}|\,0\,\rangle_n|\,\psi(r_{i-1})\,\rangle|\,0\,\rangle_{n_o} \\
&= \sum_{x\in\{0,1\}^{n-n_o}}^{n} \langle\, x\,|\,\psi\,\rangle|\,f(x)\,\rangle_n|\,x\,\rangle_{n-n_o}|\,g(x)\,\rangle_{n_o} && \text{(Simulate Circuit)} \\
|\,\mu(r_i)\,\rangle &= U_c(\alpha_i)|\,\nu(r_i)\,\rangle && \text{(Apply Phases)} \\
&= \prod_{j=n+1}^{2n} e^{i\alpha_i(\mathbb{1}-\sigma_j^z)/2} \sum_{x\subset\{0,1\}^n} |\,f(x)\,\rangle_n|\,x\,\rangle_{n-n_o}|\,g(x)\,\rangle_{n_o} \\
&= \sum_{x\in\{0,1\}^{n-n_o}} \left(\sum_{j=n+1}^{2n} e^{i\alpha_i x_j}\right)|\,f(x)\,\rangle_n|\,x\,\rangle_{n-n_o}|\,g(x)\,\rangle_{n_o} \\
|\,0\,\rangle_n|\,\phi(r_i)\,\rangle|\,0\,\rangle_{n_o} &= U_{circ}^{\dagger}|\,\mu(r_i)\,\rangle && \text{(Undo Simulation)} \\
|\,\psi(r_i)\,\rangle &= \prod_{j=1}^{n-n_o} e^{-i\beta_i\sigma_j^x}|\,\phi(r_i)\,\rangle && \text{(Apply Mixing)}
\end{aligned}$$

Here, U_{circ} implements the simulation of the faulty circuit such that $f(x)$ is the valid configuration over the wire bits that $|\,x\,\rangle$ specifies from the non-output fault bits, while $g(x)$ are the required faults on the output bits such that $x \oplus g(x) \oplus f(x)$ is a valid configuration over the $2n$ bits.

4.5. Approach 5: Bounded Fault Count with Oracle Circuit Simulator

In this section, rather than restricting ourselves to the subspace of all fault configurations, we wish to restrict ourselves to the fault configurations up to a maximum number of faults. To accomplish this task, we can use the XY mixer also discussed in Section 4.2 by utilizing ancilla qubits in a complimentary way. Here, we have $n - n_o$ non-output fault flag bits (the same as in Section 4.4) and n_o ancilla qubits to allow for representation of all state configurations with faults less than or equal to n_o.

The cost function remains the same as that used in Section 4.4, and the same procedure with the simulation of the circuit to find the faults on the end bits can be used, except for the aforementioned replacement of the mixing operator.

The initial state is then $|\psi\rangle = \binom{n}{n_o}^{-1/2} \sum_{x\in\{0,1\}^{n-n_o} \text{ s.t. } |x|_1 \le n_o} \sum_{y\in\{0,1\}^{n_o} \text{ s.t. } |y|_1 = n_o - |x|_1} |x\rangle|y\rangle$, similar to the state mentioned in Section 4.2. Note that since we also have implied faults, the maximum number of faults that can be expressed is between n_o and $2n_o$. The initialization of this state is discussed in more detail in Section 4.6.

4.6. Size of the Relevant Constrained Space and Summaries for the Approaches

In each of the approaches delineated in Section 3, the size of the constrained space of interest which the evolution of the wave function is limited to differs. In Table 2 and Figure 2, each approach is summarized by the type of mixing operator, the type of cost function, the size of the constrained space, and the complexity of each round.

Table 2. Depending on our selection of mixing and phase-separating operators, we can constrain the evolution of the wave function to constrained spaces of differing sizes.

Approach	Mixing Operator	Cost Function	Size of Constrained Space	Round Complexity
1	Pauli X	Ising	$\mathcal{O}(2^{2n})$	$\mathcal{O}(1)$
2	XY mixer and X	Ising	$\mathcal{O}(2^{n-n_o}(n+n_o)^{n_o})$	$\mathcal{O}(1)$
3	Gate-based diffusors	Pauli Z	$\mathcal{O}(2^{n-n_o})$	$\mathcal{O}(1)$
4	Pauli X	Circuit Oracle	$\mathcal{O}(2^{n-n_o})$	$\mathcal{O}(C_p)$
5	XY mixer	Circuit Oracle	$\mathcal{O}(n^{n_o})$	$\mathcal{O}(C_p)$

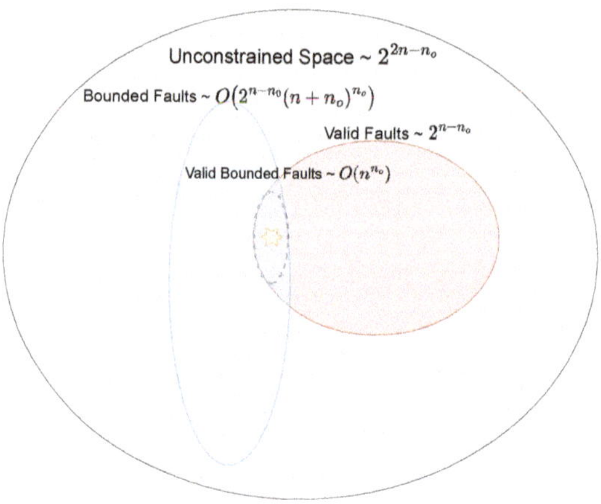

Figure 2. A visual representation of the subspaces that the wave function is kept within during evolution through each QAOA approach.

While the approaches in Sections 4.3 and 4.4 differ greatly in the type of mixing and phase separation operators used, they constrain the system to the same subspace. Consider the exploration of this space under these two different approaches. The latter begins with a uniform superposition over all valid fault configurations, and the neighborhood of each computational basis state under the action of each Pauli X operator in the mixer is a state that is a bit flip away, similar to a high-dimensional hypercube. The former begins with a single feasible state, and the neighborhood of each state under the action of the mixing operator is dependent on the available transformations around each gate to move it to a new fault configuration.

Moreover, while the cost functions associated with these two approaches are *equivalent*, the resulting phase separation operators for implementing these cost functions are very different. For example, while each call to the cost function runs in $\mathcal{O}(1)$ for the fault counting in the former, each call to the cost function in the latter will require simulating the corresponding circuit, which has a particular depth C_p. For example, for the distribution of the circuits introduced in Section 5, the depth of the classical circuit grows as $\mathcal{O}(\sqrt{n})$ if we choose the diameter and depth to be equal. (This relationship holds for the family considered for the experiments in this paper.)

Approaches 2 and 5 require the preparation of a particle number-conserving state studied in many areas of quantum computation and quantum chemistry [26–29]. We refer the reader to the appendix of [23] for a discussion of this state in the context of a QAOA with the XY mixer. In general, for a uniform superposition over n qubits preserving a number k, the state can be constructed with $\binom{n}{k} = \mathcal{O}\left(n^k\right)$ CNOT gates [29], which can be prohibitive for a circuit with a large bound on the number of faults. However, the authors of [26] provided a projective measurement method that grows polynomially with n and independent of k for large n values. Alternatively, one can use an approach similar to Approach 3, where the initial state is a computational basis state in the feasible space. The initial state selection for an QAOA remains an important area of current research [23], including warm starts [30,31]. Moreover, the number of minimum faults for many circuits of interest can be much less than n_o, and one could adapt the approaches to utilize this smaller space.

5. Random CFD Instances with Balanced Width and Depth

To demonstrate how these different approaches practically perform in the CFD problem, we introduce a family of random instances that scale with a single size parameter and allow for detailed analysis at small sizes. Figure 3 shows the first few such circuits with increasing sizes. The central feature is that both the depth of the circuit and the number of inputs or outputs (width) scale together with the size and number of wires of the circuit. We randomly select the inputs for the whole circuit and apply faults to the outputs such that every output is faulty. We randomly select the inputs and gates at each spot from the relevant gate set for every size to generate the instances used in Section 6.

The valid fault configurations for an instance of the smallest circuit in the family are in Figure 1. Unlike all the other circuits, this has only one output, and so we modified the model for this small circuit for our experiments such that placing a fault on the output wire required two faults, whereas every other location required one.

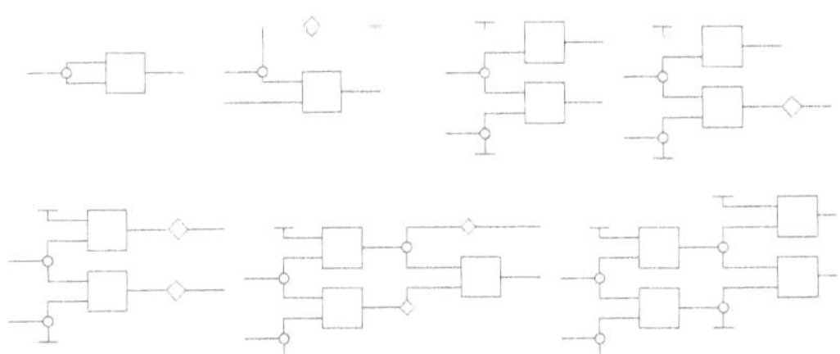

Figure 3. Diagrams for circuit instances of the CFD problem considered in Section 6, depending on the number of qubits, from these small, local, and dense circuits. Every box is a two intput/one output gate, every dot is a one input/two output gate, and every diamond is a one intput/one output gate. If a top wire has a $\top$ and a bottom wire has a $\perp$ at the same depth, they refer to the same wire (which has been wrapped around).

While at large scales we expected the performance of any specific ansatz strategy to decrease with the problem size, at the small sizes used for our simulations, the performance could vary by problem size in a more complicated fashion. For all instances, the maximum number of faults needed was two, since there were two outputs. We generated 100 instances that were filtered such that the minimum fault explanation required a single fault.

Approach 3, unlike all the other approaches, would be initialized in a solution state without this filtering. For larger-sized circuits of this family, the chance of a randomly selected instance having a minimum fault explanation that saturates this bound is increasingly diminished, but this filtering is an important step for the small-sized circuits of this family.

For the filtered data sets of different sizes, the specific topology of the circuits can still lead to important differences in fault configurations. For example, the circuit depicted at the bottom middle of Figure 3 has much more diversity in the typical size (or degeneracy) of the solution space compared with the smaller sizes. Solution degeneracy has been seen to have a beneficial impact on a variety of optimization problems for QAOAs.

6. Performance with Different Parameter Optimizations

Using the family of CFD instances from the previous section, we consider the performance of QAOA strategies with different methods of parameter optimization: BRUTE, INTERP, LINANGOPT, and LINCOEFOPT. Each of the first three requires the expected cost of the final wave function to update the angle parameters. For implementation on a quantum computer, the expected cost of the final wave function has to be sampled with repeated measurements, and there will be a trade-off between repeated runs to accurately compute this value and run the protocol with updated parameters based on the approximation [6]. The angles were selected from the interval $[-\pi, \pi]$.

For BRUTE, we chose 100 random seeds and ran the Nelder–Mead algorithm with 100 iterations to optimize each choice, using the final Hamiltonian as the cost function and selecting the choice that minimized the cost function the most. For INTERP, we used the interpolation function called INTERP in [6], which showed good performance from this method in their results. We used the Nelder–Mead algorithm (with 100 random seeds and 100 iterations each) on $p = 2$ and then for $p > 2$, beginning with the linear interpolation from $p - 1$ and optimizing with 100 iterations for this result. For LINANGOPT, we started the protocol with a linear ramp for each angle (i.e., for round $k \in [1, p]$, $\alpha_k = k\pi/p$ and $\beta_k = \pi - k\pi/p$) and then optimized the angles (with 200 iterations). For LINCOEFOPT, we used a coefficient $\Gamma \in \{9/10, 1/2, 1/4, 1/8, 1/16\}$ and used the same linear ramp but replaced α_k, β_k with $\alpha_k\Gamma, \beta_k\Gamma$ and then optimized Γ over 20 iterations before selecting the best performing Γ.

In each situation described, Approach 3 (with an initial state cost function) is different from the other approaches, since it has three angles to select for a single round k. As the initial starting point for LINANGOPT and LINCOEFOPT (with Γ), it begins with $\gamma_k = \pi - k\pi/p$, $\alpha_k = \Theta(k \leq p)(2k\pi/p) + \Theta(k > p)(\pi - 2k\pi/p)$ (reaching a maximum around $p/2$ and minimums at 0 and p), and $\beta_k = k\pi/p$. Note that Approach 3 was also considered without an initial state cost function, and the results support that this seemed to benefit its performance.

The results from [6] suggest that the Nelder–Mead algorithm can perform as well as other optimization algorithms, such as the Broyden–Fletcher–Goldfarb–Shanno algorithm. Utilizing other optimizers for these tailored ansätzes is an interesting area of future study [21,32,33]. We report the results with p set to 2 and 3 for BRUTE, 5 for INTERP, 5 and 10 for LINANGOPT, and 50 for LINCOEFOPT.

The relative simulation range capable on a workstation grows depending on the size of the relevant constrained space for the problem and so the more constrained approaches have an increased simulation range, as such we report results on larger instances for these approaches for each parameter selection. Figure 4 details the performance of each ansatz with each parameter selection strategy.

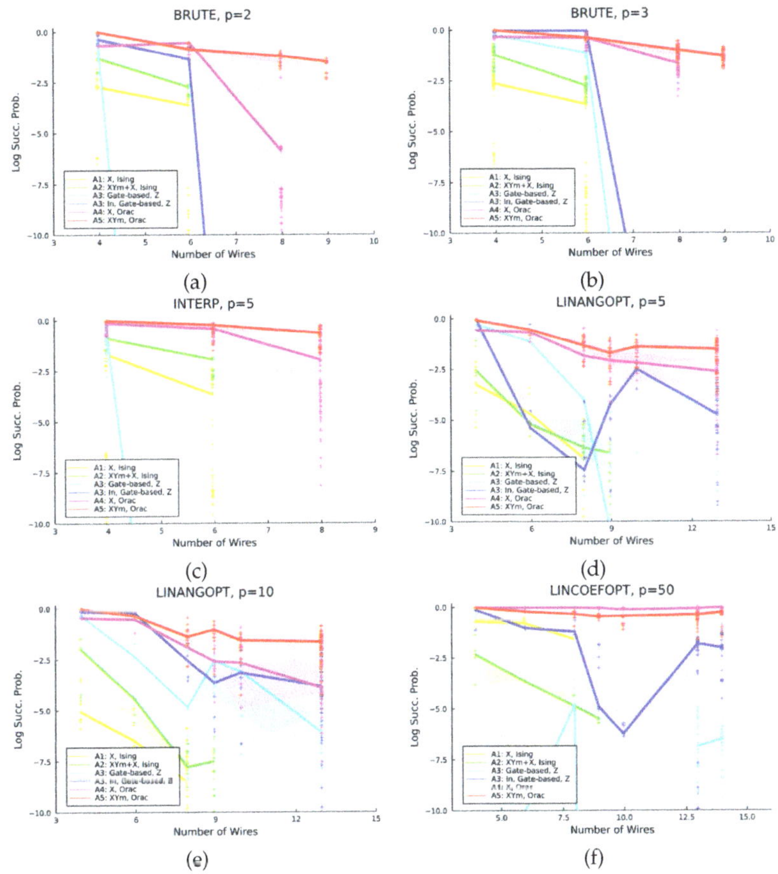

Figure 4. Performance of ansätzes with different parameter selections. The solid lines indicate the performance on the median of the instances, while the ribbons correspond to the lower and upper quantiles. Markers correspond to the success probabilities of individual instances.

The results support that ansätzes which exploit a more constrained space by tailoring the operators used to the problem structure generally perform better in the CFD problem and therefore are important methods for improving the practical applicability of QAOAs and other variational quantum algorithms. Indeed, Approaches 4 and 5 consistently performed the best, and Approach 3 performed comparably with some parameter selections for certain sizes. Surprisingly though, Approach 1 performed quite strongly for LINCOEFOPT with $p = 50$. The performance across these different metrics generally supports that while a linear tramp function might be well suited for certain approaches, such as Approaches 1 and 4, it is interesting to consider different functions to parameterize the angles for other approaches. Utilizing an initial state cost function showed advantages for Approach 3 in each parameter selection method except for LINANGOPT, where the benefit was not as clear.

The performance showed high variance under BRUTE and INTERP for most approaches. Approach 3 in particular seemed to struggle more at very low p values, perhaps because the initial state had full support for a particular solution and had to use mixing operators to explore the space, while the other approaches began with a uniform superposition over all states in the particular subspace. Since INTERP utilizes the results from BRUTE at $p = 2$, this difficulty can translate to this approach as well. While INTERP can alleviate the high cost associated with brute force evaluation to find good parameters with stepwise optimization as p is scaled higher, the parameters found at low p values can potentially be associated with a local minimum that may be the best cost minimization the algorithm can accomplish at this depth, and then the algorithm is subsequently stuck around this choice at higher p values.

Approach 3 also showed striking performance differences between instance sizes, especially for LINANGOPT with $p = 5$ and LINCOEFOPT with $p = 50$. Approach 3 is initialized to a computational basis state with faults on the outputs, and so the distance, in terms of the number of mixing operators, to find a minimum state as well as the degeneracy of the solution space may play a more acute role compared with other approaches. For example, as noted in Section 5, the instances with 13 wires had instances with higher degeneracy than that at lower sizes. This typical degeneracy growth with the problem size for the circuits of interest is one reason leveraging quantum algorithms may be beneficial.

Note that the results were based on the number of rounds p, but the actual depth of a quantum circuit to implement each of the different approaches will differ, especially for larger circuit instances. Moreover, Approaches 2 and 5 used a starting state that required more involved preparation before the procedure could begin.

7. Conclusions

One of the most compelling areas for utilizing variational quantum algorithms on NISQ devices arises from solving optimization problems, including those with hard constraints. The quantum alternating operator ansatz (QAOA) and constrained quantum annealing (CQA) are methods that can enforce those constraints naturally throughout the protocol or anneal. Designing approaches that can usefully use the structures of different optimization problems remains an important task for developing state-of-the-art quantum algorithms.

Designing mixing operators and phasing operators for a constrained space can be more general than satisfying a global hard constraint, such as satisfying many local constraints (such as the valid configurations around a faulty gate [3], as in Section 4.3), a practical bound on the maximum value a counting problem can yield (Sections 4.2 and 4.5), or simply finding a way to represent a Hamiltonian that is difficult to implement without ancillas (Sections 4.4 and 4.5).

In this paper, we constructed several general approaches to exploit constrained quantum evolution to solve the CFD problem, some of which had superpolynomially smaller constraint subspaces. While some of these approaches may be related to protocols that could be implemented on a quantum annealer, others are more challenging and therefore better suited for QAOAs or digital adiabatic simulations. We introduced a family of random circuits that are parameterized by a single size parameter, which can be useful for benchmarking future NISQ devices. Simulations of QAOA protocols with optimized parameters, interpolated and optimized parameters, and linear interpolation suggest that more advanced ansätzes can give better performance by utilizing the underlining structure of an optimization problem. As such, designing and experimenting with more novel operators for solving optimization problems remains an important area for future research. Nonetheless, the initial states of several approaches are more involved to prepare, and the unitaries necessitated for each ansatz require further analysis under specific quantum architectures.

There are many interesting areas of future work that arise from the constructions considered in this paper. It would be interesting to explore approaches such as Approach 5 with an initial state in the computational basis to relieve the cost of preparing a highly entangled initial state. Since the number of minimum faults needed for a circuit can be much smaller than the upper bound given, it would be of interest to explore several of the approaches where this is utilized to form a more constrained ansatz, especially in Approach 5. For example, if the minimum number of faults needed is known to scale logarithmically, the constrained space can then scale subexponentially for Approach 5. Given the rich and growing literature of approaches to find suitable parameters for QAOAs, it would be interesting to utilize such approaches for the ansätzes introduced here, especially those that are less cost prohibitive for intermediate p values, where the advantage of more tailored ansätzes could be more pronounced compared with more generic ansätzes using the same parameter selection approach. Given that near-term quantum devices are likely to be noisy and have inaccuracies in the application of gates, it would be interesting to compare these ansätzes in this regime and consider modifications. The performance of each ansatz varied over the instances, and it would be interesting to analyze what kind of features of an instance can be predictive of the performance of an ansatz. Finally, it would be of interest to consider other optimization problems in which similar structures can be exploited to tailor ansätzes.

Author Contributions: Conceptualization, H.L., F.M.S. and E.R.; Data curation, H.L.; Formal analysis, H.L., F.M.S. and E.R.; Funding acquisition, E.R.; Project administration, E.R.; Software, H.L.; Supervision, F.M.S. and E.R.; Visualization, H.L.; Writing—original draft, H.L., F.M.S. and E.R.; Writing—review & editing, H.L., F.M.S. and E.R. All authors have read and agreed to the published version of the manuscript.

Funding: We are grateful for the support from the NASA Ames Research Center and from DARPA under IAA 8839, Annex 128. The research is based upon work (partially) supported by the Office of the Director of National Intelligence (ODNI), Intelligence Advanced Research Projects Activity (IARPA) and the Defense Advanced Research Projects Agency (DARPA), via the U.S. Army Research Office contract W911NF-17-C-0050. H.L. was supported by the USRA Feynman Quantum Academy and funded by the NAMS R&D Student Program under contract no. NNA16BD14C.

Data Availability Statement: The data presented in this study are available on request from the corresponding author.

Acknowledgments: The authors are grateful for the support from the NASA Ames Research Center. The authors thank P. A. Lott and S. Grabbe for their helpful discussions.

Conflicts of Interest: The authors declare no conflict of interest.

References

1. Hadfield, S.; Wang, Z.; O'gorman, B.; Rieffel, E.G.; Venturelli, D.; Biswas, R. From the quantum approximate optimization algorithm to a quantum alternating operator ansatz. *Algorithms* **2019**, *12*, 34. [CrossRef]
2. Perdomo-Ortiz, A.; Feldman, A.; Ozaeta, A.; Isakov, S.V.; Zhu, Z.; O'Gorman, B.; Katzgraber, H.G.; Diedrich, A.; Neven, H.; de Kleer, J.; et al. Readiness of quantum optimization machines for industrial applications. *Phys. Rev. Appl.* **2019**, *12*, 014004. [CrossRef]
3. Leipold, H.; Spedalieri, F.M. Quantum Annealing with Special Drivers for Circuit Fault Diagnostics. *Sci. Rep.* **2022**, *12*, 11691. [CrossRef] [PubMed]
4. Farhi, E.; Goldstone, J.; Gutmann, S. A quantum approximate optimization algorithm. *arXiv* **2014**, arXiv:1411.4028.
5. Wang, Z.; Hadfield, S.; Jiang, Z.; Rieffel, E.G. Quantum approximate optimization algorithm for maxcut: A fermionic view. *Phys. Rev. A* **2018**, *97*, 022304. [CrossRef]
6. Zhou, L.; Wang, S.T.; Choi, S.; Pichler, H.; Lukin, M.D. Quantum approximate optimization algorithm: Performance, mechanism, and implementation on near-term devices. *Phys. Rev. X* **2020**, *10*, 021067. [CrossRef]
7. Hadfield, S.; Hogg, T.; Rieffel, E.G. Analytical Framework for Quantum Alternating Operator Ans\" atze. *arXiv* **2021**, arXiv:2105.06996.
8. Bravyi, S.; Kliesch, A.; Koenig, R.; Tang, E. Hybrid quantum-classical algorithms for approximate graph coloring. *arXiv* **2020**, arXiv:2011.13420.
9. Hadfield, S.; Wang, Z.; Rieffel, E.G.; O'Gorman, B.; Venturelli, D.; Biswas, R. Quantum approximate optimization with hard and soft constraints. In Proceedings of the Second International Workshop on Post Moores Era Supercomputing, Denver, CO, USA, 12–17 November 2017; pp. 15–21.
10. Farhi, E.; Harrow, A.W. Quantum supremacy through the quantum approximate optimization algorithm. *arXiv* **2016**, arXiv:1602.07674.
11. Preskill, J. Quantum computing in the NISQ era and beyond. *Quantum* **2018**, *2*, 79. [CrossRef]
12. Harrigan, M.P.; Sung, K.J.; Neeley, M.; Satzinger, K.J.; Arute, F.; Arya, K.; Atalaya, J.; Bardin, J.C.; Barends, R.; Boixo, S.; et al. Quantum approximate optimization of non-planar graph problems on a planar superconducting processor. *Nat. Phys.* **2021**, *17*, 332–336. [CrossRef]
13. Cerezo, M.; Arrasmith, A.; Babbush, R.; Benjamin, S.C.; Endo, S.; Fujii, K.; McClean, J.R.; Mitarai, K.; Yuan, X.; Cincio, L.; et al. Variational quantum algorithms. *Nat. Rev. Phys.* **2021**, *3*, 625–644. [CrossRef]

14. Bittel, L.; Kliesch, M. Training variational quantum algorithms is np-hard. *Phys. Rev. Lett.* **2021**, *127*, 120502. [CrossRef] [PubMed]
15. Arrasmith, A.; Cerezo, M.; Czarnik, P.; Cincio, L.; Coles, P.J. Effect of barren plateaus on gradient-free optimization. *Quantum* **2021**, *5*, 558. [CrossRef]
16. Cerezo, M.; Sone, A.; Volkoff, T.; Cincio, L.; Coles, P.J. Cost function dependent barren plateaus in shallow parametrized quantum circuits. *Nat. Commun.* **2021**, *12*, 1–12.
17. Holmes, Z.; Sharma, K.; Cerezo, M.; Coles, P.J. Connecting ansatz expressibility to gradient magnitudes and barren plateaus. *PRX Quantum* **2022**, *3*, 010313. [CrossRef]
18. Crooks, G.E. Performance of the quantum approximate optimization algorithm on the maximum cut problem. *arXiv* **2018**, arXiv:1811.08419.
19. Hen, I.; Spedalieri, F.M. Quantum annealing for constrained optimization. *Phys. Rev. Appl.* **2016**, *5*, 034007. [CrossRef]
20. Hen, I.; Sarandy, M.S. Driver Hamiltonians for constrained optimization in quantum annealing. *Phys. Rev. A* **2016**, *93*, 062312. [CrossRef]
21. Shaydulin, R.; Hadfield, S.; Hogg, T.; Safro, I. Classical symmetries and the Quantum Approximate Optimization Algorithm. *arXiv* **2020**, arXiv:2012.04713.
22. Leipold, H.; Spedalieri, F. Constructing driver Hamiltonians for optimization problems with linear constraints. *Quantum Sci. Technol.* **2021**. [CrossRef]
23. Wang, Z.; Rubin, N.C.; Dominy, J.M.; Rieffel, E.G. X y mixers: Analytical and numerical results for the quantum alternating operator ansatz. *Phys. Rev. A* **2020**, *101*, 012320. [CrossRef]
24. Kremenetski, V.; Hogg, T.; Hadfield, S.; Cotton, S.J.; Tubman, N.M. Quantum Alternating Operator Ansatz (QAOA) Phase Diagrams and Applications for Quantum Chemistry. *arXiv* **2021**, arXiv:2108.13056.
25. Jha, N.K.; Gupta, S. *Testing of Digital Systems*; Cambridge University Press: Cambridge, MA, USA, 2002.
26. Childs, A.M.; Farhi, E.; Goldstone, J.; Gutmann, S. Finding cliques by quantum adiabatic evolution. *arXiv* **2000**, arXiv:quant-ph/0012104.
27. Ortiz, G.; Gubernatis, J.E.; Knill, E.; Laflamme, R. Quantum algorithms for fermionic simulations. *Phys. Rev. A* **2001**, *64*, 022319. [CrossRef]
28. Bergholm, V.; Vartiainen, J.J.; Möttönen, M.; Salomaa, M.M. Quantum circuits with uniformly controlled one-qubit gates. *Phys. Rev. A* **2005**, *71*, 052330. [CrossRef]
29. Gard, B.T.; Zhu, L.; Barron, G.S.; Mayhall, N.J.; Economou, S.E.; Barnes, E. Efficient symmetry-preserving state preparation circuits for the variational quantum eigensolver algorithm. *NPJ Quantum Inf.* **2020**, *6*, 1–9. [CrossRef]
30. Egger, D.J.; Mareček, J.; Woerner, S. Warm-starting quantum optimization. *Quantum* **2021**, *5*, 479. [CrossRef]
31. Cain, M.; Farhi, E.; Gutmann, S.; Ranard, D.; Tang, E. The QAOA gets stuck starting from a good classical string. *arXiv* **2022**, arXiv:2207.05089.
32. Khairy, S.; Shaydulin, R.; Cincio, L.; Alexeev, Y.; Balaprakash, P. Learning to optimize variational quantum circuits to solve combinatorial problems. In Proceedings of the AAAI Conference on Artificial Intelligence, New York, NY, USA, 7–12 February 2020; Volume 34, pp. 2367–2375.
33. Sung, K.J.; Yao, J.; Harrigan, M.P.; Rubin, N.C.; Jiang, Z.; Lin, L.; Babbush, R.; McClean, J.R. Using models to improve optimizers for variational quantum algorithms. *Quantum Sci. Technol.* **2020**, *5*, 044008. [CrossRef]

algorithms

MDPI

Article

A Novel Intelligent Method for Fault Diagnosis of Steam Turbines Based on T-SNE and XGBoost

Zhiguo Liang [1], Lijun Zhang [1,2,3,*] and Xizhe Wang [1]

1 National Center for Materials Service Safety, University of Science and Technology Beijing, Beijing 100083, China
2 Innovation Group of Marine Engineering Materials and Corrosion Control, Southern Marine Science and Engineering Guangdong Laboratory (Zhuhai), Zhuhai 519080, China
3 Research Institute of Macro-Safety Science, University of Science and Technology Beijing, Beijing 100083, China
* Correspondence: ljzhang@ustb.edu.cn

Abstract: Since failure of steam turbines occurs frequently and can causes huge losses for thermal plants, it is important to identify a fault in advance. A novel clustering fault diagnosis method for steam turbines based on t-distribution stochastic neighborhood embedding (t-SNE) and extreme gradient boosting (XGBoost) is proposed in this paper. First, the t-SNE algorithm was used to map the high-dimensional data to the low-dimensional space; and the data clustering method of K-means was performed in the low-dimensional space to distinguish the fault data from the normal data. Then, the imbalance problem in the data was processed by the synthetic minority over-sampling technique (SMOTE) algorithm to obtain the steam turbine characteristic data set with fault labels. Finally, the XGBoost algorithm was used to solve this multi-classification problem. The data set used in this paper was derived from the time series data of a steam turbine of a thermal power plant. In the processing analysis, the method achieved the best performance with an overall accuracy of 97% and an early warning of at least two hours in advance. The experimental results show that this method can effectively evaluate the condition and provide fault warning for power plant equipment.

Keywords: fault diagnosis; steam turbine; t-distribution stochastic neighborhood embedding (t-SNE); extreme gradient boosting (XGBoost); clustering

1. Introduction

Thermal power plays an important role in power generation. Thermal power generation consumes enormous amounts of available coal energy, resulting in a shortage of coal energy. In order to conserve energy consumption, reduce pollution and protect the environment, thermal power plants should adopt advanced scientific and technological means to reduce energy efficiency loss, and strengthen research on fault diagnosis of main power generation (e.g., steam boilers and turbines) [1–3].

In recent years, the rapid development of information technologies, computer technologies and other new technologies has brought new progress in equipment condition monitoring and fault diagnosis [4,5]. The application of machine learning in intelligent diagnosis has achieved good results. The main machine learning algorithms include support vector machines (SVM) [6,7] and its improved algorithms, decision trees, its improved algorithms [8,9], artificial neural network (ANN), and its improved algorithms [10,11], etc. These algorithms can achieve better classification results for data sets with a large number of fault tags. Deng et al. [12] used the improved particle swarm optimization (PSO) algorithm to optimize the parameters of least squares support vector machines (LS-SVM) to construct an optimal LS-SVM classifier, which is used to classify the fault. In Sun's research [13], a fault diagnosis method based on wavelet packet analysis and SVM was proposed. Firstly, the wavelet packet transform was used to decompose and denoise the signal, and the original fault feature vector was extracted for reconstruction. The improved SVM algorithm was used to diagnose the fault based on the new fault feature vector. Wu et al. [14] proposed a deep transfer learning method based on the hybrid domain adversarial learning (HDAL) strategy for rotating machines in nuclear power plants.

Since failure of steam turbines occurs frequently and causes huge losses in thermal plants, it is important to identify the fault in advance. Thermal power plants use big data technology to deeply mine data value [15–18], which also makes itself more optimized, safer, and more economical. The steam turbine is one of the most important equipment in thermal power plants [19,20]. A large amount of steam turbine data, such as condition monitoring data, fault data and so on, has been accumulated in power plant automation systems, which contain characteristic data about the steam turbine fault condition. Accurate fault diagnosis can find the fault in time, repair it in advance, and ensure normal production. However, due to data acquisition and artificial records, the fault records cannot be directly related to the automatic acquisition of time series data. More seriously, due to the low efficiency and low quality of manual recording, the sample data with a large number of labels cannot be directly obtained. In addition, the turbine has high reliability and is in normal operation for a long time, which makes it difficult to provide a large amount of faulty sample data. Since the signals collected by the automatic system are nonlinear and non-stationary, the fault features are often drowned by external factors such as noise and the traditional signal processing; thus, analysis technology is severely limited. Therefore, an effective method for feature extraction and fault diagnosis for steam turbines is needed for this condition.

After analyzing the recent progress, a novel fault diagnosis method based on t-distribution stochastic neighborhood embedding (t-SNE), K-means clustering, synthetic minority over-sampling technique (SMOTE) and extreme gradient boosting (XGBoost) is proposed in this paper. Since the vibration signal collected by samplers had a high dimensional feature and the data could not be visualized, t-SNE was used to map the high-dimensional data to the low-dimensional space. Most of the data collected from the thermal plant was unlabeled, so the data clustering method of K-means was used in the low-dimensional space to distinguish the fault data from the normal data for automatic fault identification. The imbalance problem in the data was processed by the SMOTE algorithm to obtain the steam turbine characteristic data set with fault labels. Finally, the XGBoost algorithm was used to solve this multi-classification problem. When the steam turbines were detected by the trained model in this paper, the prediction information fed back to the thermal power plant immediately. This early warning information for a predictive failure will give the thermal power plant enough time to deal with the problems in advance. During this time, the plant could use other methods to reasonably determine when to take action. Compared with the above literature, the differences between the proposed method and other studies are shown in Table 1. The main objective of the proposed method was to develop a novel procedure for actual power plant data.

Table 1. Research comparison of the proposed method.

	Proposed Method	Other Literatures
Data set source	Actual data from the actual plant	Experimental data or numerical simulation data
Data length	Larger (months or even years)	Smaller (hours or days)
Fault label	Partly missing or being blurred	Identified by the experiment
Fault verification	Based on real faults in the plant	Based on simulated faults
Iterative strategy for research	Determined by the actual operation of the plant	Unable to iterate
Significance of research	Solving practical problems	Continuous improvement of research algorithms

The rest of this paper is organized as follows. Section 2 discusses methods. Section 2.1 introduces and discusses the performance indicator extraction based on t-SNE and K-means. Section 2.2 introduces the imbalanced data recognition model based on SMOTE and XGBoost. A model evaluation method is presented in Section 2.3. Section 3 presents the data experiment and results and discussion of the proposed method. Finally, conclusions are drawn in Section 4.

2. Methods

2.1. *Performance Indicator Extraction Based on t-SNE and K-Means*

The t-SNE algorithm is a nonlinear dimensionality reduction algorithm that maps multi-dimensional data into two or more dimensions by the similarity of high-dimensional data [21,22]. It has been applied to many fields, including image processing [23], genetics [24], and materials science [25]. In this paper, the input of t-SNE is signal features extracted by data acquisition equipment. According to the similarity of signal features, these features are further reduced. The main algorithm is as follows and the source code of the t-SNE algorithm is in Appendix A.

(1) The conditional probability of distribution $p_{j|i}$ between the corresponding data x_i and x_j in the high-dimensional space is calculated to represent the similarity between the data. The high-dimensional data, x_i and x_j, correspond to the mapping points y_i and y_j in a low dimension and $q_{j|i}$ is their similar conditional probability distribution. The initial value is $Y^{(0)} = \{y_1 \quad y_2 \quad \cdots \quad y_n\}$. $p_{j|i}$ and $q_{j|i}$ are calculated as follows.

$$p_{j|i} = \frac{\exp(-\|x_i - x_j\|^2/2\sigma_i^2)}{\sum_{k\neq i}\exp(-\|x_i - x_k\|^2/2\sigma_i^2)} \tag{1}$$

$$q_{j|i} = \frac{\exp(-\|y_i - y_j\|^2)}{\sum_{k\neq i}\exp(-\|y_i - y_k\|^2)} \tag{2}$$

where σ_i is the Gaussian distribution variance centered on x_i.

(2) Calculating the joint probability density p_{ij} of high dimensional samples.

$$p_{ij} = \frac{p_{j|i} + p_{i|j}}{2n} \tag{3}$$

(3) Calculating the joint probability density q_{ij} of the low dimensional samples.

$$q_{ij} = \frac{\left(1 + \|y_i - y_j\|^2\right)^{-1}}{\sum_{k\neq l}\left(1 + \|y_k - y_l\|^2\right)^{-1}} \tag{4}$$

(4) Calculating the loss function C and its gradient. C is defined by the Kullback–Leibler (KL) distance to evaluate the similarity degree of joint probability density p_{ij} and q_{ij}.

$$C = KL = \sum_i \sum_j p_{ij} \log \frac{p_{ij}}{q_{ij}} \tag{5}$$

$$\frac{\delta C}{\delta y_i} = 4\sum_j (p_{ij} - q_{ij})(y_i - y_j)\left(1 + \|y_i - y_j\|^2\right)^{-1} \tag{6}$$

(5) Iterative updating.

$$Y^{(t)} = Y^{(t-1)} + \eta\frac{\delta C}{\delta y} + \alpha(t)\left(Y^{(t-1)} - Y^{(t-2)}\right) \tag{7}$$

where t is the number of iterations, η is the learning rate, and $\alpha(\cdot)$ is the momentum factor.

(6) Returning to (4) and (5) until the number of iterations is reached.

After obtaining the low-dimensional data output by the t-SNE algorithm, the K-means clustering algorithm [26] was used to classify the data into two categories. This algorithm is used to classify fault dangerous intervals. When a single fault hazardous interval is identified, the data is divided into fault data and normal data. However, the lack of failure records leads to an imbalance problem.

2.2. Imbalanced Data Recognition Model Based on SMOTE and XGBoost

Sampling methods are very popular for balancing the class distribution. Over- and under-sampling methodologies have received considerable attention to counteract the effect of imbalanced data sets. The SMOTE algorithm is simple and efficient, has good anti-noise ability, and can improve the generalization of the model [27,28]. The formal procedure is as follows.

The minority class is over-sampled by taking each minority class sample and inserting synthetic examples along the line segments connecting any/all of the k minority class nearest neighbors. Depending on the amount of over-sampling required, neighbors are randomly selected from the k nearest neighbors. Synthetic samples are generated as follows: take the difference between the feature vector of sample and its nearest neighbor; multiply this difference by a random number between 0 and 1, and add it to the feature vector under consideration. This results in the selection of a random point along the line segment between two specific features. This approach effectively forces the decision region of the minority class to become more general [29].

Boosting is a machine learning technique that can be used for regression and classification problems. It generates a weak learner at each step and accumulates them in the overall model. If the weak learner for each step is based on the gradient direction of the loss function, it can be called gradient boosting decision tree (GBDT) [30]. The difference with GBDT is that only the first derivative of the loss function is used to compute the objective function. The XGBoost approximates the loss function using the second order Taylor expansion. The main algorithm is as follows and the source code of the XGBoost algorithm is in Appendix A.

Assume that a data set is $D = \{(x_i, y_i)\}(|D| = m, x_i \in R^n, y_i \in R)$, then we obtain n observations with m features each and with a corresponding variable y. Let $\hat{y}$ be defined as a result given by an ensemble represented by the generalized model as follows:

$$\hat{y}_i = \phi(\boldsymbol{x}_i) = \sum_{k=1}^{K} f_k(\boldsymbol{x}_i), f_k \in F \tag{8}$$

where f_k is a regression tree, and $f_k(\boldsymbol{x}_i)$ represents the score given by the k-th tree to the i-th observation in data. In order to functions f_k, the following regularized objective function should be minimized:

$$L(\phi) = \sum_i l(\hat{y}_i, y_i) + \sum_k \Omega(f_k) \tag{9}$$

where l is the loss function. To prevent too large complexity of the model, the penalty term Ω is included as follows:

$$\Omega(f_k) = \gamma T + \frac{1}{2}\lambda\|\omega\|^2 \tag{10}$$

where γ and λ are parameters controlling penalty for the number of leaves T and magnitude of leaf weights ω respectively. The purpose of $\Omega(f_k)$ is to prevent over-fitting and to simplify models produced by this algorithm.

An iterative method is used to minimize the objective function. The objective function that minimized in j-th iterative to add f_j is:

$$L^{(j)} = \sum_{i=1}^{n} l\left(y_i, \hat{y}_i^{(t-1)} + f_j(\boldsymbol{x}_i)\right) + \Omega(f_j) \tag{11}$$

Equation (11) can be simplified by using the Taylor expansion. Then, a formula can be derived for loss reduction after the tree split from a given node:

$$L_{split} = \frac{1}{2}\left[\frac{\left(\sum_{i\in I_L} g_i\right)^2}{\sum_{i\in I_L} h_i + \lambda} + \frac{\left(\sum_{i\in I_R} g_i\right)^2}{\sum_{i\in I_R} h_i + \lambda} - \frac{\left(\sum_{i\in I} g_i\right)^2}{\sum_{i\in I} h_i + \lambda}\right] - \gamma \tag{12}$$

where I is a subset of the available observations in the current node and I_L, I_R are subsets of the available observations in the left and right nodes after the split. The functions g_i and h_i are defined as follows:

$$g_i = \partial_{\hat{y}^{(j-1)}} l\left(y_i, \hat{y}^{(j-1)}\right) \tag{13}$$

$$h_i = \partial^2_{\hat{y}^{(j-1)}} l\left(y_i, \hat{y}^{(j-1)}\right) \tag{14}$$

The XGBoost algorithm has many advantages: it prevents over-fitting by increasing the complexity and compression of the loss function; it optimizes the number of iterations through cross-validation; and it improves the computational efficiency of the model through parallel processing. This algorithm is implemented in the "xgboost" package for the "Python" language provided by the creators of the algorithm.

2.3. Model Assessment Method

The confusion matrix [31] is a classical method for evaluating the results of classification models:

$$C_q = \begin{bmatrix} N_{11} & N_{12} & \cdots & N_{1k} \\ N_{21} & N_{22} & \cdots & N_{2k} \\ \vdots & \vdots & \ddots & \vdots \\ N_{k1} & N_{k2} & \cdots & N_{kk} \end{bmatrix} \tag{15}$$

where N_{ij} represents the probability that class i is divided into class j on the verification set.

Accuracy, recall, and F1 score [32] play a role in the evaluation of the classification model. Through these complementary evaluation indexes, with the results of the confusion matrix, the algorithm model can be evaluated, optimized and screened, and the optimal algorithm model suitable for the data can be obtained.

Accuracy refers to the ratio of the predicted correct number in the test results of the test set to the total number of samples, which is expressed as follows.

$$Accuracy = \frac{\sum_i N_{ii}}{\sum_i \sum_j N_{ij}} \tag{16}$$

The precision of class i indicates the ratio between the number of class i predicted correctly and the number of class i predicted in the test set results, which is expressed as follows:

$$Precision = \frac{N_{ii}}{\sum_j N_{ij}} \tag{17}$$

Recall refers to the ratio between the number of correct class i predicted in the test results of the test set and the number of class i. The equation is as follows:

$$Recall = \frac{N_{ii}}{\sum_i N_{ij}} \tag{18}$$

F1-score is calculated by precision and recall. Since these two values are not intuitive enough, they are more intuitive after conversion. The larger the value, the better the result. The formula is as follows:

$$F_1 = \frac{2PR}{P + R} \tag{19}$$

where P is the accuracy and R represents the recall rate.

Through the accuracy rate, recall rate, and F1-score, which can reflect the quality of classification results, we can adjust and optimize the classification model.

To better understand the proposed fault diagnosis of the steam turbine process, we summarize the main procedures as follows.

Step 1: Extraction of performance indicators. The t-SNE algorithm is used for dimension reduction. Then, cluster analysis is performed on the low-dimensional data. With the fault records, the fault data and normal data of the clustering result are distinguished.

Step 2: Imbalanced data detection model. The imbalance problem in the data is processed by the SMOTE algorithm. We used the XGBoost algorithm to solve this multi-classification problem.

Step 3: Model evaluation method. The confusion matrix is used to evaluate the results of classification models.

Figure 1 shows a schematic diagram of the proposed fault diagnosis of the steam turbine process in this paper.

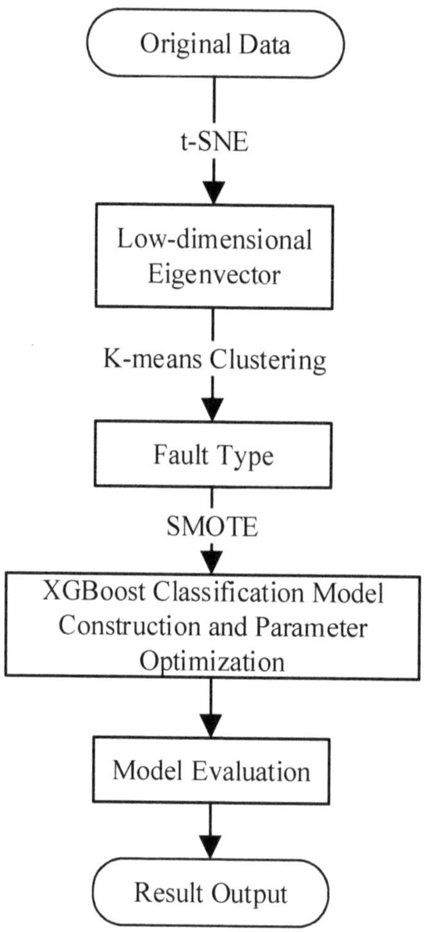

Figure 1. Flow chart of model construction.

3. Experiments, Results and Discussion

3.1. Introduction of Data Set

The data set in this paper was derived from the time series data of Steam Turbine 2 in a thermal power plant in China. The data set include the following two parts.

(1) One was from the supervisory control and data acquisition (SCADA) system. The original sampling period of the SCADA system was less than one millisecond. The data set was the interval sampling data of every one second.

(2) The other was the fault information from the manual record and the system application and product (SAP). The fault information mainly came from the manual record of the power plant, including the fault content and the recorded time. However, some of the fault information was not part of the equipment operation faults and could not be effectively identified by the automated acquisition system. Therefore, in this paper, the fault information was filtered.

After excluding measurement points with severe data loss or no data records, the steam turbine data set contained 34 variables, such as the time stamp, operating condition parameters and status parameters. The acquisition time was eight months, and the size of the effect data was approximately 340,000.

Table 2 shows the statistical information of the steam turbine data set. In addition, more detailed information of the data set can be seen in Appendix B, Table A1.

Table 2. Statistical information of the data set on steam turbines.

Data Set	Sample Size	Time Range
Steam turbine	340,468	January to August in 2018

The fault information was obtained from the fault records manually recorded by the power plant, including the fault content and recording time. Since some fault records were not plant operation faults and could not be effectively identified by the data, the available fault information was screened. The fault records selected for use are shown in Table 3

Table 3. Five types of faults in the fault record.

No.	Fault Discovery Time
1	3 Feb 2018 2:07
2	11 Feb 2018 6:19
3	13 Mar 2018 7:28
4	10 Jun 2018 7:44
5	7 Aug 2018 23:17

3.2. Setting Labels for Different or Normal Faults

We used the fault detection time in the data record to determine the time that the fault occurred. The data of 8~24 h before and after each fault record of the steam turbine were intercepted for analysis. First, the t-SNE algorithm described in the previous section was adopted to map the 34-dimensional data to a two-dimensional space. Then, the K-means clustering method was used to separate the fault data from the normal data. The processing results of the algorithm are visualized in Figure 2. Green data points represent normal data, and other colors represent different fault data points.

The time-series data after clustering was compared to fault records to distinguish fault data from normal data. As shown in Figure 3, each figure is a data graph of different faults arranged by time. In the figure, the time of the red line is the actual time recorded for the five types of faults.

Table 4 shows the information of failure data for five types. Compared to the time of fault records, it can be seen that this method can distinguish fault data and normal data of steam turbines, and it has a certain predictive ability.

3.3. Dealing with Data Imbalance

After labelling the data, the problem to be solved was the data imbalance.

The total number of fault data was 5118 and the number of normal data was 335,350. The ratio of normal data to faulty data was approximately 67:1, which is a very high imbalance. The imbalance needed to be processed before building a classification model. Immediate imbalance processing of this data set could introduce noise, which would affect the accuracy of subsequent classification algorithms.

The normal data were sampled in sections, and the data of one day every four days were extracted and reassembled into the normal data. The SMOTE algorithm was used to deal with the unbalanced data of the newly formed data, and the resulting sample data set is shown in Table 5.

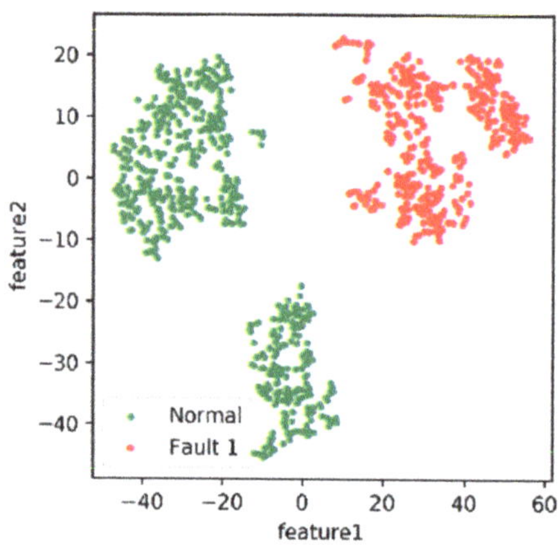

(**a**)

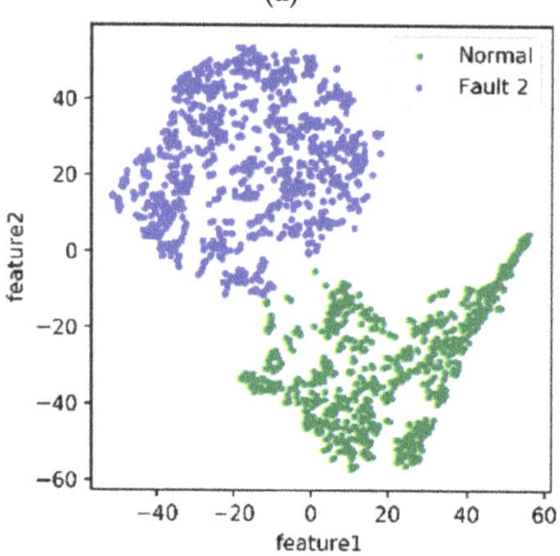

(**b**)

Figure 2. *Cont.*

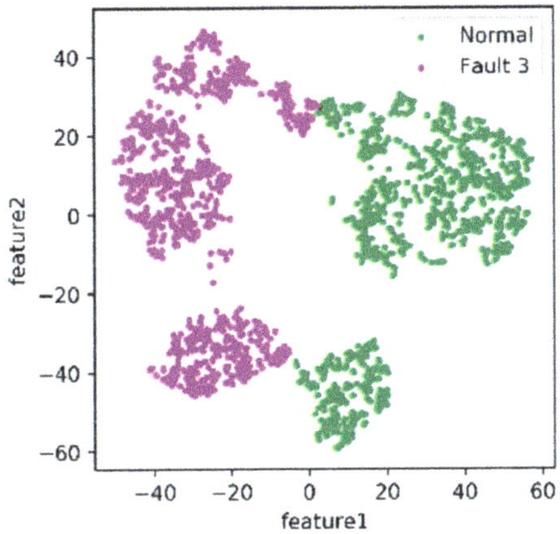

(**c**)

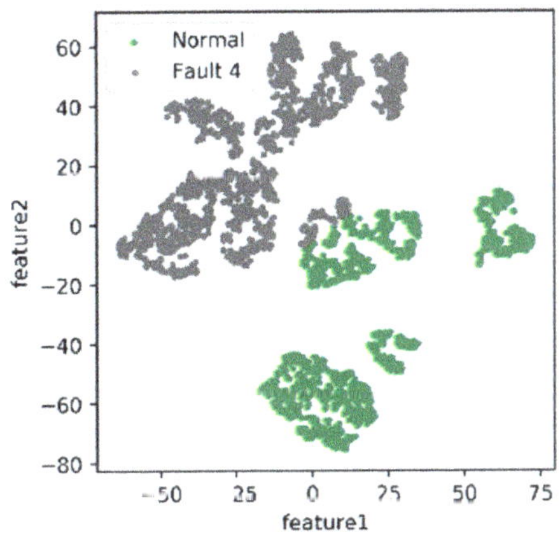

(**d**)

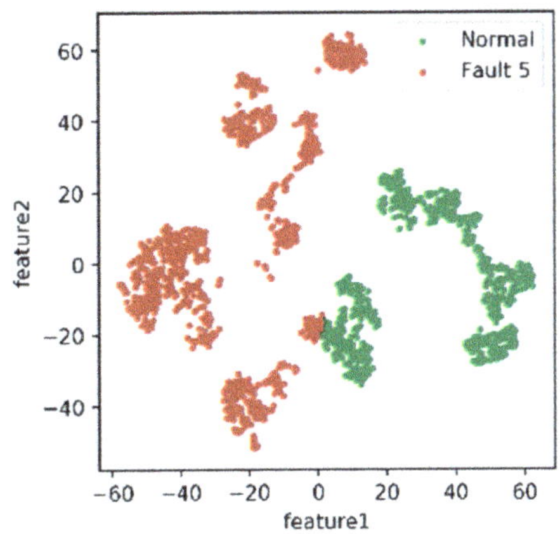

(**e**)

Figure 2. Two-dimensional features of five faults. (**a**) Two-dimensional fusion features of Fault 1. (**b**) Two-dimensional fusion features of Fault 2. (**c**) Two-dimensional fusion features of Fault 3. (**d**) Two-dimensional fusion features of Fault 4. (**e**) Two-dimensional fusion features of Fault 5.

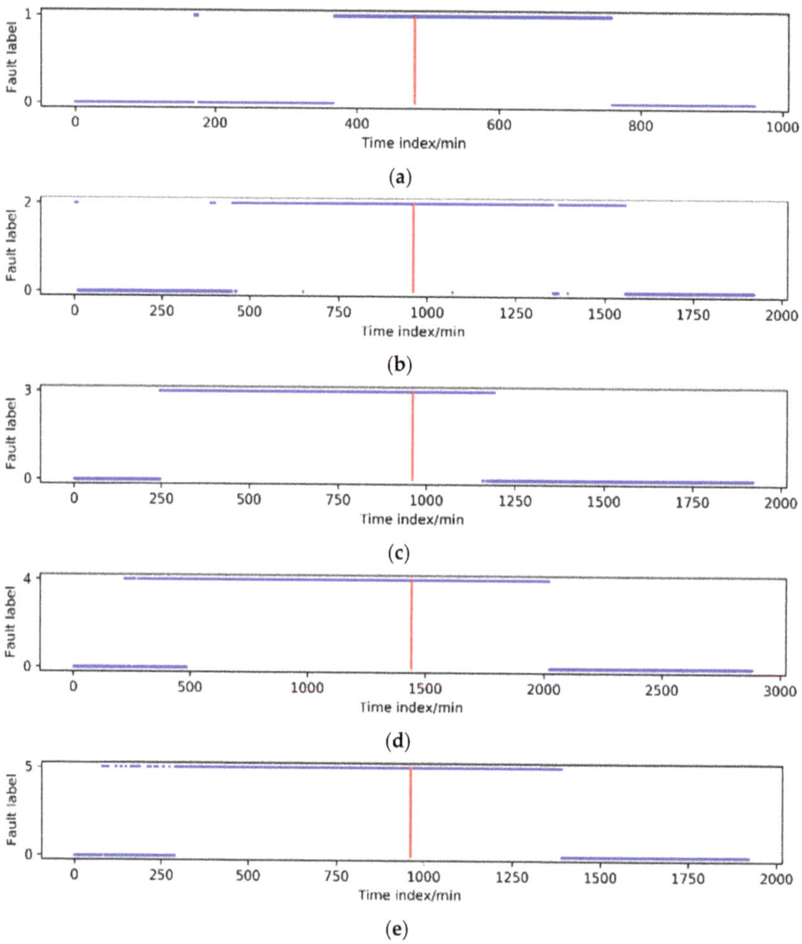

Figure 3. Time series data of five faults. (**a**) Clustering results of Fault 1 based on time series. (**b**) Clustering results of Fault 2 based on time series. (**c**) Clustering results of Fault 3 based on time series. (**d**) Clustering results of Fault 4 based on time series. (**e**) Clustering results of Fault 5 based on time series.

Table 4. Five types of fault data information table.

No.	Start Time	End Time	Advanced Time (min)
1	3 Feb 2018 0:14	3 Feb 2018 6:45	113
2	10 Feb 2018 22:02	11 Feb 2018 16:16	497
3	12 Mar 2018 19:32	13 Mar 2018 11:10	716
4	9 Jun 2018 14:53	10 Jun 2018 17:25	1011
5	7 Aug 2018 12:07	8 Aug 2018 6:25	670

Table 5. The amount of fault data.

	Original Data	by SMOTE
Normal	78,513	78,513
Fault 1	392	5832
Fault 2	1095	16,823
Fault 3	939	14,402
Fault 4	1593	24,655
Fault 5	1099	16,801
Ratio	15:1	1:1

3.4. Test Results

After optimizing the data imbalance in the previous section, the XGBoost algorithm could be used for fault diagnosis. The data set was divided into a training set and a test set and divided according to the ratio of 3:7. The results of the confusion matrix are shown in Table 6.

Table 6. Results of confusion matrix.

Confusion Matrix	Predicted Result (%)					
	0	1	2	3	4	5
0	97.06	0.08	1.09	0.67	0.37	0.73
1	0.06	99.94	0	0	0	0
2	1.24	0	98.76	0	0	0
3	2.36	0	0	97.64	0	0
4	0.41	0	0	0	99.59	0
5	0.27	0	0	0	0	99.72

To better calculate the performance of the model, precision, recall rate and F1-score were calculated, and the calculation results are shown in Table 7.

Table 7. Precision, recall and F1-score results.

Fault Label	Precision	Recall Rate	F1-Score
0	99.18%	96.80%	97.98%
1	98.74%	100.00%	99.37%
2	94.54%	99.02%	97.07%
3	96.52%	97.63%	97.07%
4	98.52%	99.70%	99.11%
5	96.58%	99.72%	98.13%

Tables 6 and 7 show the classification results of the model for five faults of the steam turbine. As is well-known, for a classification model, if precision, recall and F1-score have higher values at the same time without considering other factors, the model is considered to have better performance. The model based on the XGBoost classifier had high accuracy in fault diagnosis of steam turbines and could identify the different types of faults.

3.5. Results and Discussion

In this paper, we developed a novel procedure for the actual data of the power plant, and obtained the expected results for the power plant. In order to further illustrate the superiority of the proposed method in this paper over other methods, it is necessary to discuss the following issues.

(1) Computational efficiency.

The research object of this paper was a power plant's big data, so the complexity of the algorithm was one of the important issues to be considered. The complexity of the T-SNE algorithm used in the research method of this paper is large. In general, applying the T-SNE algorithm for dimensionality reduction for a data set of millions of samples may take several hours. The number of samples calculated in this paper was about 340,000, and the training time of the model including the dimensionality reduction algorithm was less than one hour. Such computational efficiency is perfectly acceptable for an enterprise-level data application system. In addition, since the probability of serious faults in power plant enterprises is often low, we generally recommend that power plants update the training model every six months with new data, and the time to update the model here is at most a few hours. For the calculation time of the final classification model, achievement of the real-time effect can be considered (generally no more than 1 s).

(2) Comparison with other algorithms.

The purpose of this research paper was to develop a procedure of fault diagnosis and prediction for the power plant data. For the data dimensionality reduction algorithm, we chose the t-SNE algorithm. In the research process, we also compared a principal component analysis (PCA) algorithm at the same time. Although, the PCA method had a faster computational speed, it was still less effective than nonlinear dimensionality reduction algorithms, such as t-SNE, for complex data of the power plant due to the linear dimensionality reduction method [33].

For the final classification algorithm, in addition to the XGBoost algorithm, we also compared algorithms such as SVM and random forest (RF). From the application effect of the data in this paper, the computational results of the XGBoost algorithm and the RF algorithm were better than SVM; moreover, considering that the XGBoost algorithm borrows from RF and can support column sampling processing, which can not only reduce overfitting, but also reduce computational effort [34], the XGBoost algorithm was finally chosen in this paper.

(3) Improvement of the algorithm.

For a fault diagnosis and prediction system that is really applied to the power plant, the most important purpose was to be able to detect and warn about the dangerous faults in advance based on the large historical data. In this paper, the algorithm was trained with more than 300,000 samples of data for nearly eight months, and the algorithm had some limitations. However, in the actual application system, we used more than seven years of historical data of the power plant to train the used model, which proved to have a good application effect.

Furthermore, in addition to the application data set in this paper, we also validated the pneumatic feed pump data set for this power plant. The results also showed that the method proposed in this paper was also applicable to other equipment in the power plant. In general, the accuracy of 90% of the actual data can meet the needs of the enterprise management. Therefore, the research algorithm in this paper has been practically applied in the power plant and has achieved satisfactory results.

4. Conclusions

A model based on t-SNE and XGBoost was proposed to detect the early failure of steam turbines. The model with high accuracy was verified by the data of steam turbine units of thermal power plants in China.

(1) The uncertainty problem of feature extraction in the unlabeled data set was solved using t-SNE and K-means. This method can distinguish fault data and normal data, and it has a certain foresight because it can distinguish the time when the fault occurs, which is earlier than the fault record of manual inspection, making it more suitable for practical application in fault diagnosis of steam turbines.

(2) The problem of data imbalance caused by fewer fault records was solved by using the SMOTE algorithm, which is of great significance to the fault diagnosis of the steam turbine and other mechanical equipment with fewer faulty samples.

(3) In the identification of new data, the accuracy and other indicators of the model based on XGBoost reached more than 97%, which shows that this method has high value in turbine fault diagnosis.

Author Contributions: Conceptualization, L.Z. and X.W.; methodology, L.Z. and X.W.; software, X.W.; validation, Z.L., L.Z. and X.W.; formal analysis, L.Z.; investigation, X.W.; resources, L.Z.; data curation, L.Z.; writing—original draft preparation, X.W.; writing—review and editing, Z.L. and L.Z.; supervision, L.Z.; project administration, L.Z.; funding acquisition, L.Z. All authors have read and agreed to the published version of the manuscript.

Funding: This research was supported by Innovation Group Project of Southern Marine Science and Engineering Guangdong Laboratory (Zhuhai) of China (No. 311021013), National Natural Science Foundation of China (No. 51775037), and Fundamental Research Funds for Central Universities of China (No. FRF-BD-18-001A).

Institutional Review Board Statement: Not applicable.

Informed Consent Statement: Not applicable.

Data Availability Statement: Data is contained within the article.

Acknowledgments: The authors thank the National Center for Materials Service Safety for support of the simulation and data platform.

Conflicts of Interest: The authors declare no conflict of interest.

Appendix A

The following source code for reference is the t-SNE algorithm.

Algorithm A1. T-SNE algorithm.

```
#!/usr/bin/env python
# coding: utf-8

import os
import sys
os.chdir (os.path.split (os.path.realpath (sys.argv [0]))[0])

import numpy
from numpy import *
import numpy as np

from sklearn.manifold import TSNE
from sklearn.datasets import load_iris
from sklearn.decomposition import PCA
import matplotlib.pyplot as plt

import pandas as pd

df1 = pd.read_excel ('D:/data/gz5.xlsx')

df1.label.value_counts ()

def get_data (data):
        X = data.drop (columns = ['time', 'label']).values
        y = data.label.values
        n_samples, n_features = X.shape
        return X, y, n_samples, n_features

X1, y1, n_samples1, n_features1 = get_data (df1)

X_tsne = TSNE (n_components = 2,init = 'pca', random_state = 0).fit_transform (X1)

def plot_embedding (X, y, title = None):
        x_min, x_max = np.min(X, 0), np.max(X, 0)
        X = (X − x_min) / (x_max − x_min)
```

Algorithm A1. T-SNE algorithm.

```
    plt.figure ()
    ax = plt.subplot (111)
    for i in range (X.shape [0]):
        plt.text (X [i, 0], X [i, 1], '.',
                  color = plt.cm.Set1 (y[i] * 3/10.),
                  fontdict = {'weight': 'bold', 'size': 9})
    plt.xticks ([]), plt.yticks ([])
    if title is not None:
        plt.title (title)


plot_embedding (X_tsne, y1)

from sklearn.cluster import KMeans
from sklearn.externals import joblib
from sklearn import cluster

estimator = KMeans (n_clusters = 2)

res = estimator.fit_predict (X_tsne)
lable_pred = estimator.labels_

centroids = estimator.cluster_centers_

inertia = estimator.inertia_

from pandas import DataFrame
XA = DataFrame (res)
XA.to_csv ('D:/data/gz5out.csv')
```

The following source code for reference is the XGBoost algorithm.

Algorithm A2. XGBoost algorithm.

```
#!/usr/bin/env python
# coding: utf-8

from xgboost import plot_importance
from matplotlib import pyplot as plt

import xgboost as xgb
from sklearn.model_selection import train_test_split
from sklearn.metrics import accuracy_score
import numpy as np
import pandas as pd
from xgboost.sklearn import XGBClassifier

# load data
data = pd.read_csv ('D:/data/suanfa/kyq.csv')
x, y = data.loc [:,data.columns.difference (['label'])].values, data ['label'].values
x_train, x_test, y_train, y_test = train_test_split (x, y, test_size = 0.3)

data.label.value_counts ()

params ={'learning_rate': 0.1,
        'max_depth': 2,
        'n_estimators':50,
        'num_boost_round':10,
```

Algorithm A2. XGBoost algorithm.

```
            'objective': 'multi:softprob',
            'random_state': 0,
            'silent':0,
            'num_class':6,
            'eta':0.9
        }

model = xgb.train (params, xgb.DMatrix (x_train, y_train))
y_pred = model.predict (xgb.DMatrix (x_test))
yprob = np.argmax (y_pred, axis = 1) # return the index of the biggest pro

model.save_model ('testXGboostClass.model')

yprob = np.argmax (y_pred, axis = 1) # return the index of the biggest pro

predictions = [round (value) for value in yprob]

# evaluate predictions
accuracy = accuracy_score(y_test, predictions)
print ("Accuracy: %.2f%%" % (accuracy * 100.0))

plot_importance (model)
plt.show ()

xgb1 = XGBClassifier (
        learning_rate = 0.1,
        n_estimators = 20,
        max_depth = 2,
        num_boost_round = 10,
        random_state = 0,
        silent = 0,
        objective = 'multi:softprob',
        num_class = 6,
        eta = 0.9
        )

xgb1.fit (x_train, y_train)

y_pred1 = xgb1.predict_proba (x_test)

yprob1 = np.argmax (y_pred1, axis = 1) # return the index of the biggest pro

from sklearn.metrics import confusion_matrix
confusion_matrix (y_test.astype ('int'), yprob1.astype ('int'))

from sklearn.metrics import classification_report
print ('Accuracy of Classifier:',xgb1.score (x_test, y_test.astype ('int')))
print (classification_report (y_test.astype ('int'), yprob1.astype ('int')))
```

Appendix B

Table A1. Variable name.

No.	Description
F0	Time stamp
F1	Turbine Speed
F2	Main Steam Pressure

Table A1. *Cont.*

No.	Description
F3	Reheat Steam Pressure
F4	Main Steam Temp
F5	Bearing Bushing 11
F6	Bearing Bushing 12
F7	Bearing Bushing 21
F8	Bearing Bushing 22
F9	Bearing Bushing 31
F10	Bearing Bushing 32
F11	Bearing Bushing 41
F12	Bearing Bushing 42
F13	Bearing Bushing 51
F14	Bearing Bushing 61
F15	Bearing Vibration 1X
F16	Bearing Vibration 1Y
F17	Bearing Vibration 1Z
F18	Bearing Vibration 2X
F19	Bearing Vibration 2Y
F20	Bearing Vibration 2Z
F21	Bearing Vibration 3X
F22	Bearing Vibration 3Y
F23	Bearing Vibration 3Z
F24	Bearing Vibration 4X
F25	Bearing Vibration 4Y
F26	Bearing Vibration 4Z
F27	Bearing Vibration 5X
F28	Bearing Vibration 5Y
F29	Bearing Vibration 5Z
F30	Bearing Vibration 6X
F31	Bearing Vibration 6Y
F32	Bearing Vibration 6Z
F33	Turbine Differential Expansion
F34	Rotor Eccentricity

References

1. Yu, J.; Jang, J.; Yoo, J.; Park, J.H.; Kim, S. A fault isolation method via classification and regression tree-based variable ranking for drum-type steam boiler in thermal power plant. *Energies* **2018**, *11*, 1142. [CrossRef]
2. Madrigal, G.; Astorga, C.M.; Vazquez, M.; Osorio, G.L.; Adam, M. Fault diagnosis in sensors of boiler following control of a thermal power plant. *IEEE Lat. Am. Trans.* **2018**, *16*, 1692–1699. [CrossRef]
3. Wu, Y.; Li, W.; Sheng, D.; Chen, J.; Yu, Z. Fault diagnosis method of peak-load-regulation steam turbine based on improved PCA-HKNN artificial neural network. *Proc. Inst. Mech. Eng. O J. Risk Reliab.* **2021**, *235*, 1026–1040. [CrossRef]
4. Cao, H.; Niu, L.; Xi, S.; Chen, X. Mechanical model development of rolling bearing-rotor systems: A review. *Mech. Syst. Signal Process.* **2018**, *102*, 37–58. [CrossRef]
5. Xu, Y.; Zhen, D.; Gu, J.; Rabeyee, K.; Chu, F.; Gu, F.; Ball, A.D. Autocorrelated Envelopes for early fault detection of rolling bearings. *Mech. Syst. Signal Process.* **2021**, *146*, 106990. [CrossRef]
6. Kazemi, P.; Ghisi, A.; Mariani, S. Classification of the Structural Behavior of Tall Buildings with a Diagrid Structure: A Machine Learning-Based Approach. *Algorithms* **2022**, *15*, 349. [CrossRef]
7. Shi, Q.; Zhang, H. Fault Diagnosis of an Autonomous Vehicle With an Improved SVM Algorithm Subject to Unbalanced Datasets. *IEEE Trans. Ind. Electron.* **2021**, *68*, 6248–6256. [CrossRef]
8. Zhang, P.; Gao, Z.; Cao, L.; Dong, F.; Zhou, Y.; Wang, K.; Zhang, Y.; Sun, P. Marine Systems and Equipment Prognostics and Health Management: A Systematic Review from Health Condition Monitoring to Maintenance Strategy. *Machines* **2022**, *10*, 72. [CrossRef]
9. Li, X.; Wu, S.; Li, X.; Yuan, H.; Zhao, D. Particle swarm optimization-Support Vector Machine model for machinery fault diagnoses in high-voltage circuit breakers. *Chin. J. Mech. Eng.* **2020**, *33*, 6. [CrossRef]
10. Zan, T.; Liu, Z.; Wang, H.; Wang, M.; Gao, X.; Pang, Z. Prediction of performance deterioration of rolling bearing based on JADE and PSO-SVM. *Proc. Inst. Mech. Eng. C J. Mech. Eng. Sci.* **2020**, *235*, 1684–1697. [CrossRef]
11. Fink, O.; Wang, Q.; Svensen, M.; Dersin, P.; Lee, W.-J.; Ducoffe, M. Potential, challenges and future directions for deep learning in prognostics and health management applications. *Eng. Appl. Artif. Intell.* **2020**, *92*, 103678. [CrossRef]

12. Deng, W.; Yao, R.; Zhao, H.; Yang, X.; Li, G. A novel intelligent diagnosis method using optimal LS-SVM with improved PSO algorithm. *Soft Comput.* **2019**, *23*, 2445–2462. [CrossRef]
13. Sun, H.; Zhang, L. Simulation study on fault diagnosis of power electronic circuits based on wavelet packet analysis and support vector machine. *J. Electr. Syst.* **2018**, *14*, 21–33.
14. Wang, Z.; Xia, H.; Yin, W.; Yang, B. An improved generative adversarial network for fault diagnosis of rotating machine in nuclear power plant. *Ann. Nucl. Energy* **2023**, *180*, 109434. [CrossRef]
15. Kang, C.; Wang, Y.; Xue, Y.; Mu, G.; Liao, R. Big Data Analytics in China's Electric Power Industry. *IEEE Power Energy Mag.* **2018**, *16*, 54–65. [CrossRef]
16. Ma, Y.; Huang, C.; Sun, Y.; Zhao, G.; Lei, Y. Review of Power Spatio-Temporal Big Data Technologies for Mobile Computing in Smart Grid. *IEEE Access* **2019**, *7*, 174612–174628. [CrossRef]
17. Lai, C.S.; Locatelli, G.; Pimm, A.; Wu, X.; Lai, L.L. A review on long-term electrical power system modeling with energy storage. *J. Clean. Prod.* **2021**, *280*, 124298. [CrossRef]
18. Dhanalakshmi, J.; Ayyanathan, N. A systematic review of big data in energy analytics using energy computing techniques. *Concurr. Comput. Pract. Exp.* **2021**, *34*, e6647. [CrossRef]
19. Li, W.; Li, X.; Niu, Q.; Huang, T.; Zhang, D.; Dong, Y. Analysis and Treatment of Shutdown Due to Bearing Vibration Towards Ultra-supercritical 660MW Turbine. *IOP Conf. Ser. Earth Environ. Sci.* **2019**, *300*, 42006–42008. [CrossRef]
20. Ashraf, W.M.; Rafique, Y.; Uddin, G.M.; Riaz, F.; Asin, M.; Farooq, M.; Hussain, A.; Salman, C.A. Artificial intelligence based operational strategy development and implementation for vibration reduction of a supercritical steam turbine shaft bearing. *Alex. Eng. J.* **2022**, *61*, 1864–1880. [CrossRef]
21. van der Maaten, L.; Hinton, G. Visualizing Data using t-SNE. *J. Mach. Learn. Res.* **2008**, *9*, 2579–2605.
22. Gisbrecht, A.; Schulz, A.; Hammer, B. Parametric nonlinear dimensionality reduction using kernel t-SNE. *Neurocomputing* **2015**, *147*, 71–82. [CrossRef]
23. Wang, H.-H.; Chen, C.-P. Applying t-SNE to Estimate Image Sharpness of Low-cost Nailfold Capillaroscopy. *Intell. Autom. Soft Comput.* **2022**, *32*, 237–254. [CrossRef]
24. Xu, X.; Xie, Z.; Yang, Z.; Li, D.; Xu, X. A t-SNE Based Classification Approach to Compositional Microbiome Data. *Front. Genet.* **2020**, *11*, 620143. [CrossRef]
25. Yi, C.; Tuo, S.; Tu, S.; Zhang, W. Improved fuzzy C-means clustering algorithm based on t-SNE for terahertz spectral recognition. *Infrared Phys. Technol.* **2021**, *117*, 103856. [CrossRef]
26. Gutierrez-Lopez, A.; Gonzalez-Serrano, F.-J.; Figueiras-Vidal, A.R. Optimum Bayesian thresholds for rebalanced classification problems using class-switching ensembles. *Pattern Recognit.* **2023**, *135*, 109158. [CrossRef]
27. Arora, J.; Tushir, M.; Sharma, K.; Mohan, L.; Singh, A.; Alharbi, A.; Alosaimi, W. MCBC-SMOTE: A Majority Clustering Model for Classification of Imbalanced Data. *CMC-Comput. Mater. Contin.* **2022**, *73*, 4801–4817. [CrossRef]
28. Kumar, A.; Gopal, R.D.; Shankar, R.; Tan, K.H. Fraudulent review detection model focusing on emotional expressions and explicit aspects: Investigating the potential of feature engineering. *Decis. Support Syst.* **2022**, *155*, 113728. [CrossRef]
29. Guo, S.; Chen, R.; Li, H.; Zhang, T.; Liu, Y. Identify Severity Bug Report with Distribution Imbalance by CR-SMOTE and ELM. *Int. J. Softw. Eng. Knowl. Eng.* **2019**, *29*, 139–175. [CrossRef]
30. Duan, G.; Han, W. Heavy Overload Prediction Method of Distribution Transformer Based on GBDT. *Int. J. Pattern Recognit. Artif. Intell.* **2022**, *36*, 2259014. [CrossRef]
31. Liu, X.; Liu, W.; Huang, H.; Bo, L. An improved confusion matrix for fusing multiple K-SVD classifiers. *Knowl. Inf. Syst.* **2022**, *64*, 703–722. [CrossRef]
32. Maldonado, S.; López, J.; Jimenez-Molina, A.; Lira, H. Simultaneous feature selection and heterogeneity control for SVM classification: An application to mental workload assessment. *Expert Syst. Appl.* **2020**, *143*, 112988. [CrossRef]
33. Anowar, F.; Sadaoui, S.; Selim, B. Conceptual and empirical comparison of dimensionality reduction algorithms (PCA, KPCA, LDA, MDS, SVD, LLE, ISOMAP, LE, ICA, t-SNE). *Comput. Sci. Rev.* **2021**, *40*, 100378. [CrossRef]
34. Khan, N.; Taqvi, S.A.A. Machine Learning an Intelligent Approach in Process Industries: A Perspective and Overview. *ChemBioEng Rev.* **2023**. [CrossRef]

algorithms

MDPI

Article

Wind Turbine Predictive Fault Diagnostics Based on a Novel Long Short-Term Memory Model

Shuo Zhang, Emma Robinson and Malabika Basu *

School of Electrical and Electronic Engineering, Technological University Dublin, D07 H6K8 Dublin, Ireland; d18128381@mytudublin.ie (S.Z.); emma.robinson@tudublin.ie (E.R.)
* Correspondence: malabika.basu@tudublin.ie; Tel.: +353-851418201

Abstract: The operation and maintenance (O&M) issues of offshore wind turbines (WTs) are more challenging because of the harsh operational environment and hard accessibility. As sudden component failures within WTs bring about durable downtimes and significant revenue losses, condition monitoring and predictive fault diagnostic approaches must be developed to detect faults before they occur, thus preventing durable downtimes and costly unplanned maintenance. Based primarily on supervisory control and data acquisition (SCADA) data, thirty-three weighty features from operational data are extracted, and eight specific faults are categorised for fault predictions from status information. By providing a model-agnostic vector representation for time, Time2Vec (T2V), into Long Short-Term Memory (LSTM), this paper develops a novel deep-learning neural network model, T2V-LSTM, conducting multi-level fault predictions. The classification steps allow fault diagnosis from 10 to 210 min prior to faults. The results show that T2V-LSTM can successfully predict over 84.97% of faults and outperform LSTM and other counterparts in both overall and individual fault predictions due to its topmost recall scores in most multistep-ahead cases performed. Thus, the proposed T2V-LSTM can correctly diagnose more faults and upgrade the predictive performances based on vanilla LSTM in terms of accuracy, recall scores, and F-scores.

Keywords: operation and maintenance (O&M); wind turbines (WTs); predictive fault diagnostic; supervisory control and data acquisition (SCADA); Time2Vec (T2V); Long Short-Term Memory (LSTM); T2V-LSTM

1. Introduction

The global wind energy installations expanded by about 14% annually from 2001 to 2020 [1]. The total wind power capacity increased from 650.8 GW in 2019 to 742.7 GW in 2020, with a spectacular growth of 53% (over 90 GW) since 2019 [2,3]. Due to plentiful wind resources and abundant construction sites in offshore areas, more wind farms are installed with increased seabed depths and remote distances to shore [4]. Using the same commercial wind turbine (WT), offshore power production is at least 1.34 times more than the onshore site with the highest wind energy potential due to stronger and more uniform wind resources in offshore areas [5]. However, offshore WT installation costs are about 2.64 times those of their onshore counterpart [6]. And harsher weather conditions are challenging for the operation and maintenance (O&M) tasks of offshore WTs. Moreover, O&M costs account for a large fraction of total lifecycle costs, with 10–15% and 25–30% for onshore and offshore wind farms, respectively [6,7]. Unexpectedly, sudden faults from high-risk WT components contribute significantly to the increase in O&M costs related to downtimes and discounted revenues [8]. To reduce O&M costs and enhance system reliability, condition monitoring (CM), fault diagnosis, and prognosis are of prior importance through the detection of certain faults before they reach catastrophic fault severity levels. Hence, O&M costs can be decreased along with maintenance interval optimisation [9].

Condition Monitoring System (CMS) can facilitate system failure prevention and WT availability improvement through early-stage fault detections. To diagnose fault-free conditions of WT components, such as the gearbox and drivetrain, CMS has been implemented via vibration analysis [10], oil analysis [11], electrical signature analysis [12], and acoustic emission analysis [13]. CMS-based monitoring is capable of both fault diagnosis and prognosis with a high-frequency resolution, but this approach is more expensive compared to supervisory control and data acquisition (SCADA) [14]. Thus, SCADA systems become more favourable for WT operators to apply the CM technique due to cheaper costs; however, these have a low-frequency resolution [15]. SCADA data are normally collected under a 10 min sampling rate. A number of data-driven studies on SCADA-based monitoring have been utilised for performance monitoring of WT operational conditions in recent years without retrofitting additional sensors.

Stetco et al. [16] investigated the machine learning (ML) applications for CM in WTs, including CM for diagnosis and CM for prognosis. Diagnosis focuses on real-time fault identifications, whilst prognosis is to predict the faults before their occurrences [17].

Classification is a supervised ML approach, applicable for fault detection, diagnosis, and prognosis, to train a classifier by predicting its categorised outputs based on input variables, thus differentiating between healthy and faulty operations. Lu et al. [18] proposed an online fault diagnosis for WT planetary gearbox faults employing a self-powered wireless sensor for signal acquisition. Leahy et al. [19] applied support vector machine (SVM) models to detect, diagnose, and predict faults in a 3 MW direct-drive turbine. However, the classification results on feeding and air-cooling faults had deficient performances due to the problematic classification of the SVM hyperplane. Naik and Koley [20] adopted the k-nearest neighbour (*k*-NN) classifier-based protection to detect and classify multiple types of faults in AC/HVDC transmission systems by varying fault resistance and inception angles with a classification accuracy of 100%. Marti-Puig et al. [21] investigated several automatic feature selection approaches based on the *k*-NN classifier for fault prognostics with the use of 36 sensor variables on gearbox and transmission systems. Artificial Neural Network (ANN) was trained by Ibrahim et al. [22] for WT mechanical faults with a median accuracy between 93.5% and 98% in fault detection. For various classification tasks, SVM [18,19,23], *k*-NN [20,21], ANN [22,24,25], and RF [25,26] are commonly used with SCADA, simulation, or experimental data. Most importantly, accurate fault diagnosis is the prerequisite for developing any prediction model.

ANN has been widely applied to the ML approach for supervised classification learning [27]. The typical ANN architecture, multi-layer perception (MLP), is a feed-forward multi-layered neural network consisting of an input layer, several hidden layers, and an output layer. The ANN prediction results are determined by data size, data pre-processing, selected neural network structures under their optimum activation functions, etc. [16]. Due to its robustness towards poor-quality data with noise and system disturbances, a well-trained ANN model can still make wise predictions, which cannot be achieved by other ML classifiers [6]. With the escalation of quantitative data sizes and complexity, ANN is a model with ideal predictive results but a slow convergence speed.

Compared to ANN, the Recurrent Neural Network (RNN) is a more promising neural network model for time- and sequence-based tasks because its recurrent structure captures the temporal dependency among inputs with sequential characteristics to predict the next scenario [28]. RNN is a class of deep-learning neural networks designed for variable-length sequence inputs by remembering important events and allowing the previous values as inputs to predict future outputs with recurrent connections in hidden layers. RNN overcomes the over- and under-fitting issues and reduces the convergence time compared to ANN. However, vanishing gradients, caused by error information flowing backward, are large barriers to the success of vanilla RNNs because of the resultant oscillating weights or loss of long-term dependencies [29]. To address vanishing gradients, Long-Short-Term Memory (LSTM), proposed by Hochreiter and Schmidhuber [29], is a remarkable RNN model to control the information flow with additional interacting layers. Based on SCADA data, Chen et al. [30] verified the outperformance of LSTM over ANN and autoencoder (AE) for anomaly detection. The integrated LSTM-AE model further improved the detection accuracy due to the raw input processed by AE and the time feature managed by LSTM. Based on both single-sensor and multi-sensor signals, LSTM outperformed RNN and ANN on the classification of 11 faults on the wind wheel, bearing, bearing support, and rotor [31]. For a case study of fault classification on inner, outer, and ball faults from rolling bearings [32], LSTM demonstrated higher accuracy than ANN and SVM, and stacked LSTM further enhanced the prediction accuracy. The advantages of LSTM have been validated according to multiple time-series fault diagnosis tasks [30–32].

The time-series events can occur either synchronously or asynchronously. However, most of the RNN or LSTM models fail to make use of time as a feature by considering all inputs to be synchronous. Kazemi et al. [33] proposed a model-agnostic vector representation for time, known as Time2Vec (T2V), to be integrated with the LSTM model to refurbish the architecture with the consumption of time features. The key contributions in this paper can be generalised as follows:

- A feature selection method, Recursive Feature Elimination (RFE) [34], is conducted along with an RF classifier for WT fault prediction. The weights of each feature are computed under the RF classifier, and the RFE application reserves the optimal number of features in order of their significance levels to maintain a balance between prediction accuracy and computational costs.
- By integrating Time2Vec into LSTM, this approach, T2V-LSTM, has been validated to outperform LSTM with a stationary Time2Vec activation function based on several synchronous datasets [33]. In this paper, the data points related to downtimes are removed to reserve only fault-free and fault data provided by the SCADA system for the purpose of fault and no-fault predictions. Thus, a non-stationary Time2Vec activation function is demanded to deal with the yielded asynchronous data.
- A novel deep-learning neural network model, T2V-LSTM, with an optimal non-stationary activation function, is modelled to improve the model performance of LSTM, successfully detecting over 84.97% of faults in advance. The comparative studies between T2V-LSTM, LSTM, and other ML classifiers are investigated for overall and individual fault predictions based on performance metrics, including accuracy, recall scores, precision scores, and F-scores [16].

The paper is organised as follows. Section 2 provides the SCADA operational and status data, and the modelling process is introduced with data pre-processing, feature engineering, and fault prognosis. The methodology studies of T2V-LSTM and the processes of model optimisation are presented in Section 3. Section 4 investigates the comparative predictive results from T2V-LSTM, LSTM, and other classifiers, and Section 5 presents a discussion of this investigation. The key results and contributions are summarised in Section 6.

2. SCADA Data

The available data were collected from a 7 MW demonstration offshore WT, owned by the Offshore Renewable Energy (ORE) Catapult [35]. This WT is a three-bladed upwind turbine mounted on a jacket support structure with a total height of 196 m, from blade tip to sea level, located at Levenmouth, Fife, Scotland, UK. The regarded cut-in, rated, and cut-off wind speeds were 3.5 m/s, 10.9 m/s, and 25 m/s, respectively [36]. More detailed information about this WT can be seen in Figure 1. For this turbine, the collected data had two separate groups: operational SCADA data and status data. The investigated datasets of both groups cover a 17-month period from May 2018 to September 2019.

2.1. Operational Data and Status Data

The collected SCADA operational data include alarm data, control information, electrical signals, pressure data, temperature data, turbine data, miscellaneous signals, and other signals.

Properties	Values
Wind class	IEC Class 1A
Rotor diameter	171.2 m
Capacity	7 MW
Hub height	110.6 m
Blade length	83.5 m
Total height	196 m blade tip to sea level
Generator	PMG (3.3 kV)
Converter	Full power conversion
Drive train	Medium speed (400 rpm)
Rated frequency	50 Hz
Rotor speed	5.9 ~ 10.6 rpm
Wind speed	3.5 ~ 25 m/s
Rated wind speed	10.9 m/s
Design life	25 years
Certification	DNV

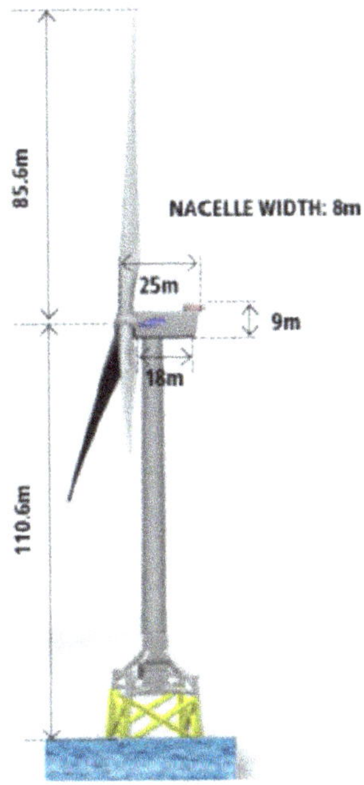

Figure 1. Levenmouth offshore wind turbine [35].

The SCADA system operates at a 10 min sampling rate by monitoring instantaneous parameters, such as wind speed, pitch angle, rotor speed, yaw error, electrical power, currents, voltages, temperatures, and pressures. Taking Table 1 as an example, the minimum, maximum, mean, standard deviation, and ending values of wind speed are collected with the corresponding timestamps. The original dataset includes more than 2000 features and approximately 70,000 data points with regard to the 17 months to be studied.

Table 1. Ten-minute SCADA operational data.

StartTime	WindSpeed _mps_Min	WindSpeed _mps_Max	WindSpeed _mps_Mean	WindSpeed _mps_Stdev	WindSpeed _mps_EndVal
21/05/2018 22:00:00	3.577394	10.11077	6.8690084	1.3447459	5.802108
21/05/2018 22:10:00	3.062414	10.03982	6.7177955	1.108204	6.073331
21/05/2018 22:20:00	4.69204	9.636992	7.1981784	1.0209401	8.475427

The information about requested shutdowns, faults, or warning events is provided by status data. As seen in Table 2, fault and warning events are tracked with respect to their corresponding event codes, on-times, and off-times. There are miscellaneous operating states under the abnormal or faulty conditions of the WT. According to Kusiak and Li [37], the status of fault data is assigned as follows:

$$\begin{gathered} If\ T_{SCADA}(t) < T_{fault} < T_{SCADA}(t+1),\ then \\ Event.Code(t) = Event.Code(t+1) = Event.Code\left(T_{fault}\right) \end{gathered} \quad (1)$$

where $T_{SCADA}(t+1)$ denotes the one-step behind (or 10 min behind) SCADA data since both timestamps, t, and $t+1$, have 10 min intervals.

Table 2. SCADA status data.

TimeOn	TimeOff	Event Code	Event Description
21/05/2018 19:38:33	21/05/2018 19:38:39	286	(Demoted) Yaw Hydraulic Pressure Diff Too Large
21/05/2018 20:26:02	21/05/2018 20:26:10	543	Gearbox Cooling Line Pressure Too Low
21/05/2018 20:26:12	21/05/2018 20:29:20	543	Gearbox Cooling Line Pressure Too Low

The 10 min period is applied to capture any fault occurrences. For example, in Table 2, the operational period from "21/05/2018 20:20:00" to "21/05/2018 20:30:00" should be labelled as "Gearbox Cooling Line Pressure Too Low" with its event code of 543 due to its fault occurrence within the 10 min time band.

As seen in Figure 2, the frequency of occurrences of each status varies. Any event code above zero indicates an abnormality. The majority are fault event codes only occurring a few times, but the faults under the event codes 399, 435, 570, and 1219 have occurred more than 800 times within this period. Some event codes, such as 12 and 97, denoting SCADA shutdown request and yaw error, respectively, are not associated with a defined fault status despite their appearances being 932 and 1290, respectively. Aside from these two examples, the majority of event codes are merely warnings, irrelevant to faults, so many event codes are of minor interest in this paper. Additionally, the event codes relating to downtime due to maintenance actions, noise curtailments, and requested owner stops in Figure 2 are to be excluded.

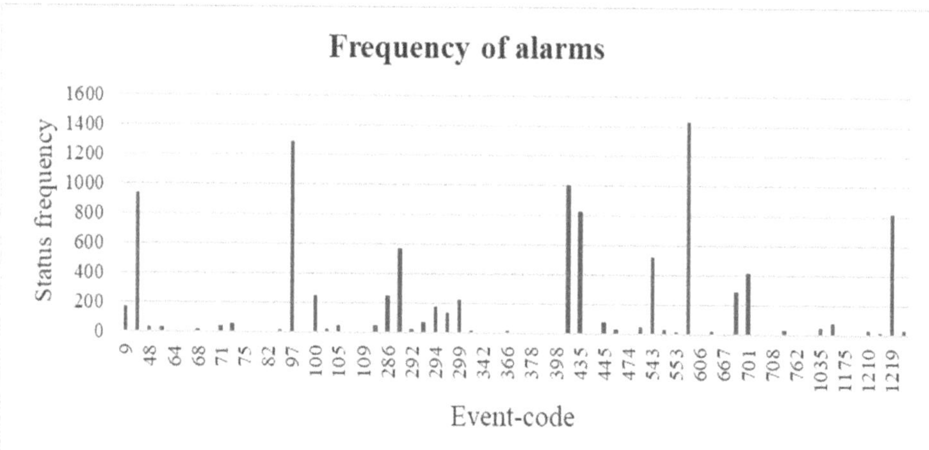

Figure 2. Frequency of alarms.

By excluding the data related to downtimes and faults with very limited frequency, only a small number of faults can be reserved according to their relatively frequent occurrences, as seen in Table 3. "HPU 2 Pump Active For Too Long" relates to a fault that occurred in the hydraulic pump unit (HPU), while "PcsOff" and "PcsTrip" relate to shut-off faults and circuit trips within the power conditioning system (PCS), respectively. The deep-learning model must train the classifiers for the specific fault instances defined in Table 3. Hence, the reserved SCADA data can be classified into nine categories: (1) fault-free; (2) HPU 2 pump active fault; (3) Blade 3 slow response; (4) pitch system fatal fault; (5) gearbox cooling pressure fault; (6) (Demoted) gearbox pressure 2 fault; (7) PcsOff fault; (8) PcsTrip fault; (9) sub-pitch fatal fault. The quantity of fault-free cases is much larger than that of any individual fault case, leading to an imbalance in the investigated dataset.

Table 3. Fault distributions.

Event Code	Frequency	Description
0	42,598	Fault-free
290	565	HPU 2 pump active for too long
399	998	Blade 3 too slow to respond
435	826	Pitch system fatal error
543	522	Gearbox cooling line pressure too low
570	1436	(Demoted) gearbox filter manifold pressure 2 shutdown
700	701	PcsOff *1
701	417	PcsTrip *2
1219	816	Sub-pitch priv fatal error has occurred more than 3 times

*1 PcsOff represents the shut-off faults of power conditioning system. *2 PcsTrip represents the circuit trips within power conditioning system.

2.2. Feature Engineering

The major occurrences of the faults are on the HPU, blade, pitch system, gearbox, PCS, and sub-pitch system (see Table 3), and a huge number of original features are CountFalse/CountTrue states, apparently irrelevant to those faults. This leads to the principal selection of 60 relevant features, which are only a small subsection of the original 2000 features. Among the 60 features, the deviations of pitch angles, as well as the deviations of sub-pitch positions from blades 1 and 2, 2 and 3, and 3 and 1 are considered because of possible blade angle asymmetry or blade angle implausibility, studied by Kusiak and Verma [38].

Feature engineering aims to reduce dimensionality by eliminating features with lower significance and improving the computational efficiency of deep-learning neural networks. RFE [34] has been commonly applied to fit the model by recursively removing irrelevant or redundant features.

Firstly, an estimator for accurate online fault diagnosis is required to cooperate with RFE for dimensionality reduction. Apart from detecting the abnormality, fault diagnosis can determine the specific fault types with an advanced multi-level fault classification. The accuracy is used to evaluate the performance of classifiers by:

$$Accuracy = \frac{1}{k}\sum_{i=1}^{k}\frac{TP_i + TN_i}{TP_i + FP_i + FN_i + TN_i} \tag{2}$$

where k is the total number of classes, TP_i donates true positive in class i, when both prediction and actuality are faulty, whilst TN_i donates true negative in class i, when both prediction and actuality are fault-free. FP_i signifies false positive in class i, when the actual fault-free condition is wrongly predicted to be faulty, whilst FN_i signifies false negative in class i, when the actual faulty condition is wrongly predicted to be fault-free.

ML approaches, such as Decision Tree (DT), k-NN, SVM, RF, ANN, and Gradient Boost (GB), are compared for fault diagnosis. As seen in Figure 3, RF is evidently the finest model among all in terms of its best accuracy (0.98607386). Hence, the RF classifier is chosen to conduct RFE using a 10-fold cross-validation for the test set. Based on the RFE process in Figure 4, the best accuracy (0.9888) is observed by selecting 33 optimal features out of 60 for the fault diagnosis task under RF classification.

As seen in Figure 5, the weighted importance of each feature is depicted under the RF classification. According to the optimal solution given in Figure 4, the 33 top-ranking features in Figure 5 are reserved for predictive fault diagnosis models. The features, such as "AverageMeasuredPtchAngle1_Max", "GBoxFilterPres2_Mean", etc., have advanced significance levels. However, the features with lower significance levels than "ManualPtchStateCounter_EndVal" are excluded in predictive fault diagnosis studies for the purpose of dimensionality reduction.

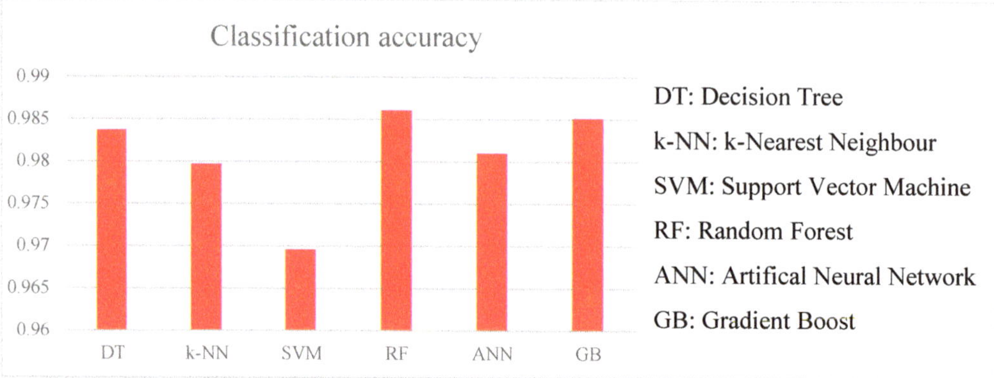

Figure 3. Comparison of classification accuracy.

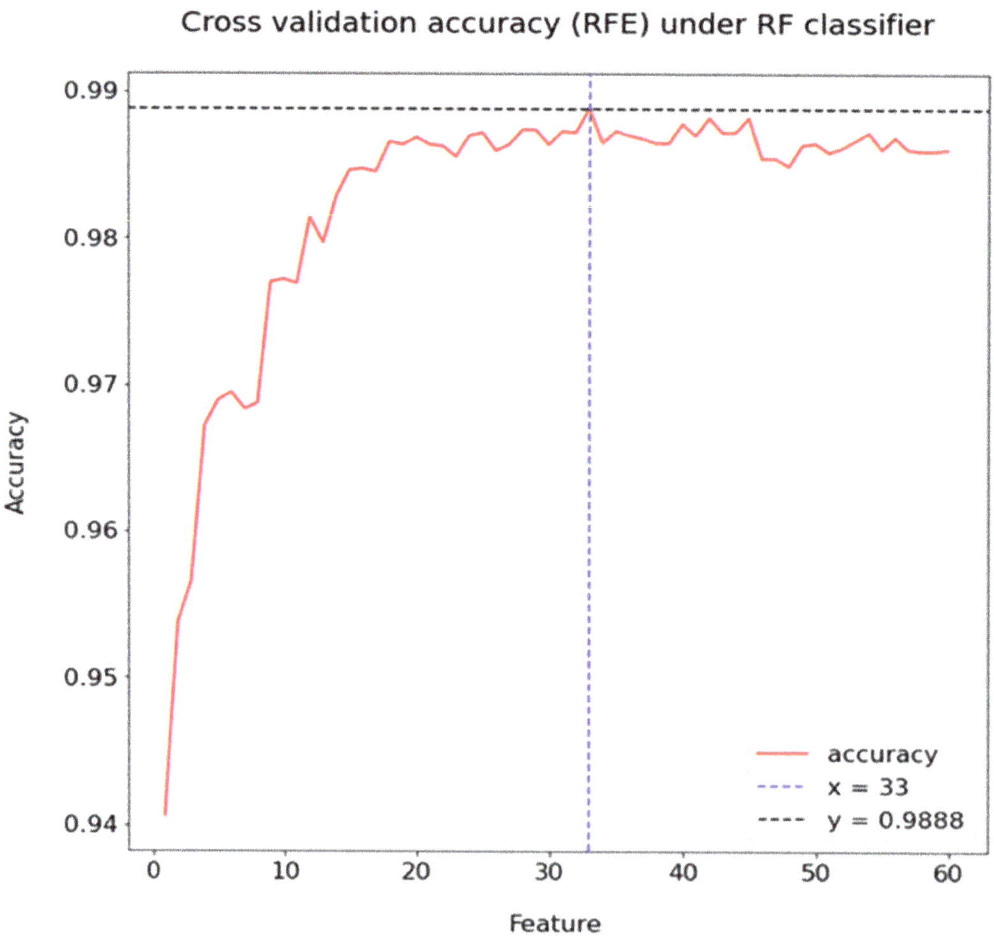

Figure 4. Cross-validation scores plotted against the number of features.

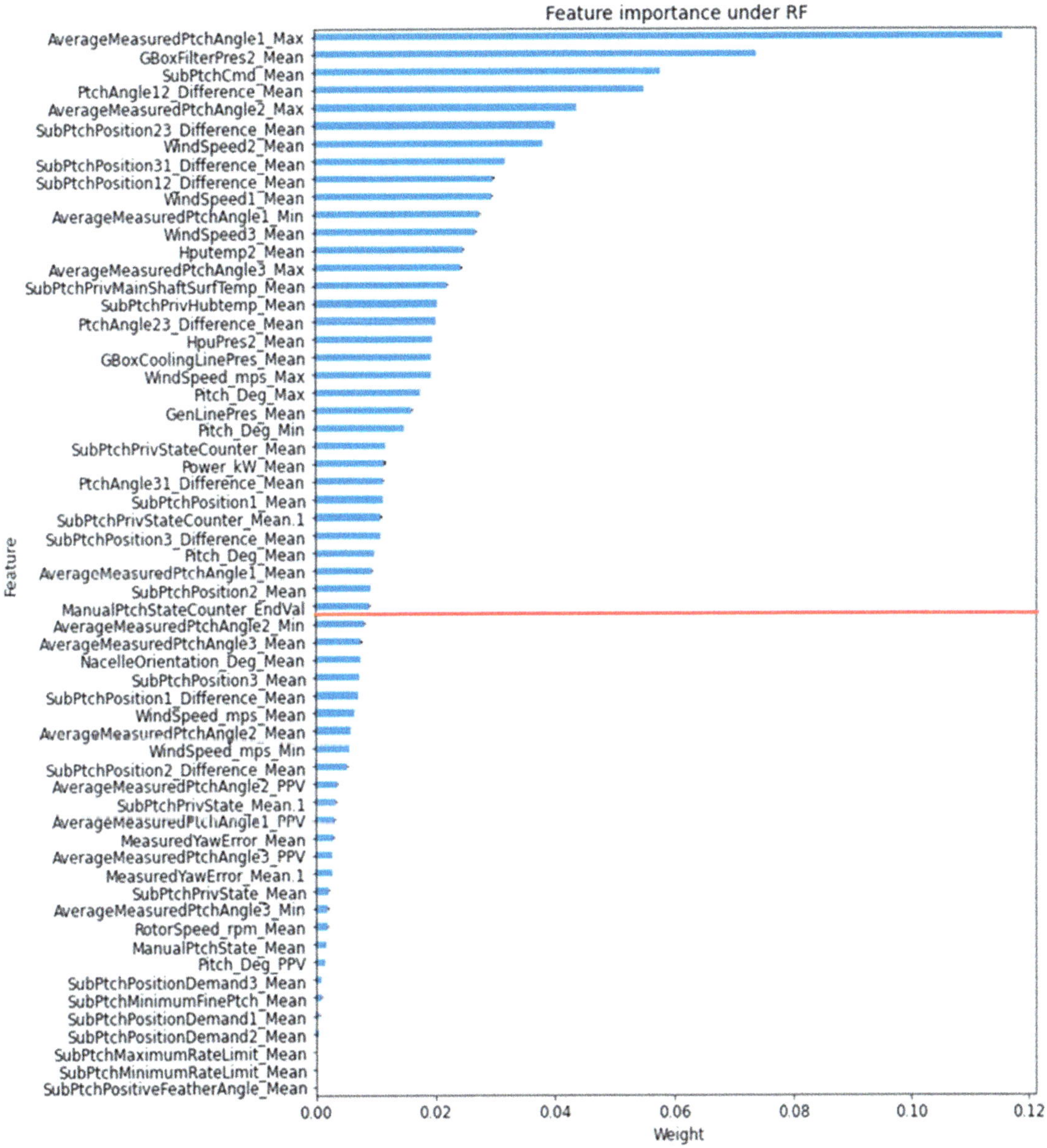

Figure 5. Feature importance under RF classifier (the 33 features above the red line are reserved).

2.3. Predictive Fault Diagnosis

Fault diagnosis aims at accurately identifying the fault types within a WT in a real-time application. However, it is insufficient to prevent damage caused by some severe failures only through online fault diagnosis. Then, fault prognosis is recommended by providing the predictive fault diagnosis prior to the fault occurrence, which decreases the maintenance fees and extends machinery life.

The observed dataset for online fault diagnosis is expressed by $\{X_t, Y_t\}$, where X_t and Y_t are the given input data and the resultant diagnosed fault class. For example, as the SCADA data are collected at 10 min intervals, the 10 min, 20 min, and 30 min ahead fault predictions can be achieved with the modified datasets, $\{X_{t-1}, Y_t\}$, $\{X_{t-2}, Y_t\}$, and $\{X_{t-3}, Y_t\}$, respectively, based on the original dataset, $\{X_t, Y_t\}$. Thus, the predictive performances under n-step in advance will be determined using the modified dataset, $\{X_{t-n}, Y_t\}$.

3. Methods

3.1. LSTM

As vanilla RNNs, with only input gates and output gates, suffer from vanishing or exploding gradients caused by error back-flow problems, the main challenge for vanilla RNNs is to handle the long-term dependencies.

To secure the long-term dependencies, LSTM additionally inserted forget gates for the update and control of cell states, regulating the information flow [29]. LSTM can handle the imbalanced data and efficiently captures a sequence of time-lagged observations as inputs for time-series classification to predict specific faults at any given time ahead. The original LSTM model can be precisely stated as follows:

$$f_j = \sigma\left(W_f x_j + U_f h_{j-1} + b_f\right) \quad (3)$$

$$i_j = \sigma(W_i x_j + U_i h_{j-1} + b_i) \quad (4)$$

$$O_j = \sigma(W_o x_j + U_o h_{j-1} + b_o) \quad (5)$$

$$\overline{C}_j = \sigma_c(W_c x_j + U_c h_{j-1} + b_c) \quad (6)$$

$$C_j = f_j \odot C_{j-1} + i_j \odot \overline{C}_j \quad (7)$$

$$h_j = \sigma_h(C_j) \odot O_j \quad (8)$$

Herein, x_j is the neuron input at the timestamp j; h_{j-1} is the cell state at the previous timestamp; $j-1$, f_j, i_j, and O_j stand for the forget, input, and output gates, respectively, all determined across the sigmoid nonlinearity, σ, with the given weights W_f, W_i, W_o, W_c, U_f, U_i, U_o, U_c, and the assigned biases, b_f, b_i, b_o, b_c. The memory cell, $\overline{C}_j$, from Equation (6) is estimated through an activation function, σ_c, which is a hyperbolic tangent layer, *Tanh*, by default. Then, the current cell state C_j in Equation (7) is updated regarding the previous cell state, C_{j-1}, and the estimated cell state, $\overline{C}_j$, with the element-wise product operator, $\odot$. Finally, the output vector, h_j, in Equation (8), also known as a hidden layer, is obtained from the element-wise product of the output gate, O_j, and the cell state, C_j, across an activation function, σ_h, which is also *Tanh* by default.

Based on the dependencies in LSTM, the forget gate, f_j, controls the fraction of C_{j-1}, to store in C_j, filtering h_{j-1} and x_j through the sigmoid gate, σ. The input gate, i_j, controls the fraction of the estimated memory cell, $\overline{C}_j$, provided to C_j through the sigmoid nonlinearity, σ; the output gate, O_j, controls the fraction of C_j flowing into the output vector, h_j, through σ_h. Therefore, the LSTM architecture can be drawn in Figure 6.

3.2. Time-LSTM-1

Regarding Equation (7), C_{j-1} covers the information at the previous timestamp, reflecting the long-term interest, and x_j is the last consumed item, hardly reflecting on current recommendations. Then, Time-LSTM, proposed by Zhu et al. [39], equips LSTM with time gates to store time intervals in C_j, C_{j+1}, $\cdots$, controlling the fraction of x_j on current recommendations. Time-LSTM-1 [39] only adds one time gate, T_j, to LSTM by:

$$T_j = \sigma(W_t x_j + \sigma(U_t \Delta t_j) + b_t) \tag{9}$$

where Δt_j is defined as the time interval for the jth event by $\Delta t_j = t_{j+1} - t_j$, implemented across a sigmoid function, σ, and T_j is also determined through σ with the assigned weights, W_t and U_t, and the given bias, b_t. Δt_j can also be recognised as the duration between the current and the last event. Based on the basic LSTM architecture from Equations (3)–(8), Equations (7) and (5) can be revised to:

$$C_j = f_j \odot C_{j-1} + i_j \odot T_j \odot \overline{C}_j \tag{10}$$

$$O_j = \sigma(W_o x_j + U_o h_{j-1} + V_o \Delta t_j + b_o) \tag{11}$$

where V_o is the added weight to calculate O_j in Time-LSTM-1. Then, both the input gate, i_j, and the time gate, T_j, control the fraction of the estimated memory cell, $\overline{C}_j$, provided to the current memory cell, C_j, in Equation (10). As T_j, containing the information of interval, Δt_j, is provided to C_j, and then transferred to C_{j+1}, C_{j+2}, $\cdots$, the time gate, T_j, benefits the long-term interests, C_j, C_{j+1}, $\cdots$, of the LSTM model by storing Δt_j.

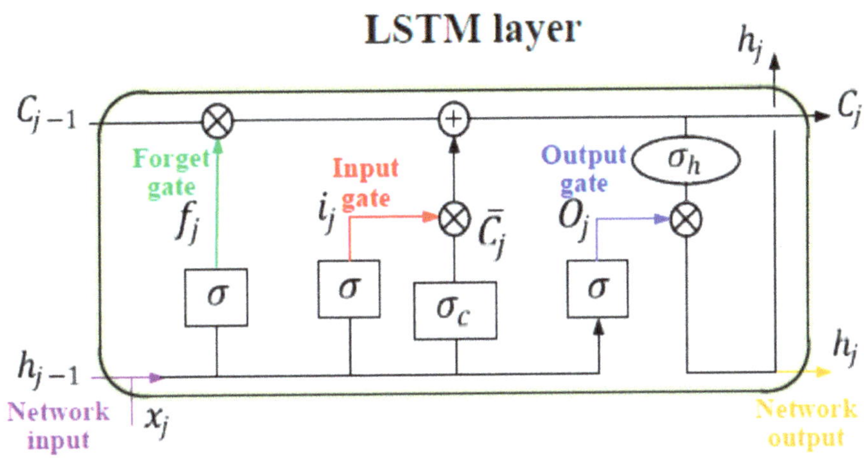

Figure 6. LSTM architecture.

3.3. *Time-LSTM-3 and T2V-LSTM Models*

For Time-LSTM-1, the single time gate T_j is mainly controlled by Δt_j. Zhu et al. [39] developed two alternative Time-LSTM models, Time-LSTM-2 and Time-LSTM-3, both containing double time gates, $T1_j$ and $T2_j$. $T1_j$ controls the influence of the last consumed item, x_j, on current recommendations, while $T2_j$ stores Δt_j for later recommendations. Based on T_j in Equation (9), $T1_j$ and $T2_j$ can be expressed by:

$$T1_j = \sigma(W_{t1} x_j + \sigma(U_{t1} \Delta t_j) + b_{t1}) \tag{12}$$

$$T2_j = \sigma(W_{t2} x_j + \sigma(U_{t2} \Delta t_j) + b_{t2}) \tag{13}$$

where W_{t1}, W_{t2}, U_{t1}, and U_{t2} are given weights and b_{t1} and b_{t2} are given biases. Among three LSTM models with time gates, Time-LSTM-3 is validated with the best predictions by coupling input and forget gates, inspired by the LSTM variant from Greff et al. [40] and the cell state, C_j, in Equation (7) under Time-LSTM-3 can be modified by:

$$C_j = (1 - i_j) \odot C_{j-1} + i_j \odot \overline{C}_j \tag{14}$$

Hence, Time-LSTM-3 has a shorter processing time than Time-LSTM-2 due to its simpler architecture and fewer parameters to calculate. By removing the forget gate, Equation (14) can be modified by:

$$\widetilde{C}_j = (1 - i_j \odot T1_j) \odot C_{j-1} + i_j \odot T1_j \odot \overline{C}_j \tag{15}$$

$$C_j = (1 - i_j) \odot C_{j-1} + i_j \odot T2_j \odot \overline{C}_j \tag{16}$$

where $\widetilde{C}_j$ is a new cell state to store the result. The output gate, O_j, in Equation (5) and the output vector, h_j, in Equation (8) can be replaced by:

$$O_j = \sigma(W_o x_j + U_o h_{j-1} + V_o \Delta t_j + b_o) \tag{17}$$

$$h_j = \sigma_h\left(\widetilde{C}_j\right) \odot O_j \tag{18}$$

Here, both i_j and $T1_j$ are filters for $\overline{C}_j$, while $T2_j$ stores Δt_j, transferred to C_j, C_{j+1}, C_{j+2}, $\cdots$, for modelling the long-term interests for later recommendations. $\widetilde{C}_j$ is implemented through an activation function, σ_h, influencing the current recommendations.

A model-agnostic vector representation for time, known as Time2Vec, is used to rebuild the architectures of Time-LSTM with the consumption of time features under either stationary or non-stationary activation functions. For this reason, Time2Vec replaces the time interval, Δt_j, by a model-agnostic vector, $T2V(\Delta t_j)$, as follows:

$$T2V(\Delta t_j)[i] = \begin{cases} \omega_i \cdot \Delta t_j + \varphi_i, \; if \; i = 0 \\ \mathcal{F}(\omega_i \cdot \Delta t_j + \varphi_i), \; if \; 1 \le i \le k \end{cases} \tag{19}$$

where $T2V(\Delta t_j)[i]$ is the ith element of $T2V(\Delta t_j)$, $\mathcal{F}$ can be any stationary or non-stationary activation functions, such as *Sine* and *Tanh*, and ω_i and φ_i are learnable parameters. Then, in a T2V-LSTM model, all time vectors, Δt_j, should be replaced by Time2Vec elements, $T2V(\Delta t_j)$, so the time gates, $T1_j$ and $T2_j$, in Equations (12) and (13), respectively, and the output gate, O_j, in Equation (17) are modified as follows:

$$T1_j = \sigma\left(W_{t1} x_j + \sigma(U_{t1} \cdot T2V(\Delta t_j)) + b_{t1}\right) \tag{20}$$

$$T2_j = \sigma\left(W_{t2} x_j + \sigma(U_{t2} \cdot T2V(\Delta t_j)) + b_{t2}\right) \tag{21}$$

$$O_j = \sigma\left(W_o x_j + U_o h_{j-1} + V_o \cdot T2V(\Delta t_j) + b_o\right) \tag{22}$$

For T2V-LSTM, the output vector, h_j, is still controlled according to Equation (18). Therefore, based on Equations (15)–(22), the architecture of Time-LSTM-3 or T2V-LSTM can be plotted in Figure 7. Time2Vec, determined by its selected activation function, has three major advantages: being capable of learning both periodic and non-periodic activation functions, having invariance to time rescaling, and being simple to combine a representation for time with multiple neural networks [33].

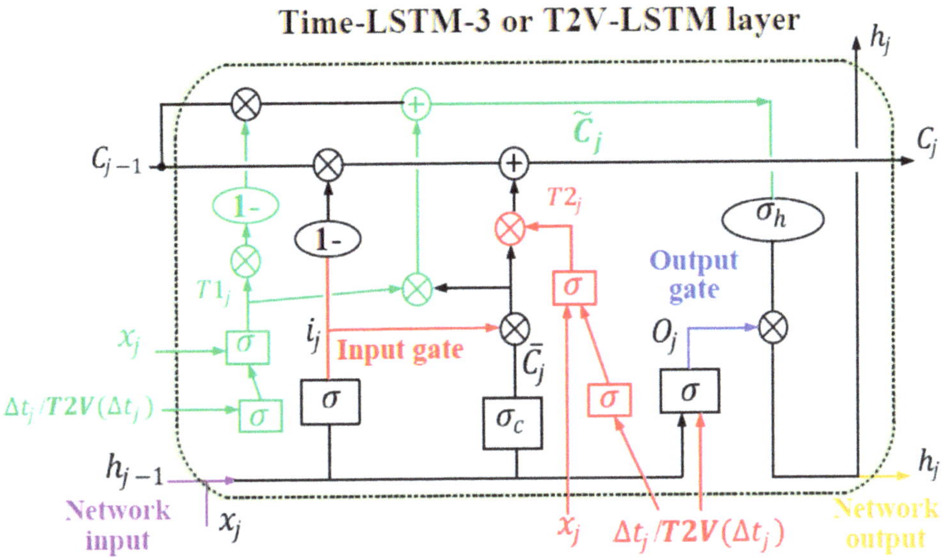

Figure 7. Time-LSTM-3 or T2V-LSTM architecture.

3.4. Validations

To evaluate the performances of neural networks and other ML classifiers, it is important to select the appropriate evaluation metrics. The accuracy in Equation (2) is commonly applied, but the overall accuracy of classification results on datasets with a significant imbalance is inappropriate for determining the predictive performance due to far more quantitative fault-free samples than faulty samples. The evaluation of overall fault predictions (FPs) is reflected by the macro precision (MAP) in Equation (23), and FNs are captured by the macro recall (MAR) in Equation (24). Moreover, the performance metrics, micro precision (MIP) and micro recall (MIR), are applied for fault diagnosis on individual faults, as seen in Equations (25) and (26), respectively.

$$MAP = \frac{1}{k}\sum_{i=1}^{k} \frac{TP_i}{TP_i + FP_i} \tag{23}$$

$$MAR = \frac{1}{k}\sum_{i=1}^{k} \frac{TP_i}{TP_i + FN_i} \tag{24}$$

$$MIP = \sum_{i=1}^{l} \frac{TP_i}{TP_i + FP_i} \tag{25}$$

$$MIR = \sum_{i=1}^{l} \frac{TP_i}{TP_i + FN_i} \tag{26}$$

$$F - score = 2 \times \frac{Precision \times Recall}{Precision + Recall} \tag{27}$$

where k is the total number of classes, and l is the specific fault class. The F-score in Equation (27) is applied as the harmonic mean of precision and recall scores for both overall and individual fault diagnosis methods.

3.5. Model Optimisation

The objective of any neural network is to minimize the cost functions for the most accurate prediction performance by optimising the weights and biases with appropriate activation functions [41]. The Time2Vec activation function, $\mathcal{F}$, in Equation (19), as well as the activations functions of the LSTM layer, σ_c and σ_h, in Figure 7, are pivotal to the design of LSTM or T2V-LSTM classifiers by affecting their predictive performance.

GridSearchCV [42] is a hyper-parameter optimisation method based on a given neural network model to optimise the individual model for each combination of hyper parameters, such as the number of epochs, batch sizes, and activation functions. The optimization of hyper parameters intends to maximise prediction accuracy by minimising the cost functions and training times of neural networks. The tunes of hyper parameters are achieved by GridSearchCV, which adopts the k-fold cross-validation (CV) to train and test the neural network by grid-searching the combination of hyper parameters to generate the highest average score across k repeated times. The hyper parameters tuned for T2V-LSTM can be seen in Table 4.

Table 4. Hyper-parameter optimisation through GridSearchCV.

Hyper Parameter	Grid	Optimisation
Batch size	10, 20, 25, 40, 50, 60, 80, 100	25
Number of Epochs	10, 20, 25, 40, 50, 60, 80, 100	100
Activation function ($\mathcal{F}$)	*Elu, Relu, Sigmoid, Sine* (only Time2Vec), *Softmax, Softplus, Softsign, Tanh*	*Tanh*
Activation function (σ_c)	*Elu, Relu, Sigmoid, Softmax, Softplus, Softsign, Tanh*	*Tanh*
Activation function (σ_h)	*Elu, Relu, Sigmoid, Softmax, Softplus, Softsign, Tanh*	*Softmax*

The optimum activation functions for both Time2Vec, $\mathcal{F}$, and the hidden layer, σ_c, are given by *Tanh*, seen in Equation (28), while the optimal activation function for the final classification output layer, σ_h, is yielded by *Softmax* in Equation (29).

$$Tanh(x) = \frac{e^x - e^{-x}}{e^x + e^{-x}} \tag{28}$$

$$Softmax(x)_i = \frac{e^{x_i}}{\sum_{j=1}^{N} e^{x_j}} \tag{29}$$

The softmax activation function [43] is a combination of sigmoid functions applied for multivariate classification tasks by normalising the outputs with probabilities of each class ranging from 0 to 1, so the target class is expressed by the highest probability.

4. Results

4.1. Overall Performance Metrics

In this subsection, the fault prediction models are extracted from timestamps $t-1$ (10 min) to $t-21$ (210 min). The detailed predictive performances under six classifiers are summarised in Figure 8 in terms of accuracy, MAP, MAR, and F-score with respect to Equations (2), (23), (24), and (27), respectively.

As seen in Table 5, all six classifiers have an upper accuracy of over 94% due to their correct predictions on fault-free cases from the imbalanced dataset. However, the resultant MARs and F-scores have poorer ranges of (0.61156, 0.92622) and (0.71038, 0.93537), respectively, and SVM especially has the poorest MIR range (0.61156, 0.84711). As MAPs (over 0.84) have better ranges than MARs (over 0.61), the resultant F-scores are promoted by precision scores, thereby representing more FNs than FPs. Among all, T2V-LSTM has correctly predicted more fault statuses than other classifiers due to its optimum MAR range.

Moreover, T2V-LSTM also has the finest ranges of accuracy and F-score despite its poorer MAP range in comparison to RF.

Figure 8. (**a**) Accuracy, (**b**) MAP, (**c**) MAR, and (**d**) F-score for fault predictions under six classifiers from $t-1$ (10 min) to $t-21$ (210 min).

Table 5. Validation scores for overall fault prediction.

Scores		Classifier (Overall Fault)						
		LSTM	**T2V-LSTM**	**RF**	**ANN**	**SVM**	**KNN**	**ALL**
Accuracy	MIN	0.97079	**0.9742954**	0.96222	0.96273	0.94477	0.96284	0.94477
	MAX	0.98441	**0.9864767**	0.97791	0.9777	0.96697	0.97213	0.98648
MAP	MIN	0.87643	0.8912656	**0.92785**	0.86133	0.84729	0.89391	0.84729
	MAX	0.94347	0.9469835	**0.97052**	0.9422	0.90898	0.92044	0.97052
MAR	MIN	0.82667	**0.8497778**	0.70844	0.74844	0.61156	0.736	0.61156
	MAX	0.91911	**0.9262222**	0.872	0.88978	0.84711	0.84089	0.92622
F-score	MIN	0.86151	**0.8788294**	0.80383	0.82085	0.71038	0.81275	0.71038
	MAX	0.92694	**0.935368**	0.90707	0.9067	0.87351	0.8739	0.93537
Execution time (s)	MIN	299.0876	**309.44707**	281.5733	232.2455	174.6638	148.6676	148.6676
	MAX	337.6192	**346.63702**	322.1635	281.5004	326.7903	186.6617	346.63702

As seen in Figure 8, the time index under 10 min per timestamp in the x-axis denotes the test cases at timestamp $t-n$. All classification approaches demonstrate their best accuracy, MAR, and F-score initially at $t-1$, but their predictive results progressively attenuate over time.

As seen in Figure 8b, RF has the best MAPs over time, implying its distinction of diagnosing fault-free conditions precisely with fewer FPs. By comparison, T2V-LSTM has successfully predicted more faults than other classifiers due to its relatively highest MARs in all test cases (see Figure 8c). Recall scores are always prior to precision scores in fault classification models because of the recall and precision scores relating to undetected failures and false fault alarms, respectively [19]. As a result, T2V-LSTM reflects its superiority over all other classifiers across overall fault predictions in terms of accuracy, MAR, and F-score (see Figure 8a,c,d)).

Apart from the best overall prediction scores, the proposed method, T2V-LSTM, requires the longest execution time, as seen in Table 5. However, the maximum execution time of T2V-LSTM (346.63702 s) is still below the minimum 10 min ahead prediction window. Thus, all six classification models can be implemented before any prediction window in all cases under the 10 min SCADA resolution.

4.2. Performance Metrics upon Individual Faults

Herein, individual faults, depicted in Table 3, are examined across timestamps $t-1$ (10 min) to $t-21$ (210 min) by performance metrics, MIP, MIR, and F-score, with respect to Equations (25)–(27), respectively. The time-domain fault prediction scores for six classification approaches across individual faults are summarised in Figures 9–12. (Demoted) gearbox pressure 2 faults, Blade 3's too-slow response, gearbox cooling pressure faults, and sub-pitch fatal faults witness successful predictions due to the minimum MIR exceeding 86.27% under the proposed T2V-LSTM indicator, studied in Appendix A. Thus, in this paper, the studies on those four individual faults are of less interest.

Figure 9. (**a**) MIP, (**b**) MIR, and (**c**) F-score for predictions on HPU 2 pump active faults from $t-1$ to $t-21$.

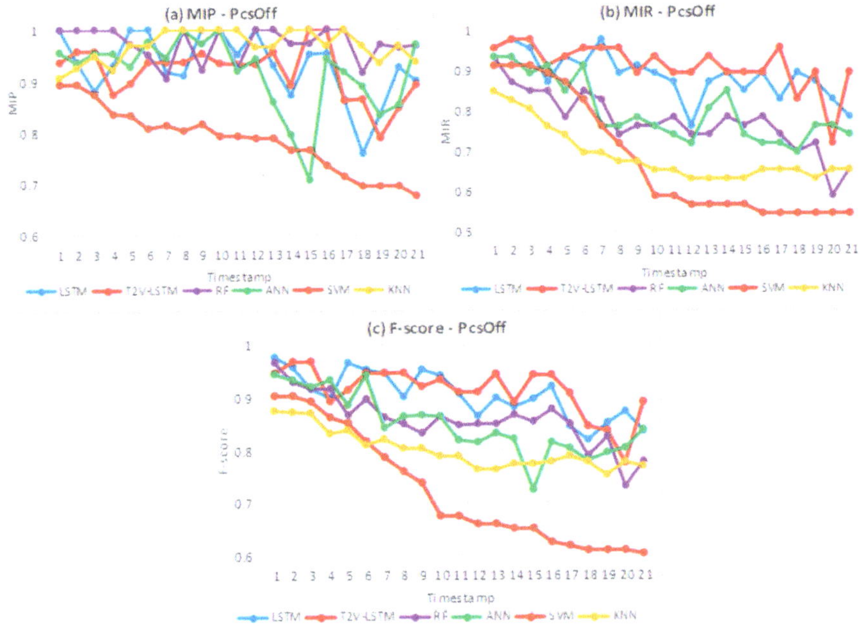

Figure 10. (**a**) MIP, (**b**) MIR, and (**c**) F-score for predictions on PcsOff faults from $t-1$ to $t-21$.

Figure 11. (**a**) MIP, (**b**) MIR, and (**c**) F-score for predictions on PcsTrip faults from $t-1$ to $t-21$.

Figure 12. (**a**) MIP, (**b**) MIR, and (**c**) F-score for predictions on pitch fatal faults from $t-1$ to $t-21$.

4.2.1. HPU 2 Pump Active

As seen in Table 6, it is most appealing that the maximum MIP under SVM has reached full score, whilst its minimum MIR is the poorest by approaching zero. Thus, SVM is inapplicable for fault diagnosis on HPU 2 pump active. Regarding predictions on fault-free cases, both LSTM models have inferior MIP ranges compared to RF. However, T2V-LSTM is superior to all other classifiers in its best MIR range (0.7657, 0.9189), which consequently leads to its best fault prediction with the fewest FNs and the optimum range of F-score under T2V-LSTM (0.7555, 0.9026).

Table 6. Validation scores for HPU 2 pump active.

Scores		Classifier (HPU 2 Pump Active)						
		LSTM	**T2V-LSTM**	**RF**	**ANN**	**SVM**	**KNN**	**ALL**
MIP	MIN	0.71277	0.744	**0.7561**	0.56667	0.59375	0.54839	0.54839
	MAX	0.90385	0.9065421	0.91837	0.93902	**1**	0.78641	1
MIR	MIN	0.6036	**0.7657658**	0.35135	0.20721	0	0.27928	0
	MAX	**0.91892**	**0.9189189**	0.82883	0.82883	0.90991	0.72973	0.91892
F-score	MIN	0.65366	**0.7555556**	0.49682	0.33577	0.01786	0.38554	0.01786
	MAX	0.88312	**0.9026549**	0.85581	0.81778	0.84519	0.75701	0.90265

Figure 9 exhibits the time-domain prediction results in advance of HPU 2 pump active faults. As seen in Figure 9b,c, SVM has the steepest downtrend in its MIR and F-score, while T2V-LSTM goes beyond other classifiers in most test cases. Although T2V-LSTM is the best predictor for HPU2 pump active faults by correctly predicting 76.57~91.89% of faults, HPU 2 pump active beholds smaller MIR ranges, compared to the predictive results on the four specific faults in Table A1.

4.2.2. PcsOff

As seen in Table 7, SVM still has the lowest minimum and maximum values in MIPs, MIRs, and F-scores, thereby the worst prediction results. Except for SVM, all other classifiers have reached full MIP scores, and KNN and RF outscore their counterparts in MIP ranges, with all MIPs surpassing 0.9. Both LSTM models outscore all other classifiers in MIR ranges, but LSTM has a higher minimum MIR and F-score than T2V-LSTM due to a substandard MIR (0.7173913) and F-score (0.7764706) under T2V-LSTM at $t-2$, seen in Figure 10b.

Table 7. Validation scores for PcsOff.

Scores		Classifier (PcsOff)						
		LSTM	T2V-LSTM	RF	ANN	SVM	KNN	ALL
MIP	MIN	0.75926	0.7884615	0.90476	0.70833	0.67568	**0.90698**	0.67568
	MAX	**1**	**1**	**1**	**1**	0.89362	**1**	1
MIR	MIN	**0.76087**	0.7173913	0.58696	0.69565	0.54348	0.63043	0.54348
	MAX	**0.97826**	**0.9782609**	0.93478	0.93478	0.91304	0.84783	0.97826
F-score	MIN	**0.82**	0.7764706	0.72973	0.7234	0.60241	0.75325	0.60241
	MAX	**0.97778**	0.9677419	0.96629	0.94505	0.90323	0.8764	0.97778

The time-domain predictive results ahead of PcsOff faults are illustrated in Figure 10. The degraded performances under both LSTM models can be recognisably obtained after $t-17$. As seen in Figure 10a, RF and ANN have more optimal predictions on fault-free cases by their MIPs exceeding 0.9 in all cases.

As seen in Figure 10b, both LSTM models have the highest MIRs before $t-17$, despite the poor MIR under LSTM (0.76087) at $t-12$, and T2V-LSTM outclasses all other models due to its MIRs surpassing 0.89.

However, the curtailments in MIRs under both LSTM models are visualised after $t-18$. Thus, both LSTM models can roughly predict over 80% of fault cases.

Consequently, both LSTM models have more balanced F-scores over other classifiers (see Figure 10c). Although LSTM obtains better ranges in MIR and F-score than T2V-LSTM (see Table 7), T2V-LSTM has predicted fault cases more correctly with respect to its greater MIRs in most test cases from Figure 10b.

4.2.3. PcsTrip

As seen in Table 8, the MIP range (0.75342, 1) is expressively upper than the MIR range (0.48148, 0.88889). Hence, the predictions on PcsTrip faults witness relatively lower recall scores than precision scores, resulting in more FNs than FPs. Thus, F-scores are increased by relatively better MIPs. However, SVM still has the worst prediction results on fault cases due to its poorest MIR range. Both LSTM models have satisfying MIPs by surpassing 0.8, but they are outclassed by RF, which has the most correct predictions on fault-free cases due to its highest minimum MIP. Both LSTM models have better MIR ranges and, thereby, more accurate fault predictions. Moreover, T2V-LSTM yields more correct predictions on fault cases with fewer FNs and generates the resultant optimum range on F-scores.

Regarding the time-domain prediction results in Figure 11, the MIPs under both LSTM models underperform RF, ANN, and KNN, whilst T2V-LSTM has superiority on MIRs in most test cases. Therefore, T2V-LSTM is the best fault predictor for PcsTrip faults with its best MIRs, leading to the fewest FNs and most balanced F-scores in Figure 11c.

Table 8. Validation scores for PcsTrip.

Scores		Classifier (PcsTrip)						
		LSTM	T2V-LSTM	RF	ANN	SVM	KNN	ALL
MIP	MIN	0.8	0.8024691	**0.92308**	0.77922	0.78	0.75342	0.75342
	MAX	0.95238	0.969697	0.98361	**1**	0.97826	0.96552	1
MIR	MIN	0.74074	**0.7530864**	0.65432	0.62963	0.48148	0.62963	0.48148
	MAX	0.83951	**0.8888889**	0.81481	0.81481	0.75309	0.79012	0.88889
F-score	MIN	0.7871	**0.8024691**	0.78519	0.75177	0.59542	0.71429	0.59542
	MAX	0.88312	**0.9056604**	0.88591	0.88	0.80263	0.81013	0.90566

4.2.4. Pitch Fatal Faults

In addition to the predictions on PcsTrip faults, the predictive results on pitch fatal faults are yielded with an even lower recall range (0, 0.69481) than the corresponding precision range (0, 0.8871), seen in Table 9. By excluding the poorest predictor, SVM, the MIPs and MIRs under other classifiers go beyond 0.53 and 0.22, respectively. Hence, for pitch fatal faults, MIPs are much greater than their corresponding MIRs, resulting in more FNs than FPs, so F-scores are downgraded by relatively poorer MIRs.

Table 9. Validation scores for pitch fatal faults.

Scores		Classifier (Pitch Fatal Faults)						
		LSTM	T2V-LSTM	RF	ANN	SVM	KNN	ALL
MIP	MIN	0.53548	0.5419355	0.64286	0.53409	0	**0.69412**	0
	MAX	0.79661	0.8076923	**0.8871**	0.82692	0.7931	0.82222	0.8871
MIR	MIN	0.4026	**0.4415584**	0.31169	0.22078	0	0.33117	0
	MAX	0.66883	**0.6948052**	0.50649	0.58442	0.45455	0.48052	0.69481
F-score	MIN	0.50196	**0.5291829**	0.43439	0.33663	0.03704	0.45133	0.03704
	MAX	0.70383	**0.7430556**	0.60938	0.66176	0.54902	0.60656	0.74306

The time-domain predictions prior to pitch fatal faults are seen in Figure 12. T2V-LSTM is the best fault predictor by having superior MIRs, and LSTM is just second to T2V-LSTM, whilst the other classifiers yield the MIRs below 0.5 in most cases from Figure 12b. It is noteworthy that MIRs under both LSTM models attenuate over time, obtaining lower than 0.5 after $t - 17$. By comparison, MIPs mainly surpass 0.5, except for the test cases under SVM in Figure 12a.

Accordingly, as seen in Figure 12c, all F-scores are decreased by their lower MIRs, but both LSTM models outperform other classifiers due to their observably better recall scores in Figure 12b, and T2V-LSTM is still the best fault predictor with the best MIRs and F-scores for pitch fatal faults. However, compared with other faults, pitch fatal faults witness much lower MIRs, and the diagnosed fault cases attenuate over a longer prediction time. Particularly, since $t - 17$, the predictions on pitch fatal faults are yielded with minor reliability because of MIRs going below 50%; thus, half of the faults cannot be correctly diagnosed due to yielding more FNs than TPs.

5. Discussion

By conducting RFE to remove irrelevant and redundant information from full operational SCADA data, 33 top-ranked features in Figure 5 are reserved for fault predictions.

LSTM has been preferable for prognostics on imbalanced data owing to its ability to store the time-lagged information and exploit the time dependency. LSTM has better recall scores (both MARs and MIRs) and overall predictions than traditional ML classifiers with respect to the results in Sections 4.1 and 4.2. However, there is also a dependence across time among data, and the time feature of inputs can be either synchronous or asynchronous [33], but vanilla LSTM always fails to recognise time itself as a feature by assuming all inputs to be synchronous. As the data points related to downtimes or maintenance actions are removed, the modelling dataset is asynchronous. Hence, the Time2Vec is adopted to remodel the LSTM architectures into T2V-LSTM (see Figure 7) by way of Time2Vec consuming the time feature under non-stationary activation functions.

The Time2Vec activation function and the other hidden layer of T2V-LSTM in Figure 7 are chosen by *Tanh*, which maps the inputs into a range $(-1, 1)$. Like *Sigmoid*, the derivative of *Tanh* is expressed by itself, but the mapping range of *Tanh* is broader than that of *Sigmoid* $(0, 1)$. The classification output layer is selected by *Softmax* because its calculated probabilities determine the target classes with given inputs, chiefly implemented for multi-level classifications. The proposed T2V-LSTM model (with a Time2Vec function of *Tanh*) has been certified to upgrade the prediction accuracy of LSTM and outperform all other classifiers on both overall and individual fault predictions.

5.1. Overall Performance Metrics

Based on SCADA data with a 10 min sampling rate, T2V-LSTM provides the best adaptability in terms of accuracy, MARs, and F-scores across all timestamps, despite its smaller MAPs compared to RF and ANN (see Figure 8). Hence, the fewest unnecessary maintenance actions can be led by RF, while T2V-LSTM identifies the highest quantity of fault cases, followed by LSTM.

Integrated with Time2Vec, T2V-LSTM outscores vanilla LSTM with regard to accuracy, MAPs, MARs, and F-scores at almost all timestamps in Figure 8. Before $t-3$, T2V-LSTM has its distinguished predictions in terms of accuracy (over 98.5%), MARs (over 91%), and F-scores (over 92.5%). T2V-LSTM marginally attenuates its accuracy, MARs, and F-scores over time by correctly predicting over 87.5% of faults before $t-16$. However, since $t-17$, T2V-LSTM has an unexpected decline in its MARs, and it can only capture 84.97% of faults at $t-19$, while by comparison, MAPs under T2V-LSTM exceed 89% in all cases. Hence, overall fault predictions are validated with fewer FPs than FNs.

5.2. Individual Performance Metrics

Individual faults, studied in Section 4.2, witness the most advanced predictions from T2V-LSTM due to its best MIRs and F-scores across most test cases over time. T2V-LSTM has mostly better prediction scores compared to vanilla LSTM, and its resultant F-scores are well adjusted due to its more balanced MIPs and MIRs across Figures 9–12. Regarding the fault studies in Appendix A, T2V-LSTM catches over 86.27% of fault cases and over 88.28% of fault-free cases.

HPU 2 pump active faults exhibit a satisfactory percentage of caught faults via MIRs, mostly over 80%, as seen in Figure 9b. PcsOff faults have both excellent MIPs and MIRs over 89% before $t-16$, but the predicted MIRs have significant relegations by scoring 0.826087 at $t-18$ and 0.717391 at $t-20$, as seen in Figure 10b.

Under T2V-LSTM, all above-mentioned faults have balanced precision and recall scores, but PcsTrip and pitch fatal faults see curtailed predictions over time and greater MIPs than MIRs, resulting in both their F-scores downgraded by poorer MIRs. Fewer PcsTrip faults are correctly predicted over time regarding its maximum MIR (88.88%) and minimum MIR (75.30%) at timestamps $t-3$ and $t-18$, respectively, as seen in Figure 11b. It is noticeable that the MIRs on pitch fatal faults are even poorer, deteriorating initially from 69.48% to 44.15% over time, as seen in Figure 12b. The forecasts over 40 min ahead on pitch fatal faults show poor results with the least MIRs (below 60%) among all individual faults, and over half of the faults cannot be correctly diagnosed after $t-17$.

T2V-LSTM under a non-stationary *Tanh* function shows its peak effectiveness for both overall and individual fault predictions, according to its overall best accuracy, recall scores (both MARs and MIRs), and F-scores. However, the significant mitigations in accuracy, MARs, and F-scores from Figure 8 are mainly reflected by the attenuated MIRs and F-scores from pitch fatal faults since $t-4$ (40 min) in Figure 12b,c.

5.3. Confusion Matrix

T2V-LSTM is the best-performing classifier for both overall fault predictions and specific fault predictions. Then, an additive classification step is to visualise the predictions of 10 min, 30 min, 1 h, 2 h, and 3 h in advance via the confusion matrices under T2V-LSTM in Figure 13. The fault-free and fault cases in Figure 13 are represented by their corresponding event codes in Table 3.

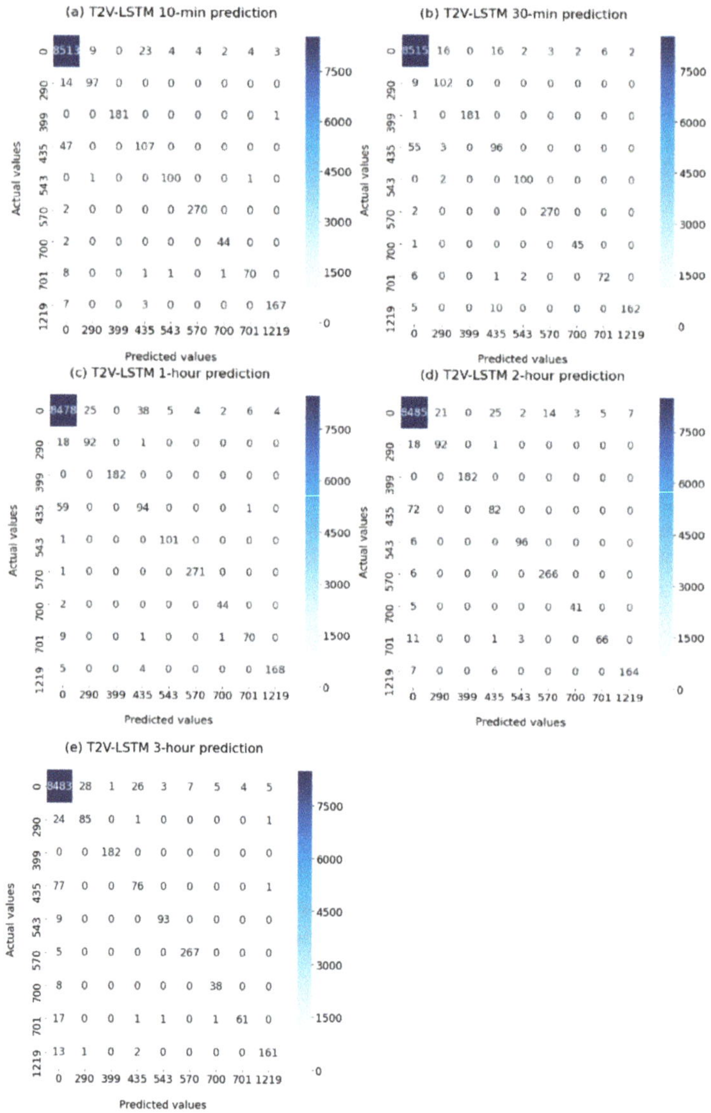

Figure 13. Confusion matrices under T2V-LSTM at five timestamps: (**a**) $t-1$ (10 min); (**b**) $t-3$ (30 min); (**c**) $t-6$ (1 h); (**d**) $t-12$ (2 h); (**e**) $t-18$ (3 h).

Except for more FNs than FPs from PcsTrip (event code 701) and pitch fatal faults (event code 435), the balances between recall and precision scores are established with regard to their unbiased FPs and FNs from confusion matrices in Figure 13.

The most frequent (Demoted) gearbox pressure 2 faults (event code 570) witness successful fault predictions with few FNs but obtain the 14 FPs at $t-12$ from Figure 13d. More accurate predictions can be witnessed on the Blade 3 slow response (event code 399) by yielding, at most, 1 FN or FP. Gearbox cooling pressure faults (event code 543) have great fault-free predictions due to minor FPs, but the relevant misdiagnosed fault cases increasing with time, 6 and 9 FNs at timestamps $t-12$ and $t-18$, as seen in Figure 13d,e, respectively.

Sub-pitch fatal faults (event code 1219) have TPs ranging from 161 to 168, with a maximum of 7 FPs, resulting in MIPs over 95%. Since the fewest TPs are obtained at $t-18$ in Figure 13e with 16 misdiagnosed fault cases, the minimum MIR reaches 90.96%.

HPU 2 pump active faults (event code 290) obtain the best prediction at $t-3$ with the maximum 102 TPs, 9 FNs, and a total of 21 FPs, so the resultant MIP and MIR reach 82.92% and 91.89%, respectively. However, the worst prediction at $t-18$ is yielded with a minimum of 85 TPs, 26 FNs, and 29 FPs in total, leading to the poorest MIP (74.56%) and MIR (76.57%). Hence, the predictions on HPU 2 pump active faults witness less success over a longer prediction horizon.

In addition to the HPU 2 pump active faults, the prediction scores on the least frequent PcsOff faults (event code 700) gradually worsen over time. The best prediction on PcsOff is at $t-3$, when only 1 FN and 2 FPs are obtained to confirm its notable MIP (95.74%) and MIR (97.82%). However, the worst prediction at $t-18$ generates 38 TPs with a total of 6 FPs and 8 FNs, thereby yielding the resultant MIP (86.36%) and MIR (82.60%).

Regarding PcsTrip faults (event code 701), MIPs are always satisfactory concerning the maximum 7 FPs at $t-6$, whilst MIRs decline over time. The best prediction on PcsTrip faults at $t-3$ is provided with 72 TPs, 6 FPs, and 9 FNs, leading to the resultant MIP (92.30%) and MIR (88.88%). By comparison, the worst case at $t-18$ yields relatively poorer results with 61 TPs, 4 FPs, and 20 FNs, leading to an agreeable MIP (93.84%) but an undervalued MIR (75.30%). Hence, the pre24dictions on PcsTrip have excellent precision scores, but the resulting F-scores are brought down by gradually declined MIRs.

In addition to PcsTrip faults, the subsequent F-scores of pitch fatal faults (event code 435) are declined by poorer recall scores. Among all faults, the pitch fatal faults witness the most misdiagnosed fault cases, yielding the maximum FNs throughout the time. Initially, at $t-1$, the MIR (69.48%) is acceptable due to 107 TPs out of 154 total fault cases, whilst the MIP (79.85%) is much greater owing to a total of 27 FPs. With a longer prediction horizon, more fault cases are wrongly predicted, accompanied by reduced TPs and increased FNs, which are shown in Figure 12. It is considerable that the prediction at $t-18$ yields an MIR of merely 49.35%, along with its relevant MIP scoring 72.38%. Hence, pitch fatal faults have observed extremely lower MIRs in comparison to other faults, and their recall scores are exceptionally exceeded by the relevant precision scores.

6. Conclusions

By integrating the vanilla LSTM model with a model-agnostic vector representation for time, Time2Vec, a novel neural network model, T2V-LSTM, is developed to predict multivariate faults with a 7 MW offshore wind turbine based on SCADA data. This approach has shown its efficacy on both overall and specific fault predictions by outperforming LSTM and other ML classifiers in most test cases. It has been proven that all classification models can be implemented prior to the next prediction window in all cases under the 10 min SCADA resolution. Using a feature selection method, RFE, to assess the importance of features for dimension reduction, 33 optimal features are extracted to improve the prediction accuracy and computing efficiency of neural networks. Regarding the T2V-LSTM prediction results, the following conclusions can be noted:

- As there are eight specific faults and massive data imbalances studied in this research, T2V-LSTM can successfully predict all faults 160 min before their occurrence with an overall recall score (MAR) of over 87.5%. T2V-LSTM outperforms LSTM and other classifiers in terms of accuracy, recall scores (both MARs and MIRs), and F-scores in all test cases, but with a longer lagged time, the MAR abruptly falls to roughly 85%.

- T2V-LSTM has satisfactory predictions on (Demoted) gearbox pressure 2 faults, Blade 3 slow response, gearbox cooling faults, and sub-pitch fatal faults, due to its minimum MIP over 88.28% and minimum MIR over 86.27%, shown in Appendix A. Approximately 80% of the HPU 2 pump active faults are correctly predicted along with the relevant MIPs scoring roughly 80%. PcsOff faults exhibit excellent prediction results 160 min before the occurrence, with both recall and precision scores over 89%, but the significantly curtailed MIPs and MIRs take place over a longer prediction horizon. The F-scores on those faults are balanced due to their unbiased and promising precision and recall decisions.
- However, the balance between MIPs and MIRs is demolished under PcsTrip and pitch fatal faults due to their F-scores being brought down by poorer recall scores. PcsTrip and pitch fatal faults behold upper MIP ranges than MIR ranges and degraded predictions over time. PcsTrip faults are successfully predicted 30 min in advance due to their optimal MIR (88.88%), but the minimum MIR (75.30%) is obtained 3 h before occurrence. By comparison, MIRs on pitch fatal faults have an even more critical downtrend, reducing from 69.48% to 44.15% over time. Particularly, over half of pitch fatal faults are misdiagnosed >170 min before occurrence. The curtailments in MIRs on pitch fatal faults over 40 min ahead predominately contribute to the significant degradations of overall accuracy, MARs, and F-scores. Hence, the poorest predictions on pitch fatal faults bear a considerable burden for overall prediction accuracy.
- The confusion matrices visually study the balance between recall and precision scores by predicting the faults 10, 30, 60, 120, and 180 min in advance. Apart from PcsTrip and pitch fatal faults having more biases in FNs over FPs, the other faults can acquire the balanced F-scores due to their FNs roughly equalising FPs. For those faults with balanced F-scores, the resultant MIPs and MIRs mostly surpass 80%, except for the MIP (74.56%) and MIR (76.57%) from the 3 h ahead prediction on HPU 2 pump active faults. PcsTrip faults mainly have excellent MIPs over 90%, but the degradations on their MIRs are expected over time. Hence, the prediction curtailments provided by HPU 2 pump active faults and PcsTrip faults over a longer prediction horizon also contribute to the degradation of overall performance metrics.
- As T2V-LSTM fails to predict over 40% of pitch fatal faults 40 min prior to occurrence, future studies should critically focus on building a performance curve of pitch angle to improve the predictions on pitch fatal faults.

Author Contributions: Conceptualisation, S.Z.; methodology, S.Z.; software, S.Z.; validation, S.Z.; formal analysis, S.Z.; investigation, S.Z.; resources, S.Z.; data curation, E.R.; writing—original draft preparation, S.Z.; writing—review and editing, S.Z., E.R. and M.B.; visualisation, S.Z., E.R. and M.B.; supervision, E.R. and M.B.; project administration, M.B.; funding acquisition, M.B. All authors have read and agreed to the published version of the manuscript.

Funding: This research was funded by the Sustainable Energy Authority of Ireland, Grant ref: SEAI 18/RDD/213.

Data Availability Statement: Restrictions apply to the availability of these data. Data were obtained from ORE Catapult and are available at https://ore.catapult.org.uk/what-we-do/offshore-renewable-energy-research/platform-for-operational-data-pod/ (accessed on 23 November 2023) with the permission of ORE Catapult.

Acknowledgments: We are grateful to ORE Catapult for giving us the permission to use the SCADA datasets.

Conflicts of Interest: The authors declare no conflict of interest.

Appendix A

As seen in Table A1, the predictive results on (Demoted) gearbox pressure 2 faults, Blade 3's too-slow response, gearbox cooling pressure faults, and sub-pitch fatal faults are validated across timestamps $t-1$ (10 min) to $t-21$ (210 min) by the minimums and maximums of their performance metrics. Both LSTM models manage to predict over 86.27% of fault cases, outperforming their ML counterparts.

Although LSTM has the finest minimum MIP, MIR, and F-score in Table A1, T2V-LSTM still outperforms LSTM in fault diagnosis because of greater MIRs in most test cases, as seen in the time-domain MIR results from Figure A1.

Table A1. Validation scores for (Demoted) gearbox pressure 2 faults, Blade 3's too-slow response, gearbox cooling pressure faults, and sub-pitch fatal faults.

Scores		Classifier (Four Other Individual Faults)						
		LSTM	T2V-LSTM	RF	ANN	SVM	KNN	ALL
MIP	MIN	0.90654	0.8828829	**0.90789**	0.84444	0.8038	0.85106	0.8038
	MAX	1	1	1	1	0.99435	0.99425	1
MIR	MIN	**0.88136**	0.8627451	0.67647	0.71186	0.70621	0.7451	0.67647
	MAX	1	1	1	1	0.96703	0.98901	1
F-score	MIN	**0.90698**	0.9035533	0.77528	0.82353	0.75758	0.82162	0.75758
	MAX	1	1	1	1	0.9805	0.97814	1

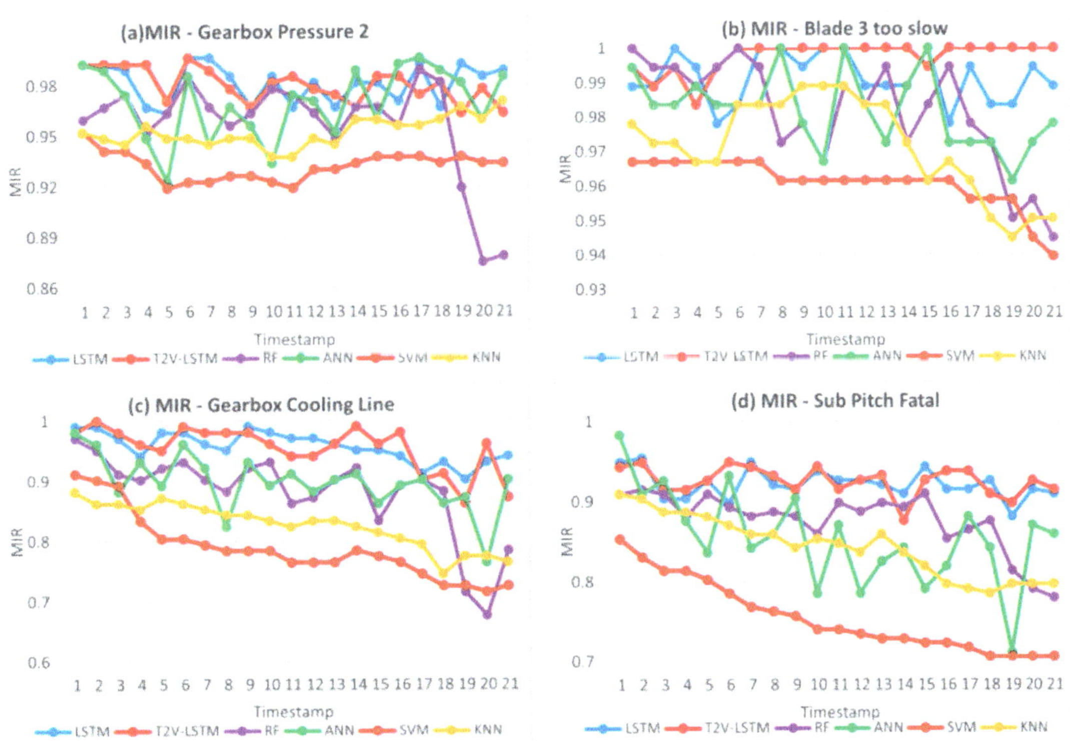

Figure A1. MIP, MIR, and F-score from $t-1$ to $t-21$: (**a**) (Demoted) gearbox pressure 2 faults; (**b**) Blade 3's too slow response; (**c**) gearbox cooling pressure faults; (**d**) sub-pitch fatal faults.

References

1. Singh, U.; Rizwan, M.; Malik, H. Wind Energy Scenario, Success and Initiatives Towards. *Energies* **2022**, *15*, 2291. [CrossRef]
2. Sommer, B.; Pinson, P.; Messner, J.W.; Obst, D. Online Distributed Learning in Wind Power Forecasting. *Int. J. Forecast.* **2021**, *37*, 205–223. [CrossRef]
3. Maldonado-Correa, J.; Solano, J.C.; Rojas-Moncayo, M. Wind Power Forecasting: A Systematic Literature Review. *Wind Eng.* **2021**, *45*, 413–426. [CrossRef]
4. Kaldellis, J.K.; Apostolou, D.; Kapsali, M.; Kondili, E. Environmental and Social Footprint of Offshore Wind Energy Comparison with Onshore Counterpart. *Renew. Energy* **2016**, *92*, 543–556. [CrossRef]
5. Al-Hinai, A.; Charabi, Y.; Kaboli, S.H.A. Offshore Wind Energy Resource Assessment across the Territory of Oman: A Spatial-Temporal Data Analysis. *Sustainability* **2021**, *13*, 2862. [CrossRef]
6. Gao, Z.; Liu, X. An Overview on Fault Diagnosis, Prognosis and Resilient Control for Wind Turbine Systems. *Processes* **2021**, *9*, 300. [CrossRef]
7. Zhang, S.; Robinson, E.; Basu, M. Hybrid Gaussian Process Regression and Fuzzy Inference System Based Approach for Condition Monitoring at the Rotor Side of a Doubly Fed Induction Generator. *Renew. Energy* **2022**, *198*, 936–946. [CrossRef]
8. Leite, G.dN.P.; Araújo, A.M.; Rosas, P.A.C. Prognostic Techniques Applied to Maintenance of Wind Turbines: A Concise and Specific Review. *Renew. Sustain. Energy Rev.* **2018**, *81*, 1917–1925. [CrossRef]
9. Sun, Y.; Kang, J.; Sun, L.; Jin, P.; Bai, X. Condition-Based Maintenance for the Offshore Wind Turbine Based on Long Short-Term Memory Network. *Proc. Inst. Mech. Eng. Part O J. Risk Reliab.* **2022**, *236*, 542–553. [CrossRef]
10. Koukoura, S.; Peeters, C.; Helsen, J.; Carroll, J. Investigating Parallel Multi-Step Vibration Processing Pipelines for Planetary Stage Fault Detection in Wind Turbine Drivetrains Investigating Parallel Multi-Step Vibration Processing Pipelines for Planetary Stage Fault Detection in Wind Turbine Drivetrains. *J. Phys. Conf. Ser.* **2020**, *1618*, 022054. [CrossRef]
11. Raposo, H.; Farinha, J.T.; Fonseca, I.; Galar, D. Predicting Condition Based on Oil Analysis—A Case Study. *Tribol. Int.* **2019**, *135*, 65–74. [CrossRef]
12. Zappalá, D.; Sarma, N.; Djurović, S.; Crabtree, C.J.; Mohammad, A.; Tavner, P.J. Electrical & Mechanical Diagnostic Indicators of Wind Turbine Induction Generator Rotor Faults. *Renew. Energy* **2019**, *131*, 14–24. [CrossRef]
13. Yang, W.; Peng, Z.; Wei, K.; Tian, W. Structural Health Monitoring of Composite Wind Turbine Blades: Challenges, Issues and Potential Solutions. *IET Renew. Power Gener.* **2017**, *11*, 411–416. [CrossRef]
14. Yang, W.; Tavner, P.J.; Crabtree, C.J.; Feng, Y.; Qiu, Y. Wind Turbine Condition Monitoring: Technical and Commercial Challenges. *Wind Energy* **2014**, *17*, 673–693. [CrossRef]
15. Tautz-Weinert, J.; Watson, S.J. Using SCADA Data for Wind Turbine Condition Monitoring—A Review. *IET Renew. Power Gener.* **2017**, *11*, 382–394. [CrossRef]
16. Stetco, A.; Dinmohammadi, F.; Zhao, X.; Robu, V.; Flynn, D.; Barnes, M.; Keane, J.; Nenadic, G. Machine Learning Methods for Wind Turbine Condition Monitoring: A Review. *Renew. Energy* **2019**, *133*, 620–635. [CrossRef]
17. Sahnoun, M.; Baudry, D.; Mustafee, N.; Louis, A.; Smart, P.A.; Godsiff, P.; Mazari, B. Modelling and Simulation of Operation and Maintenance Strategy for Offshore Wind Farms Based on Multi-Agent System. *J. Intell. Manuf.* **2019**, *30*, 2981–2997. [CrossRef]
18. Lu, L.; He, Y.; Wang, T.; Shi, T.; Li, B. Self-Powered Wireless Sensor for Fault Diagnosis of Wind Turbine Planetary Gearbox. *IEEE Access* **2019**, *7*, 87382–87395. [CrossRef]
19. Leahy, K.; Hu, R.L.; Konstantakopoulos, I.C.; Spanos, C.J.; Agogino, A.M.; Sullivan, D.T.J.O. Diagnosing and Predicting Wind Turbine Faults from SCADA Data Using Support Vector Machines. *Int. J. Progn. Health Manag.* **2018**, *9*, 1–11.
20. Naik, S.; Koley, E. Fault Detection and Classification Scheme Using KNN for AC/HVDC Transmission Lines. In Proceedings of the 2019 International Conference on Communication and Electronics Systems (ICCES), Coimbatore, India, 17–19 July 2019; pp. 1131–1135. [CrossRef]
21. Marti-Puig, P.; Blanco-M, A.; Cárdenas, J.J.; Cusidó, J.; Solé-Casals, J. Feature selection algorithms for wind turbine failure prediction. *Energies* **2019**, *12*, 453. [CrossRef]
22. Ibrahim, R.K.; Tautz-Weinert, J.; Watson, S.J. *Neural Networks for Wind Turbine Fault Detection via Current Signature Analysis*; Wind Europe: Hamburg, Germany, 2016.
23. Kandukuri, S.T.; Senanyaka, J.S.L.; Huynh, V.K.; Robbersmyr, K.G. A Two-Stage Fault Detection and Classification Scheme for Electrical Pitch Drives in Offshore Wind Farms Using Support Vector Machine. *IEEE Trans. Ind. Appl.* **2019**, *55*, 5109–5118. [CrossRef]
24. Malik, H.; Mishra, S. Artificial Neural Network and Empirical Mode Decomposition Based Imbalance Fault Diagnosis of Wind Turbine Using TurbSim, FAST and Simulink. *IET Renew. Power Gener.* **2017**, *11*, 889–902. [CrossRef]
25. Yang, X.; Zhang, Y.; Lv, W.; Wang, D. Image Recognition of Wind Turbine Blade Damage Based on a Deep Learning Model with Transfer Learning and an Ensemble Learning Classifier. *Renew. Energy* **2021**, *163*, 386–397. [CrossRef]
26. Zhang, D.; Qian, L.; Mao, B.; Huang, C.; Huang, B.; Si, Y. A Data-Driven Design for Fault Detection of Wind Turbines Using Random Forests and XGboost. *IEEE Access* **2018**, *6*, 21020–21031. [CrossRef]
27. Helbing, G.; Ritter, M. Deep Learning for Fault Detection in Wind Turbines. *Renew. Sustain. Energy Rev.* **2018**, *98*, 189–198. [CrossRef]
28. Chung, J.; Gulcehre, C.; Cho, K.; Bengio, Y. Empirical Evaluation of Gated Recurrent Neural Networks on Sequence Modeling. *arXiv* **2014**, arXiv:1412.3555.

29. Hochreiter, S.; Schmidhuber, J. Long Short-Term Memory. *Neural Comput.* **1997**, *9*, 1735–1780. [CrossRef]
30. Chen, H.; Liu, H.; Chu, X.; Liu, Q.; Xue, D. Anomaly Detection and Critical SCADA Parameters Identi Fi Cation for Wind Turbines Based on LSTM-AE Neural Network. *Renew. Energy* **2021**, *172*, 829–840. [CrossRef]
31. Lei, J.; Liu, C.; Jiang, D. Fault Diagnosis of Wind Turbine Based on Long Short-Term Memory Networks. *Renew. Energy* **2019**, *133*, 422–432. [CrossRef]
32. Yu, L.; Qu, J.; Gao, F.; Tian, Y. A Novel Hierarchical Algorithm for Bearing Fault Diagnosis Based on Stacked LSTM. *Shock Vib.* **2019**, *2019*, 2756284. [CrossRef]
33. Kazemi, S.M.; Goel, R.; Eghbali, S.; Ramanan, J.; Sahota, J.; Thakur, S.; Wu, S.; Smyth, C.; Poupart, P.; Brubaker, M. Time2Vec: Learning a Vector Representation of Time. *arXiv* **2019**, arXiv:1907.05321.
34. Granitto, P.M.; Furlanello, C.; Biasioli, F.; Gasperi, F. Recursive Feature Elimination with Random Forest for PTR-MS Analysis of Agroindustrial Products. *Chemom. Intell. Lab. Syst.* **2006**, *83*, 83–90. [CrossRef]
35. ORE Catapult. Levenmouth 7MW Demonstration Offshore Wind Turbine Specification Sheet. 2016, Volume 44, pp. 7–8. Available online: https://ore.catapult.org.uk/app/uploads/2018/01/Levenmouth-7MW-demonstration-offshore-wind-turbine.pdf (accessed on 10 September 2023).
36. Serret, J.; Rodriguez, C.; Tezdogan, T.; Stratford, T.; Thies, P. Code Comparison of a NREL-Fast Model of the Levenmouth Wind Turbine with the GH Bladed Commissioning Results. In Proceedings of the ASME 2018 37th International Conference on Ocean, Offshore and Arctic Engineering, Madrid, Spain, 17–22 June 2018; Volume 10. [CrossRef]
37. Kusiak, A.; Li, W. The Prediction and Diagnosis of Wind Turbine Faults. *Renew. Energy* **2011**, *36*, 16–23. [CrossRef]
38. Kusiak, A.; Verma, A. A Data-Driven Approach for Monitoring Blade Pitch Faults in Wind Turbines. *IEEE Trans. Sustain. Energy* **2011**, *2*, 87–96. [CrossRef]
39. Zhu, Y.; Li, H.; Liao, Y.; Wang, B.; Guan, Z.; Liu, H.; Cai, D.; Science, C. What to Do Next: Modeling User Behaviors by Time-LSTM. *IJCAI* **2017**, *17*, 3602–3608. [CrossRef]
40. Greff, K.; Srivastava, R.K.; Koutn, J.; Steunebrink, B.R. LSTM: A Search Space Odyssey. *IEEE Trans. Neural Netw. Learn. Syst.* **2016**, *28*, 2222–2232. [CrossRef]
41. Suzuki, K. *Artificial Neural Networks—Methodological Advances and Biomedical Applications*; Intech: Rijeka, Croatia, 2011; Available online: https://www.intechopen.com/books/citations/artificial-neural-networks-methodological-advances-and-biomedical-applications (accessed on 10 September 2023).
42. Brownlee, J. How to Grid Search Hyperparameters for Deep Learning Models in Python with Keras. 2016. Available online: https://machinelearningmastery.com/grid-search-hyperparameters-deeplearning-models-python-keras (accessed on 10 September 2023).
43. Sharma, S. Activation functions in neural networks. *Towards Data Sci.* **2020**, *4*, 310–316. [CrossRef]

algorithms

MDPI

Article

BENK: The Beran Estimator with Neural Kernels for Estimating the Heterogeneous Treatment Effect

Stanislav Kirpichenko [†], Lev Utkin [†], Andrei Konstantinov and Vladimir Muliukha [*]

Higher School of Artificial Intelligence Technologies, Peter the Great St. Petersburg Polytechnic University, 195251 St. Petersburg, Russia; kirpichenko.sr@edu.spbstu.ru (S.K.); utkin_lv@spbstu.ru (L.U.); konstantinov_av@spbstu.ru (A.K.)
[*] Correspondence: vladimir.muliukha@spbstu.ru
[†] These authors contributed equally to this work.

Abstract: A method for estimating the conditional average treatment effect under the condition of censored time-to-event data, called BENK (the Beran Estimator with Neural Kernels), is proposed. The main idea behind the method is to apply the Beran estimator for estimating the survival functions of controls and treatments. Instead of typical kernel functions in the Beran estimator, it is proposed to implement kernels in the form of neural networks of a specific form, called neural kernels. The conditional average treatment effect is estimated by using the survival functions as outcomes of the control and treatment neural networks, which consist of a set of neural kernels with shared parameters. The neural kernels are more flexible and can accurately model a complex location structure of feature vectors. BENK does not require a large dataset for training due to its special way for training networks by means of pairs of examples from the control and treatment groups. The proposed method extends a set of models that estimate the conditional average treatment effect. Various numerical simulation experiments illustrate BENK and compare it with the well-known T-learner, S-learner and X-learner for several types of control and treatment outcome functions based on the Cox models, the random survival forest and the Beran estimator with Gaussian kernels. The code of the proposed algorithms implementing BENK is publicly available.

Keywords: treatment effect; survival analysis; Nadaraya–Watson regression; Beran estimator; neural network; meta-learner

1. Introduction

Survival analysis is an important and fundamental tool for modeling applications when using time-to-event data [1], which can be encountered in medicine, reliability, safety, finance, etc. This is a reason why many machine learning models have been developed to deal with time-to-event data and to solve the corresponding problems in the framework of survival analysis [2]. The crucial peculiarity of time-to-event data is that a training set consists of censored and uncensored observations. When time-to-event exceeds the duration of an observation, we have a censored observation. When an event is observed, i.e., time-to-event coincides with the duration of the observation, we deal with an uncensored observation.

Many survival models are able to cover various cases of time-to-event probability distributions and their parameters [2]. One of the important models is the Cox proportional hazards model [3], which can be regarded as a semi-parametric regression model. There are also many parametric and nonparametric models. When considering machine learning survival models, it is important to point out that, in contrast to other machine learning models, their outcomes are functions, for instance, survival functions, hazard functions or cumulative hazard functions. For instance, the well-known effective model called the random survival forest (RSF) [4] predicts survival functions (SFs) or cumulative hazard functions.

An important area of survival model application is the problem of treatment effect estimation, which is often solved in the framework of machine learning problems [5]. The treatment effect shows how a treatment may be efficient depending on characteristics of a patient. The problem is solved by dividing patients into two groups called treatment and control, such that patients from the different groups can be compared. One of the popular measures of efficient treatment that is used in machine learning models is the average treatment effect (ATE) [6], which is estimated on the basis of observed data about patients, such as the mean difference between outcomes of patients from the treatment and control groups.

Due to the difference between characteristics of patients and their responses to a particular treatment, the treatment effect is measured using the conditional average treatment effect (CATE), which is defined as the mean difference between outcomes of patients from the treatment and control groups, conditional on a patient feature vector [7]. In fact, most methods of CATE estimation are based on constructing two regression models for controls and treatments. However, two difficulties in CATE estimation can be met. The first one is that the treatment group is usually very small. Therefore, many machine learning models cannot be accurately trained on the small datasets. The second difficulty is fundamental. Each patient cannot be simultaneously in the treatment and control groups, i.e., we either observe the patient outcome under the treatment or control, but never both [8]. Nevertheless, to overcome these difficulties, many methods for estimating CATE have been proposed and developed due to the importance of the problem in many areas [9–13].

One of the approaches for constructing regression models for controls and treatments is the application of the Nadaraya–Watson kernel regression [14,15], which uses standard kernel functions, for instance, the Gaussian, uniform or Epanechnikov kernels. In order to avoid selecting a standard kernel, Konstantinov et al. [16] proposed to implement kernels and the whole Nadaraya–Watson kernel regression by using a set of identical neural subnetworks with shared parameters, with a specific way of the network training. The corresponding method called TNW-CATE (Trainable Nadaraya–Watson regression for CATE) is based on an important assumption that domains of the feature vectors from the treatment and control groups are similar. Indeed, we often treat patients after being in the control group, i.e., it is assumed that treated patients came to the treatment group from the control group. For example, it is difficult to expect that patients with pneumonia will be treated with new drugs for stomach disease. The neural kernels (kernels implemented as the neural network) are more flexible, and they can accurately model a complex location structure of feature vectors, for instance, when the feature vectors from the control and treatment group are located on the spiral, as shown in Figure 1, where small triangular and circle markers correspond to the treatment and control groups, respectively. This is another important peculiarity of the TNW-CATE. Results provided in [16] illustrated outperformance of the TNW-CATE in comparison with other methods when the treatment group was very small and the feature vectors had complex structure.

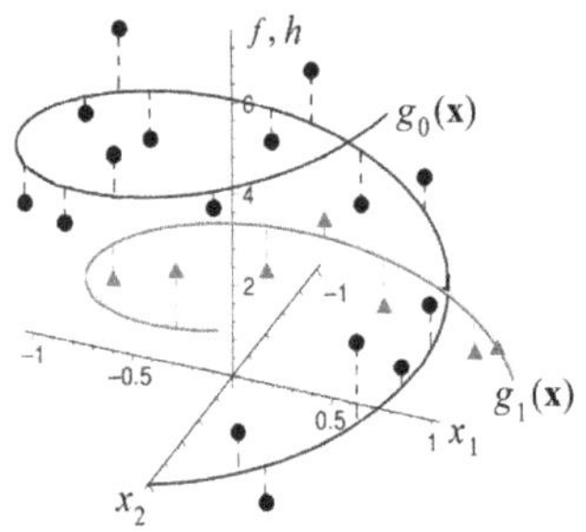

Figure 1. An example of the control $g_0(\mathbf{x})$ and treatment $g_1(\mathbf{x})$ functions, which are unknown, and of the control (circle markers) and treatment (triangle markers) data points, which are observed.

Following the ideas behind the TNW–CATE, we propose the CATE estimation method, called BENK (the Beran Estimator with Neural Kernels), dealing with censored time-to-event data in the framework of survival analysis. The main idea behind the proposed method is to apply the Beran estimator [17] for estimating SFs of treatments and controls and to compare them for estimating the CATE. One of the important peculiarities of the Beran estimator is that it takes into account distances between feature vectors by using kernels which measure the similarity between any two feature vectors. On the one hand, the Beran estimator can be regarded as an extension of the Kaplan–Meier estimator. It allows us to obtain SFs that are conditional on the feature vectors, which can be viewed as outcomes of regression survival models for the treatment and control groups. On the other hand, the Beran estimator can also be viewed as an analogue of the Nadaraya–Watson kernel regression for survival analysis. However, typical kernels, for example, the Gaussian one, cannot cope with the possible complex structure of data. Therefore, similarly to the TNW–CATE model, we propose to implement kernels in the Beran estimator by means of neural subnetworks and to estimate CATE by using the obtained SFs. The whole neural network model is trained in an end-to-end manner.

Various numerical experiments illustrate BENK and its peculiarities. They also show that BENK outperforms many well-known meta-models: the T-learner and the S-learner, the X-learner for several control and treatment output functions based on the Cox models, the RSF and the Beran estimator with Gaussian kernels.

BENK is implemented using the framework PyTorch with open code. The code of the proposed algorithms can be found at https://github.com/Stasychbr/BENK (accessed on 27 October 2023).

The paper is organized as follows. Section 2 is a review of the existing CATE estimation models, including CATE estimation survival models, the Nadaraya–Watson regression models and general survival models. A formal statement of the CATE estimation problem is provided in Section 3. The CATE estimation problem in the case of censored data is stated in Section 4. The Beran estimator is considered in Section 5. A description of BENK is provided in Section 6. Numerical experiments illustrating BENK and comparing it with other models can be found in Section 7. Concluding remarks are provided in Section 8.

2. Related Work

Estimating CATE. One of the important approaches to implement personalized medicine is the treatment effect estimation. As a result, many interesting machine learning models have been developed and implemented to estimate CATE. First, we have to point out an approach which uses the Lasso model for estimating CATE [18]. The SVM was also applied to solve the problem [19]. A unified framework for constructing fast tree-growing procedures for solving the CATE problem was provided in [20]. McFowland et al. [21] estimated CATE by using the anomaly detection model. A set of meta-algorithms or meta-learners, including the T-learner, the S-learner and the X-learner, were studied in [12]. Many other models related to the CATE estimation problem are studied in [22,23].

The aforementioned models are constructed by using machine learning methods, which are different from neural networks. However, neural networks became a basis for developing many interesting and efficient models [24–27].

Due to the importance of the CATE problem, there are many other publications devoted to this problem [28–31].

The next generation of models that solve the CATE estimation problem is based on architectures of transformers with the attention operations [32–34]. The transfer learning technique was successfully applied to the CATE estimation in [35,36]. Ideas of using the Nadaraya–Watson kernel regression in the CATE estimation were studied in [37]. These ideas can lead to the best results under the condition of large numbers of examples in the treatment and control groups. At the same time, a small amount of training data may lead to overfitting and unsatisfactory results. Therefore, the problem of overcoming this possible limitation motivated researchers to introduce a neural network of a special architecture, which implements the trainable kernels in the Nadaraya–Watson regression [16].

Machine learning models in survival analysis. The importance of survival analysis applications can be regarded as one of the reasons for developing many machine learning methods that deal with censored and time-to-event data. A comprehensive review of machine learning survival models is presented in [2]. A large portion of models use the Cox model, which can be viewed as a simple and applicable survival model that establishes a relationship between covariates and outcomes. Various extensions of the Cox model have been proposed. They can be conditionally divided into two groups. The first group remains the linear relationship of covariates and includes various modifications of the Lasso models [38]. The second group of models relaxes the linear relationship assumption accepted in the Cox model [39].

Many survival models are based on using the RSFs, which can be regarded as powerful tools, especially when models learn on tabular data [40,41]. At the same time, there are many survival models based on neural networks [42,43].

Estimating CATE with censored data. Censored data can be regarded as an important type, especially for estimating the treatment effect because many applications are characterized by time-to-event data as outcomes. This peculiarity is a reason for developing many CATE models that deal with censored data in the framework of survival analysis [44–46]. Modifications of the survival causal trees and forests for estimating the CATE based on censored observational data were proposed in [44]. An approach combining a treatment-specific semi-parametric Cox loss with a treatment-balanced deep neural network was studied in [47]. Nagpal et al. [48] presented a latent variable approach to model the CATE under assumption that an individual can belong to one of the latent clusters with distinct response characteristics. The problem of CATE estimation by focusing on learning (discrete-time) treatment-specific conditional hazard functions was studied in [49]. A three-stage modular design for estimating CATE in the framework of survival analysis was proposed in [50]. A comprehensive simulation study presenting a wide range of settings, describing CATE by taking into account the covariate overlap, was carried out in [51]. Rytgaard et al. [52] presented a data-adaptive estimation procedure for estimation of the CATE in a time-to-event setting based on generalized random forests. The authors proposed a two-step procedure for estimation, applying inverse probability weighting to construct time-point-specific weighted outcomes as input for the forest. A unified framework for counterfactual inference, applicable to survival outcomes and formulation of a nonparametric hazard ratio metric for evaluating the CATE, were proposed in [53].

In spite of many works and results devoted to estimating the CATE with censored data, these methods are mainly based on assumptions of a large number of examples in the treatment group. Moreover, there are no results implementing the Nadaraya–Watson regression by means of neural networks.

3. CATE Estimation Problem Statement

According to the CATE estimation problem, all patients are divided into two groups: control and treatment. Let the control group be the set $\mathcal{C} = \{(\mathbf{x}_1, f_1), \dots, (\mathbf{x}_c, f_c)\}$ of c patients, such that the i-th patient is characterized by the feature vector $\mathbf{x}_i = (x_{i1}, \dots, x_{id}) \in \mathbb{R}^d$ and the i-th observed outcome $f_i \in \mathbb{R}$ (time to event, temperature, the blood pressure, etc.). It is also supposed that the treatment group is the set $\mathcal{T} = \{(\mathbf{y}_1, h_1), \dots, (\mathbf{y}_t, h_t)\}$ of t patients, such that the i-th patient is characterized by the feature vector $\mathbf{y}_i = (y_{i1}, \dots, y_{id}) \in \mathbb{R}^d$ and the i-th observed outcome $h_i \in \mathbb{R}$. The indicator of a group for the i-th patient is denoted as $T_i \in \{0, 1\}$, where $T_i = 0$ ($T_i = 1$) corresponds to the control (treatment) group.

We use different notations $\mathbf{x}_i$ and $\mathbf{y}_i$ for controls and treatments in order to avoid additional indices. However, we use the vector $\mathbf{z} \in \mathbb{R}^d$ instead of $\mathbf{x}$ and $\mathbf{y}$ when estimating the CATE.

Suppose that the potential outcomes of patients from the control and treatment groups are F and H, respectively. The treatment effect for a new patient with the feature vector $\mathbf{z}$ is estimated by the individual treatment effect, defined as $H - F$. The fundamental problem of computing the CATE is that only one of the outcomes f or h for each patient can be observed. An important assumption of unconfoundedness [54] is used to allow the untreated patients to be used to construct an unbiased counterfactual for the treatment group [55]. According to the assumption, potential outcomes are characteristics of a patient before the patient is assigned to a treatment condition, or, formally, the treatment assignment T is independent of the potential outcomes for F and H that conditional on the feature vector $\mathbf{z}$, which can be written as

$$T \perp \{F, H\} \mid \mathbf{z}. \tag{1}$$

The second assumption, called the overlap assumption, regards the joint distribution of treatments and covariates. This assumption claims that a positive probability of being both treated and untreated for each value of $\mathbf{z}$ exists. This implies that the following holds with probability 1:

$$0 < \Pr\{T = 1 \mid \mathbf{z}\} < 1. \tag{2}$$

Let $\mathbf{Z}$ be the random feature vector from $\mathbb{R}^d$. The treatment effect is estimated by means of CATE, which is defined as the expected difference between two potential outcomes, as follows [56]:

$$\tau(\mathbf{z}) = \mathbb{E}[H - F \mid \mathbf{Z} = \mathbf{z}]. \tag{3}$$

By using the above assumptions, CATE can be rewritten as

$$\tau(\mathbf{z}) = \mathbb{E}[H \mid \mathbf{Z} = \mathbf{z}] - \mathbb{E}[F \mid \mathbf{Z} = \mathbf{z}]. \tag{4}$$

The motivation behind unconfoundedness is that nearby observations in the feature space can be treated as having come from a randomized experiment [7].

Suppose that functions $g_0(\mathbf{z})$ and $g_1(\mathbf{z})$ express outcomes of the control and treatment patients, respectively. Then, they can be written as follows:

$$f = g_0(\mathbf{z}) + \varepsilon,\ h = g_1(\mathbf{z}) + \varepsilon, \tag{5}$$

where ε is noise governed by the normal distribution with the zero expectation.

The above imply that the CATE can be estimated as

$$\tau(\mathbf{z}) = g_1(\mathbf{z}) - g_0(\mathbf{z}). \tag{6}$$

An example illustrating the controls (circle markers), treatments (triangle markers) and corresponding unknown function g_0 and g_1 are shown in Figure 1.

4. CATE with Censored Data

Before considering the CATE estimation problem with the censored data, we introduce basic statements of survival analysis. Let us define the training set D_0, which consists of c triplets $(\mathbf{x}_i, \delta_i, f_i)$, $i = 1, \ldots, c$, where $\mathbf{x}_i^{\mathrm{T}} = (x_{i1}, \ldots, x_{id})$ is the feature vector characterizing the i-th patient from the control group, f_i is the time to the event concerning the i-th control patient and $\delta_i \in \{0, 1\}$ is the indicator of censored or uncensored observations. If $\delta_i = 1$, then the event of interest is observed (the uncensored observation). If $\delta_i = 0$, then we have the censored observation. Only the right-censoring is considered when the observed survival time is less than or equal to the true survival time. Many applications of survival analysis deal with the right-censored observations [2]. The main goal of survival machine learning modeling is to use set D_0 to estimate probabilistic characteristics of time F to the event of interest for a new patient with the feature vector $\mathbf{z}$.

In the same way, we define the training set D_1, which consists of d triplets $(\mathbf{y}_i, \gamma_i, h_i)$, $i = 1, \ldots, s$, where $\mathbf{y}_i^{\mathrm{T}} = (y_{i1}, \ldots, y_{id})$ is the feature vector characterizing the i-th patient from the treatment group, h_i is the time to the event concerning the i-th treatment patient and $\gamma_i \in \{0, 1\}$ is the indicator of censoring.

The survival function (SF), denoted $S(t \mid \mathbf{z})$, can be regarded as an important concept in survival analysis. It represents the probability of survival of a patient with the feature vector $\mathbf{z}$ up to time t, that is, $S(t \mid \mathbf{z}) = \Pr\{T > t \mid \mathbf{z}\}$. The hazard function, denoted $\lambda(t \mid \mathbf{z})$, can be viewed as another concept in survival analysis. It is defined as the rate of an event at time t given that no event occurred before time t. It is expressed through the SF as follows:

$$\lambda(t \mid \mathbf{z}) = -\frac{\mathrm{d}}{\mathrm{d}t} \ln S(t \mid \mathbf{z}). \tag{7}$$

The integral of the hazard function, denoted $H(t \mid \mathbf{x})$, is called the cumulative hazard function and can be interpreted as the probability of an event at time t given survival until time t, i.e.,

$$\Lambda(t \mid \mathbf{z}) = \int_0^t \lambda(r \mid \mathbf{z}) dr. \tag{8}$$

It is expressed through the SF as follows:

$$\Lambda(t \mid \mathbf{z}) = -\ln(S(t \mid \mathbf{z})). \tag{9}$$

The above functions for controls and treatments are written with indices 0 and 1, respectively, for instance, $S_0(t \mid \mathbf{z}) = \Pr\{F > t \mid \mathbf{z}\}$ and $S_1(t \mid \mathbf{z}) = \Pr\{H > t \mid \mathbf{z}\}$.

In order to compare survival models, Harrell's concordance index, or the C-index [57], is usually used. The C-index measures the probability that, in a randomly selected pair of examples, the example that failed first had a worst predicted outcome. It is calculated as the ratio of the number of pairs correctly ordered by the model to the total number of admissible pairs. A pair is not admissible if the events are both right-censored or if the earliest time in the pair is censored. The corresponding survival model is supposed to be perfect when the C-index is 1. The case when the C-index is 0.5 says that the survival model is the same as random guessing. The case when the C-index is less than 0.5 says that the corresponding model is worse than random guessing.

In contrast to the standard CATE estimation problem statement given in the previous section, the CATE estimation problem with censored data has another statement, which is due to the fact that outcomes in survival analysis are random times to an event of interest having some conditional probability distribution. In other words, predictions corresponding to a patient characterized by vector $\mathbf{z}$ in survival analysis provided by a survival machine learning model are represented in the form of functions of time, for instance, in the form of SF $S(t \mid \mathbf{z})$. This implies that the CATE $\tau(\mathbf{x})$ should be reformulated by taking into account the above peculiarity. It is assumed that SFs as well as hazard functions for control and treatment patients, estimated by using datasets D_0 and D_1, will have indices 0 and 1, respectively.

The following definitions of the CATE in the case of censored data can be found in [58]:

1. Difference in expected lifetimes:

$$\tau(\mathbf{z}) = \int_0^{t_{\max}} (S_1(t \mid \mathbf{z}) - S_0(t \mid \mathbf{z}))\mathrm{d}t = \mathbb{E}\{T_1 - T_0 \mid X = \mathbf{z}\}; \tag{10}$$

2. Difference in SFs:

$$\tau(t, \mathbf{z}) = S_1(t \mid \mathbf{z}) - S_0(t \mid \mathbf{z}); \tag{11}$$

3. Hazard ratio:

$$\tau(t, \mathbf{z}) = \lambda_1(t \mid \mathbf{z}) / \lambda_0(t \mid \mathbf{z}). \tag{12}$$

We will the first integral definition of the CATE. Let $0 = t_0 < t_1 < \ldots < t_n$ be the distinct times to an event of interest, which are obtained from the set $\{f_1, \ldots, f_c\} \cup \{h_1, \ldots, h_s\}$. The SF provided by a survival machine learning model is a step function, i.e., it can be represented as $S(t \mid \mathbf{z}) = \sum_{j=1}^{n} S^{(j)}(\mathbf{z}) \cdot \chi_j(t)$, where $\chi_j(t)$ is the indicator function, taking a value of 1 if $t \in [t_{j-1}, t_j]$; $S^{(j)}(\mathbf{z})$ is the value of the SF in interval $[t_{j-1}, t_j]$. Hence, the following holds:

$$\begin{aligned}\tau(\mathbf{z}) &= \int_0^{t_{\max}} (S_1(t \mid \mathbf{z}) - S_0(t \mid \mathbf{z}))\mathrm{d}t \\ &= \sum_{j=1}^{n} \left(S_1^{(j)}(\mathbf{z}) - S_0^{(j)}(\mathbf{z})\right)(t_j - t_{j-1}). \end{aligned} \tag{13}$$

5. Nonparametric Estimation of Survival Functions and CATE

The idea to use the nonparametric kernel regression for estimating SFs and other concepts of survival analysis has been proposed by several authors [59,60]. One of the interesting estimators is the Beran estimator [17] of the SF, which is defined as follows:

$$S(t \mid \mathbf{x}) = \prod_{f_i \le t} \left\{1 - \frac{W(\mathbf{x}, \mathbf{x}_i)}{1 - \sum_{j=1}^{i-1} W(\mathbf{x}, \mathbf{x}_j)}\right\}^{\delta_i}, \tag{14}$$

where $W(\mathbf{x}, \mathbf{x}_i)$ are the kernel weights, defined as

$$W(\mathbf{x}, \mathbf{x}_i) = \frac{K(\mathbf{x}, \mathbf{x}_i)}{\sum_{j=1}^{n} K(\mathbf{x}, \mathbf{x}_j)}. \tag{15}$$

The above expression is given for the controls. The same estimator can be written for treatments, but $\mathbf{x}$, δ_i, f_i are replaced with $\mathbf{y}$, γ_i, h_i, respectively.

The Beran estimator can be regarded as a generalization of the Kaplan–Meier estimator because the former is reduced to the latter if the kernel weights take values $W(\mathbf{x}, \mathbf{x}_i) = 1/n$. It is also interesting to note that the product in (14) only takes into account uncensored observations, whereas the weights are normalized by using uncensored as well as censored observations.

By using (14) and (13), we can construct a neural network that is trained to implement the weights $W(\mathbf{z}, \mathbf{x}_i)$, $W(\mathbf{z}, \mathbf{y}_i)$ and to estimate SFs $S_1(t \mid \mathbf{z})$ and $S_0(t \mid \mathbf{z})$ for computing $\tau(\mathbf{z})$.

6. Neural Network for Estimating CATE

Let us consider how the Beran estimator with neural kernels can be implemented by means of a neural network of a special type. Our first aim is to implement kernels $K(\mathbf{x}, \mathbf{x}_i)$ by means of a neural subnetwork, which is called the neural kernel and is a part of the whole network for implementing the Beran estimator. The second aim is for this network to learn on the control data. Having the trained kernel, we can apply it to compute the conditional survival function for controls, as well as for treatments, because the kernels in (14) do not directly depend on times to events f_i or h_i. However, in order to train the kernel, we have to train the whole network because the loss function is defined through SF $S_0(t \mid \mathbf{x})$, which represents the probability of survival of a control patient up to time t, which is estimated by means of the Beran estimator. This implies that the whole network contains blocks of the neural kernels for computing kernels $K(\mathbf{x}, \mathbf{x}_i)$, normalization for computing the kernel weights $W(\mathbf{x}, \mathbf{x}_i)$ and the Beran estimator in accordance with (14). In order to realize a training procedure for the network, we randomly select a portion (n examples) from all control training examples and form a single specific example from n selected ones. This random selection is repeated N times to have N examples for training. Thus, for every $\mathbf{x}_i$, $i = 1, \dots, c$, from the control group, we add another vector $\mathbf{x}_k$ from the same set of controls. By composing n pairs of vectors $(\mathbf{x}_i, \mathbf{x}_k)$, $k = 1, \dots, n$, and including other elements of training examples (δ_i, f_i), we obtain one composite vector of data, representing one new training example for the entire neural network. Such new training examples can be constructed for each $i = 1, \dots, c$. The formal construction of the training set is considered below.

Having the trained neural kernel, it can be successfully used for computing SF $S_0(t \mid \mathbf{z})$ of controls and SF $S_1(t \mid \mathbf{z})$ of treatments for arbitrary vectors of features $\mathbf{z}$, again applying the Beran estimator.

Let us consider the training algorithm in detail. First, we return to the set of c controls $\mathcal{C} = \{(\mathbf{x}_i, \delta_i, f_i),\ i = 1, \dots, c\}$. For every i from set $\{1, \dots, c\}$, we construct N subsets $\mathcal{C}_i^{(r)}$, $r = 1, \dots, N$, having n examples randomly selected from $\mathcal{C} \backslash (\mathbf{x}_i, \delta_i, f_i)$, which have indices from the index set $\mathcal{I}^{(r)}$, i.e., the subsets $\mathcal{C}_i^{(r)}$ are of the form

$$\mathcal{C}_i^{(r)} = \{(\mathbf{x}_k^{(r)}, \delta_k^{(r)}, f_k^{(r)}),\ k \in \mathcal{I}^{(r)}\},\ r = 1, \dots, N. \tag{16}$$

Here, N and n can be regarded as tuning hyperparameters. Upper index r indicates that the r-th example $(\mathbf{x}_k^{(r)}, \delta_k^{(r)}, f_k^{(r)})$ is randomly taken from $\mathcal{C} \backslash (\mathbf{x}_i, \delta_i, f_i)$, i.e., there is an example $(\mathbf{x}_j, \delta_j, f_j)$ from $\mathcal{C}$ such that $\mathbf{x}_k^{(r)} = \mathbf{x}_j$, $\delta_k^{(r)} = \delta_j$, $f_k^{(r)} = f_j$. Each subset $\mathcal{C}_i^{(r)}$, jointly with $(\mathbf{x}_i, \delta_i, f_i)$, forms a training example $\mathbf{a}_i^{(r)}$ for the control network as follows:

$$\mathbf{a}_i^{(r)} = \left(\mathcal{C}_i^{(r)}, \mathbf{x}_i, \delta_i, f_i\right),\ i = 1, \dots, c,\ r = 1, \dots, N. \tag{17}$$

The number of possible examples $\mathbf{a}_i^{(r)}$ is $c \cdot N$, and these examples are used for training the neural network, whose output is the estimate of SF $\tilde{S}_0(t \mid \mathbf{x}_i)$.

The architecture of the neural network, consisting of n subnetworks that implement the neural kernels, is shown in Figure 2. Examples $\mathbf{a}_i^{(r)}$ produced from the dataset of controls are fed to the whole neural network, such that each pair $(\mathbf{x}_i, \mathbf{x}_k^{(r)})$, $k \in \mathcal{I}^{(r)}$, is fed to each subnetwork, which implements the kernel function. The output of each subnetwork is kernel $K(\mathbf{x}_i, \mathbf{x}_k^{(r)})$. All subnetworks are identical and have shared weights. After normalizing the kernels, we obtain n weights $W(\mathbf{x}_i, \mathbf{x}_k^{(r)})$, which are used to estimate SFs by means of the Beran estimator in (14). The block of the whole neural network that implements the Beran estimator uses all weights $W(\mathbf{x}_i, \mathbf{x}_k^{(r)})$, $k \in \mathcal{I}^{(r)}$, and the corresponding values $\delta_k^{(r)}$ and $f_k^{(r)}$, $k \in \mathcal{I}^{(r)}$. As a result, we obtain SF $\tilde{S}_0(t \mid \mathbf{x}_i)$. In the same way, we compute SFs $\tilde{S}_0(t \mid \mathbf{x}_k)$ for all $k = 1, \dots, c$. These functions are the basis for training. In fact, the normalization block and the block that implements the Beran estimator can be regarded as part of the neural network, and they are trained in an end-to-end manner.

According to (13), expected lifetimes are used to compute the CATE $\tau(\mathbf{z})$. Therefore, the whole network is trained by means of the following loss function:

$$L = \frac{1}{c^* \cdot N} \sum_{i \in \mathcal{C}^*} \sum_{k=1}^{N} \left(\tilde{E}_k^{(i)} - f_k^{(i)}\right)^2. \tag{18}$$

Here, $\mathcal{C}^*$ is a subset of $\mathcal{C}$, which contains only uncensored examples from $\mathcal{C}$, c^* is the number of elements in $\mathcal{C}^*$; $f_k^{(i)}$ is the time to an event of the k-th example from the set $\mathcal{C}^* \backslash (\mathbf{x}_i, \delta_i, f_i)$ and $\tilde{E}_k^{(i)}$ is the expected lifetime computed through SF $\tilde{S}_0(t \mid \mathbf{x}_k)$, obtained by integrating the SF:

$$\tilde{E}_k^{(i)} = \sum_{j=1}^{n} (f_j^{(i)} - f_{j-1}^{(i)}) \tilde{S}_0(f_j^{(i)} \mid \mathbf{x}_k). \tag{19}$$

The sum in (18) is taken over uncensored examples from $\mathcal{C}$. However, the Beran estimator uses all the examples.

One of the loss functions, which takes into account all data (censored and uncensored), is the C-index. However, our aim is not to estimate the SF or the CHF. We aim to estimate the difference between the predicted time to event and the expected time to event. Therefore, we use the standard mean squared error (MSE) loss function. But the censored times introduce bias into MSE and, therefore, they are not used.

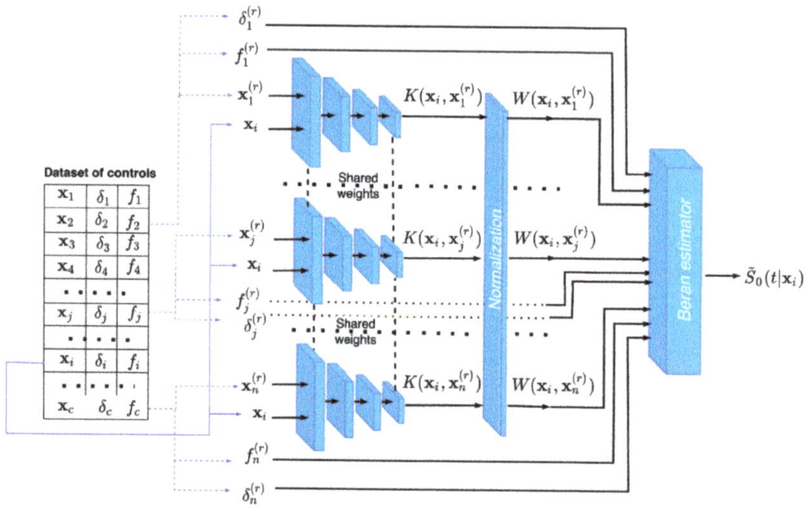

Figure 2. The neural network training on examples $\mathbf{a}_i^{(r)}$, composed of controls, for producing the Beran estimator in the form of SF $\tilde{S}_0(t \mid \mathbf{x}_i)$.

It is important to point out that our aim is to train subnetworks with shared training parameters, which are the neural kernels. By having the trained neural kernels, we can use them to compute kernels $K(\mathbf{z}, \mathbf{x}_i)$ and $K(\mathbf{z}, \mathbf{y}_i)$ and then to compute estimates of SFs $\tilde{S}_0(t \mid \mathbf{z})$ and $\tilde{S}_1(t \mid \mathbf{z})$ for controls and treatments, respectively, i.e., we realize the idea of transferring tasks from the control group to the treatment group. Let $t_1^{(0)} < t_2^{(0)} < \ldots < t_c^{(0)}$ and $t_1^{(1)} < t_2^{(1)} < \ldots < t_s^{(1)}$ be the ordered time moments corresponding to times $f_1, \ldots, f_c$ and $h_1, \ldots, h_s$, respectively. Then, the CATE $\tau(\mathbf{z})$ can be computed through SFs $S_1(t \mid \mathbf{z})$ and $S_0(t \mid \mathbf{z})$, again by using the Beran estimators with the trained neural kernels, i.e., in accordance with (13), it holds that

$$\tau(\mathbf{z}) = \sum_{j=1}^{s} (t_j^{(1)} - t_{j-1}^{(1)}) \tilde{S}_1^{(j)}(\mathbf{z}) - \sum_{k=1}^{c} (t_k^{(0)} - t_{k-1}^{(0)}) \tilde{S}_0^{(k)}(\mathbf{z}), \tag{20}$$

where $\tilde{S}_1^{(j)}(\mathbf{z})$ is the estimation of the SF of treatments on the interval $[t_{j-1}^{(1)}, t_j^{(1)})$, $\tilde{S}_0^{(k)}(\mathbf{z})$ is the estimation of SF of controls in interval $[t_{k-1}^{(0)}, t_k^{(0)})$ and it is assumed that $t_0^{(0)} = t_0^{(1)} = 0$.

The illustration of the neural networks that predict $K(\mathbf{z}, \mathbf{x}_i)$ and $K(\mathbf{z}, \mathbf{y}_i)$ for a new vector $\mathbf{z}$ of features is shown in Figure 3. It can be seen from Figure 3 that the first neural network consists of c subnetworks, such that pairs of vectors $(\mathbf{z}, \mathbf{x}_i)$, $i = 1, \ldots, c$, are fed to the subnetworks, where $\mathbf{x}_i$ is taken from the dataset of controls. Predictions of the first neural network are c kernels $K(\mathbf{z}, \mathbf{x}_i)$, which are used to compute $\tilde{S}_0(t \mid \mathbf{z})$ by means of the Beran estimator (14). The same architecture has the neural network for predicting kernels $K(\mathbf{z}, \mathbf{y}_i)$, used for estimating the treatment SF $\tilde{S}_1(t \mid \mathbf{z})$. This network consists of s subnetworks and uses vectors $\mathbf{y}_i$ from the dataset of treatments. After computing estimates $\tilde{S}_0(t \mid \mathbf{z})$ and $\tilde{S}_1(t \mid \mathbf{z})$, we can find the CATE $\tau(\mathbf{z})$.

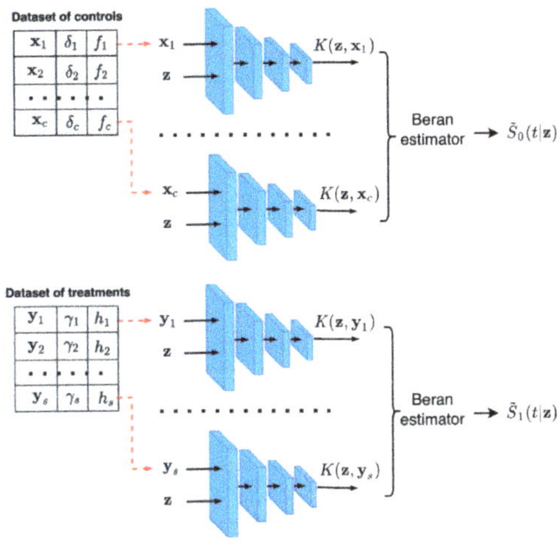

Figure 3. Neural networks consisting of the c and s trained neural kernels, predicting new values of kernels $K(\mathbf{z},\mathbf{x}_i)$ and $K(\mathbf{z},\mathbf{y}_i)$ that correspond to controls and treatments for computing estimates of $S_1(t \mid \mathbf{z})$ and $S_0(t \mid \mathbf{z})$, respectively.

Phases of training and computing CATE $\tau(\mathbf{x})$ by means of neural kernels are schematically shown as Algorithms 1 and 2, respectively.

Algorithm 1 The algorithm for training neural kernels

Require: Datasets $\mathcal{C}$ of c controls and $\mathcal{T}$ of s treatments, number N of generated subsets $\mathcal{C}_i^{(r)}$ of $\mathcal{C}$, number of examples in generated subsets n
Ensure: Neural kernels $K(\cdot,\cdot)$ for their use in the Beran estimator for control and treatment data

```
for i = 1, i ≤ c do
    for r = 1, r ≤ N do
        Generate subset C_i^(r) ⊂ C \ (x_i, y_i)
        Form example a_i^(r) = (C_i^(r), x_i, δ_i, f_i)
    end for
end for
Train the weight sharing neural network with the loss function given in (18) on the set of examples a_i^(r)
```

Algorithm 2 The algorithm for computing CATE for a new feature vector $\mathbf{z}$

Require: Trained neural kernels, datasets $\mathcal{C}$ and $\mathcal{T}$, testing example $\mathbf{z}$
Ensure: CATE $\tau(\mathbf{x})$

```
for i = 1, i ≤ c do
    Form pair (z, x_i) of vectors by using the dataset C of controls
    Feed pair (z, x_i) to the trained neural kernel and predict K(z, x_i)
end for
for i = 1, i ≤ s do
    Form pair (z, y_i) of vectors by using the dataset T of treatments
    Feed pair (z, y_i) to the trained neural kernel and predict K(z, y_i)
end for
Compute W(z, x_i), i = 1, ..., c, W(z, y_i), i = 1, ..., s
Estimate S̃_0(t | x_k) and S̃_1(t | y_k) using (14)
Compute τ(x) using (20)
```

---

7. Numerical Experiments

Numerical experiments for studying BENK and its comparison with available models are performed by using simulated datasets because the true CATEs are unknown due to the fundamental problem of causal inference for real data [8]. This implies that control and treatment datasets are randomly generated in accordance with predefined outcome functions.

7.1. CATE Estimators for Comparison and Their Parameters

For investigating BENK and its comparison, we use nine models, which can be united in three groups (the T-learner, the S-learner, the X-learner), such that each group is based on three base models for estimating SFs (the RSF, the Cox model, the Beran estimator with Gaussian kernels). The models are given below in terms of survival models:

1. The T-learner [12] is a model which estimates the control SF $S_0(t \mid \mathbf{z})$ and the treatment SF $S_1(t \mid \mathbf{z})$ for every $\mathbf{z}$. The CATE in this case is defined in accordance with (13);
2. The S-learner [12] is a model which estimates SF $S(t \mid \mathbf{z}, T)$ instead of $S_0(t \mid \mathbf{z})$ and $S_1(t \mid \mathbf{z})$, where the treatment assignment indicator $T_i \in \{0,1\}$ is included as an additional feature to the feature vector $\mathbf{z}_i$. As a result, we have a modified dataset

$$\mathcal{D} = \{(\mathbf{z}_1^*, \delta_1, f_1), \dots, (\mathbf{z}_c^*, \delta_c, f_c), (\mathbf{z}_{c+1}^*, \gamma_1, h_1), \dots, (\mathbf{z}_{c+s}^*, \gamma_s, h_s)\}, \tag{21}$$

where $\mathbf{z}_i^* = (\mathbf{x}_i, T_i) \in \mathbb{R}^{d+1}$ if $T_i = 0$, $i = 1, \dots, c$, and $\mathbf{z}_{c+i}^* = (\mathbf{y}_i, T_i) \in \mathbb{R}^{d+1}$ if $T_i = 1$, $i = 1, \dots, t$. The CATE is determined as

$$\tau(\mathbf{z}) = \sum_{j=1}^{s} (t_j^{(1)} - t_{j-1}^{(1)}) \tilde{S}^{(j)}(\mathbf{z}, 1) - \sum_{k=1}^{c} (t_k^{(0)} - t_{k-1}^{(0)}) \tilde{S}^{(k)}(\mathbf{z}, 0); \tag{22}$$

3. The X-learner [12] is based on computing the so-called imputed treatment effects and is represented in the following three steps. First, the outcome functions $g_0(\mathbf{x})$ and $g_1(\mathbf{y})$ are estimated using a regression algorithm. Second, the imputed treatment effects are computed as follows:

$$D_1(\mathbf{y}_i) = h_i - g_0(\mathbf{y}_i),\ D_0(\mathbf{x}_i) = g_1(\mathbf{x}_i) - f_i. \tag{23}$$

Third, two regression functions $\tau_1(\mathbf{y})$ and $\tau_0(\mathbf{x})$ are estimated for imputed treatment effects $D_1(\mathbf{y})$ and $D_0(\mathbf{x})$, respectively. The CATE for a point $\mathbf{z}$ is defined as a weighted linear combination of the functions $\tau_1(\mathbf{z})$ and $\tau_0(\mathbf{z})$ as $\tau(\mathbf{z}) = \alpha\tau_0(\mathbf{z}) + (1-\alpha)\tau_1(\mathbf{z})$, where $\alpha \in [0,1]$ is a weight that is equal to the ratio of treated patients. The original X-learner does not deal with censored data. Therefore, we propose a simple survival modification of the X-learner. It is assumed that $g_0(\mathbf{y}_i)$ and $g_1(\mathbf{x}_i)$ are expectations $E_0(\mathbf{y}_i)$ and $E_1(\mathbf{x}_i)$ of the times to an event corresponding to control and treatment data, respectively. Expectations $E_0(\mathbf{y}_i)$ and $E_1(\mathbf{x}_i)$ are computed by means of one of the algorithms for determining estimates of SFs $S_0(t \mid \mathbf{z})$ and $S_1(t \mid \mathbf{z})$. The functions $\tau_1(\mathbf{y})$ and $\tau_0(\mathbf{x})$ are implemented using the random forest regression algorithm for all the basic models.

Estimations of SFs $S_0(t \mid \mathbf{z})$ and $S_1(t \mid \mathbf{z})$ as well as $S(t \mid \mathbf{z}, T)$ are carried out by means o the following survival regression algorithms:

1. The RSF parameters of random forests used in experiments are the following:
   - The numbers of trees are 10, 50, 100, 200;
   - The depths are 3, 4, 5, 6;
   - The smallest values of examples which fall in a leaf are 1 example, 1%, 5%, 10% of the training set.

   The above values for the hyperparameters are tested, choosing those leading to the best results;

2. The Cox proportional hazards model [3], which is used with the elastic net regularization with the 3 to 1 ratio coefficient L_1/L_2;
3. In contrast to the proposed BENK model, we use the Beran estimator with the standard Gaussian kernels. Values 10^i, $i = -4, \ldots, 3$, and also values 0.5, 5, 50, 200, 500, 700 of the bandwidth parameter of the Gaussian kernel are tested, choosing those leading to the best results.

In sum, we have nine models for comparison, whose notations are given in Table 1.

Table 1. Notations of the models, depending on meta-learners and base models.

	Meta-Model		
Survival regression algorithms	T-learner	S-learner	X-learner
Beran estimator	T-Beran	S-Beran	X-Beran
Cox model	T-Cox	S-Cox	X-Cox
RSF	T-SF	S-SF	X-SF

7.2. Generating Synthetic Datasets

As has been described above, we consider generating the artificial complex feature spaces and outcomes in the numerical experiments. All the vectors of features, including controls $\mathbf{x}$ and treatments $\mathbf{y}$, are generated by means of three functions: the spiral function, the bell-shaped function and the circular function. The idea to use these functions stems from the goal to obtain complex structures of data, which are poorly processed by many standard methods. The above functions are defined through a parameter ξ as follows:

1. Spiral functions: The feature vectors, having dimensionality d and being located on the Archimedean spirals, are defined for even d as

$$\mathbf{x} = (\xi \sin(\xi), \xi \cos(\xi), \ldots, \xi \sin(\xi \cdot d/2), \xi \cos(\xi \cdot d/2)), \tag{24}$$

and for odd d as

$$\mathbf{x} = (\xi \sin(\xi), \xi \cos(\xi), \ldots, \xi \sin(\xi \cdot \lceil d/2 \rceil)). \tag{25}$$

Values of ξ are uniformly generated from the interval $[0, 10]$ for all numerical experiments;

2. Bell-shaped functions: Features are represented as a set of almost non-overlapping Gaussians. As ξ is uniformly generated in the numerical experiments, we can define $\xi_{\min}$ and $\xi_{\max}$ as corresponding bounds of the uniform distribution. Therefore, the feature vector of dimensionality d is represented as

$$\begin{aligned} \mathbf{x} &= (x_0, x_1, \ldots, x_{d-1}), \\ \sigma &= \frac{\xi_{\max} - \xi_{\min}}{6d}, \ \mu = \frac{\xi_{\max} - \xi_{\min}}{d-1}, \\ x_i &= \frac{1}{\sigma\sqrt{2\pi}} \cdot \exp\left(\frac{-(\xi - i \cdot \mu)^2}{2\sigma^2} \right), \ i = 1, \ldots, d-1. \end{aligned} \tag{26}$$

Therefore, each feature x_i corresponds to its own region in the ξ distribution;

3. Circular functions: The corresponding feature space is generated by using only the even numbers of features. The feature vectors are located on the two-dimensional circles as follows:

$$
\begin{aligned}
c_{num} &= \frac{d}{2}, \; c_{range} = \frac{\xi_{\max} - \xi_{\min}}{c_{num}}, \\
\mathbf{x} &= (x_1^1, x_1^2, x_2^1, x_2^2, \dots, x_{c_{num}}^1, x_{c_{num}}^2), \\
x_i^1 &= \sin\left(\frac{2\pi(\xi - (i-1) \cdot c_{range})}{c_{range}}\right) \cdot \mathbf{I}_i, \\
x_i^2 &= \cos\left(\frac{2\pi(\xi - (i-1) \cdot c_{range})}{c_{range}}\right) \cdot \mathbf{I}_i, \\
\mathbf{I}_i &= \mathbf{I}\{(i-1) \cdot c_{range} \leq \xi < i \cdot c_{range}\}, \; i = 1, \dots, c_{num},
\end{aligned} \tag{27}
$$

where $\mathbf{I}_i$ is an indicator function.

Each pair of features $(x_i^{(1)}, x_i^{(2)})$ corresponds to their own two-dimensional circle and to their own region in the ξ distribution.

In all experiments, feature vectors $\mathbf{y}$ are generated in the same way as vectors $\mathbf{x}$. However, for feature vectors $\mathbf{x}$ and $\mathbf{y}$, from the control and treatment groups, the corresponding times to events f and h are different and are generated by using the Weibull distribution, as follows:

$$
f(\xi) = -\left(\frac{\log(u)}{0.0005 \cdot \exp(1.6 \cdot \xi)}\right)^{1/2}, \tag{28}
$$

$$
h(\xi) = -\left(\frac{\log(u)}{0.005 \cdot \exp(0.8 \cdot \xi)}\right)^{1/2}, \tag{29}
$$

where u is the random variable, uniformly distributed on the interval $(0, 1)$; values f and h larger than 2000 are clipped to this value.

This way for generating f and h is in agreement with the Cox model. Hence, we can use the Cox model as a base model among RSFs and the Beran estimator with Gaussian kernels in the numerical experiments.

The proportion of censored data, denoted as p, is taken as 33% of all observations in the experiments. Hence, parameters of censoring δ_i and γ_i are generated from the binomial distribution with probabilities $\Pr\{\delta_i = 1\} = \Pr\{\gamma_i = 1\} = 0.67$, $\Pr\{\delta_i = 0\} = \Pr\{\gamma_i = 0\} = 0.33$.

The Precision in Estimation of Heterogeneous Effects metric (PEHE), proposed in [61], is used to reduce the variance in the numerical experiments. According to [61], this metric evaluates the ability of each method to capture treatment effect heterogeneity.

If we label the test dataset as $\mathcal{Z}$, then the PEHE can be defined as follows:

$$
\begin{aligned}
\text{PEHE}(\mathcal{Z}) &= \sqrt{\frac{1}{N_z} \sum_{\mathbf{z} \in \mathcal{Z}} (\mathbb{E}[(h - f) \mid \mathbf{z}(\xi)] - \tau(\mathbf{z}))^2}, \\
\mathbb{E}(f \mid \mathbf{z}(\xi)) &= \frac{1}{\sqrt{0.0005 \cdot \exp(1.6 \cdot \xi)}} \Gamma\left(\frac{3}{2}\right), \\
\mathbb{E}(h \mid \mathbf{z}(\xi)) &= \frac{1}{\sqrt{0.005 \cdot \exp(0.8 \cdot \xi)}} \Gamma\left(\frac{3}{2}\right),
\end{aligned} \tag{30}
$$

where N_z is the size of the set $\mathcal{Z}$, taken for all numerical experiments as $N_z = 1000$.

The proportion of treatments and controls in most experiments is 20%, except for experiments studying how the proportion of treatments impacts the CATE, where the proportion of treatments and controls is denoted as q. For example, if 100 controls are generated for an experiment with $q = 0.2$, then 20 treatments are generated in addition to controls, such that the total number of examples is 120. The generated feature vectors in all experiments consist of 10 features; the volume of the $\mathcal{C}$ set is 300 unless otherwise stated.

To select optimal hyperparameters of BENK, additional validation examples are generated, such that they belong to only the control group, and the size of this additional validation set is 50% of the set $\mathcal{C}$ size. After the BENK neural network training, this validation set is concatenated with $\mathcal{C}$ for other models, which are trained using cross-validation with three splits. For studying the dependencies, we repeat the numerical experiments 100 times and provide the mean values across these 100 iterations.

Each subnetwork is a fully connected neural network consisting of five layers, with corresponding activation functions ReLU6, ReLU6, ReLU6, Tanh, Softplus. Inputs for each subnetwork are represented in the form $\|\mathbf{x}_i - \mathbf{x}_j\|$ to ensure the symmetry property of kernels. The non-negativity property of neural kernels is achieved by using the activation function Softplus in the last layer of the subnetworks, which ensures that the output is always positive.

7.3. Study of the BENK Properties

In all pictures illustrating results of numerical experiments, dotted curves correspond to the T-learner (triangle markers), the S-learner (triangle markers) or the X-learner (the circle marker) under the condition of using the Beran estimator with the Gaussian kernels. Dash-and-dot curves correspond to the Cox models. Dashed curves with the same markers correspond to the same models implemented using RSFs. The solid curve with cross markers corresponds to BENK. The PEHE metric is used to represent results of experiments. The smaller the values of the PEHE, the better the obtained results. To avoid clutter of curves on the figures, we pick the best model for each T-,S- or X-learner obtained in each experiment.

First, we study different CATE estimators using different numbers c of controls, taking the values 100, 200, 300, 500, 1000. The number of treatments t is determined as 20% of the number of controls. Values of n are equal to $\min\{t, 100\}$. Figures 4–6 illustrate how values of the PEHE metric depend on the number c of controls for different estimators when different functions are used for generating examples. Figure 4 shows the difference between the PEHE metric of BENK and other models in the experiment, with the feature vectors located around the spiral. The T-SF, S-Beran and X-SF models are provided in Figure 4 because they show the best competitive metric values. In order to illustrate how the variance in results depends on the amount of input data, the error bars are also depicted in Figure 4. It can be seen from Figure 4 that the variance in results is reduced with the number of controls. This property of results indicates that the neural network is properly trained. We do not add the error bars to other graphs so as to not mask the relative positions of the corresponding curves. Figure 5 illustrates similar dependencies when the bell-shaped function is used for generating the feature vectors. The selected models in this case are T-Cox, S-SF and X-Cox. Figure 6 illustrates the relationship between different models obtained on the circular feature space. The competitive algorithms given in the picture are T-Beran, S-Beran and X-Beran. It can be seen from Figures 4–6 that the proposed model BENK provides better results in comparison with other models. The largest relative difference between BENK and other models can be observed when the feature vectors are generated in accordance with the spiral function. This function produces the most complex data structure, such that other studied models cannot cope with it.

Another interesting question is how the CATE estimators depend on the proportion q of treatments and controls in the training set. Particularly, for the proposed BENK model, we try to study whether an increasing number of treatments (the set $\mathcal{T}$) provides better CATE results with an unchanged number of controls (the set $\mathcal{C}$). The corresponding numerical results are shown in Figures 7–9. One can see from Figures 7–9 that the enhancement in the PEHE is sufficient in comparison with other CATE estimators when q is changed from 10% to 20% in the experiments with the spiral and bell-shaped functions. Moreover, we again observe the outperformance of BENK in comparison with other estimators.

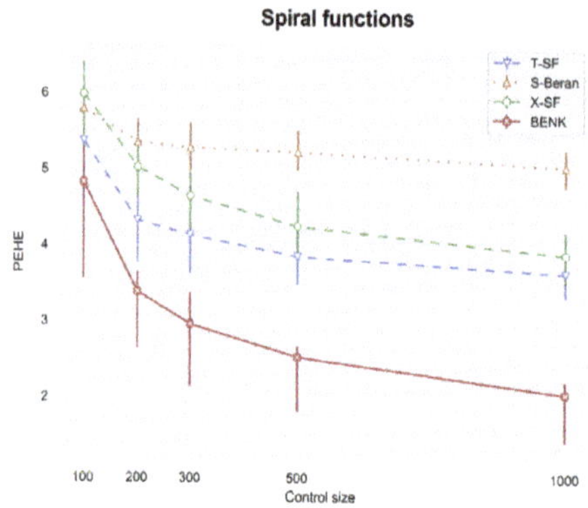

Figure 4. The PEHE metric as a function of the number of the controls when the spiral function is used for generating examples.

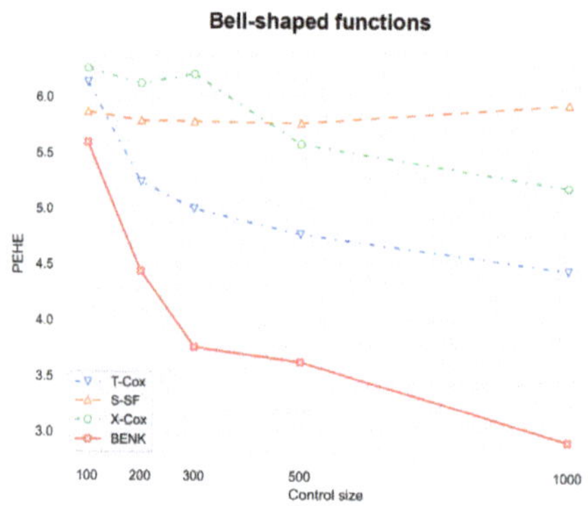

Figure 5. The PEHE metric as a function of the number of controls when the bell-shaped function is used for generating examples.

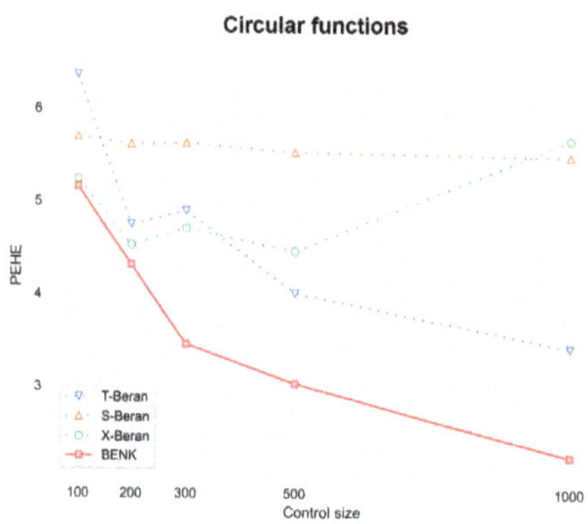

Figure 6. The PEHE metric as a function of the number of controls when the circular function is used for generating examples.

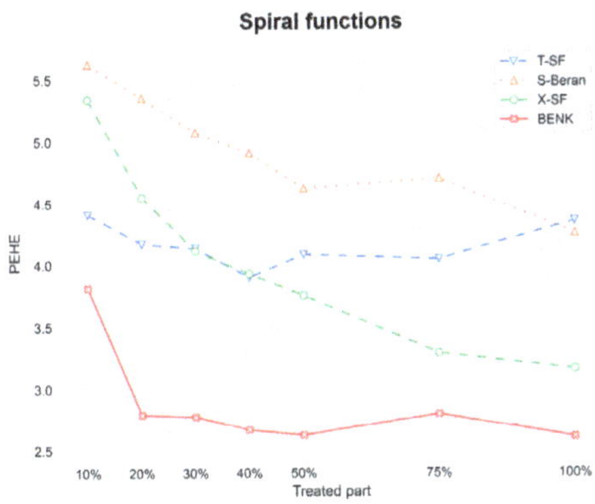

Figure 7. The PEHE metric as a function of the part of treatments when the spiral function is used for generating examples.

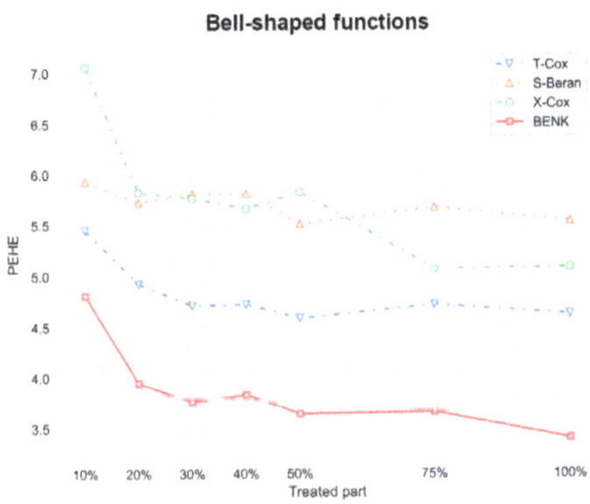

Figure 8. The PEHE metric as a function of the part of treatments when the bell-shaped function is used for generating examples.

In the previous experiments, the amount of the censored data was taken $p = 33\%$ of all observations. However, it is interesting to study how this amount impacts the PEHE of the CATE estimators. Figures 10–12 illustrate the corresponding dependencies when different generating functions are used. It can be seen from Figures 10–12 that the PEHE metrics for all estimators, including BENK, increase with the amount of censored data.

Table 2 aims to quantitatively compare results under the following conditions: $c = 400$, $s = 40$, $p = 0.2$, $m = 20$, $N = 1000$. One can see from Table 2 that BENK provides outperforming results. Let us compare results obtained for BENK with the results provided by other models in Table 2. For comparison, we can apply the standard t-test. The obtained p-values for all pairs of models are shown in the last column. We can see from Table 2 that all p-values are smaller than 0.05. Hence, we can conclude that the outperformance of BENK is statistically significant. It is interesting to note from Table 2 that methods based on the Cox model (T-Cox, S-Cox, X-Cox) show worse results. This can be explained by the weak assumption of the linear relationship of features, which takes place in the Cox model. This assumption contradicts the complex spiral, bell-shaped and circular functions and does not allow us to obtain better results. It should be pointed out that T-NW provides the best result for the bell-shaped generating function among results given by methods other than BENK. This is explained by the fact that the bell-shaped function is close to the Gaussian function; therefore, the method based on using Nadaraya–Watson kernel regression does not crucially differ from BENK. It is also interesting to note that the efficient methods such as the S-learner and the X-learner often provide worse results in comparison with the T-learner, which is rather weak in standard CATE tasks. This is due to peculiarities of survival data, which differ from the standard regression and classification data.

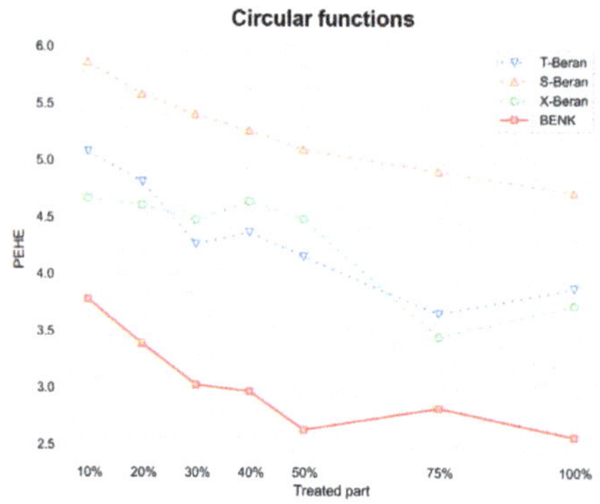

Figure 9. The PEHE metric as a function of the part of treatments when the circular function is used for generating examples.

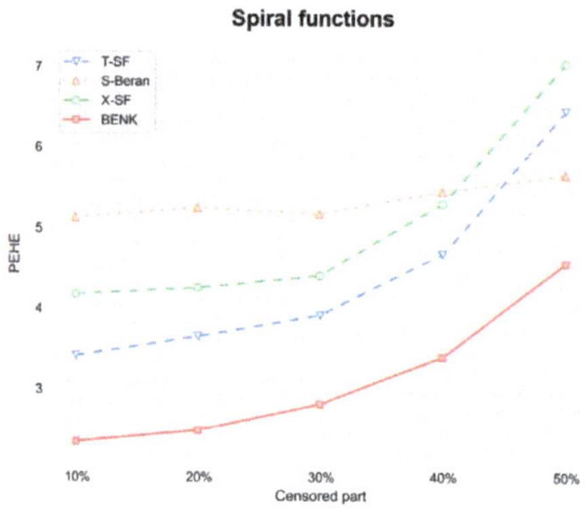

Figure 10. The PEHE metric as a function of the amount of censored observations in the training dataset when the spiral function is used for generating examples.

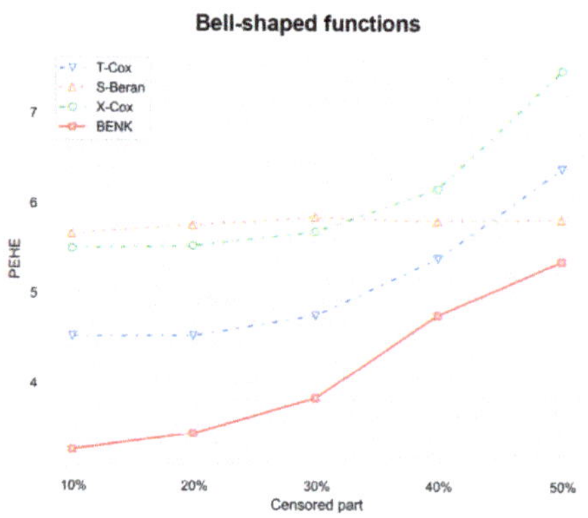

Figure 11. The PEHE metric as a function of the amount of censored observations in the training dataset when the bell-shaped function is used for generating examples.

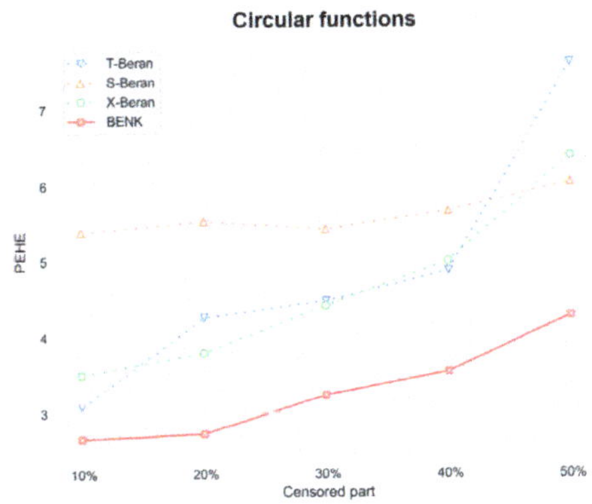

Figure 12. The PEHE metric as a function of the amount of censored observations in the training dataset when the circular function is used for generating examples.

Table 2. The PEHE values of CATE for different models obtained via different generating functions and the corresponding p-values.

	Generating Functions			
Model	**Spiral**	**Bell-Shaped**	**Circular**	**p-Value**
T-NW	5.876	4.868	5.713	0.0457
S-NW	5.759	5.868	5.946	0.0121
X-NW	4.985	5.090	6.317	0.0149
T-Cox	6.198	6.518	6.126	0.0128
S-Cox	5.959	5.941	5.963	0.0112
X-Cox	6.331	7.396	8.357	0.0178
T-SF	3.721	5.563	6.460	0.0401
S-SF	5.959	5.900	5.882	0.0035
X-SF	4.853	6.339	7.176	0.0154
BENK	2.373	3.288	3.570	

It should be noted that we did not provide results of various deep neural network extensions of the CATE estimators because they have not been successful. The problem is that neural networks require a large amount of data for training and the considered small datasets have led to overfitting the networks. This is why we studied models which provide satisfactory predictions under condition of small amounts of data.

8. Conclusions

A new method called BENK for solving the CATE problem under the condition of censored data has been presented. It extends the idea behind TNW–CATE proposed in [16] to the case of censored data. In spite of many similar parts of TNW-CATE and BENK, they are different because BENK is based on using the Beran estimator for training and can be successfully applied to survival analysis of controls and treatments. However, TNW–CATE and BENK use the same idea to train neural kernels: implementation as neural networks instead of using standard kernels.

It is also interesting to point out that BENK does not require oneto have a large dataset for training, even though the neural network is used for implementing the kernels. This is due to a special way that is proposed to train the network, which considers pairs of examples from the control group for training, as in Siamese neural networks. Our experiments have illustrated the outperforming characteristics of BENK. At the same time, we have to point out some disadvantages of BENK. First, it has many tuning parameters, including parameters of the neural network and parameters of training n and N, such that the training time may be significantly increased in comparison with other methods of solving the CATE problem. Second, BENK assumes that the feature vector domains are similar for controls and treatments. This does not mean that they have to totally coincide, but the corresponding difference in domains should not be very large. A method which could take into account a possible difference between the feature vector domains for controls and treatments can be regarded as a direction for further research. An idea behind the method is to combine the domain adaptation models and BENK.

Another direction for further research is to study robust versions of BENK when there are anomalous observations that may impact training the neural network. An idea behind the robust version is to use attention weights for feature vectors and also to introduce additional attention weights for predictions.

It should be noted that the Beran estimator is one of several estimators that are used in survival analysis. Moreover, we have studied only the difference in expected lifetimes as a definition of the CATE in the case of censored data. There are other definitions, for instance, the difference in SFs and the hazard ratio, which may lead to more interesting models. Therefore, BENK implementations and studies using other estimators and definitions of the CATE can be also considered as directions for further research.

The proposed method can be used in applications that are different from medicine. For example, it can be applied to selection and control of the most efficient regimes in the Internet of Things. This is also an interesting direction for further research.

Author Contributions: Conceptualization, S.K., L.U. and A.K.; methodology, L.U. and V.M.; software, S.K. and A.K.; validation, S.K., V.M. and A.K.; formal analysis, A.K. and L.U.; investigation, L.U., A.K. and V.M.; resources, A.K. and V.M.; data curation, S.K. and V.M.; writing—original draft preparation, L.U. and A.K.; writing—review and editing, S.K. and V.M.; visualization, A.K.; supervision, L.U.; project administration, V.M.; funding acquisition, V.M. All authors have read and agreed to the published version of the manuscript.

Funding: The research is partially funded by the Ministry of Science and Higher Education of the Russian Federation as part of World-Class Research Center program: Advanced Digital Technologies (contract No. 075-15-2022-311. dated 20 April 2022).

Institutional Review Board Statement: Not applicable.

Informed Consent Statement: Not applicable.

Data Availability Statement: Data are contained within the article.

Conflicts of Interest: The authors declare no conflicts of interest.

References

1. Hosmer, D.; Lemeshow, S.; May, S. *Applied Survival Analysis: Regression Modeling of Time to Event Data*; John Wiley & Sons: Hoboken, NJ, USA, 2008.
2. Wang, P.; Li, Y.; Reddy, C. Machine Learning for Survival Analysis: A Survey. *ACM Comput. Surv. (CSUR)* **2019**, *51*, 110.
3. Cox, D. Regression models and life-tables. *J. R. Stat. Soc. Ser. (Methodol.)* **1972**, *34*, 187–220. [CrossRef]
4. Ishwaran, H.; Kogalur, U. Random Survival Forests for R. *R News* **2007**, *7*, 25–31.
5. Shalit, U.; Johansson, F.; Sontag, D. Estimating individual treatment effect: Generalization bounds and algorithms. In Proceedings of the 34th International Conference on Machine Learning (ICML 2017), Sydney, Australia, 6–11 August 2017; pp. 3076–3085.
6. Fan, Y.; Lv, J.; Wang, J. DNN: A Two-Scale Distributional Tale of Heterogeneous Treatment Effect Inference. *arXiv* **2018**, arXiv:1808.08469v1.
7. Wager, S.; Athey, S. Estimation and inference of heterogeneous treatment effects using random forests. *J. Am. Stat. Assoc.* **2018**, *113*, 1228–1242. [CrossRef]
8. Kunzel, S.; Stadie, B.; Vemuri, N.; Ramakrishnan, V.; Sekhon, J.; Abbeel, P. Transfer Learning for Estimating Causal Effects using Neural Networks. *arXiv* **2018**, arXiv:1808.07804v1.
9. Acharki, N.; Garnier, J.; Bertoncello, A.; Lugo, R. Heterogeneous Treatment Effects Estimation: When Machine Learning meets multiple treatment regime. *arXiv* **2022**, arXiv:2205.14714.

10. Hatt, T.; Berrevoets, J.; Curth, A.; Feuerriegel, S.; van der Schaar, M. Combining Observational and Randomized Data for Estimating Heterogeneous Treatment Effects. *arXiv* **2022**, arXiv:2202.12891.
11. Jiang, H.; Qi, P.; Zhou, J.; Zhou, J.; Rao, S. A Short Survey on Forest Based Heterogeneous Treatment Effect Estimation Methods: Meta-learners and Specific Models. In Proceedings of the 2021 IEEE International Conference on Big Data (Big Data), Orlando, FL, USA, 15–18 October 2021; pp. 3006–3012.
12. Kunzel, S.; Sekhon, J.; Bickel, P.; Yu, B. Metalearners for estimating heterogeneous treatment effects using machine learning. *Proc. Natl. Acad. Sci. USA* **2019**, *116*, 4156–4165. [CrossRef]
13. Zhang, W.; Li, J.; Liu, L. A Unified Survey of Treatment Effect Heterogeneity Modelling and Uplift Modelling. *ACM Comput. Surv.* **2022**, *54*, 162. [CrossRef]
14. Nadaraya, E. On estimating regression. *Theory Probab. Its Appl.* **1964**, *9*, 141–142. [CrossRef]
15. Watson, G. Smooth regression analysis. *Sankhya Indian J. Stat. Ser. A* **1964**, *26*, 359–372.
16. Konstantinov, A.; Kirpichenko, S.; Utkin, L. Heterogeneous Treatment Effect with Trained Kernels of the Nadaraya–Watson Regression. *Algorithms* **2023**, *16*, 226. [CrossRef]
17. Beran, R. *Nonparametric Regression with Randomly Censored Survival Data*; Technical Report; University of California: Berkeley, CA, USA, 1981.
18. Jeng, X.; Lu, W.; Peng, H. High-dimensional inference for personalized treatment decision. *Electron. J. Stat.* **2018**, *12*, 2074–2089.
19. Zhou, X.; Mayer-Hamblett, N.; Khan, U.; Kosorok, M. Residual Weighted Learning for Estimating Individualized Treatment Rules. *J. Am. Stat. Assoc.* **2017**, *112*, 169–187. [CrossRef]
20. Athey, S.; Tibshirani, J.; Wager, S. Generalized random forests. *arXiv* **2019**, arXiv:1610.0171v4.
21. III, E.M.; Somanchi, S.; Neill, D. Efficient Discovery of Heterogeneous Treatment Effects in Randomized Experiments via Anomalous Pattern Detection. *arXiv* **2018**, arXiv:1803.09159v2.
22. Chen, R.; Liu, H. Heterogeneous Treatment Effect Estimation through Deep Learning. *arXiv* **2018**, arXiv:1810.11010v1.
23. Yao, L.; Lo, C.; Nir, I.; Tan, S.; Evnine, A.; Lerer, A.; Peysakhovich, A. Efficient Heterogeneous Treatment Effect Estimation With Multiple Experiments and Multiple Outcomes. *arXiv* **2022**, arXiv:2206.04907.
24. Curth, A.; van der Schaar, M. Nonparametric Estimation of Heterogeneous Treatment Effects: From Theory to Learning Algorithms. In Proceedings of the International Conference on Artificial Intelligence and Statistics, Virtual, 13–15 April 2021; pp. 1810–1818.
25. Du, X.; Fan, Y.; Lv, J.; Sun, T.; Vossler, P. Dimension-Free Average Treatment Effect Inference with Deep Neural Networks. *arXiv* **2021**, arXiv:2112.01574.
26. Nair, N.; Gurumoorthy, K.; Mandalapu, D. Individual Treatment Effect Estimation through Controlled Neural Network Training in Two Stages. *arXiv* **2021**, arXiv:2201.08559.
27. Qin, T.; Wang, T.Z.; Zhou, Z.H. Budgeted Heterogeneous Treatment Effect Estimation. In Proceedings of the 38th International Conference on Machine Learning, Virtual, 18–24 July 2021; Volume 139, pp. 8693–8702.
28. Chu, Z.; Li, S. Continual treatment effect estimation: Challenges and opportunities. In Proceedings of the Machine Learning Research. AAAI Bridge Program on Continual Causality, Washington, DC, USA, 7–8 February 2023; pp. 11–17.
29. Kennedy, E.H. Towards optimal doubly robust estimation of heterogeneous causal effects. *Electron. J. Stat.* **2023**, *17*, 3008–3049.
30. Krantsevich, N.; He, J.; Hahn, P.R. Stochastic tree ensembles for estimating heterogeneous effects. In Proceedings of the International Conference on Artificial Intelligence and Statistics, Valencia, Spain, 25–27 April 2023; pp. 6120–6131.
31. Verbeke, W.; Olaya, D.; Guerry, M.A.; Van Belle, J. To do or not to do? Cost-sensitive causal classification with individual treatment effect estimates. *Eur. J. Oper. Res.* **2023**, *305*, 838–852. [CrossRef]
32. Guo, Z.; Zheng, S.; Liu, Z.; Yan, K.; Zhu, Z. CETransformer: Casual Effect Estimation via Transformer Based Representation Learning. In Proceedings of the Pattern Recognition and Computer Vision (PRCV 2021), Beijing, China, 29 October–1 November 2021; Lecture Notes in Computer Science; Springer: Cham, Switzerland, 2021; Volume 13022, pp. 524–535.
33. Melnychuk, V.; Frauen, D.; Feuerriegel, S. Causal Transformer for Estimating Counterfactual Outcomes. In Proceedings of the International Conference on Machine Learning, Baltimore, MD, USA, 17–23 July 2022.
34. Zhang, Y.F.; Zhang, H.; Lipton, Z.; Li, L.E.; Xing, E.P. Exploring Transformer Backbones for Heterogeneous Treatment Effect Estimation. *arXiv* **2022**, arXiv:2202.01336.
35. Aoki, R.; Ester, M. Causal Inference from Small High-dimensional Datasets. *arXiv* **2022**, arXiv:2205.09281.
36. Zhou, G.; Yao, L.; Xu, X.; Wang, C.; Zhu, L. Learning to Infer Counterfactuals: Meta-Learning for Estimating Multiple Imbalanced Treatment Effects. *arXiv* **2022**, arXiv:2208.06748.
37. Park, J.; Shalit, U.; Scholkopf, B.; Muandet, K. Conditional Distributional Treatment Effect with Kernel Conditional Mean Embeddings and U-Statistic Regression. In Proceedings of the 38 th International Conference on Machine Learning, Virtual, 18–24 July 2021; Volume 139, pp. 8401–8412.
38. Witten, D.; Tibshirani, R. Survival analysis with high-dimensional covariates. *Stat. Methods Med. Res.* **2010**, *19*, 29–51. [CrossRef]
39. Widodo, A.; Yang, B.S. Machine health prognostics using survival probability and support vector machine. *Expert Syst. Appl.* **2011**, *38*, 8430–8437. [CrossRef]
40. Ibrahim, N.; Kudus, A.; Daud, I.; Bakar, M.A. Decision tree for competing risks survival probability in breast cancer study. *Int. J. Biol. Med. Res.* **2008**, *3*, 25–29.

41. Wright, M.; Dankowski, T.; Ziegler, A. Unbiased split variable selection for random survival forests using maximally selected rank statistics. *Stat. Med.* **2017**, *36*, 1272–1284. [CrossRef]
42. Haarburger, C.; Weitz, P.; Rippel, O.; Merhof, D. Image-based Survival Analysis for Lung Cancer Patients using CNNs. In Proceedings of the 2019 IEEE 16th International Symposium on Biomedical Imaging (ISBI 2019), Venice, Italy, 8–11 April 2019.
43. Katzman, J.; Shaham, U.; Cloninger, A.; Bates, J.; Jiang, T.; Kluger, Y. DeepSurv: Personalized treatment recommender system using a Cox proportional hazards deep neural network. *BMC Med. Res. Methodol.* **2018**, *18*, 24. [CrossRef] [PubMed]
44. Cui, Y.; Kosorok, M.R.; Sverdrup, E.; Wager, S.; Zhu, R. Estimating heterogeneous treatment effects with right-censored data via causal survival forests. *J. R. Stat. Soc. Ser. Stat. Methodol.* **2023**, *85*, 179–211.
45. Hou, J.; Bradic, J.; Xu, R. Treatment effect estimation under additive hazards models with high-dimensional confounding. *J. Am. Stat. Assoc.* **2023**, *118*, 327–342. [CrossRef]
46. Hu, L.; Ji, J.; Liu, H.; Ennis, R. A flexible approach for assessing heterogeneity of causal treatment effects on patient survival using large datasets with clustered observations. *Int. J. Environ. Res. Public Health* **2022**, *19*, 14903. [CrossRef] [PubMed]
47. Schrod, S.; Schäfer, A.; Solbrig, S.; Lohmayer, R.; Gronwald, W.; Oefner, P.; Beissbarth, T.; Spang, R.; Zacharias, H.; Altenbuchinger, M. BITES: Balanced Individual Treatment Effect for Survival data. *Bioinformatics* **2022**, *38*, i60–i67.
48. Nagpal, C.; Goswami, M.; Dufendach, K.; Dubrawski, A. Counterfactual Phenotyping with Censored Time-to-Events. In Proceedings of the 28th ACM SIGKDD Conference on Knowledge Discovery and Data Mining, Washington, DC, USA, 14–18 August 2022.
49. Curth, A.; Lee, C.; van der Schaar, M. SurvITE: Learning Heterogeneous Treatment Effects from Time-to-Event Data. In Proceedings of the 35th Conference on Neural Information Processing Systems (NeurIPS 2021), Online, 6–14 December 2021; pp. 1–14.
50. Zhu, J.; Gallego, B. Targeted estimation of heterogeneous treatment effect in observational survival analysis. *J. Biomed. Inform.* **2020**, *107*, 103474. [CrossRef] [PubMed]
51. Hu, L.; Ji, J.; Li, F. Estimating heterogeneous survival treatment effect in observational data using machine learning. *Stat. Med.* **2021**, *40*, 4691–4713. [PubMed]
52. Rytgaard, H.; Ekstrom, C.; Kessing, L.; Gerds, T. Ranking of average treatment effects with generalized random forests for time-to-event outcomes. *Stat. Med.* **2023**, *42*, 1542–1564.
53. Chapfuwa, P.; Assaad, S.; Zeng, S.; Pencina, M.; Carin, L.; Henao, R. Enabling Counterfactual Survival Analysis with Balanced Representations. In Proceedings of the CHIL '21: Proceedings of the Conference on Health, Inference, and Learning, Virtual, 8–10 April 2021; ACM: New York, NY, USA, 2021; pp. 133–145.
54. Rosenbaum, P.; Rubin, D. The central role of the propensity score in observational studies for causal effects. *Biometrika* **1983**, *70*, 41–55. [CrossRef]
55. Imbens, G. Nonparametric estimation of average treatment effects under exogeneity: A review. *Rev. Econ. Stat.* **2004**, *86*, 4–29.
56. Rubin, D. Causal inference using potential outcomes: Design, modeling, decisions. *J. Am. Stat. Assoc.* **2005**, *100*, 322–331. [CrossRef]
57. Harrell, F.; Califf, R.; Pryor, D.; Lee, K.; Rosati, R. Evaluating the yield of medical tests. *J. Am. Med Assoc.* **1982**, *247*, 2543–2546. [CrossRef]
58. Chapfuwa, P.; Assaad, S.; Zeng, S.; Pencina, M.; Carin, L.; Henao, R. Survival analysis meets counterfactual inference. *arXiv* **2020**, arXiv:2006.07756.
59. Pelaez, R.; Cao, R.; Vilar, J. Nonparametric estimation of the conditional survival function with double smoothing. *J. Nonparametr. Stat.* **2022**, 34, 1063–1090. [CrossRef]
60. Tutz, G.; Pritscher, L. Nonparametric estimation of discrete hazard functions. *Lifetime Data Anal.* **1996**, *2*, 291–308. [CrossRef]
61. Hill, J. Bayesian nonparametric modeling for causal inference. *J. Comput. Graph. Stat.* **2011**, *20*, 217–240.

MDPI AG
Grosspeteranlage 5
4052 Basel
Switzerland
Tel.: +41 61 683 77 34

Algorithms Editorial Office
E-mail: algorithms@mdpi.com
www.mdpi.com/journal/algorithms

www.ingramcontent.com/pod-product-compliance
Lightning Source LLC
Chambersburg PA
CBHW061557210926
51850CB00009B/2127